D1603527

EDMUND BURKE IN AMERICA

EDMUND BURKE IN AMERICA

The Contested Career of the Father of Modern Conservatism

DREW MACIAG

CORNELL UNIVERSITY PRESS
Ithaca and London

First published 2013 by Cornell University Press

Printed in the United States of America

Library of Congress Cataloging-in-Publication Data

Maciag, Drew, 1954–
Edmund Burke in America : the contested career of the father of modern conservatism / Drew Maciag.
p. cm.
Includes bibliographical references and index.
ISBN 978-0-8014-4895-9 (cloth : alk. paper)
1. Conservatism—United States—History. 2. Political science—United States—Philosophy. 3. Burke, Edmund, 1729–1797. I. Title.
JC573.2.U6M335 2013
320.520973—dc23 2012040406

Cornell University Press strives to use environmentally responsible suppliers and materials to the fullest extent possible in the publishing of its books. Such materials include vegetable-based, low-VOC inks and acid-free papers that are recycled, totally chlorine-free, or partly composed of nonwood fibers. For further information, visit our website at www.cornellpress.cornell.edu.

Cloth printing 10 9 8 7 6 5 4 3 2 1

To Jeanne

The social nature of man impels him to propagate his principles, as much as physical impulses urge him to propagate his kind. The passions give zeal and vehemence. The understanding bestows design and system. The whole man moves under the discipline of his opinions.

—Edmund Burke
Letters on a Regicide Peace

Contents

Preface

This book rests on the premise that American opinions about Edmund Burke provide unique insights into the history of political thinking in the United States.

Most of the opinion gathered here is related to formal political thought but is not limited to it; instead it extends to encompass the wider intellectual environment within which political attitudes are shaped and expressed. In the case of Burke and America, this includes not only direct engagement with Burke's writings, but also American reactions to Burke's reputation, his status, the events of his life, or his stands on particular issues; it also includes American responses to the views of other Americans on such matters. Commentary that on its most immediate level is about Burke always reveals a deeper background of competing ideas, worldviews, prejudices, and frames of reference, which inform and control the more self-consciously articulated elements of American political discourse.

While the book's arrangement is chronological—beginning in Burke's day and ending in our own—its historiographical motivation lies two-thirds of the way through, with the post–World War II revival of interest in Burke and his inauguration as the "father of conservatism." During the last couple of decades, interest in the history of American conservatism has exploded, sparked by the nation's rightward political drift. In turn, the roots of the conservative Republican resurgence have been traced back to Barry Goldwater, Joseph McCarthy, and Sunbelt populism; crucially, they have also been traced to intellectuals who articulated conservative doctrines since the war. As this study will show, the Burkean revival was part and parcel of that larger resurgence, though its challenge to established liberalism was also a variation on the long-standing ideological contest over American ideals that had been endemic since the birth of the Republic. Hence, this book opens a new window into the history of American conservatism and into conservatism's dynamic relationship with the nation's dominant liberalism.

In contrast to Louis Hartz's famous claim that the American liberal tradition reigned supreme because it incorporated key conservative elements (respect for property, the Constitution, religion, the rule of law, economic competition) and therefore faced no serious threats from alternative creeds, the evidence discussed herein indicates a more contentious interplay of divergent beliefs. Actually, the liberal tradition has survived and retained primacy only by continual struggle against repeated and varied conservative assaults. Neither the political context for—nor the internal consistency of—liberalism or conservatism has held constant throughout American history, but the prevalent traits of both persuasions are discernible in retrospect. Even before the terms themselves came into general use, their generic profiles were evident. In ideal (almost impressionistic) forms: Conservatism houses a general preference for order, stability, hierarchy, religious orthodoxy, institutional authority, social conformity, property rights, discipline, and established cultural standards. Liberalism houses a general preference for innovation, progress, fairness, reform, democracy, equality, equity, humanitarianism, flexibility, tolerance, personal fulfillment, and experimentation. Each of these constituent values is itself open to interpretation, and not every value applies (or applies with equal weight) to all conservatives or to all liberals; moreover, conservative-liberal distinctions are usually drawn by de-emphasizing opposing values, rather than by rejecting them outright. Still, these two alternative value systems—whether functioning as clear ideologies or as diffuse sensibilities—have driven the core disputes of American political thinking for over two centuries. Hence the words "conservative" and "liberal" will appear periodically throughout this book, even at the risk of occasional linguistic anachronism.

A parallel development in recent scholarship has been the recognition that the political beliefs of Americans are often shaped by some particular understanding of the *meaning* of historical texts (the Declaration of Independence and Constitution are most obvious, but there are many others). Once again, this understanding tends to break along ideological fault lines. Left and Right interpretations champion different values; the "moral" of important texts varies with the predilections of the reader. The figures in this book have grafted the words of Edmund Burke to the standard stock of "American scripture." No less than the writings of his perennial counter-authority Thomas Paine, Burke's writings have served as a basis for refining and for explicating the "promise of American life." But unlike Paine, who retained an excessive confidence in rationality, Burke understood that politics and government were products (perhaps consequences) of much deeper cultural currents. It was no coincidence that Burke was one of the first writers in English to use the word "civilization," or that he placed so much emphasis on the imaginative "decent drapery of life," and "pleasing illusions" of a people.

On that score, Burke bore a passing resemblance to Tocqueville, who recognized (less romantically) that democracy was not just a system of government, but also a way of describing a wider national culture. The *ideal* of democracy captured the spirit behind the collective American personality. Yet democracy—both the system and the spirit—has proven to be contentious. Not only has it had to reinvent itself on a practical level every few generations; it has had to redefine and re-justify itself in the national consciousness as well. That process of symbolic adjustment—carried on by advocates on both sides of the ideological divide, employing doses of Burkean wisdom as circumstances required—provides the historical plotline of this book.

Finally, a brief word about the book's cast of characters: the sole criterion for their selection was that they each had something to say regarding Burke, *which also illuminated the landscape of political thinking in the America of their time.* Despite the (mostly) elite status of its participants, this story is not exactly "trickle down" history. The bulk of the writing examined here aimed at understanding transitions in American society that boiled up from below: the decline of deference and demand for greater democracy; the rise of exceptionalism and lure of the frontier; the quest for social and economic justice, for the expansion of individual and group rights, and for increased flexibility in social and cultural norms. These writings were at heart about responses, adaptations, and accommodations to change. American commentary on Burke was usually political, but it engaged politics on a symbolic rather than tactical level. It dealt with the general condition of society. It displayed suppositions about human nature, reason, group dynamics, leadership, progress, tradition, and other fundamentals. Specific issues were less important than underlying principles. Indeed, this book may be viewed as a selective history of the United States, with alternative national visions as its theme and the reaction to Burke's writings as its evidence.

Legend has it that when the novelist James Joyce was asked "How long did it take you to write *Ulysses*?" he responded, "Ten years. But in a sense, all my life." Exactly the same response applies to *Edmund Burke in America.* While this book took six years to research and write, it could never have been accomplished had I not spent the previous twenty years reading and thinking about Western civilization, American ideals, modern political thought, the Enlightenment, ideology, national leadership, and related matters. If all parties responsible for this book (whether during the "six years" or the prior "all my life") were to be acknowledged here, there would be little room for the text. Instead, I will simply note the tiny handful of persons who were most directly connected to this project (plus one). At the University of

Rochester, Robert Westbrook inspired me to pursue a topic and an approach to scholarship that excited me, even though both the subject and the method were, at the time, far from the academic vogue. Stewart Weaver was a valuable guide to the British perspective (most of what I first wrote about Burke and his environment has since been dropped, but the insights I gained from the effort enriched my analysis of Burke's American legacy). I also benefited enormously from the publication advice of Joan Shelly Rubin. At Cornell University Press, Michael McGandy expressed immediate interest in this project, and sustained his commitment to it during an unusually lengthy path to publication. Finally, a special word of thanks goes to Richard Adelstein of Wesleyan University, who had nothing directly to do with this book. But he had a great deal to do with my being in a position to write it.

EDMUND BURKE IN AMERICA

Introduction

In Search of Icons

In a 2005 *New Yorker* interview, a neoconservative Pentagon official defended the Bush administration's invasion of Iraq by invoking the name of the eighteenth-century British politician Edmund Burke.[1] Burke's relevance may not have been obvious to most readers. But those who understood the esoteric codes of ideological discourse got the message. Forget that Burke had no practical knowledge of the Middle East, and knew nothing about weapons of mass destruction, Islamic fundamentalism, military strategy, or democratic nation building. None of that mattered. Paying homage to Burke was more a profession of faith than an explanation of policy. To certain conservative intellectuals, the use of Burke's philosophy to justify the toppling of Saddam Hussein made sense: not because the situation called for it, or the "facts on the ground" justified it, but because the ritualistic mention of Burke, the "father of conservatism," had by 2005 established itself as a standard rhetorical ploy.

It is an irony of modern intellectual history that liberals have inherited a larger and more convincing list of "fathers" than conservatives have. Liberals, who (ideally) are future-oriented innovators, barely make use of their own family tree. Conservatives, who desperately need great old names to help them defend traditional orthodoxies, have found few effective matches for Locke, Jefferson, Mill, Dewey, and other tradition-shattering icons. Consequently, they have been forced to stretch Edmund Burke beyond measure.

Since the Second World War, Burke has been employed to counter virtually all left-of-center thought. Yet the current conservative appropriation of Burke's legacy in America is only the latest chapter in a long, symbolic enterprise.

American commentary on Burke has always revealed more about the intermittent traumas of American life than it has about the historical Edmund Burke. Readers of Burke tend to find what they are seeking: wisdom, inspiration, verification of personal beliefs, and a wealth of quotable prose. Still, Burke in America has been an anomaly. Even during the revolutionary era, Burke had apparently switched sides between 1776 and 1789. In his first incarnation, he was a "friend of liberty" aligned with colonial America's nascent liberal tradition. In his second incarnation, Burke's royalist sympathies and his rejection of French revolutionary idealism placed him in stark opposition to that same tradition. Little wonder that after 1800 most Americans treaded lightly when citing Burke for political gain. For the next century and a half (until the Cold War hysteria of the 1950s) there was no dominant American school of thought on Burke. Yet patterns emerged in the way Burke continued to be discussed. In retrospect, the polemical need for Burke in America reveals deep, ever-present fissures in the national culture.

Inventing American Tradition

Long after independence, the United States remained tied to British civilization. But individual Americans, as well as politicians and historians, found it convenient to deny this. In part this was a necessary consequence of breaking free from the mother country. Yet over time, America's cultivation of its own uniqueness became a handy emotive force (akin to patriotism) that could be employed by anyone in support of various agendas. The easy acceptance of new truths suggesting that Americans were God's chosen people, that their society stood as a city on a hill, that they were expected to fulfill their manifest destiny, that they lived in a classless society endowed with a frontier spirit, and that, in some vague yet materially verifiable way (as with the great expositions of the late nineteenth century, or the space race of the mid-twentieth) their nation was leading all others into the future, tended to focus attention on the new and different. While this might seem to have been a rejection of tradition, it was something more complicated: the creation of new traditions, which, because of their redemptive nature, required the ritual rejection of old traditions. The Old World was therefore viewed as corrupt, exhausted, ossified, oppressive, and backward. Obvious connections with it had to be severed, ignored, or downplayed. America has always been exceptionalist in this sense, and American historians have generally written from within this context. Given such an environment, it is understandable that Burke—an exponent of British traditionalism—has been mostly absent in the telling of American history.

By contrast, we accept the influence in America of (Burke's friend) Adam Smith in the economic sphere, and of (Burke's adversary) Thomas Paine in the political sphere, and of John Locke in both the economic and political. But that is partly because such figures have been distilled down to one or two basic principles, which, since they have been widely accepted, appear to be almost self-evident. The "invisible hand" of the market, and the "right" of free citizens to construct their own government, are examples of this. In the case of Burke, however, it is not so easy to reduce his thoughts to a single idea. And, since his work has been neither understood nor accepted as widely, his influence has not been as clear-cut. It is also worth noting that while Locke, Smith, and Paine were viewed as apostles of progress, Burke after 1790 was often viewed as representing the anchor of tradition (on this point he *was* reducible to a single idea). This put him at odds with America's exceptionalist self-image. The ideas of Paine were adopted by Americans to help them forge into new territory, but the ideas of Burke were used as counterweights by those who felt uncomfortable with either the speed or direction of change. To this very day, Burke's champions are acting in this mold.

Burke's American legacy belongs to the same genus as that of Henry David Thoreau. This is not to suggest that their philosophies were similar—quite the contrary. Yet despite their incompatible ideas, both men represented the losing side in their respective battles with progress. Both embody a road not taken, yet neither has been forgotten. Their separate legacies retain followings, and their partisans have experienced occasional, partial victories. Both men's worldviews conflicted with the dominant forces of their times—forces now recognizable as the beginnings of modernization. Both men possessed a transcendental aspect that was central to their beliefs. In addition, the writings of both men appeal to the literary as well as the intellectual sense, and so have retained their attraction on more than one level. Like Burke, Thoreau cannot easily be reduced to a single idea, and he was never a participant in the American parade of progress as exemplified by Gilded Age industrial development or twentieth-century modernization. Instead, his philosophy inspired alternatives, such as "back to nature" movements, civil disobedience, and social nonconformity. In a similar way Burke has been used to justify opposition to excessive democracy and to an overreliance on reason, as well as to the power of the plutocracy, creeping socialism, utopian radicalism, and moral relativism. Again, these contrarian movements and ideas sometimes resulted in limited success, but they rarely constituted the dominant social or intellectual currents of the nation.

Burke's reputation, like Thoreau's, has ebbed and flowed with succeeding generations. Furthermore, Burke's image underwent alterations over time. Different ages spawned different uses for his legacy. Because Burke's work was known for its eloquence, and Burke was considered to be one of the great English rhetoricians, he was quoted (in or out of context) in support of stands on widely varied issues. This was done in the same vein in which advocates quoted the Bible or Shakespeare, and it had the effect of summoning the weight of ageless wisdom. It also revealed the speaker or writer to be erudite, and to be acting in harmony with the established Anglo-American tradition. Generally, Burke's admirers in America saw themselves as moral-cultural guardians who were formulating a philosophy of responsible leadership by a natural aristocracy. In turn, this philosophy was expected to save America from self-destructive behavior, as well as from those characters who endorsed or encouraged such behavior.

This was certainly a noble mission, which was undertaken with (I believe) seriousness and sincerity. But however good their intentions, American Burkeans quickly learned that they were unlikely to prevail. The exceptionalist environment proved too resistant to the innate traditionalism of the Burkean message. In reaction to this, the Burkean perspective became transformed into a perennial counterpoint that was played against the major themes of egalitarianism and competitive material progress. If Burkeanism had been a political party, it would have represented the loyal opposition—strong enough to influence the agenda, not strong enough to set it. The main thread that united Burkeans was a devotion to America as a civilization that was both derived from, and still in communication with, traditional Western (or European) civilization, of which the British branch was by far the most germane. This helps explain why such American Burkeans as Edward Everett, E. L. Godkin, and Russell Kirk were Anglophiles as well. Hence the founding of the United States represented an incremental development rather than a revolutionary departure. For Burkeans, severing ties with the established, accepted, or (what might even be called) "authorized" past would inevitably result in an unraveling of the social fabric in the present. Burkeans in America were not defending British royalty or nobility; they were defending the accumulated experience and wisdom of centuries—now transplanted to American soil.

Cultural Politics

Burke today is a controversial figure. Because he has been canonized by conservative intellectuals, he has not attracted as much attention from other scholars (literary interest in Burke's aesthetic theory is an exception that lies beyond our concerns here). Typically, the left-of-center constituency views Burke as an antimodern who picked the wrong side in the French Revolution. As a result, he is considered to be either irrelevant or harmful to the contemporary intellectual and political landscape, and thus not worthy of further examination. But such denial does not alter the record of history. It only ignores it.

Many scholars have classified Burke as an early romantic, thanks to his emotional rejection of cold reason. Within limits that characterization is apt. But for our purposes, it is more central that Burke was astute in his recognition—contrary to Paine, Jefferson, Franklin, and other early moderns—that reason was usually more servant than master. Portions of Burke's antirevolutionary tracts described a British society in which intellect was but a self-conscious superstructure, built atop a sturdier mass of beneficial "prejudice." When he wrote of "all the Super-added ideas, furnished from the wardrobe of a moral imagination, which the heart owns, and the understanding ratifies," and of "a bland assimilation, [that] incorporate[s] into politics the sentiments which beautify and soften private society,"[2] he was placing long-accepted, unexplored beliefs, practices, and feelings at the base of the cultural (and psychological) pyramid. Politics or political theories were meaningless—or dangerous—without them. Elsewhere, he suggested that behavior sprang in part from unknown—perhaps unknowable—sources. Admittedly, Burke most famously applied his "cultural perspective" in a narrowly traditionalist direction; but the possibilities for alternative angles abounded, and he displayed more flexibility when discussing the cultural milieu of colonial America and India. In today's postmodern environment, the subjectivity and subservience of reason are taken for granted, and cultural history has demonstrated that the influences behind social belief systems are broader and more complex than classic intellectual or political history had previously assumed. Among other things, this new awareness supports the need for a more *contextual* reading of both Burke and the Americans who engaged his writings.

If the existence of a "national culture" had not yet been fully discovered in Burke's time, neither had the concept of "political ideology." In retrospect, Burke seems to have been instrumental in anticipating the former and creating the latter.[3] Curiously, America's twenty-first-century political climate has managed a virtual merging of the two—though the polarizations and subdivisions of politics now mirror the fragmentation of culture. As the bumper stickers "Question Authority" and "God Said It. I Believe It. That Ends It" indicate, personal outlooks on life that are at heart cultural can have predictable political consequences. This mixture of sensibility and ideology is not entirely new (less intense versions of it can be found as far back as the Jacksonian era; and it was, for example, a vital component of late nineteenth-century Populism). But the widespread recognition and systematic partisan exploitation of it as a ubiquitous, extra-rational force is recent. So too is the scholarly attention now paid to factors that relate to political behavior but are outside the usual orbit of "political thought" or "theory."[4] For this story of Burke in America, alternative conceptions of national ideals form the necessary bridge between culture and ideology. That is why most of the commentary on Burke's political philosophy (even from prominent politicians) took place outside the political arena itself. By the time matters got to the Senate floor or the campaign trail, general sentiments had been translated into specific issues, and social-cultural inclinations had yielded to politics proper.

Past battles over the nature of freedom, liberty, equality, progress, justice, opportunity, and related ideals revealed alternative hopes for America as a civilization. Like Burke, all of the figures examined in this book approached political thought as a reflection of more-comprehensive belief systems. (Or at least it is nearly impossible to read them today without drawing that conclusion.) Thus they viewed laws, court decisions, and government policies as codifications of the unwritten rules, standards, and aspirations of society. In certain cases they spoke in political terms, yet their associated intellectual leanings may be sensibly discerned; in other cases their discussion was social or cultural, but the political ramifications are evident; some figures spoke of both cultural and political matters. Since these ideological battles and cultural wars are still with us, the generational debates over Burke's writings remain essential to our understanding of the perpetual tension between competing sets of American ideals.

Chapter 1

Burke in Brief

A "Philosophical" Primer

Edmund Burke (1729–97) is usually described as a British political philosopher. But he was, in the first instance, an active politician who spent most of his adult life as a member of Parliament. Whatever "philosophy" Burke expounded was extracted by others from his pamphlets, letters, and orations, which were produced in the heat of political battle. This, in part, explains why he has been susceptible to differing interpretations. Burke was a prolific speaker and writer who today is remembered chiefly as a critic of the French Revolution and as the "father of conservatism." In historical context, however, he had little in common with many conservatives of his own day, and almost nothing in common with conservatism as it is practiced today. It would be less anachronistic and more accurate to call Burke a progressive-traditionalist instead, since certain kinds of conservatism are antitraditionalist, ahistorical, and certainly not progressive. Burke's traditionalism employed an idealized conception of the past as a guide for managing change in the present. The goal was not to prevent change; it was to assure the right kind of change.

In fact, Burke called for a good deal of change during his lifetime. And far from being a conservative by the standards of his day, he was more the genuine reformer. In British terms, he was a Whig, not a Tory. On such issues as American liberty, the condition of Ireland, religious toleration, the abolition of slavery, and the governance of India, Burke opposed the archconservative power structure and—at considerable political risk—called for more humane policies (in present-day usage, he would have been "liberal" or "progressive" on such issues). Granted, this is not the whole story; on other matters—radical revolution in particular—Burke took the conservative side. But even his conservatism was—and still is—subject to qualification.

Burke's Image

Few important historical figures have been more ill-served by concise summation than Edmund Burke. The richness of his Whig vision has been diluted by an oversimplification of his political views and by a fixation on the most reactionary elements of his thought. While the present conservative stereotype of Burke was constructed by a right-wing constituency during the early Cold War, it could not have taken hold without the acquiescence of the broader intellectual community. Postwar conservatives may have needed a patron saint to guide them out of the wilderness, but liberals and radicals also benefited by finding a convenient straw man to embody the alleged backwardness of conservative positions. Even ideologically neutral writers found, and still find, that it is expedient to classify Burke as a narrow defender of outdated beliefs. Textbooks, for instance, give brief mention to Burke for the sake of obstruction—that is, to demonstrate to late-modern students why the historical path to secular democracy, pluralism, and egalitarian values was not traveled as effortlessly as might be assumed in retrospect.

Yet had Burke actually been as crudely cemented to rigid ideas and practices as his current image implies, it is doubtful that his writings would have found a receptive audience for generations after his passing. Usually, brief treatments of Burke deal exclusively with the concluding chapter of his career. But if Burke had died at the age of sixty, his thought would not have been subject to such misinterpretation. Moreover, his legacy would likely have been incorporated into the tradition of progressive reform rather than conservative reaction. Be that as it may, had Burke died at sixty (which would have been in 1789, the year the French Revolution began), he would have died a much smaller man. No matter how prolific a writer, or how distinguished his political career, Burke was merely an interesting figure of secondary importance until he published his *Reflections on the Revolution in France* in 1790. Only then did he become one of the major voices of political philosophy. His remaining years were most notable for his elaborations on that great work.[1]

To better understand Burke's American image, it is helpful to look briefly at those elements of his career that formed the basis for later interpretations.

For the sake of convenience (and following a tiny nutshell biography), this summary will be divided into three topics: America and reform, reason and revolution, and Burke's Whig vision.

Nutshell Biography

Edmund Burke was born in Dublin, Ireland, in 1729, the son of a Protestant (lawyer) father and a Catholic mother. After graduating from Trinity College, he relocated to London, ostensibly to study law, but intent on a career as a man of letters. Although he achieved recognition with *A Philosophical Inquiry into the Origins of Our Ideas of the Sublime and Beautiful* (1757), he chose to enter politics. In 1765 Burke became secretary to the Marquis of Rockingham (leader of the Whigs, and briefly prime minister) and was elected to Parliament from the pocket borough of Wendover. He remained in the House of Commons for over twenty-eight years, later representing Bristol (1774–80) and the pocket borough of Malton (1781–94); in 1782–83 he twice held the subcabinet post of paymaster of the forces. Burke was a genius at political rhetoric, and his early tracts and published speeches mostly served a reform agenda, especially regarding the American crisis, the Wilkes Affair, and Whig attempts at curbing the power of King George III. After Rockingham's death in 1782, Burke's influence dwindled among Whigs; from 1783 on, his major reform crusade was an attack on Britain's exploitation of India. Following the fall of the Bastille in 1789, Burke began to break with the Whigs and oppose the revolution in France, ultimately calling for British military intervention to thwart France's European expansion. He retired from Parliament in 1794 and died at his Beaconsfield estate near London in 1797.

Burke's accomplishments may appear to have been modest. He failed to achieve high office or significant power and was rarely on the winning side of political debates. Nevertheless, he was an articulate proponent of political principles that were to have profound and long-lasting consequences. His writings and speeches were (and are) what made Burke important and exceptional. For instance, his *Thoughts on the Present Discontents* (1770) outlined the Whig opposition to the court government and defended the rise of political parties. His two major speeches on America—*Speech on American Taxation* (1774) and *Speech on Conciliation with America* (1775)—brilliantly addressed the issues of political liberty and colonial governance; his *Letter to the Sheriffs of Bristol* (1777) expanded on those themes, and also defined the proper relationship between elected representatives and their constituents. In his later antirevolutionary works, *Reflections on the Revolution in France*

(1790) and many others, Burke defended traditional practices against radicalism and rationalism, and laid a foundation for ideological conservatism. Thus it was Burke's writings, rather than his political effectiveness, that made him "immortal" and relevant to future generations.

America and Reform

Contrary to popular belief, Burke did not exactly support the American Revolution, but he sympathized with it. He believed that colonial grievances were justified, and that a combination of arrogance, corruption, and stupidity on the part of the king's government had prevented British Americans from enjoying their customary liberties. Burke strongly preferred granting America some version of autonomy short of independence. As he put it in his *Speech on Conciliation with America*: "My hold of the Colonies is in the close affection which grows from common names, from kindred blood, from similar privileges, and equal protection. These ties, which, though light as air, are as strong as links of iron."[2]

Burke seems to have found America alluring, and he even considered emigrating. In his late twenties, he wrote that he wished "shortly please God, to be in America," and at thirty-two he asked a friend: "When you look at the Atlantic do you not think of America?"[3] Around this time *An Account of the European Settlements in America* appeared, bearing no author's name but actually a collaboration of Edmund and his "cousin" Will Burke.[4] Portentously, the book observed that Englishmen in America exhibited an unusually strong "natural temper" for liberty.[5] Later, Burke stated that the colonists "must be governed according to the opinion of a free land."[6] Elsewhere he concluded that British Americans chafed against authority because they were both militant Protestants and assertive Whigs, inclined to "snuff the approach of tyranny in every tainted breeze."[7] Accordingly, during the brief ministry of the Rockingham Whigs, Britain repealed the hated Stamp Act, which had been the chief cause of American discontent. On one hand, Burke saw in America living proof of British liberty unencumbered by the damaging rule of "wicked and designing men." On the other hand, since America lacked so many of the stabilizing institutions of England, particularly a hereditary aristocracy, Burke doubted the colonies' ability to function outside the protection of the British Empire and its unwritten constitution. Nevertheless, at this early stage of the game Burke leaned in favor of liberty and kept his reservations about its consequences in check.

For example, when the radical MP John Wilkes was charged with treason for publishing a criticism of royal prerogative, Burke aligned his party with

English radicals in the name of liberty. Wilkes also supported the American colonial cause, and the Wilkes Affair was a major catalyst in shifting American opinion toward independence.[8] This episode introduced a whole cluster of reform issues—parliamentary privilege, habeas corpus, freedom of the press, the constitutionality of general warrants, the reporting of parliamentary speeches, and the rights of citizens to choose their legislative representatives—all centered on the actions of Wilkes between 1763 and 1774. On each of these matters, Burke championed (what would now be called) civil liberties and government transparency and accountability.[9] Far from the aristocratic flavor of his more famous conservative sentiments, Burke's ideas during this early crisis sounded solidly bottom-up by the standards of his day: "The House of Commons can never be a control on other parts of Government unless they are controuled [*sic*] themselves by their constituents."[10] And: "The temper of the people amongst whom he presides ought therefore to be the first study of a Statesman."[11] In his *Conciliation* speech, he declared: "I do not know a method of drawing up an indictment against a whole people. I cannot insult and ridicule the feelings of Millions of my fellow-creatures." And elsewhere he posed the question: "If any ask me what a free government is? I answer, that, for any practical purpose, it is what the people think so; and that they, not I, are the natural, lawful, and competent judges of this matter."[12] True, Burke never became a democrat as the term is used today. In the 1770s, only radicals drifted toward that persuasion. But Burke's own drift certainly pointed away from government by a "cabal" of "King's friends" and away from authoritarian notions of imperial control.

Obviously, Burke failed to prevent American independence, though he quickly accommodated himself to it, even hinting, in a private note, at a favorable outcome: "A great revolution has happened. . . . It has made as great a change . . . as the appearance of a new planet would in the system of the solar world."[13] The related Wilkes Affair, which had forged a marriage of convenience between Whigs and radicals (and of Burke and radicals), ushered in a number of liberty-enhancing reforms in Britain concerning arrest warrants, the reporting of parliamentary speeches, and freedom of the press. Finally—and perhaps difficult for Americans to comprehend—once the United States achieved independence, it seemed to fade from Burke's consciousness; since America no longer belonged to the British Empire, his concerns turned elsewhere.

It may surprise many to learn that Burke espoused a gentle rather than tough line on what today's politicians call "law and order." This included that ultimate litmus test of tough-on-crime rhetoric: the death penalty. Here Burke noted that "experience" showed "that capital punishments are not more certain to prevent crimes than inferior penalties." It was a mistake, he said, to "suppose the Gallows the only force."[14] Later, when the issue was the punishment of rioters, he argued that the number of prisoners awaiting execution (sixty-two) was excessive, and that the "carnage" of mass executions "rather resembles a Massacre than a sober" justice.[15] The next month, Burke defended two sailors condemned to hang for mutiny, and he was among those instrumental in obtaining pardons for both men.[16] While not strictly opposed to capital punishment, Burke sought to limit its use. On punishments short of the death penalty Burke likewise favored humane reform, as when he offered to support legislation to outlaw the pillory.[17] He also proposed the revision of the entire criminal code, and called especially for improvements to, or even the complete abolishment of, the system of transportation to penal colonies. In fact, on criminal law in general, the father of conservatism sometimes sounded remarkably softhearted, even calling criminals "the diseased and infirm part of our country. . . . They are under cure; and that is a state which calls for tenderness, and diligence, and great consideration."[18] Burke's reform impulse extended to civil matters. For instance, he supported a bill to prevent the permanent imprisonment of insolvent debtors—and he went even further, by proposing a "white-washing" provision allowing for the total discharge of debt. He criticized the existing law for turning a civil matter into a criminal one, which delivered into "private hands" the right "to punish without mercy and without measure."[19]

Perhaps most interesting of all reform issues was Burke's opposition to slavery. As far back as 1765 Burke opposed a plan to seat American representatives in the House of Commons, because the colonial contingent would include southern slaveholders. Burke favored abolition but realized that it was not a practical goal. He therefore applied himself to reforming the conditions of slavery, and he drew up a "Negro Code," intended to "lessen the inconveniences and evils" of slavery and the slave trade "until both shall be gradually done away." This code proposed detailed regulations for conditions aboard slave ships and in slave ports along the African coast, including who could be enslaved and how they must be treated.[20] This was a radical document for its day in the use of interventionist government, the granting of substantial legal rights to slaves, and in its basic premise that the human rights of captive Africans took precedence over the property rights of their owners. In 1792, a year and a half after publishing his *Reflections*, Burke reaffirmed his earlier belief that his code was but a temporary measure preparatory to abolition: "I should think the utter abolition to be, on the whole, more advisable than any scheme of regulation and reform. . . . I heartily wish [slavery] at an end."[21] In 1796, two years after retiring from Parliament and about fifteen months before his death, Burke wrote that one idea he "perfectly agreed with . . . was to give property to the Negroes."[22] Since he did not supply details, it is impossible to determine just how close his thoughts came to the proverbial forty acres and a mule. But that this renowned conservative, long after the French Revolution had restrained his reformist impulse, could suggest compensating not the slaveholders but the emancipated slaves deserves extra notice.

So too does Burke's favoring of religious toleration, extending to "Jews[,] Mahometans and even Pagans." Had Burke been theologically conservative, he would not likely have championed Catholicism for Ireland and France while at the same time defending the established Anglican church for England.[23] Instead Burke followed the modern secular practice of dispatching the dogmatic passions of the Reformation, Counter-Reformation, and Wars of Religion to the less-enlightened past, when "enthusiasm of religion threw a gloom over the politics; and political interests poisoned and perverted the spirit of religion on all sides." Although Burke was uncomfortable with the religious skepticism of Deism and atheism, he sought to prevent the persecution of nonestablished faiths. Burke probably felt the same Whiggish impulse against religious monopoly as he felt against political monopoly. In his *Tracts on the Popery Laws*, concerning Ireland, he warned that "by rooting out any sect, you are never secure against the effects of fanaticism; it may arise on the side of the most favored opinions."[24] Burke, whose mother and sister were Catholic, and who often stood accused of crypto-Catholicism, was firmly devoted to the repeal of the harsh penal laws that oppressed Irish Catholics. He acknowledged some practical limits to toleration, but argued that Catholicism should remain unhindered so long as it posed no threat to the government, the established church, or society. This appears to have been his approach toward minority religions in general.[25]

The story of Burke and reform contained many chapters, and it is by no means a stretch to claim that reform was the central theme of his political career prior to the French Revolution. Burke's plan for cleaning up government, which he outlined in 1780 in his *Speech on Economical Reform*, bore a family resemblance to nineteenth-century civil service reform and to later attempts at campaign finance reform and "streamlining" government. His defense of political parties was a major break with traditional political thought, which had considered such groups to be disloyal factions. Moreover, since his anti-court Whig party viewed itself as the guardian of the principles of the Glorious Revolution of 1688, its fundamental purpose was the diffusion of government power. The Old Whig contingent (and the conservative element of Burke's thought) sought to take power from the king and distribute it among an aristocratic oligarchy. The New Whig contingent (and the reformist side of Burke's personality) sought to diffuse power further among electors (voters), the House of Commons, the press, and—at least abstractly—the people.

Finally, the climax of Burke's career as a Whig reformer was his campaign to impeach Warren Hastings for abuse of power while governing British India. This matter was least relevant to issues that later concerned Americans, yet it represented the one important exception to the conservative theme of Burke's antirevolutionary final years.[26] His sustained involvement began in 1783 with the Whig attempt to rein in the East India Company, which had achieved a virtual commercial, military, and political monopoly over much of India. The British rulers of India had, according to Burke, abdicated their duty of stewardship in order to exploit the colony's resources for their own profit: "We . . . sold the blood of millions of men, for the base consideration of money." Because of this gross abuse, Burke wanted Parliament to intervene and guarantee the Indian people rights along British lines by passing a bill "intended to form the *Magna Charta* of Hindostan." The crux of the problem was that the British officials had been corrupted by the taste of absolute power and the lure of easy wealth. They "drink the intoxicating draught of authority and dominion" in an environment where "all the vices operate by which sudden fortune is acquired." Worse, Warren Hastings represented the personification of the evils of absolute power, of "usurped authority."[27] As with America, Burke feared that a heavy-handed British policy might lead to independence: "If we are not able to contrive some method of governing India *well* . . . a ground is laid for their eternal separation." Also as in the American crisis, Burke thought abuse of power jeopardized the political traditions of the mother country.[28] One writer on Burke's Indian efforts has summarized them well: "The main force of [Burke's] argument, unlike that of the *Reflections*, errs on the side of popular protest, humanitarian internationalism, and eagerness, even yearning for change."[29]

This was a crusade Burke pursued with enormous energy. His correspondence for these years contained more writing on India than on the French Revolution. By the time the trial was over, Burke was old, ill, ostracized from his Whig party because of his stand on France, and, after he resigned from Parliament in 1794, suffered the unexpected death of his only son—who had just been elected to the House of Commons. In 1795 the House of Lords issued its verdict acquitting Hastings of Burke's charges of high crimes and misdemeanors. Hastings was even given a pension. Burke died a disappointed man in 1797, and to many eyes (perhaps to his own) he died a failure. It would be an exaggeration to say that the legacy of his lifelong efforts as a

Whig reformer died with him. But certainly the legacy of his conservative efforts as an antirevolutionary traditionalist has enjoyed greater renown.

Reason and Revolution

Burke was no less a product of the Age of Reason than most well-educated men of his time. But rationalism, or "the view that reason is the only guide leading to the improvement and progress of the human race, and that adherence to religious or other 'non-rational' beliefs is outdated," was another matter.[30] Burke preferred wisdom over reason because he knew that one must be wise enough to sense the parameters within which reason can effectively operate. Beyond such parameters, thought becomes speculation. Burke's celebrated axiom on "circumstances" (stated in *Reflections*) was one demonstration of this cautionary approach. Burke agreed that "abstractly speaking . . . liberty, is good." However, "stripped of every relation, in all the . . . solitude of metaphysical abstraction," it is too broad a concept to be of practical value. Escaped murderers, highwaymen, and madmen may have achieved liberty, but certainly this did not constitute a social good. Thus when Burke observed that "circumstances . . . give in reality to every political principle its distinguishing effect . . . [and] are what render every civil and political scheme beneficial or noxious to mankind," he was arguing that the application of reason made sense only within the specifics of a given situation.[31] As one twentieth-century conservative has pointed out, this reasoning from individual circumstances "is the argument philosophically appropriate to the liberal" and "fatal to conservatism," since it relies on a situational flexibility rather than a strict adherence to explicit principles.[32] If this interpretation is valid, it confirms that Burke was not so much at odds with the Enlightenment as he was hostile to its excesses.

Burke aimed a special hostility at the French philosophes: a new aristocracy of sorts. Ultimately, Burke's objection to the "morass of metaphysic sophistry" was that the "gentlemen theorists" and "our men of speculation" insisted upon implementing their ideas. This was, of course, exactly the type of misguided meddling with the existing system that Burke found impossible to tolerate. In *Refections*, he wrote, "Far am I from denying in theory . . . the real rights of men." But their interpretation and application must stem from practical experience rather than intellectual exercise: "In that deliberation I shall always advise and call in the aid of the farmer and the physician, rather than the professor of metaphysics."[33]

Not only did Burke object to the ideas of the philosophes, but he was driven to extreme reaction by just how fashionable Enlightenment thought had become—and how it had already begun to encourage dangerous political action. He called the Enlightenment writers known as the Encyclopedists a "literary cabal" and branded them as "Atheistical fathers" who had "learnt to talk against monks with the spirit of a monk."[34] In *Thoughts on French Affairs*, Burke asserted that the French Revolution was precipitated not "upon principles merely political." Instead (and the emphasis is Burke's), "*It is a Revolution of doctrine and theoretik dogma.* It has much greater resemblance to those changes which have been made upon religious grounds." Burke specifically likened the Enlightenment to the Reformation, and, consistent with his approach to religion in general, declared that it was not the veracity of the ideas that mattered, but the effects those ideas had on society.[35] Just as the Reformation had transcended the political boundaries of Europe, so too might the secular theology of the French Revolution.

Modern readers of Burke's conservative tracts must therefore note this crucial point: Burke saw the political rationalism of the French Revolution as a threat to *British* civilization as he knew it, and as he believed it had been slowly evolving since time out of mind. Indeed, the original title of *Reflections* indicated that it was not primarily France that alarmed him. "Reflections on certain proceedings of the [London] Revolution Society, of the 4th of November, 1789, concerning the affairs of France"[36] referred to a sermon delivered at London's Old Jewry meeting hall in which the dissenting minister Dr. Richard Price favorably linked the Glorious Revolution of 1688, the American Revolution of 1776, and the French Revolution that had recently begun in 1789. To Burke, the uniting of those three events revealed a monumental and disastrous misunderstanding. For him the impetus behind the revolutions of 1688 and 1776 might have been cut from the same ideological cloth (the retrieval of British liberties), but the "affairs of France" were charting entirely new, speculative, and dangerous territory.

The apparent about-face in Burke's political philosophy in 1790 must be understood within the historical context of (what we now call) an "existential threat" to European civilization. Before the French Revolution, Burke had directed his efforts toward reforming, improving, or advancing British society, which by his standards was remarkably free and fundamentally sound. After 1790 Burke summoned all of his talent and energy to prevent the destruction of that society and its reconstruction by rationalist social engineers. That was why he closed out his days as a propagandist and war hawk.

Between 1791 and his death from stomach cancer in July 1797, Burke clarified and expanded upon the arguments he introduced in *Reflections*. Additional motivation came in the form of initially favorable responses to

French developments and revolutionary ideals within England. Even members of the aristocracy voiced optimism over the promise of liberty, equality, and fraternity taking hold across the channel. Burke's strategy for combating this "monstrous, tragi-comic scene" did not require his renunciation of earlier reform positions. But it required his commitment to nothing less than total victory in what he now saw as an unprecedented struggle for survival. Hence Burke resorted to expostulations not only against the revolution proper (that is, political and military affairs), but against the ideas and attitudes that gave rise to the revolution and continued to inspire its confidence. Thus Burke drew a sharp distinction between his own Whig impulse to reform and the Enlightenment impulse to experiment: "*To innovate is not to reform*. . . . The French revolutionists . . . refused to reform anything; and they left . . . nothing at all *unchanged*."[37] Furthermore, he began to invoke the authority of history and religion in defense of inherited civilization.

Ingeniously, Burke began to exploit what J. G. A. Pocock has called England's "tradition of relying on tradition,"[38] and he turned to mystery, habit, and intuition as antidotes to "naked reason." This strategy, presented in dramatic and often poetic prose, romanticized and sanctified "prescription," "prejudice," and ancient institutions, just as it vilified rational criticisms of them. In apparent contradiction of his earlier respect for the temper of the people, Burke now called democracy shameless, and, in his single most famous utterance he characterized the common folk as a "swinish multitude."[39] Moreover, Burke—who in nonpolitical fields exhibited a practical kinship to certain varieties of Enlightenment thought—now found it necessary to denounce creative thinking and to exalt England's "cold sluggishness" and "sullen resistance to innovation."[40] He attacked both individualism and the idealization of natural man, and called instead for a "bland assimilation" into a historically rooted organic community. Yet perhaps the most antimodern of Burke's tactics was his attack on skepticism.

Scholars have long disagreed (and certain writers have jumped to convenient conclusions) about Burke's religious views: both his personal beliefs and his thoughts on religion's societal role. Here it is enough to note that within the context of his antirevolutionary campaign, Burke jettisoned any vestiges of his own previous doubts concerning the truth of religious beliefs and clung to religion as an essential (extra-rational) force of social and political cohesion. In other words, Burke believed in belief itself. He believed it was safer to accept than to question "allowed opinions" that had long proven successful as civilizing agents. Years earlier, Burke had written: "In their closets [Anglican clergymen] may embrace what tenets they please, but for the sake of peace and order, they must inculcate from the pulpit only the religion of the state."[41] Now Burke extended his rebuke of skepticism to include secular orthodoxies as well. In discussing the unknowable origins of Britain's unwritten constitution, Burke offered advice that served as a general maxim for all inherited traditions or beliefs: "We ought to understand it according to our measure; and to venerate where we are not able presently to comprehend."[42] In this way Burke routinely employed tradition as a political trump card: it enjoyed preference by prior agreement rather than analytical merit.

Once this process of consecrating tradition and disallowing skepticism and innovation was established, there was essentially no way to go but backward. Just as Burke viewed the Glorious and American Revolutions as *restorations*, so too he chided the French for not following a similar, historically grounded course: "You might . . . have profited from our example. . . . Your constitution . . . suffered waste and dilapidation; but you possessed in some parts the walls, and in all the foundations of a noble and venerable castle. You might have repaired those walls; you might have built on those old foundations."[43] Instead, the French demolished their existing architecture and devised novel foundations. Burke's disgust with France and his fear of a rationalist domino effect only strengthened after war erupted on the Continent, which Great Britain joined in 1793. From that point forward Burke (especially in his *Letters on a Regicide Peace*) called for the military defeat of France and argued against any moves for peace without absolute victory. And absolute victory meant the restoration of the old regime.

The Edmund Burke who had been a Whig reformer and progressive thinker during less catastrophic times became obsessively single-minded and narrowly focused under the threat of a radical revolution with world-historical potential. Beginning in 1790, Burke transformed himself into one of the most eloquent and brilliant propagandists in history. Yet by its very nature, propaganda—even if it contains valid observations and propositions—must limit its scope, tone, complexity, balance, and perspective, in order to achieve its polemical goals as sharply as possible. No doubt Burke honestly believed what he said in *Reflections* and his other antirevolutionary tracts. But it is clear in retrospect that such writings gave voice solely to the conservative Old Whig half of his political vision. This made sense at the time, as Burke himself recognized when he remarked that it was "better to be despised for too anxious apprehensions, than ruined by too confident a security."[44] Yet in the long run, this tactical decision proved to be a decisive one for Burke's image. Both English radicals and Americans at large took the extremism of Burke's French Revolution essays as indicative of the whole of his thought. In pursuit of what to him was a just cause, Burke unintentionally sketched his own caricature and created his own reactionary stereotype.

Burke's Whig Vision

Despite widespread judgments to the contrary (in Burke's day and since), Burke did not "turn conservative" in old age. Rather, his Whig sensibility contained both proto-liberal and proto-conservative elements, and circumstances determined which would dominate. Even during his reform period, Burke took the occasional conservative stand. He opposed a measure that would have made divorce easier to obtain, and another that would have dropped compulsory clerical subscription to the Thirty-Nine Articles of the Anglican church.[45] Furthermore, a close reading of Burke's views on religious toleration reveals that he believed a tolerant environment would strengthen both the established church and the nation's constitution. Similarly, Burke supported American colonial protests because he saw them as Whiggish attempts at restoring traditional English liberties, which had been violated by a tyrannical regime. Perhaps more surprising, while it is well-known that Burke feared the French Revolution might spread to England, few have noticed Burke's same fear about the American Revolution. Yet he was troubled that the new popular governments established in the colonies would set a global precedent. Burke's standard reason for favoring traditional society over experimental forms was that traditional society had proven successful over long periods of time. But in reference to America in 1775, Burke announced that he feared experiments in government not because they would fail, but because they might succeed! And "that many of those fundamental principles, formerly believed infallible, are . . . not of the importance they were imagined to be." Therefore, he was "much against any further experiments, which tend to put to the proof any more of these allowed opinions, which contribute so much to the public tranquillity."[46]

Here was a foretaste of Burke's traditionalism, and of the defensive methods he would use to promote it in later years. Radicals and liberals would gladly sacrifice orthodox opinions and public tranquillity to the cause of progress and improvement; most Whigs would not. In condemning the French Revolution, Burke spoke of "all the pleasing illusions which . . . incorporated into politics the sentiments which beautify and soften," and he praised "ancient chivalry . . . which . . . had produced a noble equality . . . which mitigated kings into companions, and raised private men to be fellows with kings."[47] Of course, chivalry did no such thing, and Burke knew this. Yet he was being neither dishonest nor naive. Instead Burke believed that every civilization needed its "pleasing illusions" and "allowed opinions" to serve as what Conor Cruise O'Brien has likened to "Platonic ideals."[48] In such passages and with such language, Burke was essentially speaking in parable, a technique that can be effective only when recognized by his audience. Otherwise, as in the cases of Tom Paine, Mary Wollstonecraft, and virtually all liberal and radical critics of Burke's conservative writings (especially of his *Reflections*), Burke could only sound fantastic, ignorant, or deranged. Hence, when Burke alluded to "all the decent drapery of life" or referred to the "Nobility" as "the Corinthian capital of polished society," he was invoking the Platonic ideals of custom, class, and a "system of manners" that, for him, made a national culture "lovely" and worth preserving.[49]

Nevertheless, for the first twenty years or more of his parliamentary tenure, Burke broached *but did not push* such traditional points nor indulge in such purple prose. Instead, he consulted his conservative instinct in order to structure and qualify his support for reform. Before 1790 Burke usually backed the causes of reformers, radicals, and revolutionaries—even while claiming he was *with* them, yet not *of* them. Clearly Burke had many opportunities to align himself with the "conservatives," had that been his inclination. But he stood against conservatives more often than not. Some have interpreted Burke's Whig approach to reform as a sign of moderation; however, it is more precise to recognize this approach as a quest for balance. Burke likened it to the shifting of weight from one side of a dangerously unbalanced ship to the other.[50] While moderation, by definition, precludes resorting to extremes, Burke was willing to counterbalance any extreme roll to one side of the political spectrum with a suitably extreme shifting of weight to the opposite side. One manifestation of this was the heightened emotionalism, and exaggerated language, in certain of his writings and speeches.

Along with this quest for balance came the need for ballast: the weight of tradition, religion, constitution, crown, and especially aristocracy. While Burke was no democrat, he was devoted to a process of consensus he thought was better. Burke believed the essential spirit of democracy could be best served when the genuine will of the people was mediated by a natural aristocracy of "wise," "judicious," "sober," "decent," "mild and merciful" men. The purpose of such an elite was not to impose their own will, but to implement and guide the temper of the people in ways that were responsible and consistent with existing traditions.[51] Granted, this was easier said than done. But Burke recognized the differences between the aristocratic ideal and the value of individual flesh-and-blood aristocrats. In one of his most quoted passages, famous for its "great oaks," Burke seemed to lavish obsequious praise on the hereditary peerage: comparing commoners like himself to mere "annual plants" that "creep on the ground" and "belly into melons." But upon closer reading, it is obvious that Burke was praising the *ideal* of nobility, not the reality. As important, he was lecturing his social superiors on the necessity of living up to their inherited public duty: "Persons in your Station of Life *ought to have* long views. You people of great families and hereditary Trusts and Fortunes. . . . You *if you are what you ought to be*, are in my eye the great oaks that shade a country."[52] Throughout his life Burke was continually disappointed by his inability to find living personifications of his ideal types. But that did not prevent him from promoting the ideals.

Among the unifying themes in Burke's Whig vision was his lifelong crusade against injustice (what O'Brien calls his "great melody"). This was most obvious in his efforts against slavery and for reforms to English law, but it also motivated his support for American liberty and his prosecution of Warren Hastings. In this sense Burke was conforming to the Old Whig principle of resisting power when the powerful acted unjustly. But equally true to the same Whig vision, Burke aligned himself with institutions of order and stability (and tradition) when he sensed chaos, mob rule, or radical experimentation: that is, when those who *sought* power acted irresponsibly or unjustly.

Though Burke often praised the unwritten constitution, he was flexible in its interpretation. His view of society was historical, and he seems to have adhered to a loose version of the Whig interpretation of history; even in his nonpolitical writing he revealed a belief in progress over time. By contrast, he allowed for the potential of revolutionary events to alter the path of historical development—and not always in a direction he might have preferred. In prospect he feared such events, while in retrospect he proved adept at accommodating himself to them—once they became final and irreversible. Burke entered the modern world gingerly; suspicious of novelty, he was not enraptured with the potential of human reason, unrestrained democracy, or scientific planning to improve the lot of the average man. Yet Burke did not yearn for the past, and he never admired a prior golden age. Even in *Reflections* he did not call for an exact return to the status quo ante, but instead acknowledged the need for reforms to the old regime. Rather than being an antimodern, Burke was a curious type of half modern. While the Enlightenment mind valued change through innovation, Burke sought change with continuity. He hoped to carry the best elements of the past into a better future. He knew that no single generation could acquire enough knowledge to design civilization anew.

Given this outlook, Burke was not a conservative in the common sense of the term. As the above sampling has shown, Burke did not subscribe to the dictum of "that which is, is good." Clearly he was not a strict defender of the status quo. If for no other reason, he did not have the right personality for that kind of work. Burke simply was never happy enough with the world as he found it. This helps explain why he was always shifting from one side of the vessel to the other: now to the reformist gunwale, now to the conservative. Burke saw threats to the political good nearly everywhere he looked, and there was scarcely a moment in which he was not throwing himself into opposition against some group or some process.

A century ago, the American psychologist and philosopher William James spoke of "once-born" and "twice-born" personalities. Once-borns were more stable and contented, less tortured, "their passions are not excessive," they displayed a "systemic healthy-mindedness," and they "treat evil by ignoring it." The optimistic man of reason would seem to fit this personality type, with its nature "of a sky-blue tint." But so too might the satisfied conservative, whose world is already what it should be. By contrast, twice-borns were "persons whose existence is . . . a series of zigzags, as now one tendency and now the other gets the upper hand." They suffered feelings of separateness from their environments; a sense of belonging did not come easily. Inner peace was evasive as well, and "real deliverance, twice-born folk insist, must be of universal application." Hence, in the secular domain, twice-borns might seek to change the world: "Real wrongness in this world . . . must be squarely met and overcome by an appeal to the soul's heroic resources."[53] Certainly we recognize more of the twice-born in Burke: his shifting between reformist and conservative impulses, his reputed emotional instability, and the widely held impression among both his contemporaries and later admirers that he was an outsider in English society. Burke's tireless display of passion alone reveals that he was more suited for crusades for the preservation and betterment of British society than he was for a patient career of custodial oversight. Philosophically, the Old Whig vision may have called for a defensive stewardship of civilization. But on a practical plane, Burke's execution of this mission was an extremely aggressive one. Perhaps he was merely responding in proportion to the aggression of his adversaries, and fighting fire with fire. Though it is also possible that Burke's passionate temperament was a poor match for his Whig philosophy. To extend his own metaphor of the well-balanced ship: sometimes, in an effort to throw his weight far to one side, he threw himself overboard instead. Burke's crusades were rarely successful during his own lifetime. But regardless of his internal motivations, the record shows that Burke's political efforts were focused on controlling the tempo and direction of change. Politically, Burke was a progressive-traditionalist. Contrary to common belief, he was not focused on the classically conservative goal of cementing in place the established conditions of 1688, 1729, 1765, or 1789.[54]

Part I

Early America

Chapter 2

Old Seeds, New Soil

The Land of Paine

Benjamin Franklin once remarked that the Atlantic Ocean acted as a filter on European ideas as they traveled to America. But Franklin was exaggerating the influence of the voyage. European ideas arrived in America intact because they arrived in print. The same writings by Old World intellectuals were available on both continents, though the cultural environment into which they were received in America was distinctive. In today's political jargon, we would say that the ideas of Locke, Rousseau, Milton, Montesquieu, and Edmund Burke *resonated* differently in the colonies, compared to England or France. As one scholar put it, "Freed from the tyranny of the past, ideas, even the same ideas, flourish[ed] in a different way."[1] This transatlantic divergence was widened by the pioneering issues that confronted Americans during the watershed period of their development as a separate people.

Hence leading Americans of the founding era displayed an uncommonly strong need to find intellectual foundations for their public activities. For instance, historian Bernard Bailyn found that their surviving political pamphlets "are to an unusual degree, *explanatory*. They reveal not merely positions taken but reasons why positions were taken; they reveal motive and understanding: the assumptions, beliefs, and ideas . . . behind the manifest events of the time."[2] Perhaps because early American society was so obviously and self-consciously charting new ground, its leaders sought to justify their precedent-setting behavior. By contrast, there would have been no need to justify actions based on habit or custom—and so no need to seek ideas to support them. Ideas that encouraged breaks from traditional practices would have appeared less threatening on the western side of the Atlantic, where the institutional weight of tradition was much lighter than in Europe. Also, since the radicalism of any idea is defined mostly by those who are opposed to it, many ideas seemed less radical in colonial society because fewer entrenched powers were poised to resist them. These conditions yielded a less rigid intellectual climate overall and were particularly helpful for translating the Enlightenment sensibility into practice.[3]

Creation Myth

The United States has always viewed itself as historically unique, and it has celebrated this exceptionalism by sanctifying the process of its own self-creation. What the founding fathers accomplished was not just the construction of a new nation with a novel system of government, but the establishment of a new starting point for history. Grandiose as this claim may seem, much of American political, social, and economic behavior can be understood only in relation to this premise of a new beginning, a fresh start. While the issue of just how radical the American Revolution was is often debated, less attention has been paid to one of the revolution's truly remarkable consequences: the creation of a new archetype. Such a creation is an exceedingly rare occurrence, and by itself makes American history exceptional. The heart of this archetype combined two basic truths. First, America was a clean slate; not only was it virgin territory geographically, but politically and socially as well. Second, the creation of the United States as a "new order for the ages" did not happen by accident, nor by the slow churning of natural forces, nor by divine intervention, but instead by conscious and concerted human effort. Finally, the combination of these two truths yielded, by inference, a third: because the founders had an unspoiled landscape with which to work, and because they thought wisely about what they were doing, they created a world that was not only newer, but better. When Abraham Lincoln recalled how "our fathers brought forth on this continent, a new nation, conceived in liberty and dedicated to the proposition that all men are created equal," he was invoking all three elements of this archetype.[4] To citizens of Lincoln's day, these beliefs already seemed obvious and well-established. By then, the new American archetype had become thoroughly assimilated, much the same way as Thomas Jefferson's "self-evident truths" had become intuitively established in the minds of Americans even before he wrote them into the Declaration of Independence.

A consequence of this archetype is that while citizens of other nations speak of the mother country or the fatherland, Americans speak of the founding fathers. Their new nation was "created" or "invented" by identifiable men who acted in specific instances at known locations—and they knew what they were doing. This was human agency at its most concrete, confident, and noble, and certainly was a manifestation of the Enlightenment frame of mind—the belief that some mixture of knowledge, reason, and practical experience could enable men to improve their inherited condition in a variety of fields: government, medicine, science, commerce, technology, even religion. Thus the Enlightenment impulse to strip mystery and superstition from the world found its way into the myth of America's own beginnings. This stood in contrast to Old World myths of national origin: Italians traced their roots to the imaginary founding of Rome by Romulus or Aeneas; Germans traced theirs to ancient legends of Valhalla and the Valkyries; the English believed their civilization emerged from Anglo-Saxon tribes living "time out of mind," or even from Arthur's Camelot. But Americans eschewed such immemorial and fantastic elements altogether, and instead endowed concrete events and real persons with mythic stature. In so doing, the virtue of human agency became enculturated into the national worldview.

The leaders and the events of the revolutionary and early national periods became the prime focus for this myth-creating process, though earlier events that were portents of things to come were mythologized in similar fashion. The Puritans of seventeenth-century New England, for instance, escaped Old World corruption and injustice, came to a virgin land, and set out to create a model society, "as a city upon a hill." So too, myth has transformed the Mayflower Compact into an early constitution; thus the democracy of the Pilgrims has outshone their (in fact stronger) theocracy. Even the European "discovery" of America fits this pattern. The legend of 1492 conforms to the overarching myth of New World exceptionalism by portraying Columbus as an Enlightenment figure *before* the Enlightenment.[5] He knew the world was round, he did not fear sailing off the edge, he was not shackled by superstition or conventional thinking; his planning, navigational skill, and entrepreneurial energy yielded results; even the fact that "we speak of Christopher Columbus being the discoverer of America, although millions of human beings had occupied the continent for untold ages,"[6] perversely illustrates the belief that the New World only began to matter once calculating "civilized" men began to act upon it.

Yet if America represented the beginning, it was a newness of an "after the flood" rather than "big bang" variety. No one denied that civilization had existed in Europe for centuries. The common practice of reading and citing transatlantic sources dating back to antiquity proved this. What Americans sought to do was avoid the sins of history and the corruption of Europe by transplanting the most enlightened thinking to the New World while straining out the outmoded and fossilized ideas and practices. Here then, in the millennial designs of activist lawyers, merchants, physicians, planters, and others, were the real filters to which Ben Franklin had alluded. "Is it not the glory of the American people," asked James Madison in *The Federalist*, "that, whilst they have paid a decent regard to the opinions of former times and other nations, they have not suffered a blind veneration for antiquity, for custom, or for names, to overrule suggestions of their own good sense, the knowledge of their own situation, and the lessons of their own experience?"[7]

Historian Gordon Wood discerned this early view of the country's creation as a world-historical event when he noted the founding generation's belief that "the illimitable progress of mankind promised by the Enlightenment could at last be made coincident with the history of a single nation."[8] The true extent, form, and nature of Enlightenment thought in America may be forever debated.[9] What is relevant here is not the traceable detail, but the symbolic dedication to this idea of a better world made by thinking men. One scholar of "exceptionalism and identity" found that, in the wake of Columbus, Europeans and colonists alike believed America to be a distinctively different sort of place. But "only with the Revolution did contemporary observers begin to tout America as a social and political model and . . . to claim for it superiority over the Old World."[10] As part of the construction of this new national image making the United States not only different, but better, the authority of certain great names of European thought proved useful. On the other hand, dragging the ideas of certain other European thinkers across the Atlantic was either unnecessary or counterproductive. Newton, Locke, Montesquieu, and Adam Smith, for instance, were welcome because they represented reason, liberty, balance, and individualism. But Edmund Burke was locked out of the mainstream canon because, after *Reflections on the Revolution in France* appeared, he represented the antithesis of such values. His counter-Enlightenment reputation now required his banishment from "the empire of reason." Moreover, this was the case regardless of how legitimately reasonable, new, or exceptional the United States actually was. It also made little difference just how conservative or progressive the greater body of Burke's thought was.

Despite his early reputation as a friend of liberty, the democratic egalitarian spirit of early America did not bode well for Burke. Writings in which he indulged his conservative impulse were particularly at odds with the postrevolutionary climate. As Burke had feared, the fledgling nation had supplanted many long-held "fundamental principles" of government, "formerly believed infallible," with pragmatic alternatives. Worse yet, opinion in the United States was initially enthusiastic about the French Revolution. Prior to the Reign of Terror, most Americans assumed events in France to be similar to their own recent revolution. The warm popular reception accorded the new French ambassador "Citizen" Genet in early 1793 was a demonstration of this belief. True, certain prominent Americans quickly saw the French Revolution as a catastrophe and regarded Burke's *Reflections* with admiration. However, those who held such opinions faced ideological disadvantages that eventually led to their collective defeat politically and to their ultimate demise as a viable counterforce socially. During the early phases of the French Revolution, American leadership began its division into a Francophilic camp of Jeffersonian Republicans and an Anglophilic camp of Hamiltonian Federalists. While their struggle for influence over national policy ended in a draw, whereby some combination of their alternative approaches to government merged into a working (if philosophically frustrated) system, the battle for the national myth was clearly won by the Jeffersonians.

Although the entire process was not substantially complete until the Jacksonian era in the 1830s, it began much earlier. In fact, by George Washington's first term—during which the president decided in favor of Hamilton's policies over Jefferson's objections—it was already obvious that Americans viewed themselves as perpetually devoted to the spirit and ideals of their recent revolution. On a symbolic level this meant a Jeffersonian view of the world and of human nature. The agrarian myth of the yeoman citizen, which Jefferson articulated so memorably, served as an almost visual representation of equality, independence, economic self-sufficiency, and even of intellectual democracy, in that citizens could be trusted to govern themselves wisely because of an underlying belief in their capacity to reason. This utopian ideal housed the twin promises of competitive individualism and cooperative civic-republicanism. Hence it reinforced the belief in human agency as a force for both material progress and social order. Granted the practical world never did conform to this vision. But versions of this ideal, to which the majority of Americans subscribed throughout the antebellum period, helped determine which intellectual authorities were accepted into or rejected from the dominant national culture.

A Choice of Sages

The cases of Edmund Burke and Thomas Paine are especially telling examples of this phenomenon, not only because of the content of their work, but also because of the timing of their respective publications. Paine

(1737–1809) died ostracized by the American nation he had helped to create. Once a hero of the revolution, he had fallen victim first to religious intolerance (he was a Deist, and his *Age of Reason* rejected the Bible as the revealed word of God) and later to personal bitterness (which caused him to attack George Washington in print, with disastrous results). Given this unhappy ending, Paine, like Burke, could have been dropped from the canon and ignored by the textbooks. But exactly the opposite happened. Though subjected to unfounded abuse in the nineteenth century, Paine is widely honored for his work in justifying the philosophy of democratic revolution. *Common Sense*, *The American Crisis*, and *Rights of Man* were all written between 1776 and 1792, a period roughly bounded by the final break with Britain and the ratification of the Bill of Rights. His *Age of Reason*, however, which applied Enlightenment rationalism to religion instead of politics, arrived (1794–95) after both the war for independence and the creation of the new political order had been accomplished. From the standpoint of both content and timing there was little practical need for such a work in America. Nevertheless, *Age of Reason* did not completely damage Paine's honorable reputation as a popularizer of the New World's challenge to established thought. In a nation officially committed to a separation of church and state, the scriptural skepticism of the work proved to be of no lasting threat. Separately, Paine's petty *Letter to Washington* (1796) has been all but forgotten.[11]

Burke, on the other hand, irreversibly ruined his chances of inclusion in the American canon because *Reflections* conflicted with the new nation's symbolic ideals. But the timing here was important as well. Paine had established his reputation as a friend of democratic thought at the same time American society was creating its new archetype. His own image and the collective self-image of the American people formed together. Paine was eventually welcomed back to the fold because *Age of Reason* could be ignored (by those who objected to it) in a way that Burke's *Reflections* could not be. Among its other assets, Paine's writing—like that of Jefferson and Franklin—implicitly extolled the value of human agency. Burke too began as a friend of liberty in the 1760s and 1770s with his support of American rights during the Wilkes Affair, and with his speeches on American taxation and conciliation with the colonies. Fortunately, this was the period in which the embryonic nation was struggling to define itself, identify its first national leaders, and declare its intentions and ideals to the world. During these early volatile years Burke—though never the major figure Paine was—appeared to be on board with the colonists. So much so, that when the Boston Committee of Safety authorized thirteen armed barges for use against the British, it voted to name one of them after Burke, and when delegates to the Continental Congress dined at Philadelphia's City Tavern in 1775, they toasted Burke's health. But there followed a long period of war and peace capped by the implementation of a new political order and the realization of a new national self-image. During these years Burke's role in the American Revolution diminished to the point of negligibility. Somehow the Declaration of Independence, the war, the critical period of confederation, the Constitution, the Bill of Rights, and the rise of the founding fathers merged in the popular imagination into one unified epic drama. Whether this historical watershed was called the Revolution, the Founding, the Creation, or any other name, it retrospectively acquired the aura of a grand, Enlightenment-inspired design.[12] Unfortunately, Burke's counterrevolutionary *Reflections* appeared toward the end of this crucial formative period in American thought. By 1791, the year *Reflections* crossed the Atlantic, popular devotion to the spirit of the revolution and to its underlying assumptions about rights, expanded freedoms, and the breaking of Old World conventions was no longer subject to reversal by anyone.

Most likely a European tract like Burke's *Reflections* would never have found a large receptive American audience no matter what its date of publication. However, after the United States won independence through blood and sacrifice, and established its government under a written constitution including a bill of rights, Burke's defense of monarchy, aristocracy, and the established church, along with his veneration of an unwritten constitution and his praise of ancient chivalry, must have seemed pathetically irrelevant. Even Burke's preference for tradition conflicted with America's recent experience of "inventing itself," and his distrust of conscious design undermined the myth of the founding fathers. By implication *Reflections* condemned the value of human agency as it applied to political experimentation, dismissing it as "insolence." All this was at a time when Americans were celebrating their own successful "experiment with democracy." America had needed Tom Paine because he had been an integral part of the revolution, and it continued to value him because the larger body of his work articulated important national ideals. Burke, although sympathetic to colonial grievances, was never a major force in the revolution, because he failed to alter British policy toward America. In fact, had he done so, it would have prevented the now sanctified revolution from taking place! Burke did not support the war for independence, and he certainly did not believe the American experience stood as a model for European emulation, in Britain, France, or elsewhere. Actually, Burke's true concern for America was predicated on its being a part of the British Empire. Once that was no longer the case, Burke's attention turned away.

In the final collective judgment of the American people, Paine was remembered as an embodiment of founding-era ideals who had gone (temporarily) astray by pushing rationalism to its limits, while Burke was remembered (if at all) as a onetime ally in the struggle for liberty who had deserted the cause. It was little wonder that Paine's *Rights of Man* greatly outsold Burke's *Reflections*, or that the arch-Federalist George Cabot could later write to Alexander Hamilton: "I . . . remind you of 'Burke's Reflections' which were reprobated almost universally when they first appeared—even those who approved the Sentiments thought the avowal of them imprudent and *the publication of them untimely*."[13] From the 1790s forward, most citizens of the new nation considered themselves to be far ahead of Europe socially and politically. Any tract that claimed answers to practical problems could best be found by looking backward to tradition was not only absurd, but subversive.

During the last years of Burke's life, both the American image of Burke and the nation's image of itself were formed. Each represented opposing ideals. These original constructions set the pattern for the use and interpretation of Burke in America for the next two centuries. Because of the nation's Enlightenment heritage, progress and liberalism have dominated tradition and conservatism in the United States, and conservatism has mostly been "the thankless persuasion." This contention is most valid at the level of myth, though political reality has had to accommodate itself to it. To paraphrase Arthur Schlesinger Jr., conservatism has had to adopt the language of liberalism in order to survive.[14] Acknowledging this general rule is *not* tantamount to claiming that liberalism or progress has always triumphed. But Americans in step with the mainstream culture have had to focus on those aspects of Burke that did not threaten the national psyche: the artistry of his rhetoric, his progressive crusades, even the humane quality of some of his conservative beliefs. Alternatively, those who hailed Burke as the voice of Old World charm, or as the defender of pre-Enlightenment traditional values, received an indifferent hearing.

CHAPTER 3

Federalist Persuasions

John and J. Q. Adams

One American who scarcely praised Burke at all, who was in fact almost dismissive of him, was John Adams. This is ironic, since Adams (1735–1826) has been called an "American Burke." Actually the nation's second president was no Burkean in the proper sense: he neither consulted Burke for guidance nor invoked him for authority. Even so, there is much about Adams that seems congruent with Burke at first glance. Both men stood left of the political center while in their primes, and appeared to move to the right in their later years. Both purportedly held a dark view of human nature. Both believed in representative government, as long as this meant, in practice, a system whereby a natural elite could shape or check the majority impulse. In their political philosophy, both men were ardent constitutionalists; for them constitutions provided the framework within which all political action—and all political thought—rightfully took place. Of course, the crowning proof of their ideological unity is that both men were critical of the French Revolution from its early stages. Finally, on the personal level, both were motivated by a quest for balance, and both felt unappreciated in old age.

Not Quite Burkean

Yet, as with Burke's own image, truisms based on quick and selective readings can be misleading. While superficial similarities between Burke and Adams abound, and meaningful similarities exist, so do essential differences. The identification of John Adams as an American Burke is a distraction that reveals more about those making the claim than it does about the actual relationship between the political thought of the two statesmen.[1] Most readers who are familiar with only the stereotypes of Burke and Adams may be surprised to hear that Adams (who was Burke's junior by seven years) considered himself to be the senior partner of the two, in that he believed his own writings had served as the basis for Burke's antirevolutionary essays. Hence, at least in his own eyes, Adams was no disciple of Burke.

Adams did acknowledge Burke to be one of the great men of his age. But, consistent with his private assessments of other great men, such as Franklin, Jefferson, and Washington, he went out of his way not to sound overly impressed. This was partly due to envy, since Adams felt his own fame had unjustifiably fallen short of that enjoyed by several of his contemporaries. It also stemmed from his habitual tendency toward contentiousness. Yet whatever the reasons, Adams's surviving references to Burke certainly display no sense of awe. Their only face-to-face meeting, in London in 1783, was recorded matter-of-factly in Adams's memoirs: "I was introduced . . . to the Duke of Portland, Mr. Burke, and Mr. Fox; but finding nothing but ceremony there, I did not . . . receive anything but cold formalities."[2] Years later, Adams wrote to Jefferson that Burke and Samuel Johnson were "superstitious Slaves or Self deceiving Hypocrites." He then asked: "Is it not laughable to hear Burke call Bolingbroke a superficial writer? . . . Had I been present I would have answered him . . . in my Opinion the epithet 'Superficial' belongs to you and your friend Johnson."[3] In a letter to Benjamin Rush, Adams further opined that Burke and Fox were deficient in their knowledge of the English constitution, and that they had "uttered and published very absurd notions of the principles of government."[4] Elsewhere, Adams claimed that he had once given a copy of his treatise *A Defense of the Constitutions of Government of the United States* to an intermediary who passed it on to Burke, and that it was this exposure to Adams's political philosophy that changed Burke's own view of the French Revolution—and inspired him to write *Reflections*! Afterward, according to Adams, when a gentleman called General Washington "the greatest man in the world," Burke replied, "I thought so too, till I knew John Adams."[5]

Few if any scholars agree with Adams's assessment of his own influence on Burke's thought. Yet if nothing else, Adams's ambivalence toward Burke should be taken as a sign that retrospective attempts to force the two of them into one mold are misguided. The colorful story of Adams asking the Senate to create the title "His Highness, the President of the United States, and Protector of their Liberties" for George Washington is often taken as hilarious evidence of his preference for the trappings of Old World–style monarchy. Since this episode occurred just three months before the fall of the Bastille, it is easy to view it as Adams's first step toward Burkean traditionalism. Yet this simplistic interpretation was debunked long ago.[6] In his *Defense of the Constitutions* (written and published before the presidential-title debate) Adams avowed that, contrary to the assumptions held by European society, "in America, there are different orders of *offices* but none of *men*. Out of office, all men are of the same species." While natural inequalities of talent, virtue, courage, industry, and so on were present in all societies, Adams noted with obvious satisfaction that in his native Massachusetts there existed "as yet no appearance of artificial inequalities of condition, such as hereditary dignities, titles, magistracies, or legal distinctions; and no established marks, as stars, garters, crosses, or ribbons." Why then did Adams call for an impressive title for the nation's chief executive? One reason, according to *Defense of the Constitutions*, was that "there never was yet a people who must not have somebody or something to represent the dignity of the state, the majesty of the people, call it what you will—a doge, an avoyer, an acron, a president."[7] Since the dignity of the presidency was crucial to the legitimacy of the new government, the indicia of rank such a title would imply were comparable to the later practice of playing "Hail to the Chief." Another, less symbolic reason for elevating the image of the president was Adams's preference for a strong constitutional executive—one leader uniquely capable of unifying disparate political factions.[8] Valid reasons notwithstanding, Adams surely misjudged public opinion on this issue; not only was his title rejected, but he was ridiculed as "the Duke of Braintree" and "His Rotundity." Though succeeding generations have been no kinder to the merits of awesome titles in America, at least it should be acknowledged that Adams was no monarchist. In fact, his feelings were so deeply hurt over this false charge that he was still proclaiming his innocence nearly a quarter century later: "Now, I will forfeit my Life," he wrote Jefferson, "if you can find one Sentence in my [writings] . . . which by a fair construction, can favour the introduction of hereditary Monarchy or Aristocracy into America."[9]

Adams's concern that republican government retain enough authority to ensure order and stability had little to do with a romantic attachment to the titles or customs of ancient regimes. Like other practical leaders of his time, Adams knew that all successful revolutions progressed through two stages, the first of which comprised the overthrow of the existing order. Since this stage was essentially destructive and targeted some oppressive regime, it both required and inspired more passion than restraint. The second stage comprised the institution of a new order and was essentially constructive; its real enemy was chaos. Hence it required a cooling of the passions, and the implementation of new political, social, and economic structures that were faithful to the ideals that had motivated the first stage. The great mistake of the French was that they were unable to jettison their destructive first-stage mentality while implementing the constructive second stage of their revolution. The true greatness of such founders as Adams, Washington, and Hamilton stemmed from their ability to excel at the leadership of both phases of the American Revolution (while such others as Tom Paine, Sam Adams, Patrick Henry, and even Thomas Jefferson, had difficulty making the transition from the first phase to the second).

Burke, despite his tentative alliance with the colonists, was ultimately unhappy with both stages of the American Revolution. He did not look favorably upon Britain's loss of such an important part of its empire, and he never was comfortable with the new political order that developed in the United States—because he feared it might spread to Europe. Burke's intellectual commitment, unlike that of *any* of the American leaders, was to good government rather than necessarily to republican government, and even this was complicated by his emotional attachment to aristocracy. Most important, to him democracy was a noble ideal rather than a comprehensive way of life. Burke's worldview *included* the idea of democracy; but the new American Weltanschauung eventually came to be *defined* by the word "democracy." America's leaders, aware that the revolution had unleashed popular aspirations beyond their control, soon had to accommodate themselves to circumstances within which systems of order could not be mistaken for subversions of revolutionary-Enlightenment ideals. The flaying of John Adams during the presidential-title debate was a lesson to all: not only was Adams attacked by Jeffersonians, but even some Federalists who were ideologically close to his views (and who knew or should have known better) condemned him as a monarchist in what can only be described as a ritualist avowal of revolutionary symbolism.

Given these circumstances, it is more sensible to conclude that Adams and Burke each developed political philosophies that occasionally ran along parallel lines but contained fundamental incompatibilities. After the French Revolution, Burke's mission was to apply the brakes to the momentum of Enlightenment overreach. To him, European civilization had already exceeded its manageable pace of progress; hence his voice became one of reaction. His response was to admonish society's leaders for their naive rationalism, and to persuade them to return to a more traditional conception of reform. Burke in his last years sensed that he had outlived his own era.

Adams, by contrast, saw his mission as one of implementing Enlightenment thought in some workable, responsible manner. His voice may have been more cautionary than America's utopian democrats would have liked, but his devotion to republican government and his distrust of aristocratic power placed him within the American political mainstream and in opposition to European-style reactive conservatism. Rather than apply the brakes to political progress, Adams sought to steer it on its proper course. For example, he was one of the most forceful voices favoring bicameral legislatures, rather than the single-house versions championed by radical democrats. While this is usually viewed as a conservative strategy to check the direct will of the people, to Adams the bicameral structure fulfilled the equally important function of checking the ability of the elite to impose their will on a unicameral chamber by means of their wealth, power, status, and superior learning.[10] Unlike Burke, who feared the aristocracy least of all groups, Adams feared the aristocracy most—more than either a strong executive or the masses. He once called aristocratic power the "first danger" to the republic. Given its inevitable presence in all societies, he concluded that "all that policy and legislation can do is to check its force by force. Arm a power above it and another below it . . . both able to say to it, when it grows mad, 'Maniac! keep within your limits.'"[11]

Adams, despite his old-age crankiness (he was cranky at every age), never felt he had lived too long, nor did he feel out of place living within the order he had helped create. Granted, he complained continually that people misunderstood and did not appreciate him; once he wrote that he felt as if he "lived in an enemies Country." But this was mostly because he knew that both his colleagues and the public at large judged him to be more conservative, monarchic, aristocratic, puritan, and old-fashioned than he believed he actually was.[12] Notwithstanding Adams's lifelong capacity for self-pity and resentfulness, on the philosophical plane he remained optimistic to the end—which came twenty-nine years after Burke's death, and long after most Americans had left Burkean traditionalism behind. "I have every reason to rejoice in the happiness of my country," wrote Adams at the age of eighty-three, "which has fully equalled, though not exceeded, the sanguine anticipation of my youth." Looking toward the future, he declared: "God prosper long our glorious country, and make it a pattern to the world!"[13] Half a year later, he expressed similar sentiments in notably Enlightenment-centered language:

> We shall leave the world with many consolations. It is better than we found it. Superstition, persecution, and bigotry are somewhat abated;

> governments are a little ameliorated; science and literature are greatly improved, and more widely spread. Our country has brilliant and exhilarating prospects before it, instead of that solemn gloom in which many of the former parts of our lives have been obscured.[14]

By contrast, Burke in his final years experienced "that solemn gloom" on both a personal and public level. Unlike Adams, whose son John Quincy enjoyed a brilliant career capped by election to the presidency of the United States, Burke's only son, Richard, died shortly after his election to Parliament in 1794. Added to this family tragedy, Burke witnessed what looked to him to be the death of his belief system. When he broke from his Whig party over the issue of revolution, he was keenly aware of the generational nature of the schism. The younger, Enlightenment-smitten New Whigs had "the doctors of the modern school" to guide them, while Old Whigs like himself looked instead to "their constitutional ancestors." Burke made clear that this revolution of political thought would have to proceed without him. He abhorred the "new order" he saw "coming on" and lamented that the old "political opinions must pass away as dreams which our ancestors have worshipped as revelations."[15]

For some years prior to his demise, Burke habitually referred to his life and his traditional approach to politics and society as if they had already come to an end. His voice became both pessimistic and resigned. "Every thing appears to me in this Season to be serious and awful in the highest degree. . . . I am as a man dead." He was "ever unhappy" and could feel nothing "with real pleasure." Later he wrote, "I am very miserable—tost by publick upon private grief, and by private upon publick."[16] Burke's dejection did not stem solely from his paternal mourning over Richard's death, and he had long displayed a tendency to speak to his contemporaries as if he were an ambassador from the past. Portions of the *Appeal from the New to the Old Whigs* serve as examples of this; an even earlier example can be found (before the French Revolution) during the initial phase of the Hastings proceedings.[17]

Unlike Burke, John Adams never felt he was defending the values of a bygone age. Rather, he was trying to construct a new American system that could funnel public activity toward constructive ends. What Adams sought to accomplish with political activity was comparable to what Alexander Hamilton sought to accomplish with economic activity. That is, in recognition that self-interest, hedonism, power, and insecurity—what Adams called "the passions"—motivated behavior more than did virtue or altruism, both men sought to create systems that would tap the egotistical energies while containing the egotistical excesses. "To regulate and not eradicate [the passions] is the province of policy," wrote Adams. "It is of the highest importance . . . that they should . . . be . . . on the side of virtue."[18] Burke never stopped calling for the natural aristocracy to reclaim its leadership role by reprising virtuous behavior. To his mind, this would have encouraged the reassertion of tradition as a guiding principle of politics. Virtue and tradition were so closely linked in Burke's view that he saw the decay of each contributing to the decay of the other. Adams reluctantly concluded that virtue in America had declined markedly once independence had been won, and he was modern enough (or realistic enough) to let old warhorses lie. His view was more consistent with the New World sensibility, which assumed that America needed to learn from the lessons of European history rather than habitually continue in its tradition, which was fraught with errors. While Burke still hoped for virtue to restore good government, Adams surmised that it would have to work the other way around: "The best republics will be virtuous, and have been so; but we may hazard a conjecture, that virtues have been the effect of the well ordered constitution, rather than the cause."[19] Hence, for Adams, political behavior was best controlled by the purely practical process of dividing power among countervailing entities: a strong executive with overall responsibility for the whole nation, an independent judiciary serving for life and working within the common-law tradition and thus insulated from momentary pressures and passions, an elite senate wherein personal quests for distinction, power, and influence would cancel each other out, or at least they would be contained within a single arena, and a democratic house in which the most immediate concerns of the people could be vented. In fact, this institutional balancing of power was Adams's very reason for writing *Defense of the Constitutions* to begin with.

This reason provides a key to understanding Adams's intellectual universe as well. While he was one of the most well-read men of his time, his interest was quite narrowly focused on government. Enlightened though he was, he had none of Franklin's or Jefferson's fascination with science; he studied history and philosophy, but mostly for what they could tell him about the relationship between governance and human nature. The founding of America was, like few moments in history, a time during which the construction of a new system of government was nearly tantamount to the creation of a new society. Many of the founders must have sensed this, but Adams seems to have seized upon the opportunity to influence this process with an unmatched intensity. "You and I, my dear friend," he wrote Richard Henry Lee in 1777, "have been sent into life at a time when the greatest lawgivers of antiquity would have wished to live. How few of the human race have ever enjoyed an opportunity of making election of government . . . for themselves or their children." Nourished intellectually and motivated psychologically by the chance intersection of his own life and the birth of the nation, Adams's obsession with government never ended. Government, he believed, "is the only adequate instrument of order and subordination in society . . . since without it, neither human reason nor standing armies would ever produce that great effect."[20] Strangely, Edmund Burke (so widely acknowledged as a great political philosopher) did not express the same degree of confidence in the nuts-and-bolts structure of government as the only instrument of order and subordination in society. To him, the entire landscape of tradition and national culture—of which government was but a part—contributed to the maintenance of order. Hence his emphasis on heroic leadership and on a venerable code of conduct. As he said in *Reflections*, "There ought to be a system of manners in every nation which a well-formed mind would be disposed to relish."[21]

Both Burke and Adams would have considered an unchecked monarchy to be tyrannical, but on neither side of the Atlantic was royal absolutism a real danger. The threat to ordered liberty stemmed from other sources in both England and America. Adams (while living in London as a U.S. diplomat) published the first volume of *Defense* just before the constitutional convention in 1787, while Burke published *Reflections* in late 1790, more than a year into the French Revolution. Burke was terrified over Britain's apparent willingness to follow the French example, while Adams was similarly shocked by Shays's Rebellion (1786) and the reported lack of political stability in his newly autonomous homeland. Though both men were united in their quest for order, they were fighting different ideological battles. Burke feared speculative design. He hated the philosophes, seeing them as a pseudo-elite of wicked men, and he looked to long tradition as a means of combating their experimental rationalism. Adams, on the other hand, though often critical of the philosophes, was, in the words of one scholar, "on the whole . . . more moderate than Burke; he did not reject indiscriminately all their ideas."[22] Burke proposed sticking with (a flexible application of) the tried and true as a means of combating radical democracy and misguided egalitarianism. Adams too fought against the extreme designs fostered by the revolutionary climate of the day. But instead of calling for adherence to tradition, he advocated the construction of a completely new system of government. Moreover, not only was Adams's tolerance for political experimentation greater than Burke's, but his relationship with tradition was less constraining.

Transformation of John Adams

Adams merged tradition, experimentation, and human agency in a way that was consistent with the new American archetype of enlightened design. In his prime he possessed a rare talent for understanding the present, and so was able to discern the essence of new conditions before most others knew what was happening. He had done this earlier, when he was one of the first unyielding voices for independence. As he later recalled, the American Revolution was not the war—it was the changing of people's minds before the first shot was fired. His prescient recognition of this informed his commitment to the new nation as an intellectual reality before most of his contemporaries even began their fight to make it a political reality.[23] So too in his *Defense*, written after the war but before the Constitution or the Federal period, Adams presented what may pass as an accurate summation of the creation myth even before the creation was complete:

> The United States of America have exhibited, perhaps, the first example of governments erected on the simple principles of nature; and if men are now sufficiently enlightened to disabuse themselves of artifice, imposture, hypocrisy, and superstition, they will consider this event as an era in their history. . . . They adopted the method of a wise architect. . . . [They consulted great writers] to inquire how far both the theories and models were founded in nature, or created by fancy; and when this was done . . . [they decided] to adopt the advantages and reject the inconveniences of all. Unembarrassed by attachments to noble families, hereditary lines and successions, or any considerations of royal blood, even the pious mystery of holy oil had no more influence. . . . The people were universally too enlightened to be impressed by artifice. . . . Thirteen governments thus founded on the natural authority of the people alone, without a pretense of miracle or mystery. . . . The experiment is made, and has completely succeeded.[24]

This passage, most likely written in the fall of 1786, not only anticipated Madison's view in *The Federalist*, but, perhaps more significantly, represented the style of thinking commonly associated with Jefferson, who personified the Enlightenment, rather than Adams, who allegedly did not. Most important, few passages on government could be more counter-Burkean than this one. Unfortunately, Adams's ability to gauge the political climate with uncanny clarity soon began to erode. Up until the constitutional convention, Adams was ahead of the curve on American political thought, while after that point he fell behind it. He especially failed to adjust to the growth of the democratic sensibility. In the later half of his public career, Adams betrayed a conflicted understanding of the relationship between the people and their government. One recent intellectual biography declared him to be "against the emerging mainstream of American thinking about politics." This led to "Adams's political alienation" and made him "an intellectual anachronism who had missed the political significance and meaning of the American Revolution."[25] Adams's inner conflicts between order and innovation, stability and progress, deference and democracy, and so on, have frustrated scholars over the years. Treatments of the second president bearing such titles as "The Trouble with Adams" and "The Relevance and Irrelevance of John Adams" are really extrapolations of the unsettled nature of Adams's own mind.[26] Possibly this difficulty in sketching Adams in clear, simple lines accounted for his long-held status (until quite recently) as the "forgotten" founding father.

The totality of Adams's thinking (otherwise so hard to handle that it has been overshadowed by that of Jefferson, Hamilton, Madison, and others) was more representative of the vicissitudes of the American political outlook between 1765 and 1826 than was the thinking of any other prominent figure. At first, Adams's principles conformed to the Whiggish challenge to "corrupt" British colonial rule, as well as to the general Enlightenment challenge to traditional thought.[27] His writings during this period (1765–87) were of a liberal sensibility and coincided with the buildup to, and the accomplishment of, the first stage of the American Revolution. Adams's next period (1787–1801) corresponded to the constructive second stage of the revolution, and so his writings emphasized the need for order, and preached on the dangers of radicalism, simple democracy, Jacobinism, and unrestrained rationalism. The third and final period of Adams's intellectual evolution (early 1800s to 1826) mirrored the paradox in American thought after 1800. He, like the nation itself, wrestled with the task of reconciling the enlightened ideals that had (by then) become embedded in the collective American psyche, with the practical impossibility of implementing those ideals too literally. His writing thus alternated between idealism and realism.[28] This refusal to commit himself boldly to a single perspective amenable to partisan debate gained him few disciples in his waning years. It also explains why "few commentators on the American past have ever been altogether certain what to do with John Adams or just where to place him."[29] Adams in his prolonged and reflective retirement could have cleared up his reputation and declared his opinions unequivocally. It is certain that he (like Burke) cared about the judgment of posterity, yet he was unable to state his principles in a tidy package.

Both Adams and Burke dragged old baggage into their later years, but the bags contained different articles of faith. Burke's were stuffed with the cloak of tradition and with the tenets of Old Whig reform. Adams's bags were mixed: they held many elements of the English Whig tradition, but (as Burke noted about Americans) these elements inclined toward a rights-based philosophy, and thus against traditional authority. But Adams also carried with him an Enlightenment-based commitment to conscious design. Burke proclaimed that "to innovate is not to reform," but for Adams, the type of innovation represented by the framing of the state and federal constitutions in America was a mark of genuine progress. Adams's stance on innovation was positive yet restrained. Enlightenment radicals thought of innovation as a perpetual-motion machine of continual improvement: if the application of reason worked as well as they believed it did, then constant experimentation in all fields of human activity was sure to be its own reward—since beneficial outcomes could be adopted, and damaging outcomes could be rejected. Adams, however, was less confident that bad outcomes could be discarded so easily, and thus seemed willing to experiment only when absolutely necessary. Adams seems to have believed in periodic waves of innovation, rather than in a steady tide of it. Burke was more opposed to innovation on principle; otherwise he would not have stressed prescription and tradition. Philosophical substance aside, Burke intentionally and for overtly ideological purposes encouraged the construction of his conservative, counterrevolutionary, antirationalist (and even anti-Enlightenment) image. Adams, probably for unintentional, psychological reasons, allowed himself to be portrayed as a monarchist, antirepublican stick-in-the-mud. But while Adams's availability as a convenient target for his democratic adversaries made his reputation Burke-like, his beliefs did not quite make him Burkean.

The French Revolution

When assessing the relative harmony between the thoughts of John Adams and Edmund Burke, no single topic has greater significance than the French Revolution. Of course, the true importance of the French Revolution went much deeper than this. Americans today hardly realize the huge impact of that event on the course of politics in the United States. Without it, the first fifty years of the national history might have unfolded differently—with potential ramifications for succeeding periods. The ideological divisions spawned in America by France's upheaval provided a framework for two generations of political rivalry between various liberal and conservative factions. Divisions in American society were nothing new, but due to the passions unleashed by the revolutionary climate, existing disagreements took on greater sharpness. Debate over issues rose to a more politically philosophical plane as participants sought intellectual justification for their positions; they reexamined Enlightenment thought and redefined their views about its practical application to government.[30] Even issues that had nothing to do with France's revolution (such as competing visions of economic development) were fought over by opposing camps that were—because of the revolution—arrayed around contrasting views of constitutions, rights, equality, tradition, and popular will. In this respect, both the Federalist-Republican split and the later Whig-Democrat split were to an important degree shaped by the original French Revolution debates.[31] Specific issues and alignments would change over time, but this general revolutionary-versus-antirevolutionary dichotomy (which was soon restyled as a democratic-versus-antidemocratic dichotomy) supplied the major ideological tension in America until supplanted by the divisions between North and South.

One way of describing this activity is to say that Americans used the French Revolution as a mirror in which they saw the image of their own revolution reflected back across the Atlantic. Unique though the American Revolution was, the "self-evident truths" upon which it was predicated were assumed to be of universal application. Hence the French arena served as a political laboratory for testing the general principles of liberty. This was akin to the independent confirmation of a scientific experiment, and, in a sense, the validity of America's earlier experiment—and the robustness of republican philosophy—was at stake. No one saw this with more gravity than John Adams, since the construction of republican government was his obsession. Moreover, he shared with most Americans the hope that the United States would serve as a model for other nations to emulate. Since France unwittingly presented itself as the first country in line for this process, Adams was intent that everyone draw the right conclusions from the exercise.

It is therefore puzzling that Adams did not write much about the French Revolution. While Burke churned out hundreds of pages on its dangers in just a few years, Adams wrote only a few statements on the topic over the span of three decades. From his retirement perch, Adams bitterly lamented that the French Revolution caused the Jeffersonians "to run me down as an aristocrat and a monarchist . . . [and] produced a coldness towards me in all my old Revolutionary friends."[32] So perhaps he avoided the subject out of personal pain. It is interesting that virtually all of Adams's criticism of Burke took place in his later years—well after the French Revolution, and after Adams's alleged turn toward Burkean conservatism. While Adams himself blamed the French Revolution for his conservative reputation, apparently that reputation had already existed. Just two months after the fall of the Bastille, one Jeffersonian senator wrote: "France seems travailing in the birth of freedom. . . . Royalty, nobility and vile pageantry, by which a few of the human race lord it over and tread on the necks of their fellow mortals, seem likely to be demolished. . . . Ye gods! with what indignation do I review the late attempt of some creatures to revive this vile machinery! O Adams! Adams! what a wretch art thou!"[33] Eventually Adams did sound a critical note on the French Revolution, though he never produced a political tract dedicated to the subject. While his *Discourses on Davila* was clearly an antiradical work written with France in mind, it did not directly confront the French Revolution the way Burke's *Reflections* did. Adams's most well-known statement on the topic came not in any published forum, but in a letter to Richard Price, the British philosopher and dissenting minister whose 1789 speech "Discourse on the Love of Our Country" was the paean to the French Revolution that Burke chose to answer with *Reflections*. Adams told Price that he had spent his life fighting for liberty, "but I have learned by awful experience to rejoice with trembling." Further:

> I know that encyclopedists and economists, Diderot and D'Alembert, Voltaire and Rousseau, have contributed to this great event more than Sidney, Locke, or Hoadley, perhaps more than the American Revolution, and I own to you that I do not know what to make of a republic of thirty million atheists.
>
> Too many Frenchmen, like too many Americans, pant for equality of persons and property. The impracticality of this God Almighty has decreed, and the advocates for liberty who attempt it will surely suffer for it.[34]

Clearly this reaction sounds very close to what Burke would later write, and it was written before the publication of *Reflections*—though not before Burke formed his own negative opinion of the revolution.[35] Adams in later years reaffirmed his objections: "When I saw that the Sympathies in America had caught the French flame: I was determined to wash my own hands as clean as I could of all this foulness." He also left no doubt as to the magnitude of the danger: "The French Revolution I dreaded; because I was sure it would, not only arrest the progress of Improvement, but give it a retrograde course."[36] Elsewhere in dribs and drabs Adams revealed other criticisms: his lack of trust in the philosophes, his assertion of the need for religion, his displeasure with social leveling or with "simple democracy" (as opposed to "balanced" government of multiple branches). But most of these statements were made in private letters; nowhere did he pull all his thoughts on this important subject together in a unified, published work. Surprisingly, one of the few direct statements Adams made concerning Burke's *Reflections* was an attack on the term "swinish multitude." Writing to John Taylor, Adams called Burke's terminology "unphilosophical, immoral, irreligious, uncivil, impolitic, inhuman, and insolent." He then addressed (the dead) Burke rhetorically: "Impudent libeller [*sic*] of your species! Whom do you mean by your 'multitude?' The multitude in your country means the people of England, Scotland, and Ireland. . . . The multitude in this country means the people of the United States. The multitude means mankind." A couple of years earlier, when coming across the phrase "unyoked multitude" in his copy of Mary Wollstonecraft's *French Revolution*, Adams jotted in the margin: "Not swinish."[37] Perhaps this was an example of the American democratic sensibility working its way into Adams's psyche. Or perhaps it was yet another example of his personal ambivalence toward Burke.

Adams relegated another textual comment on *Reflections* to a private marginal note in Wollstonecraft's book. Here he criticized Burke for defending the French constitution, saying, "He certainly understood not the Constitution of the States General; nor had he considered the history of France as connected with, and springing out of, that constitution." Coming from Adams, this was a serious charge. Recall that he had earlier criticized Burke's understanding of the British constitution, and, to Adams's mind, understanding constitutions was understanding political thought. Unfortunately, since Adams did not expand upon his complaints about Burke and either the English or French constitutions, few conclusions can be drawn from his passing remarks. His remaining reference to *Reflections* came in his partial autobiography of 1812. This time he was skeptical of Burke's poetic portrait of the French queen, judging that "in his description, there is more of the orator than the philosopher."[38] Such comments are notable for their scarcity, their critical tone, and their mostly private (that is, unpublished) context. On the other hand, Adams's negative remarks on *Reflections* amounted to little more than quibbling over nonessential points. Overall it is safe to conclude that Adams sided more with Burke than with Paine in the French Revolution debate. Though even granting this, his ideas on some core matters diverged significantly from Burke's.

John Quincy Adams

In recalling his own role in the great debate, Adams seemed satisfied that his *Davila* essays, which were first published in 1790–91 in the Federalist

United States Gazette, explained his position on the French Revolution. But they did so circuitously at best. A more direct alternative to *Davila* were the *Letters of Publicola* written by his son John Quincy (1767–1848), which were also representative of the thoughts of Adams senior. These began appearing pseudonymously in a Boston newspaper soon after the *Davila* essays finished their run, and contemporaries (including Jefferson) assumed they were the work of Vice President John Adams.[39] In the face of widespread criticism of the *Publicola* essays, John Adams denied authorship but did not renounce their content. Even once the real author was known, key contemporaries refused to exonerate Adams senior from ultimate responsibility.[40] Charles Francis Adams, editor of his grandfather's papers, believed that John and John Quincy shared the same views on the subject, and John Adams in later recollections about the French Revolution placed no distance between himself and the arguments of Publicola. Whether the *Publicola* essays are technically scripture or apocrypha is less important than the practical fact that they were too well identified with John Adams's position to ignore.

Publicola did not discuss the French Revolution head-on but instead evaluated the contrasting interpretations of it found in Burke's *Reflections* and Paine's *Rights of Man*. As such, *Letters of Publicola* represented an important entry in the American branch of the great pamphlet war of the 1790s. By entering this debate, young John Quincy aided the birth of ideology in America, and his readers seemed very excited about the process. Toward the end of Publicola's newspaper run, James Monroe observed, "The contest of Burke and Paine, as reviv'd in America with the different publications on either side[,] is much the subject of discussion in all parts of this state."[41] Many years later, John Quincy's own son described this ideological "contest" as "a controversy which shook the chief governments of Christian civilization. Nowhere was it more sensibly felt than in America."[42] Like Paine, Publicola praised the "Genius of Freedom . . . snapping . . . the arbitrary system of government in France." In doing so he countered Burke's denial of the root justification for toppling the ancien régime. J. Q. Adams supported the first stage of the revolution (the overthrowing of oppressive power) and directed his criticism toward the excesses of the second stage (the establishment of an improved order). His pose was to act as a mediator between Burke's "one continued invective . . . which passes a severe and indiscriminating censure" and Paine's "applause as undistinguishing as is the censure of Mr. Burke." However, most of his text attacked certain of Paine's positions—and by extension those of his father's rival Thomas Jefferson, who had praised *Rights of Man* in print. (In fact, in defending his own position, Jefferson stoked the ideological fires of the day by implying that the Adamses' sympathetic reading of *Reflections* was subversive of American values, since "Mr. Paine's principles . . . were the principles of the citizens of the U.S.")[43] That said, unlike the rambling *Reflections* or the expansive *Rights of Man*, the *Publicola* essays were limited in scope, and focused mainly on the practical application of rights. Adams explicitly rejected hereditary nobility for America, and somewhat misleadingly asserted, "It is not my intention to defend the principles of Mr. Burke." True, Publicola avoided defending the bulk of Burke's ideas; instead, most of what Burke threw into *Reflections* was never brought up.[44]

Possibly this was a sensible strategy for avoiding the morass of speculative arguments about religion, human nature, the cloak of tradition, "pleasing illusions," and the like. Publicola's essays were more a refutation of Paine than they were an endorsement of Burke. This was a perfectly logical strategy, since Paine's *Rights of Man* clearly resonated with Americans much more than Burke's *Reflections* did. In order to counter Paine's attempt at uniting transatlantic revolutionary ideology, Publicola's goal was to differentiate the American Revolution from the French Revolution. Doing so would forestall the possibility of guilt by association. Any troubles toward which France may have been headed in 1791 could not be blamed on its emulation of America if in fact its revolution was of a separate variety. Equally important for the younger Adams, Publicola's American readers needed to be convinced that their own unique environment was inhospitable to any radical excesses that may have germinated in French soil.

"This principle, that a whole nation has a right to do whatever it pleases, cannot in any sense whatever be admitted as true," wrote Publicola. However, this apparent disavowal of democracy and human agency was modified almost immediately, and was aimed solely at Paine's unbounded belief that a democratic majority could reframe its government each generation without practical restraint. This was exactly the sentiment behind Jefferson's remark that a country needed a good revolution every twenty years or so. Publicola objected to such a misguided and disorderly concept by cautioning, "Mr. Paine seems to think it as easy for a nation to change its government, as for a man to change his coat." In some respects this was the crux of the great pamphlet wars, and it stemmed from Richard Price's contention that by virtue of the revolution of 1688, the people of England (and by extension any free people) had the right to choose their own governors, to cashier them for misconduct, and to frame a government for themselves. These rights were denied by Burke in *Reflections*, and Burke's position was in turn rejected by Paine in *Rights of Man*. When Publicola weighed in on the matter, he purported to steer a middle course. But he effectively sided with Burke in believing that any such right "ought never to be exercised but in cases of extreme urgency: Every nation has a right as unquestionable to dissolve the bands of civil society, by which they are united," but only when they "have been compelled by an unaccountable necessity." Adams further agreed with Burke that, as in the case of England's Glorious Revolution of 1688, Americans not only had no choice but to revolt, but, by means of their new constitution, they also had the right "to legislate for succeeding generations."[45] Thus while Paine and his American adherents expected their revolution to remain perpetually in its iconoclastic first stage, Adams and his Federalist allies hoped that its stabilizing second stage was here to stay. The new system designed by the founding fathers must be altered only under dire circumstances. While not plainly acknowledging the connection, Publicola tacitly and generically linked the British settlement of 1688–89 with the adoption of the U.S. Constitution—both represented constructive stages of revolution, and for purposes of political stability this was all to the good.

If on this core matter Publicola sounded similar to Burke, he made it clear in his final letter that on other issues he parted company with him. First (sounding just like his father), he complained that he had been unjustly portrayed as an advocate of hereditary rule: "The author challenges all . . . to produce a single passage to these publications which has the most distant tendency to recommend either a monarchy or an aristocracy to the citizens of these States." Then, in obvious contrast to Burke's eulogy to the British constitution, Publicola claimed he "never had the intention to defend the corruptions of the English Constitution, nor even its principles in theory, except such as were adopted by our own." Furthermore, "I have contended that our representation of the people is infinitely superior both to the French and to the English." He had earlier implied that this superiority resulted from wise choice and conscious design: "The Constitution of the United States appears to me to unite all the advantages, both of the French and of the English, while it has avoided the evils of both." So even from the anti-Paine side of the argument, America's New World knack for filtering out bad European ideas was celebrated. Despite these (and other) anti-Burkean elements, the *Publicola* letters proved too counter-republican for popular tastes. Again like his father, Publicola appeared wounded by the "torrent of abuse" his letters had generated from America's Painite majority. He decided to suspend further publication, and he hoped "the public will not take misrepresentation for reason, nor invective for argument."[46]

Six years later, in 1797, when the younger Adams was in London on diplomatic service, he wrote a series of letters to his father that shed additional light on their shared attitudes about the French Revolution and its aftermath.

Beginning with a sneer at Citizen Genet and those Americans who had been duped by him, John Quincy displayed a somewhat Burkean fear of the French Revolution's potential to leap great distances for nefarious purposes: "Our foreign and domestic Jacobins pursue with concerted exertions . . . the dissolution of our Union and the overthrow of our Constitution." He equated French republicanism with government by bayonet, and predicted that an "unqualified military government" would be the "only possible" result. Adams then engaged in a lengthy attack on revolutionary propagandists, including Paine, whom he described as "peculiarly fitted . . . to wind up the drunkenness of a club or a tavern into a frenzy." He sent his father (the new president of the United States) samples of recent pamphlets as proof that "the revolutionary prejudices and follies are still predominant." Turning his attention to the struggle between the Girondists and Jacobins, he criticized "the two great Republican factions" for "their modes of intrigue and perfidy for the destruction of each other, and the false and erroneous principles upon which their theories of liberty were respectively grounded."[47] By the late 1790s, J. Q. Adams was cynically observing a revolution that was spinning out of control because it was locked in a destructive mentality long after the old regime had been destroyed.

Obviously John Quincy was not alone in his condemnations. In September 1797 he wrote his father: "You will have seen by the public prints that Edmund Burke died in the course of the month of July. His executors have within these few days published three memorials upon French affairs written by him. . . . I have sent you a copy."[48] Adams compared the rising despotism in France to the fall of the Roman Republic under Caesar, and he compared Burke to Cicero: both men rose from humble origins to become "the most strenuous and energetic defenders of aristocracies." In another letter, Adams reported that the "object" of Burke's recently published essays had been to dissuade the British government from recognizing the revolutionary government of France as legitimate. Instead London should have aligned itself with the "emigrant princes, and the party of France opposed to [the new constitution] and adhering to the monarchy." Since this advice had been rejected, Adams now compared Burke to Cassandra: "His prophesies were true but they were not believed." Turning his attention back to the French radicals, Adams declared: "They . . . will continue to play, in the United States the same game which Mr. Burke foretells they will in *all* countries." Remarkably, John Quincy did not place all the blame for French aggression on malignant rationalism, but instead on "their uniform and constant policy . . . adopted from the monarchy under which they were bred."[49] In other words, it was expansionist French behavior carried forward from the days of the ancien régime, rather than a philosophe-inspired revolutionary mania, that was propelling the exportation of radicalism. On the one hand, John and John Quincy did seem to share Burke's paranoia about either the French Revolution or the ideas behind it spilling over borders and infecting the world. On the other hand, since both Adamses believed America to be substantially different from Europe, they at least partially believed it would be naturally immune to foreign radicalism. Still, there was no use in taking chances, and radical conspirators such as Paine remained a discomforting force. Whatever the true source and nature of the Adamses' fear of radical conspiracy, father and son stood as prominent exemplars of that fear. As one scholar put it: "A good deal of Federalist obsession with an American Jacobin plot can be attributed to the Adams family . . . [who] saw it as a grave threat to the nation."[50]

It was no coincidence that the Adamses' harsh views about French revolutionary government came during the climax of the "quasi-war" with France, which was the overwhelming crisis of John Adams's presidency. The machinations of Talleyrand in France and of political opponents at home were about to explode in the so-called XYZ Affair, in which French envoys demanded bribes and concessions from the United States government. By the time of John Quincy's letters to his father, American sympathy for the French Revolution had been waning for years. The succession of French governments, each one further removed from the idealism of 1789, had convinced most U.S. citizens that France was unlikely to follow the American example. The arrogance and corruption of the latest regime in Paris—now dramatized by the XYZ Affair—inflamed the passions not only of John and John Quincy Adams, but of popular opinion in America as well. The greatest achievement of John Adams's single term as president was his avoidance of an outright declaration of war. Thus John Quincy's bitter words about France were not driven by philosophical objections alone.

Yet while American sentiment turned against France, it did not monolithically turn against French revolutionary ideals. Just as Americans were able to separate their own national ideals from many aspects of their practical activity, so too the growing republican majority was able to deplore recent French behavior while still admiring the utopian spirit and democratic egalitarian goals of France's revolution-gone-awry. One of the most intriguing political trends of the quasi-war period was that the party that most hated the French lost popular support, while the party that was less suspicious of France gained support. Republican sympathy for France was based on a persistent fear of England, and on a general philosophical kinship with the French Revolution's Enlightenment foundations. Three years after Louis XVI met the guillotine, a still-encouraged Jefferson was able to write, "This I hope will be the age of experiments in government." But the Federalist camp, which had been cautious in its early assessments, and then quickly became critical of the revolution, had by mid-decade become disgusted with almost everything associated with France: "This is indeed as you say the Age of Experiments in Government," John Adams replied to Jefferson. "An hundred thousand Dutchmen guillotined or beknifed . . . five hundred thousand Frenchmen. . . . How many . . . must be slaughtered to convince John Bull I cannot calculate."[51] Even after the rise of Napoleon, while conservative American factions judged his despotism and military aggression to be an inevitable consequence of the revolution's flawed principles, America's republican factions viewed his rise as the final perversion of an otherwise worthy experiment. To followers of Paine, the revolution had run into problems; to followers of Burke, the revolution had always been the problem.

Hence the connection between the spirit of 1776 and the promise of 1789 became a critical point of ideological contention. If the two revolutions were of the same species, their ideas could continue to cross-fertilize each other; if the two events were of separate species, they would continue to develop endemically—and America would be safe from contagion. Here, then, at the very birth of ideology in America, was also born the nation's fear of contamination from newly conceived European designs (later to threaten in the forms of anarchism, socialism, and communism). American exceptionalism soon became a one-way street: after its formative years, America did not want or need additional Old World ideas, but Americans believed the Old World could always benefit from adopting American ideas (as could the "developing world" after the Second World War). The French Revolution could have benefited from closer attention to the U.S. example, but there was growing skepticism after 1793 that America could appropriate any theories of political or social value from France. A strange bifurcation had occurred: Republicans accepted the transatlantic unity of the Age of Revolution. However, they did this by freezing time. They merged the high ideals of the early French Revolution—liberty, equality, fraternity—with those of the successful American Revolution: life, liberty, and the pursuit of happiness. Whatever terrors and usurpations may have ensued later in France were blamed on extraneous factors. Meanwhile, Federalists dismissed the early French ideals of equality and fraternity as panaceas of a naive and dangerous rationalism. They instead focused on the horrors of the later revolution as proof that no two events with such drastically different outcomes could possibly have shared meaningful connections in principle.

This was why, after moving to Berlin in 1800, John Quincy translated and published (anonymously, in Philadelphia) a German tract by Friedrich von Gentz that sharply outlined the differences between the American and French Revolutions. Gentz had previously translated *Reflections* into German, and the key emphasis of his own tract was the classification of the American Revolution as "defensive" and the French Revolution as "offensive." This was another way of saying that the American Revolution was at heart a restoration, while the French Revolution was a radical departure from the course of Western civilization.[52] Clearly this taxonomic distinction was Adams's chief reason for spreading Gentz's argument to his own countrymen. He said as much in a letter of gratitude to Gentz, who, in Adams's view, had "so ably vindicated [the American Revolution] from the imputation of having originated, or been conducted upon the same principles as that of France. . . . You have bourne testimony to the purity of principle upon which the revolution of my country was founded."[53] Yet the principles upon which both Gentz and J. Q. Adams seemed to agree were more of the anti-Paine than pro-Burke variety. Gentz's tract was very different from Burke's *Reflections* in style, emphasis, and detail. In contrast to *Reflections*, it was brief and tightly constructed; it contained no defense of the mysterious, nor of chivalry; and it was devoid of personal animus against the philosophes and radicals. In fact, both the tone and substance of Gentz's work were more reminiscent of Burke's earlier voice as a Whig reformer during the American crisis than they were of Burke's vitriolic performance in *Reflections*. Moreover, both Gentz and Publicola did a better job of contrasting the differences between the causes or original ideologies behind the two revolutions than they did of interpreting the dynamic processes that each revolution set in motion. As important, both John and John Quincy Adams differed with Gentz and European conservatives in the way they applied the restoration argument. While all parties recognized that the restoration of traditional constitutional rights had been the impetus for the American Revolution, European conservatives saw the revolution's result as philosophical return to the values of the English constitution, while Americans (including the Adamses) saw the result as the creation of something new.

It was fitting that J. Q. Adams's translation of Gentz appeared in 1800, the year of America's first seriously contested national elections. Jefferson challenged the incumbent senior Adams for the presidency, and the election was in effect a popular referendum on the nation's competing ideologies. On both the presidential and congressional levels the Jefferson-Paine view triumphed over the Adams-Gentz-Burke view, yet the victory was more symbolic than substantive. All the institutional structures and

Federalist precedents that served as checks on majoritarianism survived. At least on a structural and constitutional level, the American Revolution remained in its mature, constructive second stage. It was on the level of national symbolism that the Jeffersonian revolution took hold and became dominant. The election of perceived idealist-democrats over perceived realist-elites did nothing to reconcile the country's high ideals with its actual governing practices, but apparently there was little awareness of any contradictions. In light of this disparity, Jefferson's inaugural sentiment, "We are all Republicans, we are all Federalists," was true in a way he could not have known. After 1800, both the government and citizenry of the United States continued to sanctify the Enlightenment-inspired values of reason, democracy, freedom, and human agency, while simultaneously engaging in behavior that to various degrees ignored those values. Instead of radical egalitarianism, a more incremental growth in the democratic ethos evolved in the early 1800s, with John Quincy Adams eventually contributing to the process. In a sense, too much can be made of this tension between symbolism and substance: no nation ever can wholly live up to its ideals, and the separation between political theory and practice did not wait until 1800 to occur in America. But to the extent that the election of a Republican regime promised to bring political practice closer to the lofty principles of the founding era, the revolution of 1800 fell short of its potential. It did, however, validate once and for all the Jeffersonian-Enlightenment perspective as the nation's dominant symbolic ideal. Conversely, the ideological referendum of 1800 rejected the view of Adams and other critics of the French Revolution that essentially challenged the national quest for utopian perfectibility.

Rights and Wrongs of Revolution

As for John Adams's only sustained attempt to confront the revolution in France, his *Discourses on Davila: A Series of Papers on Political History*, by "An American Citizen,"[54] has baffled scholars for ages. Why Adams chose to wrap his views on contemporary French affairs inside a laborious commentary on Enrico Davila's (then) 160-year-old history of the sixteenth-century French civil wars is open to endless speculation. The simplest explanation is that Adams saw the sixteenth-century feuds as a parallel to the French Revolution and believed that the lessons learned from studying those older struggles could help in understanding the newer one. Or perhaps Adams, who knew that his alleged monarchist sympathies were making him unpopular in America, felt he needed to summon some great mass of historical evidence to bolster his positions. Alternatively, since Adams never was comfortable with overt factionalism, he may have been hiding his polemical stance behind a mask of scholarly erudition. Whatever the reason, Adams, even long into his retirement, expressed pride over this "dull, heavy volume," which, he said, "still excites the wonder of its author."[55]

Scholars agree that *Davila* contained no original ideas, yet it did provide a useful window on Adams's political philosophy and his view of human nature. The major historical parallel Adams drew in *Davila* was that the disastrous civil wars (1560–98) resulted from France's unbalanced structure of government—specifically, the nobility had too much power relative to the king. Now the French Revolution was repeating the same mistake with a different twist—the people were grabbing all the power. Without some check on this simple democracy, chaos was bound to follow. Eventually, just as France's earlier chaos had yielded to royal absolutism, France's new chaos would lead to despotism (Adams later felt his view had been vindicated by the rise of Napoleon). Adams also reasserted his earlier theme from *Defense of the Constitutions*: balanced government of multiple branches was the sole practical alternative to either chaos or tyranny. But this redundant argument was not what made *Davila* interesting.

Instead—and this was one area in which Adams's emphasis diverged from Burke's—the most prominent theme in *Davila* concerned the human passions. Adams was asking: why do men behave the way they do, and how can government be structured to capitalize on such behavior? Adams began *Davila* by observing that nature furnished men "with passions, appetites, and propensities, as well as a variety of faculties, calculated both for their individual enjoyment, and to render them useful to each other in their social conditions." Chief among these was man's "passion for distinction," which itself was composed of the "desires" of emulation, ambition, jealousy, envy, and vanity.[56] Simply put, men sought to outdo each other, and craved the recognition and rewards that came with proven superiority: "Every personal quality, and every blessing of fortune, is cherished in proportion to its capacity for gratifying this universal affection for esteem, the sympathy, admiration and congratulations of the public."[57] Adams may well have been projecting his own passion for fame and greatness onto the rest of humanity, but the projection was likely valid for most political elites of his era.[58] Whether it was birth, wealth, military prowess, or any other means of distinction, Adams believed it was the passion for fame and for dominion over others that spurred elites—members of both "natural" (earned) and "artificial" (hereditary) aristocracies—to action.

Given this state of human nature, the laboratories of political experimentation in both France and America had to aim for a common result: construction of governments that funneled universal human passions into publicly beneficial behavior. Adams believed the United States was well on its way toward achieving this by 1791—so long as it could resist contamination by French radicalism. France, however, was already misapplying the lessons of history and human psychology: "If a balance of passions and interests is not scientifically concerted, the present struggle in Europe will be little beneficial to mankind, and produce nothing but another thousand years of feudal fanaticism, under new and strange names."[59] In a direct warning to both societies, Adams declared

> FRENCHMEN! Act and think like yourselves! . . . The affectation of being exempted from passions is inhuman. . . . Consider that government is intended to set bounds to passions which nature has not limited; and to assist reason, conscience, justice, and truth. . . .
>
> AMERICANS! Rejoice that from experience you have learned wisdom; and instead of whimsical and fanatical projects, you have adopted a promising essay towards a well-ordered government. Instead of following any foreign example . . . contemplate the means of restoring decency, honesty, and order in society, by preserving and completing . . . the balance of your government.[60]

Discourses on Davila—or the small portion of it that addressed the French Revolution directly—certainly opposed what the radicals were attempting to accomplish. It shared with Burke's *Reflections* both a condemnation of speculative theory and a fear that such theories, because of their superficial appeal, might spread beyond France. But while *Reflections* attacked the revolution because it departed from tradition, *Davila* attacked it because it failed to implement the laws of social science. Adams's (almost naively comprehensive) belief that a properly designed constitutional system would channel human needs and wants into socially constructive activity was in some ways prototypical of nineteenth-century scientism. It may have been faulty reasoning, but it was faulty in a forward-looking manner. It was also a byproduct of Enlightenment rationalism, though one that would be turned mostly to conservative purposes in the coming century. Burke's belief in a restoration of traditional society was, by contrast, backward looking and decidedly anti-Enlightenment in character. His recourse to pleasing illusions, chivalry, and a preference for wisdom over reason was as contradictory to Adams's argument in *Davila* as it was to the designs of the philosophes or to the humanistic liberalism of Thomas Paine.

As far as Burke, Adams, and the harmony of their opposition to the French Revolution was concerned, there was less there than met the eye. It was not enough that they opposed the radicals and generally dismissed speculative philosophy. They viewed the revolution from completely different angles, and championed entirely different—in fact hostile—alternatives. Adams proposed the application of reason in the form of (as he saw it) the methodical study of human psychology and systems of government. Burke, on the other hand, was so overcome by what he saw as a "revolution of theoretic dogma" that he traded his lifelong commitment to progressive reform for the reactive security cloak of tradition. It was no wonder that Adams's references to Burke ran the gamut from ambivalence to dismissiveness to outright disapproval.

Reputation

The key to understanding the meaning of the Adams-Burke symbolic association can only be found by understanding how the reputations of both men fit into the polemical dynamic of America in the later half of the founding era. Since ideological battles resonate better at the popular level when heroes lock horns with villains, political debates reach deeper and wider when the leading participants are seen as personifications of their cause. Burke, for a variety of reasons including his own desire to fill the role, became the embodiment of Old World antirevolutionary traditionalism. Adams, for reasons less within his control, became the embodiment of American antiradicalism, even of antidemocracy or antirepublicanism in the eyes of many. Adams's status as the only (officially) Federalist president, and thus the nation's highest ranking anti-Painite, made him an obvious choice to become the embodiment of a Burkean point of view—or at least that view as modified for American purposes—just as Thomas Jefferson's status made him the obvious embodiment of the alternative view. The inception of ideology in America required not just ideas, but big names that could be linked to those ideas. Adams fit the bill for the forces of order and continuity, as well as Jefferson did for the forces of innovation and progress. If the Republican-Enlightenment ideal was to become the dominant national vision, and so give rise to an ideology of liberalism and progress, then certainly a counter-persuasion, loosely defined as conservative, was needed in order for the dynamic process to function. In this sense, if John Adams did not exist, it would have been necessary to invent him. That is, some flesh-and-blood person had to represent the origin of the American counterpoint to the nation's utopian confidence in democracy, equality, and the sensibility of perpetual revolution. Adams was not the only name in town, but he was the most convenient.[61]

CHAPTER 4

Democratic America

The Ethos of Liberalism

What John Adams, Edmund Burke, Thomas Paine, the founding fathers, and many of their contemporaries all shared was the privilege of historical opportunity. The worldwide importance of the American and French Revolutions infused their efforts with added consequence, and in the process infused their lives with great historical value. But when the turbulent epoch in which they thrived finally passed, it was followed by a period of comparative calm. During this less-revolutionary phase of national development, the primary driving force of human agency in America shifted from a relative handful of important men to a larger and more diverse collection of citizens intent on reaping the benefits of their new social, political, and economic order.

Democratic Consensus

The Age of Revolution was essentially over in the United States by the time Thomas Jefferson took office in 1801, though not until the end of the War of 1812 would the nation feel secure enough to realize this. The peace treaty with Britain in 1815 definitively marked the end of America's founding era and the beginning of a period in which there was no longer any question that the new nation would survive and that its "experiment with democracy" would proceed.[1] The brief "Era of Good Feelings" that followed the war was but the start of a longer period of conceptual stability that peaked in the 1830s. During this period, an underlying consensus developed about the arrival of progress. Such a consensus would appear a second time after the Second World War and would inspire a sense of supreme confidence that the nation had chosen the right path. Obviously this did not mean problems had stopped occurring. But there was a widespread feeling in the country that the society had reached a sort of high plateau from which the errors of the past could be viewed with detached perspective. Issues that had long plagued society had either been resolved or were on their way toward successful resolution. In other words, the ideological conflicts that drove the historical process had been transcended. Perhaps the problems had not all been fixed, but at least the proper tools with which to fix them had finally been developed. The tools for the nation's first (antebellum) consensus were contained in the process of democratization, just as those for the second (post–World War II) consensus were to be found in the process of modernization.[2]

In the broadest terms, the mission of antebellum America was the reconciliation of democratic egalitarianism with social and political order. For the first time anywhere, representative democracy was put to the test on a large scale, and constitutional rights, competitive individualism, and free market economics were substituted for hereditary monarchy, aristocracy, and restrictive customary practices. With the tragic exception of slavery and its related doctrine of states' rights, the age-old problems of tyranny and injustice now seemed to be subject to rational democratic control. As one scholar has observed: "By creating a new kind of democratic republic, America appeared to have solved the ills that had always destroyed republics in the past." The combination of agrarian ideals, commercial opportunity, and republican institutions would "insure its progress virtually in perpetuity," so that "society . . . even while progressing, could escape historical change."[3]

By the mid-antebellum period the nation had widened the franchise to include most white males, had proven it could peacefully transfer power from one political party to another, had expanded its territory almost to the Pacific (with the Louisiana Purchase), had survived the threats of mob rule (Shays's Rebellion, the Whiskey Rebellion, Fries's Rebellion), of tyranny (the Alien and Sedition Acts), and of the reassertion of a hereditary aristocracy (the Society of the Cincinnati), and had finally ended the threat of foreign conquest (the War of 1812). Americans at last had pause to take stock of their situation and construct some meaningful understanding of it. By no means were the 1830s devoid of conflict or drama, as events such as the nullification crisis, Indian removal, Andrew Jackson's bank veto, or the Panic of 1837 easily demonstrate. But unlike those of the founding era, these events unfolded within a nonrevolutionary landscape. The fact that for all practical purposes the nation temporarily reverted to a one-party political system (the Democratic-Republicans) was an indication of this lack of clear ideological division. Beginning in the 1840s this consensus would deteriorate as the Whig Party became nationally viable and a renewed North-South conflict stemming from the Mexican War and the annexation of Texas grabbed the nation's attention and, in effect, started the historical process rolling again—this time toward civil war. But while it lasted, this generation-long period of relative stability (or at least of conceptual stability) served to solidify and enhance the model of civilization produced by the founding era.

Now that the idea of democracy is old hat, it is difficult to imagine the importance of the perceived success of democratic egalitarianism during the post-founding era.[4] But the democratization of society (and not just of government itself) appears to have been an exhilarating experience for the large majority of citizens. So much so, that not only did democracy become the major theme in American culture; it became synonymous with the nation itself—even to foreigners. Such a panacea could only lead to disappointment in the longer run, but in the short run, democratization would serve as a cultural glue in the United States much the same way that tradition served as a cultural glue in England.

Among other things, the widespread and repeated election victories of Jacksonian Democrats in the late 1820s and the 1830s signaled that Paine and Jefferson had extended their ideological supremacy over the Federalists well past the formative years of the founding era. Majority rule, even with the extant Federalist system of checks and balances, had (at least temporarily) become a practical reality. "The people are the sovereign," declared Jackson; "they can alter & amend, and the people alone . . . can dissolve this union peaceably."[5] The mediation of popular will that had served as the basis for founding-era republican thought had become outmoded; the institutional structures and theories of balance that made up John Adams's political universe no longer seemed relevant. As the Democratic journalist and poet Walt Whitman—who eulogized Tom Paine for his contributions to the nation's "ardent belief in, and substantial practice of, radical human rights"[6]—once gleefully observed: "We do not mean that our party has succeeded in every *election*, . . . [sometimes] the Conservative—under the various names—carried the day. But we mean to say our *principles* have advanced with a steady and sure progress."[7] This democratic sensibility was prominent enough to capture the attention even of non-Americans who had no particular interest in the future of the United States. Alexis de Tocqueville's (almost cloyingly famous) *Democracy in America*, written after his nine-month visit in 1831–32, was both skeptical of and impressed by conditions of everyday life. Topics such as the "Unlimited Power of the Majority in the United States and Its Consequences" and "Of Individualism in Democratic Countries," if nothing else, attested to the pervasiveness of the democratic ethos.[8] Homegrown publications on the same democratic themes—such as James Fenimore Cooper's *Notions of the Americans* (1828)—contributed to the process of not only celebrating democratic society, but also explaining it to the rest of the world. Even religion in America apparently did not escape this great wave of democratization.[9] In unison with the growth of democracy came the accession of individualism, of nationalism, geographic expansionism, commercialism, and the Americanization of the belief in progress. Not only were these phenomena related; they were intertwined and were not easily distinguishable from each other.

As forward-looking as these concepts may have been, the exceptionalism upon which they were grounded (and to which they in turn contributed) also informed a rediscovery of America's past. Now that the revolution had receded into memory and its logical development had climaxed with the "final" success of democratization, the nation's privileged path to the end of history could be viewed with satisfaction. Numerous historical societies were founded, and important commemorations of the revolution (such as the building of the Bunker Hill Monument and the beginning of the Washington Monument) took place. History made its way into the classroom and into vogue as popular literature, and the first generation of "modern" historians began to publish in the 1830s or soon thereafter. One study of history in America found that "at least as early as the Revolution, American historical writing seemed to have a different tone from its European counterpart . . . and these differences grew in the nineteenth century." Thereafter, "Americans were thinking in terms of a distinctive national character, the uniqueness of their own experience, and the ways in which the American soul differed from that of other people."[10] Culturally embedded ideas about the effect of reasoned human agency on the clean slate of North America colored the tone of historical writing regardless of the political persuasion of the historian. This exceptionalist interpretation was an offshoot of the creation-myth archetype. It would undergo several transmutations over time but would not lose its core message about the conscious construction of a better civilization in an unspoiled landscape.[11] "The keynote in American History," wrote an early twentieth-century scholar, "is found in the efforts of a virile and energetic people to appropriate and develop the wonderful natural resources of a new continent and there *to realize their ideals of liberty and government*."[12]

George Bancroft

This inventive spirit has been called the "genius" of the American character, and its emphasis on newness and progress flew in the face of the tradition and continuity that Burke so admired. Hence Burke was shunned by American writers after 1800. Even those making Burkean political arguments avoided using his name.[13] It is therefore unexpected to find the following in the letters of George Bancroft, the most important Democratic historian of the era:

> On the way back [to London] we drove through Beacons-field. At the name I cried out Edmund Burke; and straight-away we went to the Gregories, traced the ruins of the old house, which was burned down; went into his garden, studied out his walks; admired his trees; and tried to get a picture of his life. . . . His name was cherished all about; from all the villages round they came to his feasts.
>
> At the church which I entered, there was his pew, his grave, and the tablet in the wall to that part of him which was mortal. The churchyard has the tomb of Waller under a huge walnut tree: but Waller's huge monument does not move like the plain slab to Edmund Burke, who must have had a kind heart, easily touched with sympathy.[14]

Bancroft could not have chosen a metaphorically more appropriate device than to place himself in contemplation of the burned ruins of the old Burkean estate. As a nineteenth-century scholar and public intellectual, Bancroft was intrigued by the past but was ultimately more concerned with the present and future. Hence his visit to Beaconsfield presented the opportunity not only of better understanding Edmund Burke, but also of passing judgment on him.[15] In an age still concerned with personal character, separate judgments could be applied to Burke the man and to the value and consequences of his political thought. A few years after his trip to Beaconsfield, Bancroft published the middle volumes of his *History of the United States*, which has been called the most influential work of American history in the nineteenth century, and "a vote for Jackson in ten volumes." Although Bancroft had mentioned Burke at earlier points in the narrative, these new volumes on the American Revolution offered the only substantial passages about him.[16]

In Bancroft's assessment, Burke *the man* was an exceptional talent and a faithful retainer to Lord Rockingham. "He brought to his employer . . . all that he had—boundless stores of knowledge . . . wit, philosophy, imagination, gorgeous eloquence, unwearied industry, mastery of the English tongue, and, as some think, the most accomplished intellect which the nation had produced for centuries." Yet for all these attributes, Burke *the political thinker* unfortunately was "content with the applause of the aristocracy" and failed to comprehend the birth of democratic society in the Anglo-American sphere. "No man had a better heart, or more thoroughly hated oppression; but . . . his genius, under the impulse of his bewildering passions, wrought much evil to his country and to Europe." Bancroft praised Burke's reform positions on issues pertaining to America, Ireland, and "commercial freedom," but reluctantly (yet unequivocally) condemned his conservative antirevolutionary ideas as dangerously anachronistic. "His writings are a brilliant picture of the British constitution, as it existed in the best days of the eighteenth century," but both Great Britain and the United States had, by the time of Bancroft's *History*, advanced well beyond the transitional Old Whig order—with its half-modern worldview—that had thrived after the Glorious Revolution of 1688.[17]

One can easily discern Bancroft's disappointment at losing the services of Burke's masterly abilities in the cause of progress. Burke as a New Whig democrat would surely have been a potent force: "The words fell from him as burning oracles. It appeared as if he was lifted upward to gaze into futurity." "Yet," Bancroft admitted, "it was not so."

> Though more than half a century had intervened, Burke would not be wiser than the whigs of the days of King William [1689–1702]. It was enough for him if the Aristocracy applauded. He did not believe in the dawn of a new light, in the coming on of a new order. . . .
>
> As Dante is the poet who sums up the . . . spirit of the Middle Age . . . so Burke portrays . . . all the lineaments of that Old Whig Aristocracy which in its day achieved mighty things for liberty. . . .
>
> He that will study . . . the enlightened character of England in the first half of the eighteenth century . . . must give his days and nights to the writings of Edmund Burke. But time never keeps company with the mourners . . . it leaves those who stand still to their despair; and itself hurries on to fresh fields of action and scenes for ever new.[18]

Burke's best writing was to Bancroft a monument to a long-past age. That age was of great historical value because it curbed the power of monarchy and ushered in a system of constitutional balance—and so set the stage for the greater liberties of Burke's own time and ultimately for the American Revolution. As such it was worthy of respect and admiration; but by no means was it deserving of nostalgic emulation. To democratic true believers, Burke's reactionary rejection of the democratic ethos may have been worthy of esteem for its rhetorical art, yet intellectually it was only a brilliant last hurrah for political values that were already outdated. From the democratic perspective, Bancroft was exactly on the mark when he equated Burke with the "mourners" for a bygone world. As we have seen, Burke's own language turned increasingly elegiac in his final years. Burke famously chastised those who refused to repair old walls and build upon existing ancient foundations.[19] But foundations were never truly the issue. Both democrats and conservatives in America would have agreed with Burke that English liberties had served as a basis for American freedoms. The real argument was over what to build next. Unlike Burke, Bancroft held no prescriptive desire to reject recent innovations. Bancroft *in his capacity as a democratic historian* surveyed the remnants of Burke's Beaconsfield estate as he would have surveyed the ruins of the Forum or the Acropolis: it was one thing to trace archaeologically the course of civilization; it was quite another to lament the passing of structures that had served their purpose. The less direct the connection between old artifacts and the contentious issues of the present, the more those artifacts could be appreciated as benchmarks of past progress or as generalized additions to the collective architecture of Western civilization.

This seems to have served as an interpretive pattern for the nineteenth century in America. Writers of a liberal sensibility granted Burke—by virtue of his rhetoric, his concern for humanity, and his early political sagacity—a place in their historical museum; they admired his genius, but ultimately viewed him as a relic of the past. In a sad reversal of the modern penchant for praising great men for being ahead of their time, Burke instead was eulogized as a great man born too late. His Old Whig perspective had lost currency during his own lifetime, and certainly was out of step with the succeeding age of democracy. Conservative writers, on the other hand, read Burke almost as if he still lived; his ideas would always be relevant because his values were timeless. For them, it was the democratic ethos itself that had outrun the natural pace of historical development. Too much faith in "the people" had resulted in a leveling of standards and a diffusion (and *confusion*) of leadership. The exuberant optimism that accompanied the process of democratization masked what some feared to be a process of cultural decline.[20] Yet however valid such concerns about the effects of democracy may have been, they represented at the time a minority position.

Before he became a historian, George Bancroft delivered an Independence Day oration in which he expressed his personal enthusiasm for the contemporary democratic ideal: "The sovereignty of the people is the basis of the system. With the people the power resides, both theoretically and practically. The government is a democracy, a determined, uncompromising democracy; administered immediately by the people, or by the people's responsible agents."[21] In the Jefferson-Jackson mold, the young Bancroft was siding with

Tom Paine and revolution and in opposition to Edmund Burke and tradition. Soon thereafter, he would employ the "scientific" methods of modern historiographical research in the service of a politically useful narrative on the origins of democratic American society. In other words, Bancroft's *History* would come very close to presenting an "authorized" version of the saga of America, which reinforced the nation's newly formed traditions.[22] Rather than condemn Bancroft for his obvious democratic leanings, one should recognize his outlook as a natural incorporation of the widely accepted new American archetype of exceptionalism based on the good deeds and wise thoughts of freedom-loving men.[23] This in itself was a testament to the lasting impress of Enlightenment beliefs on American society, and the fact that succeeding editions of Bancroft's *History* remained popular throughout the nineteenth century demonstrated that national ideals did not change with the shifting realities of everyday life.[24]

Later, Bancroft contrasted democracy with its more conservative counterparts. "The tory clings to past abuses; the whig idolizes present possessions; democracy is the party of progress and reform," he told an audience of Massachusetts Democrats in 1836. While the Tory will "sanction" a "government of force," and the Whig "appeals to prescription; democracy lives in the consciences of the living . . . democracy enfranchises the human mind . . . [and] struggles for equal rights. . . . Democracy claims freedom as an inalienable right." Tories want slaves, Whigs prefer tenant farmers, but "democracy puts the plough in the hands of the owner."[25] Here was an analysis of—and an attitude about—the major schools of Anglo-American political thought that could have been written by Paine or Jefferson and assented to by the current president, Andrew Jackson. In fact, since the highly popular Jackson was about to complete his second term and pass the office to his handpicked successor Martin Van Buren, there is little doubt that the majority of Americans would have agreed with Bancroft's opinions as well.

But in acknowledging this we are speaking politically, not necessarily culturally. It is worth noting some scholarship that has claimed that "Bancroft had always emphasized the conservative character of American democracy." For instance, late in his career Bancroft wrote that the "gates of revolution" were shut.[26] While revisionism of this sort can be misleading, it does help us recognize that Bancroft—a genuine political liberal for his day—was more conservative in what might be called his cultural sensibility. That is, he saw himself as a defender of Western Christian civilization. In such areas as literature, religion, and morality, he was a conservator rather than a revolutionary. In this sense he could be contrasted with Paine and compared more closely to the Massachusetts Brahmins with whom he was personally associated (most of whom were political conservatives). This would explain why Bancroft could admire Burke but hate his politics. It also made Bancroft prototypical of the culturally conservative Progressives who were to carry American society from the nineteenth century into the twentieth. Obviously such a cultural sensibility opened itself to a sympathetic reading of Edmund Burke—even if much of his political stance could not be accepted.

Democratic Ambivalence

In 1837, the partisan *United States Magazine and Democratic Review*[27] articulated the broadly Jacksonian democratic creed in its very first issue: "We believe . . . in the principle of *democratic republicanism* in its strongest and purest sense. We have an abiding confidence in the virtue, intelligence, and full capacity for self-government, of the great mass of our people, our industrious, honest, manly, intelligent millions of free men." Conversely, "We are opposed to all self-styled 'wholesome restraints' on the free action of the popular opinion and free will."[28] Yet even while espousing this non-prescriptive, antiaristocratic creed, the *Democratic Review*, like Bancroft, found value in the life of Edmund Burke. In two articles about him, it chose to dwell almost exclusively on his character and ability and on his activities as a Whig reformer. The first article's sole passage on Burke's conservatism criticized him for supporting the Declaratory Act of 1766: "We conceive that Burke did not in this effort exhibit the wisdom that he manifested several years after in discussing the same question. He was for the repeal of the stamp act, but he was at the same time for an assertion of the right of Parliament to tax the colonies. . . . How this policy could have met the approval of the colonies, and produce such joy and rejoicing as it did produce, is remarkable." Since the article ventured no farther chronologically than the American crisis, the richer and more controversial segments of Burke's career were left "to another occasion."[29]

The second and more interesting article began by stating outright what Bancroft had merely hinted at in the wake of his visit to Beaconsfield: "The lives of distinguished public men" could be viewed as archaeological artifacts. "They may be . . . compared to the Egyptian pyramids . . . which although solitary relics of an empire swept away, yet remain massive and enduring monuments, evincing the power of their builders, and something of the genius of the period in which they were erected." Such an analogy "will particularly apply to the character of the statesman [Edmund Burke]." Later, the article concluded with the assertion that "[Burke's] works . . . bequeathed to us a monument which . . . may be compared to one of those old Gothic cathedrals of England . . . settled upon deep and strong foundations." Like the first article, this one concerned itself mostly with Burke's life, character, and Whig reform activities, and devoted only two of its eighteen pages to the French Revolution. That revolution's roots were traced to the "mouldering corruptions growing out of the feudal structure of the monarchy," aggravated by the return of French troops from the American Revolution, "awaken[ed] with a desire of innovation and an ardent spirit of democratic freedom." If the event turned out to be disastrous in its execution, it was due to an "absence of sound intelligence and system in the policy of its leaders." While granting that Burke was probably justified in curbing British enthusiasm for the spread of "French revolutionary patriotism," the *Democratic Review* made a quick exit from the topic with the broad assertion that "notwithstanding his opposition to social disorganization in every form, Mr. Burke was always found on the side of substantial and well regulated liberty." Like much writing on Burke during this period, this essay treaded lightly on the French Revolution and on Burke's reaction to it (even avoiding mention of *Reflections* by name—it was simply "his well known work").[30]

Such ambivalent treatment of Burke's counterrevolutionary activity seems to have been commonplace in antebellum America. One might even conclude that it took the form of a standard literary convention. For example, the less openly democratic (though respectfully progressive) *Methodist Quarterly Review* also failed to name *Reflections* in its article on Burke, and it devoted just two of twenty-four paragraphs to the French Revolution. After first honoring Burke as a Whig reformer on America, Ireland, press freedom, religious tolerance, India, and other issues in which "he made a firm stand for the rights of man," the article declared that "his speeches and writings on [the French Revolution] are brilliant and powerful as a body; but they do not show his mind nor his humanity in its best phase. . . . He was growing old, and had to some extent outlived his associations. . . . Infirmities and dislikes had, in all probability, some effect on his judgement." In an ingenious assessment of the French Revolution that both rejected and justified Burke's stand, the article stated: "We do indeed consider that France has profited by her revolutions, but the price for the advantages was an enormous one; and probably the most enthusiastic lover of liberty, could he have seen the end from the beginning, would not have signed the contract."[31]

Antebellum American writers—even democrats and progressives—seem to have let Burke off rather easily regarding the French Revolution because he was otherwise such an agreeable figure. Even if he was no democrat, he was a humane and progressive thinker who unfortunately got old, sick, and frenzied, without losing his rhetorical power. As both a Whig reformer and a rhetorician Burke could be saluted as a great man, because his accomplishments in those areas were accepted by all. Consequently, this side of Burke could be thought of in historical rather than ideological terms—and could fit comfortably into the era's progressive consensus. But as an antirevolutionary conservative Burke could not be so easily accommodated, because to do so would reprise the old Burke-Paine "contest" and reignite the ideological struggle that Americans believed democratization had ended. When compared with today's environment, in which the French Revolution controls our image of Burke, the antebellum period seems eerily devoid of that revolution's presence. When the topic did surface, not only was it dispensed with rapidly, but ambivalently as well. It would not be until the nakedly ideological battle between democratic capitalism and totalitarian communism in the twentieth century that the primary legacy of Burke became that of his *Reflections* and other antirevolutionary works.

Transcendental Perspective

Even the master essayist Ralph Waldo Emerson—whose political orientation has never been definitively established—chose to avoid treatment of the French Revolution, and instead speculated on why Burke preferred conservatism over radicalism.[32] Emerson was an early user of the term "conservative" in its modern connotation, and in his "Edmund Burke" lecture of 1835 he called Burke "the Conservative of modern times." But Emerson explained that he meant conservatism "in an exalted and quite peculiar sense, the teacher of order, peace, and elegance; the adorner of existing institutions, but, combining therewith a fire of affection, and a depth of virtuous sentiment that add heroism to his wisdom." Later, Emerson declared Burke to have been "no vulgar conservative . . . he was found a steadfast friend of liberty, of humanity, the redresser of wrong. . . . Every cause of humanity found in him its lover and defender. . . . He turned against every cruelty and selfishness."[33]

Emerson conformed to his generation's convention of soft-pedaling the French Revolution by devoting just one paragraph out of fifty to it. He also avoided citing *Reflections* by name and instead referred to it as Burke's "alarm through England and the World." Emerson's summation of Burke's position was a rather tentative one: "Whether or not Mr. Burke judged wisely in the part he took in the French Revolution is the question on which most persons according as they answer it fix their views of him. That he judged wisely for his own time and country will be by most conceded. No doubt he was unconsciously biased in his taste and imagination." The ostensible reason for withholding final judgment on the topic was that the events of Burke's lifetime were still too recent to place in proper perspective. But clearly this was a transparent excuse; neither Emerson nor other writers had any qualms about boldly siding with Burke on reform issues—some of which unfolded contemporaneously with the years of the French Revolution. Curiously, Emerson's concluding thought on the topic was very close to the noncommittal sentiment expressed by the *Methodist Review*: "I suppose the boldest lover of freedom if he love virtue also might well hesitate to decide between the continuance of tyranny and the outrageous abuses of freedom."[34]

Despite his reluctance to delve deeply into the French Revolution, Emerson nevertheless provided some of his generation's most insightful commentary on Burke. His lecture on "The Conservative" presented a general view of the dynamic philosophical, historical, and psychological tension between the forces of conservatism and innovation, while his lecture on Burke presented a more specific example of that same tension.[35] In "The Conservative" Emerson observed, "The castle, which conservatism is set to defend, is the actual state of things, good and bad. The project of innovation is the best possible state of things." In "Edmund Burke" Emerson explained that Burke's sense of "exquisite Taste," his social "attachments," and his "partiality for Establishments" (that is, for institutions) had prevented "his love of liberty and his fondness for theory" from "making him a radical Reformer." Emerson not only acknowledged the inner conflict that "swayed [Burke's] mind originally and habitually towards the side of existing order and at the same time made him from first to last a wise reformer," but identified such conflict as part of a timeless and universal phenomenon. "Conservatism and . . . Innovation, are very old, and have disputed the possession of the world ever since it was made. This quarrel is the subject of civil history. . . . The war rages not only in battlefields, in national councils, and ecclesiastical synods, but agitates every man's bosom with opposing advantages every hour." Therefore, "We are reformers in spring and summer; in autumn and winter, we stand by the old; reformers in the morning, conservers at night." To Emerson there was no such thing as either a "pure reformer" or a "pure conservative." While the accuracy of this postulate was open to challenge, at least Emerson offered a general rule about the universal human spirit that helped in understanding Edmund Burke.[36]

Yet the most interesting point Emerson made in "The Conservative" was not that everyone's thoughts alternated between opposing forces. It was instead the *indispensability* of those oppositional forces to each other. Though he did not use the terms, Emerson described a sort of "yin-yang" holistic tension that aided human advancement. Neither the conservative impulse nor the innovative impulse could exist without the other, any more than light could exist without darkness. Moreover, conservatism for Emerson provided the basis (or foundation, or trunk) from which improvements could grow:

> It is a happiness of mankind that innovation has got on so far, and has so free a field before it. The boldness of the hope men entertain transcends all former experience. . . . And this hope flowered on what tree? It was not imported from the stock of some celestial plant, but grew here on the wild crab of conservatism. It is much that this old and vituperated system of things has borne so fair a child. It predicts that amidst a planet peopled with conservatives, one Reformer may yet be born.[37]

As this peroration made clear, Emerson shared the hope of improving the human condition. But that hope was tethered to his transcendental conceptions of man and nature—conceptions that had not guided previous generations. Emerson apparently believed that the errors of the past and the corruptions of the present were essential for bringing about the counterforces of personal renewal and social reform. This view was contrary to Burke's belief in the collective wisdom of the past, and it was no coincidence that Emerson replaced Burke's great oaks with a lone crab apple tree.[38] Emerson was closer to Burke in his rejection of speculative design, as his dismissal of "some celestial plant" indicated. To the extent that transcendentalism was spiritual, idealist, romantic, and critical of rationalism, it was, if not consistent with, at least sympathetic to Burke's thought. And given Burke's reputation as a rhetorical genius, it was only natural that transcendentalists would admire him for his mastery of the English language. But members of Emerson's circle were too obsessed with the present and the future (and with the hope of discovering a new "American Adam") to accept Burke's Anglo-traditionalism, and they were too reform oriented to endorse Burke's conservative politics.[39]

New England transcendentalism flowered during the climax of Jacksonian democracy. While transcendentalism was not overtly political, its sensibility was in keeping with the underlying political spirit of the era: "The exaltation of man, of all men; the doctrine that all power, all wisdom, comes from nature, with which man must establish an original and firsthand relationship . . . the insistence that instinct is good and must be obeyed rather than curbed in accordance with conventions and authority—all these ideas were closely related to the democratic impulse."[40] Or as the first major study of transcendentalism put it: the movement "was something more than a reaction against formalism and tradition. . . . Practically it was an assertion of the inalienable worth of man; theoretically it was . . . the transference of supernatural attributes to the natural constitution of mankind."[41] Unlike democratization, transcendentalism was not a mass phenomenon. Yet even if the movement was confined to a regional literati, it sprang from the wider American climate, and (while granting transatlantic influences) it shared some existing national ideals. It was particularly suited for incorporation into the nation's self-image as a "clean slate" or "virgin land" upon which individuals could assert their unique identity and exert their personal dignity.

Although Andrew Jackson was sixty-two by the time he entered the White House, the bulk of his followers consisted of a younger generation with no firsthand knowledge of either the American Revolution or the ideological struggles of the Federalist period. Likewise the transcendentalists were born at the dawn of the new century, near the time of the triumph of Jeffersonian Democratic-Republicanism and after Edmund Burke and his age had passed into history. One important difference in the worldview of this newer generation was its lack of reliance on a natural aristocracy.[42] This new egalitarian attitude conflicted with one of the most crucial tenets of Burkean thought. Bancroft's chastisement of Burke for seeking the applause of the aristocracy—a remark he made twice in his *History*—had reflected not just his personal opinion, but the broadly held egalitarian outlook of the time.

Just as Burke had articulated the intuitive (perhaps mystical) strain of Old Whig traditionalism, the transcendentalists articulated the intuitive and mystical strain of American liberal thought. While individual members of the Concord circle opposed slavery, imperialism, bureaucratization, philistinism, and religious dogmatism, and supported early feminism, transcendentalists were political mostly in the "personal is political" sense—which might explain why Henry David Thoreau achieved renewed popularity with young Americans during the 1960s and 1970s. (Of course, Thoreau's hostility toward institutions put him in direct opposition to Burke's conception of a well-ordered society.)[43] Burkean philosophy and transcendentalism both presented challenges to an overreliance on Enlightenment rationalism in the pursuit of social progress. However, each offered different methods for stemming the rationalist tide. Burke encouraged a return to the communal traditions of the past; the American transcendentalists encouraged a celebration of individual intuition and championed the authenticity of new experience.

Transcendentalism has long enjoyed a prominent place in American thought and in American schooling. In some quarters it has been the major cultural topic of the antebellum years. Probably this sprang from its uniquely American integration of the individual and nature.[44] As such it served as an early example of the construction of a new national culture that was increasingly distinguishable from its Old World inheritance. One great exemplar of that older culture, Edmund Burke, has often been recognized as a precursor to English romanticism. In the realm of human emotion this recognition is valid. But Burke diverged from romantic thought when he failed to include the power or redemptive value of nature in his philosophy. Instead he was exclusively concerned with highly developed human societies. He did not care about English oaks because they were oaks, but because they were ideograms for great men, great families, great institutions, or great traditions. Therefore Burke on this point was not only at odds with transcendentalists, but also with America's fascination with the wilderness and the frontier. This Enlightenment-based emphasis on nature, combined with transcendentalism's intuitively individualistic and democratic leanings, yielded a clear cultural alternative to Burke's ideal of a hierarchical, institutional, and traditional commonwealth. As we have seen, Burke's conservative political thought had already been rejected from the American mainstream for ideological reasons. What transcendentalism and Jacksonian democracy (broadly defined) accomplished was to immunize the main currents of American culture against it as well—without affecting Burke's rhetorical and Whig reform legacy. Simply put, writers like Paine and Jefferson provided reasoned arguments about why Burke's antirevolutionary and traditionalist views did not fit into American politics. Writers like the transcendentalists helped create a cultural sensibility that assured Burke's Old World conservatism would not *feel right* in America. In the long run this latter, more subliminal message may have had the greater impact.

Setting the Future

Bancroft, the transcendentalists, and the Jacksonians were already living in the future to which the founding fathers had looked with such utopian vision. Their expansion of revolutionary ideals, and their weaving of the new American archetype into the broader culture, proved to be their own lasting contribution to the national identity. In this sense, Gertrude Stein's assertion that America was the first country to enter the twentieth century applies equally well to the nineteenth. With its pioneering democratic ethos, the United States in the antebellum years prepared the world for the modern age. From that time forward, the dominant strain of American cultural expression would work within this democratic exceptionalist identity. No national self-image could have been less hospitable to the exaggerated Anglo-traditionalism of Edmund Burke. Well into the twentieth century, one major writer expressed his desire to "convince our coevals that America has a *monopoly of Revolution*, that we really started the whole thing and have our chance *for the last word also*, if we are able and if we prove willing to take it."[45]

Chapter 5

American Whigs

A Conservative Response

If the mid-antebellum consensus felt somewhat like the end of history, not all Americans of the time were satisfied with the outcome. An important minority failed to accept democratization as a recipe for the good society. Many elites saw the swelling democratic tide as a threat to their own status, influence, and power, as well as to the old Federalist and classical republican reliance on constitutional balance. Under America's first two-party system, the rivalry between Federalists and Republicans had conformed to a fairly straightforward contest between hierarchical and grassroots sensibilities. To exaggerate for the sake of contrast: Federalists wanted a strong central government along with a capital-intensive (and thus a somewhat concentrated) economic system, and they wanted institutions to be controlled by a "power elite." Republicans wanted limited, decentralized government, along with an economy composed of small, autonomous (and primarily agrarian) economic units, and they wanted every possible organization to be controlled by and for "the people." Federalists expected deference; Republicans anticipated democracy. The second two-party system, comprising the Democrats and Whigs, repeated nearly the same economic dichotomy, but on the political front the picture was more confused.

Politics and Sensibility

A chief rallying cry of the early Whigs was against "King Andrew's" executive despotism.[1] One of the earliest Whig-oriented articles to employ the writings of Edmund Burke appeared in the *New England Magazine* in 1834—the first year of the Whig Party's existence.[2] Rather than using Burke's conservative writing as a defense of Whig anti-Democratic ideology, it instead used a specimen of Burke's reform writing to attack Jackson's presidential absolutism. Entitled "Thoughts on the Causes of the Present Discontents," the article alternated its own commentary on Jacksonian usurpation with excerpts from Burke's 1770 essay of the same name that had attacked the corruption and despotism of George III's court.[3] Jackson had enraged his opponents by killing the Second Bank of the United States, by his unprecedented use of the presidential veto, by his Indian removal policy, by his reputed reliance on secret advisers, and most of all by his continued success and popularity. The *New England Magazine* believed Burke's old tract was "remarkable for its perfect adaptation, in many particulars, to our country at the present time." While Burke had condemned the "king's friends," his "double-cabinet," and the "court cabal," this article criticized Jackson's "cabal, *camarilla*, kitchen-cabinet, or whatever it may be."[4] Just as members of the double-cabinet had allegedly been loyal to the king at the expense of the public good in Britain, members of the kitchen cabinet were allegedly loyal to the president at the expense of the public good in the United States. Both cabals purportedly violated the constitutions of their respective countries, because they indulged excesses of executive power. Worse, both Parliament and the Congress had acquiesced in this perversion of constitutional balance. It was a paradox of Whig principles that while the party favored a strong and active national government, its very origins lay in its opposition to an assertive head of that government. In the 1830s the presidency was still a work in progress, and Jackson's vigorous executive leadership was viewed by his adversaries as either a tyranny of the Caesar-Napoleon sort, or as an example of democracy run wild—since the president appealed to the masses over the heads of established elites.[5] Hence it was not surprising that the party most committed to a natural aristocracy and most suspicious of expansive democracy would portray Andrew Jackson as a despot.[6]

The *New England Magazine* article was as interesting for what it omitted from Burke's essay as for what it included. While it played up Burke's attack against "back-stairs influence and clandestine government," it played down his argument about the government's accountability to public opinion. While it quoted Burke's complaint about the aristocracy abdicating its independent responsibility and falling into "an abject servitude" to the corrupt court, it completely avoided Burke's defense of political parties—perhaps the most famous words in his essay.[7] Burke's *Thoughts on the Present Discontents* had been a manifesto for the Rockingham Whigs, and it stood as a decidedly left-of-center document written in the wake of the Wilkes Affair. Yet the *New England Magazine* ignored this sense of it, most likely because of the obvious democratic ramifications. In any event, the *New England Magazine* proved once again that Burke's usefulness did not depend on the French Revolution.

During the Federal period, the contest between Burke and Paine had loomed large above the American political landscape. But by the 1830s Burke was relegated to a subterranean influence on American political thought. As Daniel Walker Howe demonstrated some time ago, Whig political culture was broader and deeper than electoral politics.[8] Like their rivals the Democrats, the Whigs held certain assumptions about American society that, while they obviously influenced political behavior, also contributed to a more comprehensive sensibility that colored the Whig outlook in many fields. It was within this more conservative worldview that Burke's philosophy continued to resonate. Yet in order to be effective, conservatives were required—at least to some degree—to work in concert with liberal national ideals about which they had significant reservations. Or to put it another way, Whigs held a more constrained and traditional interpretation of those ideals. For example, advocates for the liberal sensibility exaggerated the American break with Anglo-European civilization; advocates for the conservative sensibility emphasized the continued strength of the old transatlantic ties.

One must also keep in mind that the national consensus began to unravel in the late antebellum period owing to a variety of factors. Although abolitionism has gotten most of the attention because it anticipated the Civil War, such trends as industrialization and immigration, and such social movements as temperance and women's rights, contributed to the growing perception that society was changing radically. Both liberals and conservatives were nervous about how the combined weight of such changes would alter their known world. The main difference between them was that liberals were reluctant to abandon their faith in democracy as a solution to new problems, while conservatives instinctively turned to an elite leadership instead. Not all Democrats were liberal, and Whigs were not universally conservative. Slavery was only the most dramatic issue upon which the opposite was often the case. But as a general rule most Whigs were of the more conservative, more traditional, and more elitist frame of mind. To the extent that the United States had any semblance of a natural aristocracy during the late antebellum period, the Whigs represented it. As Michael Holt's study observes: "For . . . patricians, belonging to the Whig party was the equivalent of belonging to an exclusive gentlemen's club of social peers." Even those who merely identified with the elite responded favorably to the Whig principles of "probity, respectability, morality, and reason."[9] Emerson's famous observation that the Democrats had the best program while the Whigs had the best men seems to have caught the mood of the era with exceptional clarity, if not with literal accuracy.

Toward the end of the Age of Revolution one Federalist had written to another, "I think it will be truly laughable to see the *swinish multitude* (as Mr. Burke observes) feasting on a quadruped and swilling whiskey to seditious toasts—God only knows where it will end."[10] But a few short years later Burke the nasty reactionary was gone and Burke the rhetorical genius took his place. By 1810 the (Boston) *Monthly Anthology; or, Magazine of Polite Literature* was tying Burke's oratory to Milton's poetry, and Benjamin Rush was writing to John Adams, "We do not stand in need now of Greek and Roman poets, historians, and orators. Shakespear [*sic*], Milton, Thompson, Pope, Hume, Robertson, Burke . . . and a dozen others that might be named *more* than fill their places." In the 1820s the (Philadelphia) *Port folio*—which at one time had been "strongly federalist, and reactionary to a degree"—explicitly disavowed memorializing Burke in ideological terms: "Any writer may eke out a quarto volume with declamations about [the American Revolution, the Letters of Junius, or] diatribes on the French Revolution: but a book so manufactured . . . is the life of nobody." Instead it rhapsodized over "the charms of [Burke's] rhetorical discourses, of the power of his eloquence . . . the goodness of his heart . . . the connexion between real genius and virtue." Soon thereafter, when the Whig politician Caleb Cushing needed to improve his own oratory skills, he wrote in his diary: "Burke—study of him necessary—I have injudiciously neglected him . . . rely upon a collection of necessaries, especially the orators like Demosthenes & Burke."[11] A deceptively trivial example of the degree to which Burke had been inducted into the nonideological "great books" tradition of Western literature came later in the antebellum period when Herman Melville included two epigraphs from Burke at the beginning of *Moby Dick*—along with quotations from the Bible, Shakespeare, Blackstone, Pope, and other such fonts of wisdom.[12]

Throughout the antebellum period, conservatives in America seem to have consulted and quoted Burke more than their liberal counterparts did. But they usually followed the liberal practice of concentrating on Burke's Whig reform writings and treading lightly on his antirevolutionary ones. They also seemed to appreciate him more for his rhetoric than for his ideology. Most of all they seem to have appreciated his *sensibility*, of which his rhetoric was an instrument.[13] A concise illustration of this can be found in the journal of the Whig lawyer, politician, and man of letters Richard Henry Dana.[14] Like George Bancroft, Dana made a pilgrimage to one of Burke's old residences (his London apartment) and recorded a tribute to Burke's commitment to lofty principles and traditional institutions, yet the only direct mention of a political matter was the impeachment of Warren Hastings.[15] Dana and certain other Americans of the Whig persuasion diverged from the dominant antebellum culture because, for them, Burke just felt right. Hence Burke found transatlantic relevance as an intuitive cultural counterforce against the liberalizing sensibility of tradition-breaking democratization. Since Whiggism never gained the upper hand on that ultimate cultural plateau, prominent Whigs each had to confront this reality in his own way.

Three prominent men who professed Whig conservative principles with a Burkean twist were Edward Everett, Rufus Choate, and Joseph Story. Two were lawyers, one was a scholar; two held elective office, one was a Supreme Court justice and law professor. Everett and Choate were known as great orators, with reputations approaching that of their political mentor Daniel Webster (which is why their takes on Burke were important; they were famous and respected "public intellectuals" in their day). None of the three is a household name in America today; Story remains an important figure among legal and constitutional scholars, but is virtually unknown elsewhere. The careers of all three climaxed during the decades when Edmund Burke's reputation in America had lost most of the ideological valence that had been its signature in the 1790s and had settled into a comparatively nonpartisan legacy of thoughtful statesmanship and masterly rhetoric.

Edward Everett

Today Edward Everett (1794–1865) is a minor footnote in United States history. To his ultimate discredit, he has found lasting fame as a speck of historical trivia: Everett gave the now-neglected long speech at Gettysburg just before Lincoln gave his immortal short speech. The fact that Everett's two-hour oration has been overshadowed (if not obliterated) by Lincoln's two-minute address serves as a metaphor for his life. Everett held several important positions and achieved national fame as an orator, but to no great effect, and only to be forgotten. Born in Massachusetts in 1794, Everett at the age of twenty-one was appointed to the faculty of Harvard, from which he had graduated with highest honors at seventeen. He was the first American ever to receive a Ph.D. (from Gottingen University in Germany), and, while a Harvard professor, he edited the *North American Review*—to which he contributed 118 articles. Everett held important diplomatic posts, served ten years in the U.S. Congress (1825–35), and was elected to four one-year terms as governor of Massachusetts (1836–39) before becoming president of Harvard (1846–49); he later served eight months as secretary of state (1852–53) and fifteen months in the U.S. Senate (1853–54). Everett was instrumental in the creation of the Whig Party in Massachusetts, and was an ardent unionist during the Civil War—dying just before its conclusion in 1865. Yet for all these accomplishments, Everett's life amounted to less than the sum of its parts.[16]

In this, Everett was not alone. Whig politicians have mostly been remembered for what they failed to accomplish. The two greatest Whigs—Henry Clay and Daniel Webster—are best remembered for never reaching the White House; the first Whig to become president—William Harrison—died after a month in office; the second (and last) Whig to be elected president—Zachary Taylor—died after sixteen months in office.[17] The Whig Party itself lived a mere twenty-two years and was replaced not by a successor conservative party, but by an antislavery Republican Party. Yet it is not simply a case of history being written by the winners that has relegated American Whigs to historical limbo. It was also that Whigs, even in their days of rough political parity with the Democrats, never represented the main current in U.S. history. Politically and culturally Whigs formed a countercurrent in American thought. Since countercurrents tend, over time, to become counterintuitive, they are not easily incorporated into the nation's collective memory—which must always conform to Enlightenment ideals of liberal progress.

Even by Whig standards, Everett was significant but no giant. Whatever influence he achieved in his time stemmed not from his political offices, but from his role as a great orator. Such a role is now difficult to comprehend, since grandiloquent speeches are no longer in vogue (in fact, the thought of them is somewhat comical). But today's self-consciously sophisticated dismissal of grand oratory is indicative of an increasingly cynical view of the democratic process. Americans are now conditioned to accept interest-group pressure politics as the norm—they may grouse about it, but no one expects to change it. Yet in the earlier days of the Republic, respect for oratory was tied to reverence for democracy. If reason was to guide the citizen in his political decisions, then oratory was to be an instrument of that reason. Hence the great orator was lionized in the antebellum period, and Edward Everett was one of the greatest.[18]

Everett in turn admired Edmund Burke, whom he called "the greatest political philosopher and most consummate statesman of modern Europe."

To Everett, Burke was "great, almost beyond rivalry," to the point that "no compositions in the English tongue can take precedence to those of Burke, in depth of thought, reach of forecast, or magnificence of style."[19] The fact that Everett defended Burke's reputation against those who admired his rhetoric but did not accept his political thought not only made Everett a true American Burkean, but also placed him at odds with the dominant values of his day. Unlike the nation as a whole, Everett never moved beyond the ideological struggles of the Federalist era. Far from acknowledging the reality of democratization, he displayed a John Adams–like belief that "a rightly organized state was the greatest engine of moral power known to man." He praised Charles Francis Adams for editing John Adams's *Works*, "without being inflamed by the heats of temporary controversies." In context this meant that his support for the principles of the American Revolution were coupled to his recognition that *the revolution was over.* Everett had no illusions about the general unpopularity of his beliefs. Once, he spoke of the "ostracism to which . . . conservative opinions" had "condemned" his Whig colleague Rufus Choate.[20] Fortunately, Everett did not owe his popularity as an orator to his conservative ideology. On the political score, like Burke in his final years, Everett chose to be among the last of an Old Whig breed.

True to Burke's example, Everett's Whig vision was not just rabidly conservative; it included elements of humane reform as well. Like Burke, Everett sought to lessen the use of capital punishment and eliminate imprisonment for debt. And Everett's condemnation of Jackson's Indian removal policy bore some resemblance to Burke's enlightened positions on India and Ireland. But while reform was a major theme in Burke's career, it was a minor one in Everett's. For instance, though Everett called slavery a "great evil," he saw abolitionism as an even greater threat to the nation, and he hoped the issue would fade away. In fact, Everett retired from politics just as (and in large part *because*) the debates over slavery were coming to a head in the 1850s. As Charles Francis Adams observed, "Everett did well enough in fair weather, but succumbed when the going got rough."[21]

Everett repeatedly and eloquently portrayed the nation not only as a unified whole, but as a distinctive land with a unique heritage. In doing so, he attempted to tie his conservative sensibility into the new American archetype. For instance, commemorating the American Revolution was a recurring and always effective theme for his speeches. In fact, his early fame as an orator resulted from his address welcoming the return of Lafayette in 1824. Everett served as secretary of the Bunker Hill Monument Association, and he defended both American spoken English and American literature from British criticism. Often he championed the *ideal* of democracy. Nowhere was this more evident than in his call for U.S. support for the Greek rebellion against the Turks in the early 1820s—an event he likened to the American Revolution. He contributed as well to the deification of George Washington, delivering his lecture of tribute to him 137 times in four years.[22] In this sense Everett might be viewed as a "conservative exceptionalist," and his career demonstrated that leaders of all ideological camps had to tie their beliefs into the nation's established ideals in order to be effective. Perhaps this was why Emerson once called Everett "our Cicero." With Everett and his more powerful mentor Daniel Webster, American conservatives learned for the first time to adopt (and adapt) the language of liberalism for their own purposes—a lesson the earlier Federalists never did learn.

Everett seems to have led two parallel public lives. One was as a politician. In this incarnation he represented the interests of the conservative Massachusetts elite, and he stood squarely against Jacksonian democracy in both policy and sensibility. But in his other role as a ceremonial orator he assumed a nonpartisan "consensus" persona. Everett was not particularly skilled or effective at political debate, yet he excelled at inspirational and commemorative oratory. In an Independence Day speech in 1826, Everett proclaimed that the creation of the United States represented "a maturity of political wisdom . . . and a moral courage, of which the modern world affords no other example." He then extolled the value of republican government and harshly condemned the record of European monarchy. Summoning Burke's remark that "Kings are fond of low company," Everett derided the generations of royalty entombed "in the dreary pomp of monumental marble" in Old World cathedrals, and he railed against all the "calamities" of their countless wars and "all their other uncouth pretenses for destroying mankind." By contrast, Everett looked to republican government for "the cessation of wars." And he glorified the function of human agency by praising the founding fathers as "the great benefactors of mankind." If not for them—and here he sounded like George Bancroft—the world "would have continued to be arrogated, as the exclusive inheritance of a few."[23]

But this was about as democratic as Everett got. While many Americans of the liberal sensibility wielded exceptionalism as a cultural weapon, Everett simply employed it as a widely accepted premise. As such it was neutral and ritualistic, rather than partisan and democratic. In this same spirit Everett used Burke as a bridge between the Old World and the New, as well as between progress and stability. Everett mentioned Burke more than thirty times in his major addresses; he even sneaked in a rare citation of Burke's *Abridgement of English History*.[24] In keeping with the conventional practice of his time, Everett praised Burke's character and his rhetorical powers.[25] But

Everett departed from convention when he tried to balance his exceptionalist perspective with his feelings of attachment to British civilization. In a speech at Plymouth, Massachusetts, in 1824, Everett asked, "What reflecting American does not acknowledge . . . the deep fountains of civil, intellectual, and moral truth, from which we have drawn in England?" He paid homage to the contributions of Bacon, Newton, and Locke and recalled the love of liberty exemplified by the Pilgrims, Burke, and Chatham. On a more mystical level, Everett declared, "In touching the soil of England, I seem to return, like a descendant, to the old family seat; to come back to the abode of an aged and venerable parent." Everett claimed to be no "panegyrist of England," but he recognized it as "the cradle and the refuge of free principles." In an effort to extrapolate his own sentiments to the rest of American society, Everett concluded, "I should think him cold in his love for his native land, who felt no melting in his heart for that other native country, which holds the ashes of his forefathers."[26]

It would be fruitlessly anachronistic to apply today's multicultural perspective to Everett's sentiments. But even in light of Everett's own celebrations of American exceptionalism, his gushing about the land of our "other fathers" seems out of place. Yet in this apparent contradiction, Everett was actually constructing a model of antebellum consensus that he hoped would preserve a balanced system of liberty. Everett's references to England were at different times traditionalist and exceptionalist. Everett rejected the abuses and dead-ends of British history, and praised only the intellectual, political, and cultural elements he thought represented progress—certainly the heritage of liberty was chief among these. Furthermore, in his selective incorporation of British precedent into American culture, Everett was acknowledging the young nation's need to be part of a recognizable tradition. Not surprisingly, he chose to inculcate the virtues of stability and restraint into the national character. Everett may have glamorized the first stage of the American Revolution in his commemorative oratory, but in his political activity and his intellectual thought he valued the constructive, orderly, and controlled second stage.

Hence when Everett invoked the creation myth, he did not trumpet inalienable rights. Instead he portrayed the revolution as an epic tale of classical form. In one speech he proclaimed: "The incidents, the characters, are worthy of the drama. What names, what men! Chatham, Burke, Fox, Franklin, the Adamses, Washington, Jefferson, and all the chivalry and all the diplomacy of Europe and America." Certainly this was heroic, transatlantic, and (in tone) more historically grand than politically insurrectional. Perhaps a sense of civilized glory was all that Everett was trying to convey. Elsewhere Everett saluted Burke's *Speech on Conciliation with America*, which he said "excels every thing, in the form of eloquence, that has come down to us from Greece or Rome." And he repeated Burke's lines about the transatlantic ties that were light as air but strong as links of iron. According to Everett, all of Britain's many conquests and victories over the years were but "barbarous distinctions, vulgar fame, compared with 'the peculiar glory' [the phrase was Burke's] of founding a colonial empire on the principles of liberty."[27] Here Everett seems to have been very close in thought to the patriots at the *start* of the revolution, who broke with Britain because Britain had violated its own standards of freedom. Everett seemed less willing to endorse the liberal tendencies that the revolution later unleashed.

What then of the French Revolution, and of Burke's criticism of it? As we have seen, writers and speakers in the mid-antebellum period shied away from the issue, and Everett was no exception. But in his occasional references to it, he firmly identified with Burke's position. His only sustained mention of Burke's antirevolutionary efforts was clear and emphatic: "[Burke's] all but inspired appeals and expostulations which went to the heart of England and Europe in the hour of their dearest peril, and did so much to expose the deformity and arrest the progress, of their godless philosophy,—specious, arrogant, hypocritical, and sanguinary,—which, with liberty and equality on its lips, and plunder and murder and treason in its heart, wages deadly war on France and mankind, and closed a professed crusade for republican freedom by the establishment of a military despotism."[28]

The oration that best showcased Edward Everett as the American exemplar of Burke's sensibility and language was his speech "Stability and Progress," delivered at Boston's Faneuil Hall on July 4, 1853. Though Edmund Burke's name was never invoked, his influence cannot be mistaken. The purpose of the speech was, after all, a defense of conservatism after a generation of democratization. "[One] class of men," said Everett, "received a few years ago, in England, the designation of 'conservatives,' from their disposition to maintain things just as they are. . . . These benighted individuals . . . err only in pushing a sound principle to its extremes." He then elucidated some of those sound principles; or rather, he articulated some traditional sentiments:

> The sacred tie of family, which, reaching backward and forward, binds the generations together. . . . The mystic tissue of race, woven far back in the chambers of the past . . . wraps up great nations in its broad mantle. . . . Forefather, parent, child, posterity, native land . . . these teach us not blinding worship, but duly to honor the past . . . in constitutions, in laws, in maxims, in traditions. . . .
>
> . . . If this notion [of progress] is carried too far it becomes suicidal . . . and justifies the next generation in sweeping away their work. . . .

> . . . [The founding fathers] not only looked to the future, but they explored the past. They built wisely and skilfully . . . they dug the foundation deep to the eternal rock.[29]

Just how deep—that is, how far back—Everett was willing to go to place American civilization on firm ground became apparent at Gettysburg. In the wake of their cemetery dedication speeches, Everett wrote Lincoln that he hoped he had come "as near to the central idea of the occasion in two hours as you did in two minutes." If the central idea was to revive lagging support for the northern war effort, Everett (contrary to popular belief) may have come nearer to achieving that immediate goal than Lincoln did.[30] On the other hand, the two speeches differed not only in length, but also in tone and in focus. Both speeches invoked ideals, but they were not exactly the same ones. Lincoln chose to reaffirm the ideals of the revolution: the Union was fighting to preserve its government of, by, and for the people, which had been conceived in liberty and dedicated to equality. Only once did he directly mention the current rebellion, calling it a test of the nation's endurance. Everett, on the other hand, turned his speech into a general condemnation of the right to revolt. Not only was he sharp in his recriminations against the southern extremist conspiracy that he believed started the catastrophic war, but he engaged in a historical-legal analysis on the legitimacy of revolution.

Citing the American Revolution, the English Civil War, and the Glorious Revolution as examples, Everett argued that it was "only just and proper to rebel against oppressive government," or "against tyranny." On the other hand, a rebellion of "ambitious men against a beneficent government," a rebellion that "seeks to overturn wise constitutions," was "treason." He then cataloged the horrors of the Wars of the Roses, the English Civil War, the German Wars of Reformation, the Thirty Years' War, the Italian wars since the decline of the Roman Empire, and the French civil wars, all as lessons on the consequences of destructive factionalism and internecine chaos.[31] Everett began and ended his oration with ancient Athens. In doing so, not only was he reaching back to the very beginning of Western civilization, but in a sense he was discarding the element of time completely. When he quoted from Pericles's own battlefield funeral oration, that "the whole earth is the sepulchre of illustrious men," and extended it with, "All time, he might have added, is the millennium of their glory," Everett was uniting the martyrs of Gettysburg with all those who had died gallantly throughout history.[32] In his ambition to be universal, Everett placed the emphasis away from what exactly the Gettysburg sacrifices were for. Surely the objective of teaching the illegitimate rebel leadership a lesson was insufficient to the occasion. Preserving the Union may have been sufficient, but (unlike Lincoln) Everett said nothing about what kind of union the North was fighting for. Though the Gettysburg ceremony took place almost a year after Lincoln's Emancipation Proclamation took effect, Everett did not even acknowledge that a Union victory would end slavery.

Lincoln's address, though solemn, signaled resolve and optimism. In retrospect it is possible to connect the dots from Lincoln's words at Gettysburg to his earlier words about the better angels of our nature, or his later words about malice toward none and charity for all. Lincoln's ideals can be applied to the civil rights movement of the twentieth century—or to any crusade for social justice, or for the preservation of American values. But in Everett's case, sadly, it is only possible to connect the dots from his essentially classical oration at Gettysburg to his ineffectual conservative legacy. Lincoln's ideals were timeless, progressive, and dynamic. The conservative ideals cherished by Everett, however, were static; he wanted to stop history at a point of his own choosing. Apparently the American Revolution (or more inclusively, the establishment of constitutional republican government) was one such point, and it represented for him what the Glorious Revolution had represented to the Old Whigs of Britain: a successful experiment that was over. It could thus be safely praised, hallowed, consecrated, or celebrated, as long as it was not perpetuated into the present as an ongoing, open-ended process.[33]

In fact, it did not take long for Everett's perspective to be seen as fossilized, even by some of his affectionate contemporaries. When friends and associates gathered to memorialize Everett two days after his death—which came just fourteen months after the Gettysburg ceremony—one speaker summed up his life and his sensibility with unadorned candor:

> [Everett] was naturally timid and distrustful of change. . . . He revered the past, but distrusted the future. . . . He honored precedents, but distrusted theories. . . . Hence during the vigor of this life, impressed with an honest fear of evils to come, he seemed to throw his transcendental talents in the way of progress and reform, until he was almost crushed beneath their advancing tread, and lovers of liberty and right had almost come to look upon him as an enemy to freedom and humanity.[34]

Today this passage could be applied to Burke—at least to the simplified image of him that persists in America. But unlike the continually resurrected Burke, Everett rests undisturbed in a mostly forgotten grave. Of course Burke was a more important figure historically, and this accounts for a good deal of the disparity between the reputations of the two men. But another factor might be that Burke has been incorporated into the main currents of British thought, while Everett remains out of touch with American ideals.

Rufus Choate

As expendable as Edward Everett may appear in retrospect, there is no denying he was a prime representative of the New England Brahmin establishment of his day.[35] Rufus Choate (1799–1859), on the other hand, seems to have been branded as bizarre and eccentric by his contemporaries, and he has retained that image ever since. Tall and thin, with a "prematurely wrinkled" face, Choate was said to project an "oriental" appearance. He was rumored to have used opium, and he exhibited phenomenal bursts of energy followed by bouts of debilitating fatigue. Like Everett, he was renowned for his ceremonial oratory, and also for his theatrical courtroom performances. Choate rarely handled a case of significant legal or constitutional importance. Still he was eulogized as the "Wizard of the Law" long after his death, because of his legendary ability to sway juries.[36] Even more incongruously, given his lack of concrete accomplishments, Choate was nearly elected to the American Hall of Fame in New York City in 1900. No doubt Choate was a colorful character, but his exact contributions to the nation remain elusive. Only in the last generation or so has anyone claimed him to be an important voice in the history of American conservative thought. Along with this distinction, he has also been identified as a disciple of Burke.[37]

Born in Essex, Massachusetts, in 1799, Choate was a student at Dartmouth at the time of the landmark Dartmouth College case in 1818.[38] The event sparked his interest in the law, as well as his lifelong admiration for Daniel Webster (who successfully argued the case before the Supreme Court). Choate went on to become one of the most successful and famous lawyers in Massachusetts and a prominent spokesman for Whig principles. He served in the Massachusetts legislature (1825–27) and the U.S. Congress (1830–32); he helped form the Massachusetts Whig Party in 1834 and later served in the U.S. Senate (1841–45). A "cotton" rather than "conscience" Whig, Choate endorsed the Democrat Buchanan in 1856 rather than align himself with the new Republican Party. Choate died in Halifax, Nova Scotia, in 1859, en route to Europe in search of a cure for his declining health.

If Choate's ultimate importance to U.S. history is questionable, at least he serves as a useful example for understanding the Whig reaction to democracy. By the time of the Dartmouth College lawsuit, the old Federalist elite had already long felt its control of society was threatened. One member of the old guard wrote: "We have satisfactory evidence, that democracy intends to pour her poison into our literary fountains and to train up our youth for her own purposes. . . . The other institutions of New England are to be *regenerated* to 'pure republicanism.' . . . The College will become democratic, and a set of sycophants . . . will be put in the place of some of the best men for a literary Seminary unless the stubborn arm of democracy can be arrested."[39] Choate later made it his mission to protect American society from the same sort of majoritarian threat that Dartmouth had faced during his youth. But strangely he did not devote his full energies to the task, nor did he systematically articulate his philosophy.

The political scientist Samuel Huntington once argued that strains of modern conservatism develop whenever some "challenging social force" presents a "clear and present danger" to institutions a particular group has a stake in defending. Huntington cited Burke as his prime example, and concluded, "Men are driven to conservatism by the shock of events, by the horrible feeling that a society or institution which they have approved or taken for granted and with which they have been intimately connected may suddenly cease to exist."[40] Certainly Rufus Choate saw the democratization of American society as the clear and present danger of his own time, and he saw his connection to Edmund Burke in that light. As he wrote sarcastically to Charles Sumner: "We, poor, unidealized, Tom Painified democrats, do not understand . . . [Burke's] universal wisdom . . . and are afraid of his principles." Choate also told Sumner, "I . . . embrace you for your Burkeism generally," and he encouraged Sumner to write a hundred-page article on Burke for the *North American Review*.[41] One biographer likened Choate's late-career defection to the conservative Buchanan Democrats to Burke's late-career defection from the Whigs: "Like Edmund Burke before him, [Choate] allied himself, towards the close of his life, with a party the views of which he had hitherto repudiated. Like Burke, too, he would have argued that he was absolutely consistent, absolutely true to certain basic convictions which were more important than superficial party loyalty." But also like Burke, "Choate was fighting against destiny!"[42]

Like his friend Edward Everett, Rufus Choate easily conformed to the model of the conservative as a reactive defender of threatened values or establishments. Though, in the opinion of some, Choate went farther by developing an ideological response to those threats. As one scholar put it: "Choate devised a powerful, articulate defence of America's inherited political and social order. In short, Choate performed that paramount duty of the genuine philosophic conservative—of rising to protect the existing system by enunciating a body of theory which could serve as a meaningful rationale for the status quo." Again like Everett: "Whiggery," for Choate, "still provided the best means and the soundest policies by which the Union might be preserved."[43] Note however that this view dismissed the new American archetype by interpreting Choate as a defender of an *inherited* order, and Choate did seem to deny the radical nature of the American split with Britain. He demonstrated this belief in his dismissal of the Declaration of Independence as a statement of "glittering and sounding generalities of natural right."[44] When the new Republican Party promised to execute its constitutional powers "in the spirit of the Declaration," Choate asked mockingly: "Would they venture the proposition that the Federal Government derives any powers, any one power from that source?" Consistent with other American conservatives of various eras, Choate venerated the order-inducing, property-protecting Constitution and downplayed the lofty ideals of the Declaration. "Every great party," said Choate when endorsing the Democrats in 1856, "successively becomes the savior of the Constitution." He believed the Republican Party's emphasis on slavery to be an "evil which assails the state" and that "their creed" was "revolutionary and dangerous." He added, "The fear to which I appeal is that early and provident fear which Mr. Burke so beautifully describes as being the mother of safety."[45] In this revealing speech Choate stood at odds with the mainstream American tradition on two separate points: he mocked the ideals of the revolution, and he backed the futile strategy of avoiding civil war by mollifying the South. Perversely, it was in this vein that some anti-abolitionist writers invoked Burke in response to "ultras" or "Jacobins" like Elijah Lovejoy and William Lloyd Garrison.[46]

Yet it is to Choate's ceremonial and political speeches that we must turn for clues about his Whig-conservative (and elements of Burkean) thought.[47] In preparing these speeches, Choate by his own testimony turned to Burke (among others) in search of a proven model. When planning his oratorical strategy for the advocacy of Whig candidates in 1844, he wrote in his journal: "I at once confine my rhetorical excercitations within strict and impassible limits. . . . I shall read Burke's American speeches, writing observations on them. The object is his matter, and manner." As if to convince himself that it would be personally edifying to devote time and energy to studies outside the law, he sought to "liberalize" his mind by finding "a body of digested truths" in the writings of "Cicero, Homer, Burke, and Milton." A month later he wrote of collecting "maxims and proverbs" from Burke and other "great author[s]."[48] Clearly there was here an element of the nonideological consultation of Burke for rhetorical technique and general wisdom. But Choate's speeches indicated a philosophical debt to Burke that went beyond style and the abstract search for truth.

In an address at Salem, Massachusetts, in 1833, for instance, Choate called for a body of romantic literature, in the tradition of Walter Scott, that would "speak directly to the heart and affections and imagination of the whole people" about the history of New England, supplying "a vast amount of positive information quite as authentic and valuable . . . as that which makes up the matter of professed history, but which the historian does not and cannot furnish." At first glance it might appear that Choate was in effect advertising for a James Michener of his day—a writer who could fictionalize history in order to make it more accessible and easier to grasp. But Choate was not just asking for a popularizer; he was looking for an "authorized" version of New England history (which for him meant American history) that would reach citizens on an emotional level, and "would fix deep in the general mind and memory of the whole people" his Whiggish view of the past. As he put it plainly: "It is time that literature and the arts should at least cooperate with history."[49] Choate's remarks came at exactly the time when indigenous American culture seemed to be dawning, and he was well aware of the ways that collective intuition and communal sensibilities could trump rational argument.

Perhaps Choate's most-noted speech was "The Position and Functions of the American Bar, as an Element of Conservatism in the State," which he delivered at Harvard Law School in 1845.[50] In it he demonstrated both his unease with democracy and his Burkean traditionalist sensibility. Choate rejected the ideas of "Rousseau and Locke, and our own revolutionary age . . . that the State is nothing but a contract." Then he sounded off against excessive individual freedom: "It might almost seem to be growing to be our national humor to hold ourselves free at every instant, to be and do just what we please, go where we please . . . and that the State itself were held to be no more than an encampment of tents on the great prairie, pitched at sun-down, and struck [at dawn] . . . instead of a structure, stately and eternal."[51] Obviously Choate displayed no reverence for the ethos of democracy. He did not subscribe to the popular belief that "what the majority pleases, it may ordain. What it ordains is law." Instead he asked: "But, then, as law is nothing but the will of a major number, and as that will differs from the will of yesterday, and will differ from that of to-morrow, and as all law is a restraint on natural right and independence, how can it gain a moment's hold on the reverential sentiments of the heart, and the profounder convictions of judgement?" Choate's alternative view held that law "is not the offspring of will at all. It is the absolute justice of the State, enlightened by the perfect reason of the State. That is Law." Moreover, "haste, injustice, revenge, and folly" could be excluded from the law, "by the aid of time." Time "tries all things . . . and works them pure."[52] And here he waxed Burkean in both matter and manner:

> We subject the law . . . to the tests of old experience, to the reason and justice of successive generations. . . . And then and thus we pronounce it good. . . . We would grave it deep into the heart of the undying State. We would strengthen it by opinion, by manners, by private virtue, by habit, by the awful hoar of innumerable ages.[53]

Considering the United States was roughly two generations old at the time of Choate's remarks, and that it explicitly thought of itself as a young nation, there is little doubt that Choate was invoking the much-older English common law and constitutional tradition. And it is likely that he intended this long-historical approach to apply to areas of human activity outside the law as well:

> In the way . . . it comes down to us, it seems one mighty and continuous stream of experience and reason, accumulated, ancestral . . . the grand agent of civilization . . . the guardian angel of a hundred generations, our own hereditary laws. . . . There is a deep presumption in favor of that which has endured so long. . . . There is a virtue, there is truth, in that effacing touch of time.[54]

Since conservative Whigs like Choate felt American society was suffering in the throes of malignant democratization, it was only natural for them to turn to the independent judiciary as a restraining force. Hence Choate's message about the conservative function of time and tradition could not have been delivered to a more appropriate audience than this one—the nation's premiere (and still Brahmin dominated) law school. In a later speech to the Massachusetts constitutional convention, in which he opposed the direct election of judges, Choate noted that America's "intensely republican" political system had two goals: liberty and security. And he observed that the American people loved liberty, but also held dear to "the old Anglo-Saxon instinct of property; the rational, and the credible desire to be secure in life." This desire, Choate believed, could only be "indulged" by "a learned, impartial, and honored judiciary." He then lapsed into a nautical analogy of the "noble ship" at sea. The people may love the "exhilaration of the crowding sail," but they also know the value of a good storm anchor.[55]

Edmund Burke had argued that a hereditary aristocracy served as a responsible restraining force in liberty-loving British society. Yet by the mid-antebellum period, no one in the United States could have seriously suggested such an idea. The closest practical approximation of it was a call for an independent judiciary answerable only to its own understanding of constitutions, precedents, and common-law traditions. Both the Whigs and Federalists have been identified (or accused) of paving the way for the later plutocratic challenge to the rule of egalitarian democracy. In this vein Rufus Choate has been identified as a protector of the New England business elite. But Choate also held an organic view of society that in important ways conflicted with the competitive and individualist virtues of the unfettered market. As such he was representative of certain contradictions within Whig conservatism itself. This helps in understanding why the Burkean organic-traditionalist strain of conservatism has not been the dominant variety practiced in the United States. It also helps explain why such Burkean Whigs as Rufus Choate have become historically homeless figures.

The supreme example of Choate's antiliberal sensibility can be found in a speech he delivered to the Joseph Story Association of the Harvard Law School in 1851.[56] Following a procession led by the "Brigade Band," members of the association gathered in the First Church of Cambridge, where—after an opening prayer—they were treated to Choate's "very brilliant oration." The undercurrents of his address were the inextricable problems of slavery, secession, and abolitionism. Important as these issues were, Choate chose to tie them into the even more fundamental matters of conscience, individualism, morality, and the common good. He began by denying the prevalent notion that American civilization was in a state of decline. This had been a common theme among conservatives in the wake of the revolution (recall that John Adams invoked it as early as the 1790s), but it gained new currency as the nation slid toward civil war. In an unconvincing effort to start off on an optimistic note, Choate claimed the United States was experiencing "no decay—strictly and absolutely speaking." But he immediately acknowledged that "there are phenomena which might sadden and perplex," such as "this pride in individual liberty," and "the sentiment of obligation to duty and conscience." By this Choate meant that too many citizens were listening to their own inner voices, particularly over the morality of slavery. He saw abolitionism as a threat not only to national unity, but to the supremacy of elite rule: "These ethics of agitation can accomplish nothing towards the training of good citizens. They treat us to a banquet of emotions, but do not furnish us with a practical guide to life." Choate was preaching to an already converted choir of conservative Whigs. Yet despite his call for "practical" rather than "visionary" policies, his moral contortions over slavery represented the very approach that would destroy the Whig Party five years later.[57]

Twice in his speech Choate referred to Jeremy Taylor, the British royalist bishop of the English Civil War era who has been called the Shakespeare and Spenser of the pulpit. In an effort to discredit the many Protestant ministers who were supporting the cause of abolitionism, Choate cited Taylor's dictum that although "unjust laws do not bind the conscience," only those laws that were "notorious" and that garnered "universal" agreement as to their unjust nature could rightly be disobeyed. Clearly this was an impossible standard to meet, even for the widely hated Fugitive Slave Act. But Choate was also making a larger point about the responsibility of moral leaders that was very similar to Burke's "clergy in their closets" idea.[58] That is, clerics should not encourage passion or free thought among members of their congregations—not because the status quo was sacrosanct, but because the "mass" was not qualified to deal with change in a responsible way. Not only was this contrary to the spirit of democracy—it was hostile to intellectual freedom. While Choate implied that lawyers and judges had a way of finding "actual law," which, once found, "nothing is left but to exact obedience to it," he assumed no such ability on the part of the common citizen: "Among the startling developments of a perfect and consummate freedom, men in this country feel at liberty to try everything, law, Constitution, the existence of nature and society, by the standard of their individual judgements; by their consciences, enlightened or unenlightened . . . to honor . . . in exact proportion to the darkness of their own inward light."[59] If this was not enough to demonstrate Choate's disavowal of the Enlightenment frame of mind, his view of the nation's creation certainly was.

Choate partially acknowledged the new American archetype of a society produced by conscious human agency. As he put it: "Our Union is a direct and arbitrary production of the human mind. Some nations seem moulded into nations by the divine mind; ours is the direct and visible work of our own hands." But while the American mainstream viewed this as a good thing worthy of celebration, Choate viewed it as a bad thing that fostered insecurity. While most Americans saw promise in the nation's comparative youth, Choate saw the "recency of its formation" as a threat to the nation's survival. He also saw "its artificial construction" as a weakness. In essence Choate rejected the deductive conclusion of the creation-myth syllogism: for him intentional human design in a virgin land did not necessarily yield a better society—since it discarded the beneficial support of long tradition. Choate's efforts to venerate the Constitution were defensive ones, because the Constitution itself lacked the majesty of "the effacing touch of time." Of course Choate predictably took aim at the Declaration of Independence as well; anticipating his famous "glittering . . . generalities" remark, he called it "a glittering abstraction."[60] As in his earlier speech on the conservative role of the law, Rufus Choate seemed most comfortable working within an inherited continuous tradition that avoided revolutionary change. Given that Choate's hour-and-a-half-long speech "was frequently interrupted by bursts of applause" by his Story Association audience, he was not exactly alone in this perspective.

The conservative-Whig persuasion—as exemplified by Choate—was clearly a reaction to individualism, democratization, and a decline in deference. It also represented a mutated form of exceptionalism, which memorialized the revolution as a restoration of traditional liberties and which recognized still-significant ties between the United States and British civilization (and in fact lamented that such ties were not even stronger). It contained a cultural-mystical element that saw tradition as a counterweight to both rational design and personal moral initiative. Most important—and this is seldom noticed—Whig conservatism failed to link its worldview with American ideals. In fact it came close to flouting those ideals instead. By the late antebellum period the Whig conservative ethos was already a dead man walking, though it continued to walk boldly on its own turf—especially in New England and within many of the nation's elite institutions: legal, educational, and journalistic. The Civil War would eventually kill it as a clearly recognizable phenomenon, but something of its ghost resurfaced and (as will be seen) lingered for several more generations.

Joseph Story

The most powerful of the antebellum Burkeans was Joseph Story (1779–1845), whose importance stemmed from his long tenure on the U.S. Supreme Court. Story is widely acknowledged to have been—after John Marshall—the court's most influential member during the early nineteenth century. Ironically, Story's appointment to the high court had nothing to do with his Whig conservative views. In fact, had President James Madison known better of Story's political orientation, he surely would never have nominated him. (As it was, Story had been Madison's fourth choice, and no less a figure than Thomas Jefferson had opposed him.)[61] Story was an anomalous character in several ways. Now remembered as an oracle of Federalist-Whig principles, Story came from a radical republican background. His father had been one of the "Indians" at the Boston Tea Party, and the Story family had progressed from revolutionary militancy to Jeffersonian Republicanism by the turn of the century.[62] Much of Story's important legal work coincided with the climax of democracy in the 1830s.[63]

Born in Marblehead, Massachusetts, in 1779, Story graduated from Harvard in 1798 and practiced law in Salem. He served briefly in the Massachusetts legislature and then in the U.S. House of Representatives (1808–9) as a Republican. He took his seat on the Supreme Court in 1812 and remained there until his death in 1845. From 1829 on, Story doubled as Dane Professor of Law at Harvard, where he shaped a generation of future lawyers, including Dana and Choate. Story's publications on American jurisprudence gained international attention, though not all writers agree on exactly how they embodied conservative, Whig, Federalist, or natural law principles. There is near universal agreement that Story's major impact on U.S. constitutional law was as a judicial nationalist. That is, he forcefully interpreted the Constitution as the foundation of federal power rather than as the protector of states' rights. As he once noted: "The people of the *United States*, not the distinct people of a *particular state* . . . establish[ed] a '*constitution*,' not a '*confederation*.'"[64] As a corollary to this, Story and Marshall established the Supreme Court as the final arbiter of the constitutionality of both state and federal laws. While the precedents they set in these matters were institutionally conservative (in that the judiciary was the least democratic branch of government), their long-term practical consequences could be either conservative (as many of the nineteenth-century decisions proved to be), or quite liberal and egalitarian (as many of the mid-twentieth-century decisions proved to be). Thus while Story helped assure the perpetuation of a substantial element of elite rule in America, he could not in the long run guarantee the ideology or even the sensibility of that rule. Among other things this meant that even so talented a force as Joseph Story could not impose Burke's philosophy on the United States—even had that been his intention.

Whether or not Story had a definite Burkean agenda is difficult to ascertain. Most assuredly he admired Burke, quoted him often, and some of his own positions were similar to those of Burke. Still, it is possible that some writers seeking to make Story a disciple of Burke have inferred too much from the evidence at hand.[65] That said, Burke undoubtedly was one of the important Old World thinkers to whom Story turned for intellectual support. As Story himself wrote in 1828: "I have considerable curiosity to dip into Burke's Correspondence, though probably the time is not yet arrived, in which the best can safely be published." And in 1835, "he confessed that Aristotle, Cicero, and Burke had become the polestars of his political thought, and that he found in their words proof positive of the folly of the new times."[66] Of course, what was folly to some was the will of the people to others. It was also the intrinsic messiness of the democratic process and the machinations of party politics. Story most likely chose "scientific law" over party politics because he was both psychologically and intellectually unsuited for the political arena.[67] In his early years as a legislator, Story had found it difficult to consistently toe the Republican party line. Although he eventually aligned himself unofficially with the Whigs, he did so at least in part because he believed the Whig Party to be less factional—and less overtly political—than the Democratic Party. Even then, Story worked entirely behind the scenes, and never considered himself to be a committed partisan.[68]

Like most citizens, Story had a personal investment in the national creation myth, and he largely accepted the new American archetype based on enlightened human agency. In this respect he broke with the Burkean traditionalist interpretation of political progress. But like many conservatives, he also feared the country might unravel if either individualism, sectionalism, or democracy got out of hand. As the legal historian R. Kent Newmyer put it, for Story "the Republic . . . was not the American 'folk'; it was not a Platonic and indestructible idea . . . or even a reflection of natural law. . . . Constitutional government was the work of real men, still fragile wisdom salvaged from the chaos of history by experience. Wise and good men made the Constitution; foolish ones could destroy it." Thus society required some force of unity and stabilization. While Burke had invoked the force of tradition, Story—working within a much more democratic and innovative society—invoked the force of constitutional and common law. For him, "Principles of justice were the cement that held society together in moral harmony."[69]

In his twin roles as Supreme Court justice and legal scholar, Story was himself engaging in "founding" agency when he assertively shaped the still-amorphous legal system of the antebellum age. His *Commentaries on the Constitution*—which had been derived from his Harvard Law lectures—spelled out with clarity and in considerable detail his judicial philosophy. In it, Story quoted or at least cited Burke often, but he did not always use Burke in the way one might expect.[70] Burke's influence was real, but must be kept in proper perspective. Moreover, Story almost always cited Burke tangentially; almost never did he rely on him to provide the crux of an argument.

Burke did receive pride of place in one sense: a quote from him appeared (along with one from Cicero) as an epigraph on the *Commentaries* title page. Burke's assertion that "government is a contrivance of human wisdom to provide for human wants" was hardly a contentious proposition, but it did reveal an important aspect of Story's worldview. Like John Adams before him, Story had a restrained view of democracy that led him to exaggerate the role government could play in controlling social behavior. Burke had valued Britain's unwritten constitution and its common law, but to him they were integral parts of a broader tradition that included a hereditary aristocracy, a privileged gentry, a state religion, a distinguished national literature, and a very long national history, among many other things. Story could not rely on such an established and venerated common tradition in the United States. This meant he could not rely on such a wide and mutually supportive variety of stabilizing forces. Hence the nation's written constitution and its federal judiciary would have to perform extra duty. In this respect Story held the same view about the conservative role of law in American society that was later articulated by Rufus Choate. But while Choate lacked either the motivation or the position to implement his philosophy, Story possessed both the will and the station that enabled him to do so. Curiously, unlike Choate and Everett, Story never employed Burkean language in support of his arguments. His straightforward prose style reads today as the most "modern" of the three.

Since his *Commentaries* approached the Constitution as a deliberately constructed blueprint for a completely new system of government, Story devoted a considerable part of it to exploring the nature of the state's legitimacy. Inevitably this meant dealing with the notions of "compact" and "contract," upon which so many political thinkers, from Cicero to Locke to Burke, had written. What made this subject so crucial was that it concerned the will of the people, or, as it was stated in the Declaration of Independence, the consent of the governed. Here Story quoted at length—though in a footnote—Burke's famous passage from *Reflections* about society comprising a unique sort of contract. Yet Story used what he called "one of [Burke's] most splendid performances" more to counter the strict (or exaggerated) Lockean interpretation of social contract than to adopt a strict Burkean "eternal obligation" alternative. Story's ultimate position was one of practicality rather than of theory or tradition. This stance was closely akin to Burke's "argument from circumstance," which provided a healthy degree of latitude in the face of tradition, prescription, or other such conservative constraints. As Story put it (this time citing Burke's *Appeal from the New to the Old Whigs*): the doctrine of social compact or contract "requires many limitations and qualifications, when applied to the actual conditions of nations." He pointed out that even the American Revolution did not enjoy the support of the majority of colonists, and that women, children, and several other groups never had any right to decide the great public issues that followed in the wake of independence. Nor did all men qualified to vote necessarily agree with each provision of the Constitution or with every subsequent law. Even so, all persons residing in the United States were bound to follow its laws whether or not they individually approved of them. Story concluded that the Constitution was "a fundamental *law*, and not . . . a mere contract of government, during the good pleasure of all the persons, who were originally bound by it, or assented to it." Later he likened the ratification of the Constitution to the settlement of the Glorious Revolution of 1688: "From the moment it became a constitution, it ceased to be a compact, and became a fundamental law of absolute paramount obligation." Only a majority of the minority of the population who were qualified to vote could legitimately alter the system—and then only in accordance with constitutional procedures.[71]

Commentaries addressed several topics on the "Nature of the Constitution," including federal supremacy. But the main point for our purposes was that Story argued for a practical interpretation of the will of the people, and one that encouraged stability and consistency. Story was in tune with Burke in his Whiggish conception of ordered liberty, and in his obvious sympathy for the British Whig historical interpretation. But these predilections were also held by a wide range of American leaders—most of whom were not Burkeans by any stretch. Closer to the Burkean core, Story was a more intellectually relevant figure than Everett or Choate. Both of those men subscribed to Burke's traditionalist-conservative philosophy as well as to his mystical sensibility. The fact that they often lapsed into their own approximations of Burke's prose style was an indication of this. Story, by contrast, subscribed to Burke's progressive-conservative philosophy, which hinged on his argument from circumstance, and which often surfaced in his reform writings. While Burke was no liberal, his doctrine of argument from circumstance at least opened the door to liberalism, since it rested upon reasoned choice based on critical analysis. Story's preference for this approach was demonstrated in his powerful argument against a strict-constructionist interpretation of the Constitution.

In his discussion of "Rules of Interpretation," Story defined the "large" or "free and liberal" interpretation as "rational interpretation," and he contrasted it with the "close," "strict," and "literal" method. Story admitted that there were instances when a strict interpretation yielded the best solution, but "no such presumption . . . to use the words in the most restricted sense necessarily arises" across the board. Story was in effect arguing against legal formalism, "because the rules can have no permanent interest in a free government, distinct from that of the people, of whom they are a part, and to whom they are responsible." Moreover, "that narrow construction" that would prevent the government from fulfilling its duties and "render it incompetent" must not be adopted.[72] Story warned against quibbling over the meaning of "single words" in the Constitution, which he called "mere verbal criticism." Instead he favored looking at the broader "context and subject matter." "We should never forget, that it is an instrument of government we are to construe. . . . The truest exposition . . . harmonizes with its design, its objects, and its general structure." He then referred to the "remark of Mr. Burke . . . as an admonition to all those called upon to . . . interpret a constitution. Government is a practical thing made for the happiness of mankind, and not to furnish the schemes of visionary politicians. The business of those who are called upon to administer it, is to rule, and not to wrangle. It would be a poor compensation . . . that we had frittered down [the government's] power, and at the same time had destroyed the republic."[73]

Curiously this reference was to Burke's *Letter to the Sheriffs of Bristol* of 1777. Although Burke's point about government and the schemes of visionary politicians has since been used to support arguments against ambitious government projects, Story and Burke were each pushing what they saw as progressive agendas in their respective circumstances. Burke's *Letter to the Sheriffs* was one of the conciliatory pieces he composed during the American Revolution.[74] Story, in his argument for an expansive reading of the Constitution, was increasing the power of the federal government in order to save the Republic from fractious and corrosive forces, as well as to prepare the way for the development of his version of nineteenth-century liberalism. This was consistent with the landmark Supreme Court rulings in which he participated. *Dartmouth College v. Woodward* curbed the excesses of democracy and strengthened the hand of corporations; *Martin v. Hunter's Lessee* (1816) enabled the Supreme Court to review the decisions of state courts, and thus curbed sectionalism; *McCulloch v. Maryland* (1819) favored a broad interpretation of the national government's implied powers under the Constitution, and *Gibbons v. Ogden* (1824) broadened the meaning of commerce and thus made it easier for the federal government to stop the states from interfering with it. Burke's notion that government was practical rather than visionary could have been used by either side in most American political debates.[75] Few proponents of any idea would have admitted to harboring utopian schemes. "Practicality" often turned out to be simply a specific and tangible application of the general principle of argument from circumstance. This useful approach (justifiably thought to be pervasive in America) in no small way undermined whatever organic-traditionalist sentiments remained in antebellum society.

Even when Story cited Burke's *Reflections*, he avoided invoking its mystical and reactionary traditionalism and instead quoted from it surgically in order to support his progressive-conservative agenda. For instance, in his discussion of the House of Representatives in *Commentaries*, Story employed Burke's reasoning from *Reflections* to demonstrate the practical benefits of a lower house elected directly by the people. He expanded upon this theme by explaining some of the "indirect advantages" that resulted from the "immediate agency of the people." The right to elect representatives conferred "an additional sense of personal dignity and duty upon the mass of the people." It also procured the "courtesy and sympathy" of their superiors, and diffused a "common interest, through all ranks of society." Furthermore, the public proceedings of a democratically elected house would "gradually furnish the mind with safe and solid materials for judgement upon all public affairs."[76] Here was a perfect specimen of the Whig blend of democracy and hierarchy. The people must be acknowledged as sovereign, but they must also be shaped toward responsible behavior. There was little confidence here in the people's ability to make the right decisions, but there was a recognition that some meaningful venue for their participation was required.

The most blatant examples of Story's efforts to combat the excesses of democracy came late in his life over the issues of slavery and Dorr's Rebellion. As already noted, the comparative consensus underlying the triumph of democracy began to unravel after 1840 as the result of several factors. Chief among these were the potential expansion of slavery and the increasingly strident (and popular) views of northern abolitionists. Story was typical of many conservative northern Whigs in that he found slavery morally repugnant; yet out of respect for national unity he failed to move against it. On the bench Story had a mixed record on slavery. In two high-profile cases toward the end of his career he offered what appeared to be conflicting signals. In *U.S. v. Amistad* (1841) Story voted to free forty or so Africans rather than return them to slave traders; but the judgment was decided on narrow grounds. A year later, in *Prigg v. Pennsylvania*, Story voted to void the prosecution of an agent who had captured a fugitive slave, and he invalidated the state law that had made the prosecution possible—thus enhancing the old Fugitive Slave Law of 1793. Perhaps Story was soothing his own conscience when he called his decision "a triumph of freedom."[77] Or more likely, he was simply displaying the moral and intellectual contortions in which he and other Whigs were willing to engage for the elusive goal of national harmony.

The issue of Dorr's Rebellion in Rhode Island (1841–42) did not reach the Supreme Court until after Story's death. But in his concurrent role as the senior federal circuit judge for New England, Story worked intensely to hamper the legal defense of the rebels.[78] The Dorr incident was a perfect example of a conservative reaction to a bottom-up threat, and Story responded to it in much the same way that Burke had responded to the French Revolution. In some respects Dorr's Rebellion was an unlikely candidate to draw a strong reactionary response. The Dorrites were trying to replace Rhode Island's ridiculously out-of-date royal charter of 1663 with a more democratic modern constitution. They attempted this by way of the ballot and the convention rather than by violence, and only the hard line taken by the state's governor raised the possibility of actual fighting. In fact, the existing government soon drew up a reformed constitution that significantly expanded the voter franchise—which had been the key issue all along. Yet in the wake of the rebellion's collapse and the subsequent granting of most of the rebels' demands, Story moved aggressively to punish the leaders for treason. That he did so with such relish at about the same time that he began to speak against the dangers of abolitionism can easily be interpreted as a Burke-like turn to the right in old age. But this standard grumpy-old-man syndrome, even if valid, does not account for the wide combination of factors at work.

One reason the 1820s and 1830s marked a hiatus from bitter ideological battles was that the Missouri Compromise of 1821 had temporarily suppressed the fight over slavery. Another important reason was that organized political opposition to increasingly democratic government had been in disarray since the demise of the Federalist Party. But by about 1840 those conditions were no longer fully operative: abolitionism was gearing up for its final push toward forced emancipation, and the Whig Party actually won a national election. Story linked abolitionism with Dorr's Rebellion and saw them both as evidence of "the tendency to ultraism of all sorts." Unlike his moderate and constructive tone in *Commentaries*, he began to sound more like Choate and Everett (and hence, like Burke's antirevolutionary voice): "The spirit of the age has broken loose from the strong ties, which have hitherto bound society together by the mutual cohesions and attractions of habits, manners, institutions, morals, and literature." He called for a return to the values of Burke, Adam Smith, and *The Federalist*, and a rejection of "those mad men, who . . . in the name of conscience, liberty, or the rights of man . . . are willing and ready to bid farewell to that Constitution . . . which I trust may be transmitted, unimpaired, from generation to generation for many centuries to come."[79] This was the closest Story ever got to Burkean language, and it was a genuine reflection of his passion of the moment. Apparently, some disturbing changes in political circumstances had brought such sentiments to the forefront.

Like Edmund Burke—in fact like most men—Joseph Story had found it easy to be moderate in moderate times. But as the general heat of ideology returned in the late antebellum period, the temperature of Story's opinions rose along with those of the nation at large. The direction of his thoughts was predictable. A key attribute linking abolitionism with Dorr's Rebellion was that each represented a form of bottom-up agitation outside of established institutions. Both movements, according to their opponents, subscribed to demagogic leadership (shades of wicked and designing men). Dorr's Rebellion, like the earlier insurrections by Shays, Fries, and the whiskey farmers of western Pennsylvania, was a small matter in and of itself. What rallied the forces of "law and order" in every case was the symbolic example that a successful revolt would set. Progressive conservatives like Story were adamantly opposed to reopening the American Revolution—even if doing so might realign the country closer to their own moral vision, or closer to the nation's own professed ideals. This might explain why they tried so hard to avoid a civil war. Their particular sensibility was also incapable of transferring control of the national agenda from the established elite to the democratic masses. This paternalistic streak was yet another anachronistic legacy of the Old Whig origins of American Whig conservatism.

It is not enough to say that Story's activities regarding slavery or Dorr's Rebellion represented a practical search for order. To state the obvious: fascists and divine right monarchists also have sought to impose social order, as have southern plantation aristocrats; so too had the high Federalists, and later the Republican "old guard." It is the nature of the order—and the means employed to achieve it—that defines each ideological cohort. One must keep in mind that Story (like Burke) was a Whig but not a Tory. He no doubt believed he was right without being right-wing. And with allowances for some exceptions such as the Dorr case, the larger record of his career supports such an assessment. Although Story sided with John Adams rather than Thomas Jefferson on the principle of the "paper transactions" of one generation binding another, the "binders" Story envisioned were comparatively loose ones. His rejection of a strict constructionist interpretation of the Constitution, as well as his genuine (if tepid) recognition of the sovereignty of the people, demonstrated this. These factors, when combined with his professionally dictated practice of res adjudicata, were tantamount to an endorsement of Burke's quasi-liberal principle of argument from circumstance—since a written opinion explaining the final judgment based on the merits of a particular case was its methodological equivalent. Then again, the fact that Story most trusted the secular priesthood of the federal judiciary to decide matters of monumental importance made him a Whig rather than a Democrat. Story was acting precisely in the Old Whig spirit of intermediation between the tyranny of the one and the tyranny of the many. In his particular vision, the independent federal judiciary was the institutional bulwark between executive hubris and mob rule.[80]

Here Samuel Huntington's point about conservatism responding to threats against existing institutions or social orders comes into play. During Story's early years on the court, such threats were not so obvious. Then during the Jacksonian era the threats came from both King Andrew and the mob. But by the early 1840s, with Whigs in power, the threat came mostly from the people—as abolitionism and Dorr demonstrated. One reason Story acted so aggressively as a circuit judge in the Dorr case was that he could not count on the Supreme Court under its new chief justice (the Democrat) Roger Taney to see things his way. Even Story's favorite institution seemed threatened by the encroachment of democratic ideology. At the height of the Jacksonian era, Story had made some private remarks to James Kent that in retrospect seem even more indicative of his thinking during his final years. These remarks began with his assertion that his "greatest authorities on the science of government" were Aristotle, Cicero, and Burke. While, unfortunately, he did not specify exactly which of Burke's principles were most important, he cited Aristotle and Cicero for their lack of faith in democracy. He declared Alexander Hamilton to have been the "greatest and wisest man of this country," followed by John Marshall. Furthermore, "Government is deplorable, weak, fractious, and corrupt . . . everything is sinking down into despotism, under the guise of a democratic government. . . . The Sup[reme] Court is sinking, and so is the judicial in every state." He noted that there were still men of virtue left in the Senate, but that the House was "collared" by the president, and public opinion was devoted to "Tyranny and Corruption."[81]

If ever Story's words echoed the "solemn gloom" that had descended on Edmund Burke as he worried over the future of British civilization, they certainly did so here. Yet Story's other writings from this same period did not necessarily exhibit such pessimism. Perhaps Story, like Burke, was hypersensitive to any perceived divergences from his own Platonic ideals regarding political society. Or perhaps he and Burke were both ahead of *and* behind their own times, depending on the circumstance. Clearly in terms of cultural sensibility they were both out of touch with the main currents of their respective eras.

Whigs: Closing Thoughts

American Whigs as a group embraced both backward- and forward-looking visions. In retrospect the more old-fashioned elements of Whig thought tended to predominate, and the Whigs stood as impediments to the march of progress. But in their approaches to economic policy, and to the expanded role of government, as well as in their commitment to nationalism, the Whigs were more modern than their Democratic opponents. On the issues of banking, currency, internal improvements, and the development of manufacturing, the Whigs anticipated the future more accurately than the Democrats did with their anti-bank, agrarian, and hard-money policies. The social and economic order created by industrialization would eventually mount an unexpected challenge to the individualistic egalitarianism that had been the lifeblood of the Jacksonian era. On the other hand, the rise of a plutocracy would undermine the status of the cultural, intellectual, and moral elite as exemplified by the "best men" of American Whiggery. Yet during the antebellum years these transformations still lurked largely in the future, and the main challenge to Whig control was the Democratic ascendency.

It was no coincidence that so many figures in our discussion of Burke in America were from New England, especially from Massachusetts. The Adamses, Bancroft, Emerson, Everett, Choate, and Story all lived in the Bay State. No state save Virginia had been as important to the creation of an independent United States, and no state in the antebellum period contributed more to the American cultural and intellectual renaissance. Yet in hindsight it seems that no state's political and intellectual elite worried more about the decline of their influence. Possibly this was a vestige of the old Puritan jeremiad on the decay of piety, morality, and obedience—and on the inability of church leaders to stop it. Whatever the reasons, Massachusetts elites (and to some degree those of New England generally) experienced periodic waves of regional insecurity. It had been an ideological oddity that the hotbed of radicalism during the revolution became the bastion of Federalism during the postrevolutionary era. This in part had been the consequence of a loss of sectional political clout as revealed by such reactive phenomena as the Essex Junto, the Hartford Convention, and New England's resentment of the Virginia dynasty. During the Jacksonian era, a similar loss of regional power resulted from the nation's westward expansion; influence seemed to migrate along with the population and economic activity. Worse still, the more fluid frontier societies showed less respect for the type of insular leadership that had been long established in the more settled world around Boston. By the late-Jacksonian years, the old Federalist stronghold of New England had become a Whig stronghold (though as the examples of Bancroft and the transcendentalists attest, "democratic" impulses resided there as well). In somewhat smug contrast to the crudities of western frontier society and to the affected haughtiness of southern cavalier society, the conservative Brahmin heirs of Puritan utopianism believed that since they were the most highly civilized of Americans, they were best qualified to instruct the nation on all aspects of moral philosophy.[82] That they would turn to Edmund Burke for comfort was understandable, since Burke in his own time had reacted to kindred threats to his established worldview and to his crumbling Old Whig order.

Daniel Walker Howe has noted that "Burke's approach to political morality answered the desires" of Massachusetts elites because "he had just the right strain of conservatism for them."[83] The Burkean preference for moderation, order, tradition, and leadership by a natural aristocracy was evident in many Whiggish publications of the day. So was the Burkean urge to attack usurpers with vigor and conspicuous drama, as if civilization itself were at stake. In 1835, for instance, the "conscience Whig" Charles Francis Adams published "An Appeal from the New to the Old Whigs," in which he attacked aggressive legislators for what he saw as tampering with the stability of the Constitution. Not only did Adams borrow Burke's title, but he began his "Appeal" with Burke's own words: "Specious, untried, ambiguous prospects for new advantage . . . have sacrificed the good, of which they had been in assured possession, in favor of wild and irrational expectations." Adams was no reactionary, yet his strong response to a change in constitutional interpretation (the issue at hand was the right of the Senate to block presidential removals of executive appointees) revealed his deep insecurity about the inherent disorderliness and instability of democratic government: "It would seem as if in this country nothing was destined to acquire stability. The constitution of the United States has now been in operation nearly half a century, during which period many doubtful points in its construction have been thought to have been settled. . . . Yet . . . a turn in party politics, a new concurrence of circumstances, seems all that is requisite to unsettle what was most firmly done."[84]

During the Civil War, Whiggish periodicals abandoned their antebellum practice of praising Burke ("the most minutely comprehensive . . . of human intellects—not excepting Aristotle") as a general sage who deserved "the veneration of . . . men of all parties," and revived his partisan, antirevolutionary image.[85] It was as though the war was America's punishment for not adhering to Whig principles of moderation and organic unity. With the resurgence of ideological conflict, the *North American Review* launched an aggressive defense of Burke's attack on the French Revolution: "The ancient system of French polity" had portions worth preserving, "yet . . . the Revolutionists destroyed all." Invoking the Bastille as a metaphor for the state, the article concluded that the French "preferred to break down their prison . . . and to form the stones into a different structure for the permanent benefit of the people. Well would it have been for them if equal wisdom had guided them in dealing with the edifice of a vitiated government."[86] A stranger (and a more incisive) article appeared the same year in *Littell's Living Age*, which seemed to put much of the blame for extremism on Burke himself. Although the article defended Burke's political positions, it admonished him for his own lack of balance. Burke "was the prey of an absorbing, however noble, egoism. . . . He did not care to temper one conviction of his mind with another. . . . He was equally a friend of liberty; yet his passionate denunciations revived Toryism, and were [used] as authorities for tyranny by all the despots of Europe."[87] In this respect—at least as far as personality was concerned—Burke had not been Whiggish enough for the American Whigs. That is, he gave way to an extremism that proved counterproductive.

By about 1860, not even Burkeans could agree on how best to incorporate Burke's writings into their own political philosophies. Burke in his last years seemed to have slipped into the sort of ideological "ultraism" that Joseph Story had condemned in American politics. And it was not clear what role Burke's defense of "liberty" could play in the era's most contentious of all issues: slavery. One thing was certain. As the Civil War approached, whatever fragile consensus democratization had spawned collapsed. It had not been the contrapuntal force of Whig thought that destroyed it, but the expansion of slavery and the rise of abolitionism. Then again, the spirit of Burkean moderation, organic unity, tradition, and social hierarchy—as embodied by conservative American Whigs—had not been popular enough nor effective enough to prevent disaster by forging an alternative consensus.

Part II

Transition to Modern America

Chapter 6

The Gilded Age

Eclectic Interpretations

America's political interest in Edmund Burke became less consequential after the Civil War, because of dramatic changes (both literally and figuratively) to the national landscape. During the Age of Revolution and the antebellum period, politics in its broadest sense was the central concern of American life, since the process of democratization was the defining theme. Burke therefore was always relevant in one way or another. But following the war, economics in its broadest sense became the central concern of American life—and politics, immigration, urbanization, westward migration, and even to some extent religion, became intertwined with the new defining theme of industrialization. The compatibility of monopoly capitalism with traditional Burkean philosophy was doubtful. Moreover, most Americans preferred the homegrown frontier myth of rugged individualism to the imported "pleasing illusions" of Anglo-Saxon legend. Hence Burke became a sideshow during the Gilded Age; he never completely disappeared, but he was not where the significant action was. Burkean wisdom was no longer proclaimed in great political debates or grand patriotic orations. Instead Burke was discussed mostly in the highbrow magazines and other such venues frequented by the intellectual and literary elite.

The Nation

In the aftermath of the Civil War, one of the premier organs for elevated commentary in America was the *Nation* magazine. First published in July 1865, this "Weekly Journal Devoted to Politics, Literature, Science and Art" sought to present an independent, nonsensational style of journalism "with greater accuracy and moderation than are now to be found in the daily press," and to offer literary and art criticism by distinguished writers. Indeed, a great deal of the magazine's stature derived from the highly respected figures who contributed regularly to its pages.[1] In a sense the *Nation* in its first decades became what the *North American Review* had been prior to the war: the quasi-official journal of opinion for the Whiggish northeastern elite. A number of the *Nation*'s principal contributors had migrated from the *North American Review*, including Charles Eliot Norton, who had edited the *NAR*, and Edwin Lawrence Godkin (1831–1902), who would edit and nearly personify the *Nation* for years. These were the sort of culturally conservative reformers who would later be known as "Mugwump types," and many members of their circle may also be included in what has been called the "genteel tradition."[2]

The genteel sensibility contained a mixture of New World idealism and Old World sophistication, and it housed a moral desire to bring about the heightened civilization of American society. Politically this meant fighting corruption and bossism; socially this meant vesting leadership in a disinterested gentry instead of in a plutocracy or an overly democratic mobocracy; and culturally this meant teaching the nation to appreciate, and eventually to produce, the quality of literature, art, and ideas that hitherto had been the province of Europe. Not only did genteel leadership expect to achieve this from the top down, but it expected to define what (that is, *whom*) the top should consist of. This assertive gentility represented a renewed attempt to invigorate a natural aristocracy in the United States, and it carried with it some remnants of antebellum Whig culture.

Headquartered in New York City, the *Nation*—while energetically American—looked across the Atlantic for examples of mature civilization. To be more precise, the *Nation* admired and condemned the United States and Europe for alternative reasons. It shared the mainstream liberal belief that Europe was politically oppressive and socially stagnant and that democratic America held greater promise for the future, but it also subscribed to the conclusions of Tocqueville and others that democracy bred mediocrity; thus the high culture, intellectual luster, and even political leadership of aristocratic Europe were superior. Viewed from the bottom up, American civilization was more appealing; viewed from the top down, it fell short of Old World standards.[3] Since the *Nation*'s journalistic perspective was clearly top-down, its writers no doubt believed they were undertaking a civilizing mission. They saw the American South and West as raw, violent, primitive regions, in need of forced improvement from without, and they saw much of the urban industrial North as a harsh, philistine, and fragmented society, susceptible to enlightened improvement from within.[4]

The *Nation* squeezed an impressive amount of commentary on Edmund Burke into four short reviews published between 1867 and 1879. These long-forgotten pieces contained lively remarks on Burke's political legacy, and today they serve as compact samples of the nineteenth-century treatment of Burke in America. Despite their forceful tone, they displayed an element of ambiguity about Burke not commonly found in our own times. One senses a need on the part of the *Nation* to have Burke both ways: wise and mad, resourceful and ineffectual, traditional and progressive, historically grounded and flexible; the *Nation*'s writers also stressed his quest for workable solutions over his blanket conservatism. The French Revolution was handled with kid gloves, and it was not allowed to consume the rest of what Burke wrote and said. As the opening paragraph of the first article put it: Burke's "works have for fifty years been an arsenal from which Tories and Liberals have armed themselves with almost equal confidence."[5]

Utilitarian Liberalism

E. L. Godkin's review of John Morley's *Edmund Burke: A Historical Study* (1867) would no doubt astonish many readers today. Yet its interpretation of Burke as a *utilitarian* was widely accepted during the nineteenth century, and Godkin—at the time a devout utilitarian himself—found that "there is very little in Burke's political philosophy" that the "school" of Bentham, Austin, and Mill "does not accept." He expanded this notion in a passage that surely would not have gone unchallenged in America a century later:

> Burke was undoubtedly, if not the earliest, the best known, most eloquent, and most earnest of English utilitarian politicians, and some of the most clearly cherished doctrines of their creed may be picked out even in his impassioned diatribes against the French Revolution and his impassioned eulogies of the British Constitution. At the hands of the positivists, therefore, Burke's memory is undergoing a sort of rehabilitation.[6]

Of course, today Burke's eulogies of ancient tradition are among the most commonly cited examples of a method of thought that is completely opposed to the methods derived from, or related to, utilitarianism; and modern "positivists," who are methodologically ahistorical, would have no good reason to rehabilitate Burke. But apparently nineteenth-century political scientism was so strongly prone to an all-encompassing worldview that it had to fit Burke into its system. Burke was by then firmly established as a great name in Anglo-American thought (for reasons not limited to the French Revolution) and the new creed of utilitarianism could only benefit from his association.

As for the attack on the French Revolution itself, which today forms the foundation of Burke's reputation, Godkin appeared to be sympathetic yet qualified in his judgment: "Burke's course on the French Revolution—which has long constituted the great blot on his political reputation, and which prompts, at the present day, hundreds of political writers, who probably owe to him nearly every idea of any value they have ever possessed, to sneer at him in the latter years of his life as a crazy reactionist"—was a complicated matter that had to be placed in proper perspective. "If we tear off from Burke's assaults on the Revolution the excrescences produced by his heated imagination . . . and his passionate style of oratory, we shall find a theory of national life of which the history of France for the last seventy years abundantly proves the soundness." Here Godkin was alluding to the continual political traumas France had experienced ever since the revolution, and which were ongoing at the time of his writing. He concluded with what was pretty much the standard nineteenth-century liberal mantra that the French Revolution was a good idea that got out of hand, though he differed with the liberals and sided with the conservatives in blaming the disastrous consequences not only on poor leadership, but on the abruptness and radical nature of the event: "Most calm observers are now agreed that the failure of the French to make the 'principles of '89' the basis of any permanent political system has been undoubtedly mainly due to the suddenness and completeness of the break with the past into which they were unfortunately led by the literary politicians who precipitated but were unable to control the revolution."[7]

A few years later, in 1874, the *Nation* reviewed the first volume of Burke's *Select Works*, published that year in Oxford and edited by E. J. Payne.[8] The reviewer, Albert Dicey (1835–1922), was a distinguished English jurist and a recognized authority on the British constitution. Since Dicey's magnum opus, *Lectures to the Study of the Law of the Constitution* (1885), was to become "a standard work now considered part of the British constitution," one might have expected him to share Burke's conservative veneration for prescription and precedent, rather than to highlight Burke's argument from circumstances and echo the Godkin-Morley characterization of Burke as a utilitarian. Yet the proto-liberal course was exactly the one he took.[9] Throughout his review, headlined "The 'Conservatism' of Burke," Dicey seemed to subscribe to Emerson's dictum that Burke was "no vulgar conservative." Most of his argument demonstrated the flexibility and progressive quality of Burke's thought. Presumably this explains why "conservatism" was set in quotation marks in the title, and why Dicey made a variety of attempts to take the sting out of the term:

> [Burke's] conservatism is not a mass of rules, but a spirit. . . . Burke, again, though a conservative, was at no time a Tory. . . . When Burke's conservatism is understood, it is seen to be utterly different from many beliefs or attitudes of mind which are often called conservative. Burke, for example, had little in common with the men who at the beginning of this century quoted with admiration all his anti-Revolutionary utterances. . . .
>
> The contrast between his conservatism and the mere policy of resistance . . . or the policy of fanatical reaction . . . shows what is the real worth of Burke's conservative doctrine.[10]

In a complete rejection of the standard practice of political Burkeans, Dicey warned that it was "especially futile to enlist the authority" of Burke's name "on the side of modern conservatives or modern liberals," since Burke's words always applied to specific issues and events as they stood in his own day. The unique conditions present at each moment in history precluded the practical transplantation of Burke's arguments to other times and new issues. Moreover, "It is at this point that Burke's conservatism blends with his liberalism. He, no less than Bentham, was a utilitarian. . . . Burke, like Bentham, despised the pretentious platitudes which the conservatives no less than the democrats of the last century held to be absolute principles; he, no less than Bentham, believed that government existed for the benefit of the governed." Nevertheless, Dicey qualified some of this "blend" of Burke and Bentham by noting that Burke's analysis was primarily historical while Bentham's was primarily logical. Burke presumed in favor of existing institutions; Bentham held no such presumption. Since Dicey capped his comparison by pointing out "the fundamental conservatism of Burke, and the no less fundamental anti-conservatism of the older utilitarians," one is left to wonder just how robust or viable his "utilitarianization" of Burke was to begin with.[11]

To his credit Dicey concluded his essay by acknowledging "two main criticisms" of Burke's conservatism. One of which was that Burke's presumption that existing institutions were worth preserving blinded him to situations in which "the mass of a nation are prepared to risk everything that is dear to them rather than bear a state of things which they hold to be unendurable." Obviously this applied to France in 1789. The other criticism was that "Burke underrated the extent to which abstract principles can be applied to politics." Here again Dicey's utilitarian perspective peeked through, as he celebrated the triumph of modern neoclassical economic theory over "the whole scheme of protection" that preceded it. This supposedly proved "that in some departments of politics, at least, there is far more room for the application of *a priori* principles than Burke would perhaps have been disposed to admit." Like a good enlightened modern viewing the world from his elevated and scientific perch, Dicey charitably added: "His error in this can scarcely be blamed, for the then prevalent theory of natural rights has turned out to be, as he perceived, absolutely worthless, and the questions with which he was called upon to deal were not for the most part problems of the kind to which political economy applies." By this mode of analysis, common tenets of conservatism derived from tradition were to take a backseat to universal laws of utilitarian liberalism derived from "science" (Dicey had earlier noted that Burke's politics were "an art, not a science").[12] It is little wonder that Dicey's biographer concluded that he "applied the tools of legal positivism for the purpose of deriving general principles about the subject in question. His steadfast adherence to this methodology worked well" on some occasions, but was "unsatisfactory" on others.[13] This search for general principles, or universal laws, was indicative of the scientistic spirit of the Victorian age. It clashed with Burke's belief in prescription, which in its pure form relied on no analytical method other than to ask whether a customary practice needed slight adjustment or whether it was best left alone.

If nothing else, Dicey once again demonstrated that interpretation of Burke, even before the twentieth-century conservative revival, often revealed more about the modern interpreter than about Burke himself. This phenomenon resurfaced in the *Nation* in 1879, when Dicey reviewed "Morley's Burke," but this time his emphasis was on character rather than utilitarian ideology.[14] Dicey later told Godkin that Burke was one of the writers he "read with perpetual profit & enjoyment," yet this affection was not apparent in Dicey's article.[15] Not only did he identify Burke as "an adventurer" (though one with "principles"), but he repeated the old English suspicions about the Irish Burke, who "began life with nothing, and within a few years became the owner of an estate and had pecuniary means for the existence of which it was not easy to account." He also lent partial credence to the charge of Burke's Catholic leanings, and to his unconvincing Protestantism.

But even more damaging to Burke's character, Dicey sided with New Whig critics and accused Burke of lacking "justness of mind." While Burke aimed at ending oppression, "he was not a just man" because he allowed his emotional biases to skew his political thought. For instance: "Not a single weak point in the position of the French Revolutionists escaped his glance. . . . but to the good or the better side of the revolutionary movement he was as blind as the stupidest of Tory squires." Dicey identified this lack of justness as Burke's "one great deficiency," and he credited that flaw with diminishing Burke's effectiveness during his own lifetime. For example, "His splendid diatribe against Hastings was gradually injured by its obvious want of justice to the accused." Dicey concluded by stating that although Burke was "one of the best of men, and, in many respects, the very wisest of English statesmen," many refused to tolerate him because he was an adventurer whose "astounding genius lacked the one great quality of justice."[16]

The *Nation* eventually addressed Burke and the French Revolution head-on. The occasion was the publication of the second volume of Payne's *Select Works* of Burke, which consisted entirely of *Reflections* and Payne's lengthy introduction to it. Bearing the intriguing title "Burke as a Prophet," the review confronted the issue of Burke's portentousness just as the *Nation*'s previous essay had confronted the issue of his conservatism. This time the result was less impressive, possibly because conservatism went to the core of Burke's reputation, while his predictions of catastrophe for France were simply icing on a more important cake. Nevertheless the review proved to be an interesting mixture of Victorian political science and Old Whig moral philosophy. It began by stating that "Burke's *Reflections* have a singular interest as illustrations of the extent and limits of historical prediction." But it soon added the less-scientific opinion: "With [Burke] (as with all prophets) the predictive portion of his work is of secondary importance compared with his moral teaching. . . . His foresight is grounded on the perception of the certainty of the moral laws of human nature." In this vein Burke's foresight was distinguishable from Tocqueville's; the former's was based on the "force of moral insight," while the latter's was based on "the perfection of intellectual criticism." Within Burke's "anti-Revolutionary polemics," his "intellectual criticism" was "little more than a cover of moral denunciation." His "fierce moral indignation" led him to accurately predict the "massacres and outrages" in France, but steered him wrong in the case of England. Not only had Burke been in gross error about the spread of revolutionary radicalism, but "his constitutionalism, with all its veneration for the balances, the fictions, and, to speak plainly, the dodges of the constitution, is as dead as . . . Jacobinism." Sadly, "To the feelings which led men of all creeds and nations to welcome any hope of change, he was absolutely dead." Burke possessed an "almost morbid hatred of . . . abstract truths" and thus "failed to perceive . . . that whatever the evils of the Revolution, the country people gained immensely" from it. Instead he "clung . . . to the illusion that disgust at revolutionary violence would produce enthusiasm for a restoration." The review admonished Burke's disciples for not being able "to divest themselves from the weakest part of their master's teaching." It ended by suggesting that a "decisive" passage from Tocqueville's own writings on the French Revolution "should be placed as a motto on Burke's *Reflections*."[17] The passage is worth repeating, as it dramatically illustrated Burke's profound misunderstanding of the soul of the French people:

> "Ingenious persons in our day have taken to restore the credit of the *ancien régime* . . . but I judge of the *ancien régime* not by what I imagine, but by the sentiments with which it inspired those who destroyed it. I see that during the whole course of the Revolution, oppressive and cruel as it was, the hatred of the *ancien régime* always surpassed in the hearts of all Frenchmen every other hatred, and took such deep root in their hearts that it survived even its object, and passed from a momentary passion into a sort of permanent instinct. I remark that during the most perilous vicissitudes of the last sixty years the fear of restoration of the *ancien régime* has surpassed all other fears. For me this is enough. To my mind the proof is complete."[18]

It seems that the *Nation*, with its culturally conservative, utilitarian-liberal mentality, admired Burke's genius mostly for its ability to illuminate the political principles of the modern world—rather than for its ability to sanctify established tradition. This was why Tocqueville, who was an aristocratic liberal and a child of the Age of Revolution, seemed more in step with the magazine's position than Burke, who was a Whig of the old school.[19] On topics upon which Tocqueville and Burke were in nearly complete agreement, such as their acceptance of the American Revolution, the *Nation* praised Burke unequivocally. Unlike the major issues of the revolutionary and Jacksonian periods, a time when discussion of liberty, constitutions, and democracy predominated, the issues of the Gilded Age (tariffs, currency, civil service reform, labor unrest, myriad sins of the cities, immigration, the conduct of big business) were not the ones Burke directly addressed. So possibly his continued presence was an indication of his preexisting popularity among the *Nation*'s contributors and readers (though for exactly what reasons it is difficult to say, given the ambiguity of the articles).

E. L. Godkin, the Frontier

A more comprehensive overview of Burke's career came not in the *Nation* itself, but in an introduction Godkin wrote for an American edition of Burke's selected works.[20] While this essay retained elements of political analysis from the earlier *Nation* articles, it was notably more sympathetic to Burke on the personal level, and somewhat more understanding of his Old Whig sensibility. Perhaps this resulted from the widely accepted fact that Godkin became more conservative beginning in the 1870s and became (according to some writers) reactionary by the 1890s.[21] Or perhaps it stemmed from the practical necessity of trying to sum up all of Burke's views in some reasonably unified way in just eight pages. Whatever the reason, this introduction—written in 1899—included some curious contributions to the modern presentation of Burke.

Among these was Godkin's contention that the influence of John Locke on political thought was modest, and that "to Montesquieu and to Burke we owe what I may call the dawn of political consciousness." This was instantly followed by a summation of Burke's political creed that could easily have been written by Burke's present-day admirers: "Human society was to him the most glorious product of human reason, and he could not bear to see the slightest amendment effected in it, except for overwhelming reason." Burke became "the greatest elucidator that ever has appeared in the field of government." Yet his influence was so pervasive that his contributions were easy to overlook. His "novelties" had become so "diffused" over time, that they were now the "commonplaces of modern politics." Godkin admitted that "a good deal of fault has been found with the gaudiness of Burke's rhetoric." But even allowing for disagreements over the French Revolution, he was "impossible to read . . . without being struck with the depth of his insight . . . and with the extraordinary skill with which he had rolled words of wisdom into telling aphorisms which everybody could carry about . . . without reference to the general argument." Here was an important point that contradicted the *Nation*'s earlier warning against enlisting the authority of Burke's name in support of modern causes. Snippets of Burke's masterly language could always prove useful, even when removed from the circumstances in which they were produced. As Godkin noted: "It is difficult to find a recent political essay, or a newspaper article, in which there are not traces of indebtedness to him. A very large number of maxims and assertions with which he startled the Tories of 1780 are to-day the inspiration of every stump orator or speaker at a town meeting." Godkin then uttered the well-worn opinion (intended as a show of centrist moderation, it revealed as well the opportunity for choosing alternative Burkean philosophies): "A young man who has mastered [Burke's words] is really armed against all opponents of free government, as well as against all promoters of unbridled democracy."[22]

Hence the recurring problem of classifying Burke ideologically edged no closer to solution. Conveniently, the volume Godkin was introducing included selections varied enough to show more than one side of Burke's thinking: two speeches on the American crisis, three to his Bristol constituency, one speech on Hastings, plus *The Sublime and Beautiful*, *Reflections*, and *A Letter to a Noble Lord*. Godkin declared that India and the French Revolution were "the flaws of Burke's career." While Burke had valid reasons for prosecuting Warren Hastings, he allowed his "fervour" to drive him into such a long battle that the British public lost interest. On France, "He wrote a pamphlet . . . which convulsed England, and in which, it has been justly said, he all but completely overlooked the wrongs of the wretched peasants which had had so much to do with bringing it about." Worse yet, there was "little doubt" that Burke's *Reflections* "had much to do with precipitating the twenty-years war . . . which so fatally retarded the progress of freedom and reform at home, besides covering the Continent with blood and flame."[23]

Godkin then stepped back and cut Burke enough slack to prevent the perpetual controversy over the French Revolution from damaging his reputation:

> We who live in calmer times, with riper experience and with fuller knowledge, find it easy enough to point at the defects of Burke's argumentation, and to prune his exuberance; but we must remember that every man, even the greatest, not only has the defects of his qualities, but partakes of the passions of his time. On all other topics [except France and India] it is difficult to say too much of Burke's farsightedness and judicial-mindedness.[24]

Finally, Godkin summarized Burke by stating that "both his defects and his virtues are to be ascribed . . . to his reverence for prescription." Burke's respect for "long established" society "was overwhelming. . . . Stare super antiquas vias [stand by the old ways] was the motto of his political philosophy."[25] By his tone, if not by explicit declaration, Godkin seemed to endorse Burke's belief that change must come slowly in order to preserve as well as reform society. And there were other hints outside of this essay that by 1899 Godkin was identifying with Burke in more ways than one.

Like Burke, Godkin (who was born in Ireland of English parents) was often subject to suspicion because of his Irish roots. But in Godkin's case, the essence of his cultural nationality was even more complicated. As his onetime friend Henry Cabot Lodge put it: Godkin "is by birth an Irishman, it is true, and by residence he is an American, but professionally he is an Englishman." Albert Dicey agreed with Lodge, and the fact that Godkin, after spending most of his adult life in the United States, chose to retire to England tends to confirm their judgment.[26] Again like Burke, Godkin, in his transition from reformer to conservative, left associates to paint a mixed portrait of him. "Godkin was a man of remarkable character and of strong personality," wrote *Nation* contributor Brander Matthews. "He was clear-headed, but he was never open-minded." He merely tried to "apply to America" what he had learned "in his youth in England."[27] Matthews recalled that after the early reform crusades were finished (actually, some were simply abandoned)

> Godkin found himself at sea. His political writing then lost much of its force; and in the later years of his life he had ceased to be a leader. He was impervious to every new idea in sociology or in statecraft; when he died he was limited to the beliefs he had held when he immigrated to America. His faith in the future failed him; he sank into a praiser of past times and a disparager of the present. He came to feel that a people that would no longer listen to his advice must be on the road to ruin. . . . His main regret was . . . that he would not live long enough to see the fulfillment of his prophecies of evil.[28]

Much of Matthews's assessment—including its tragic tone—might well have applied to the aged Edmund Burke. Moreover, twentieth-century writers have in large part perpetuated this view. The literary scholar Vernon Parrington concluded that "to the end of his life Godkin was a leader without a following, little more than a voice crying in the wilderness."[29] The "consensus" historian Richard Hofstadter called Godkin "an honorable conservative of the old school," yet he confirmed Matthews's characterization by citing Godkin's own words: "I came here fifty years ago with high and fond ideals about America . . . they are now all shattered, and I have apparently to look elsewhere to keep even moderate hopes about the human race alive."[30] Even Godkin's biographer William Armstrong concluded: "The narrow conservatism in which he wrapped himself in his later years cannot be accounted a force for good. . . . Godkin, to whom compassion—like sentimentality—denoted frailty, lacked the intellectual outlook the times demanded."[31] Indeed, as the turn of the century approached, Godkin testified to his own disillusionment that the United States had failed to live up to his essentially Whiggish vision. In his cynically titled *Unforeseen Tendencies of Democracy* he lamented that "no democratic state comes anywhere near their ideal.

Unexpected desires and prejudices have revealed themselves." Godkin sounded almost naively Federalist when he observed: "[Democracies] have not shown that desire to employ leading men in the management of their affairs which they were expected to show." Instead, men of quality devoted themselves to making money. "The demoralization this is producing, even among the scions of old houses, is one of the wonders of our time. . . . The aristocratic contempt for money as compared with station and honor . . . has completely vanished. The thirst for gold seems to be felt now by all classes equally."[32] Unfortunately, while such remarks revealed Godkin's preference for disinterested aristocrats, they did not explain why he sided with plutocrats on most political issues. The apparent explanation is that he feared the masses more—especially the urban immigrant masses.[33] In this Godkin was adhering to the general tendency of conservatives to trust the few rather than the many—regardless of their degree of respect for the few.

Finally, like so many cultural conservatives, Godkin had mixed feelings about the western frontier. While an early article of his in the *North American Review* had expressed cautious optimism regarding the freshening effect of national expansion, and even anticipated the argument of Frederick Jackson Turner's famous "frontier thesis," there was also a skepticism concerning the coarsening effect that individualistic pioneering had on civilization.[34] Godkin and (later) Turner both believed the availability of unoccupied land drew settlers for predominantly economic reasons, and that this behavior was consistent with human nature. Likewise both linked the patterns of migration to successive advances in transportation technology (canals, steamboats, railroads). Both shared a "melting pot" view of immigration, and both acknowledged the resentment that the mature East exhibited toward the growing frontier regions of the West.[35] Though Godkin displayed a more Burkean sensibility, it was Turner who quoted Burke directly on this very point in "The Significance of the Frontier in American History." Turner noted that

> the East has always feared the result of an unregulated advance of the frontier, and has tried to check and guide it. The English authorities would have checked settlement at the headwaters of the Atlantic tributaries. . . . This called out Burke's splendid protest: "If you stopped your grants, what would be the consequence: The people would occupy without grants. They have already occupied in many places. You cannot station garrisons in every part of these deserts. If you drive the people from one place, they will carry on their annual tillage and remove with their flocks to another. Many of the people in the back settlements are already little attached to particular

> situations. Already they have topped the Appalachian mountains. From thence they behold before them an immense plain, one vast, rich, level meadow; a square of five hundred miles. Over this they would wander without a possibility of restraint; they would change their manners with their habits of life; would soon forget a government by which they were disowned; would become hordes of English Tartars; and pouring down upon your unfortified frontiers a fierce and irresistible cavalry, become masters of your governors and your counselors, your collectors and comptrollers, and of all the slaves that adhered to them. Such would, and in no long time must, be the effect of attempting to forbid as a crime, and to suppress as an evil, the command and blessing of Providence, 'Increase and multiply.' Such would be the happy result of an endeavor to keep as a lair of wild beasts that earth which God, by an express charter, has given to the children of men."[36]

That Edmund Burke would be invited to speak with such force in what was to become the single most influential essay on American history was itself an extraordinary occurrence. This was especially so because Burke—the legendary exemplar of Old World traditional civilization—seemed to be endorsing some of the crucial premises of the exceptionalist frontier thesis: the inevitability of westward expansion, the temporary and transitory character of American communities, the economic and romantic lure of virgin land, the ability of the frontier to change the manners and habits of the people, the primitive nature of those changes, the attendant physical and social toughening, and even (in Burke's final lines) the spirit of manifest destiny. Not only were these premises misaligned with the standard pillars of Burkean philosophy, but the fact that no scholarly treatment of Turner's essay has commented on Burke's appearance testifies to the incongruity (or the complete irrelevance) of Burke's image with the dominant concerns of historians of the American West.[37] An additional oddity here was that Turner selectively quoted the "wild" part of Burke's passage and omitted Burke's adjacent plea for a more "civilized" colonization of North America. Had Turner let Burke finish his thought, he would have revealed a more traditional attitude:

> Far different, and surely much wiser, has been our policy hitherto. Hitherto we have invited our people, by every kind of bounty, to fixed establishments. We have invited the husbandman, to look to authority for his title. We have taught him piously to believe in the mysterious virtue of wax and parchment. We have thrown each tract of land, as it was peopled, into districts; that the ruling power should never be

> wholly out of sight. We have settled all we could; and we have carefully attended every settlement with government.[38]

Rarely had the contrasts between Burke's liberal and conservative impulses appeared in such sharp and close association as in this single paragraph from his *Speech on Conciliation with America.* Burke was arguing that because people crave liberty and opportunity, trying to stop frontier expansion is futile. Instead see that it progresses in a controlled way—as an extension of existing society, rather than as something new, different, and threatening. (Years earlier, he had expressed similar sentiments in his *Account of the European Settlements in America*: "I do by no means think that this sort of transplantations ought to be discouraged; I only observe . . . that the manner of their settlement ought to be regulated.")[39] As the next two hundred years would demonstrate, regulating the frontier spirit was easier said than done. Burke's own susceptibility to the "mysterious virtue of wax and parchment" was not shared by most citizens, particularly in America. This was why Turner, unlike Burke, was less interested in how the metropolis controlled the frontier than in how the frontier experience altered society at large. In this respect both Turner and Godkin revealed a compelling explanation as to why the United States could never subscribe to Burkean traditionalism. Even if it were possible to loosen the grip of Enlightenment ideas on American society, the frontier experience (and the frontier myth) precluded the possibility of reverting to a pre-individualistic mentality that was rooted in the distant past.

Godkin may have been willing to give "frontier America" a chance to improve itself, but he would judge that improvement by his own dated standards. As he grew older, and the population showed no desire to implement his genteel version of civilization, he became pessimistic and bitter. Godkin wanted not so much a diversified liberal democracy for the United States as he wanted an Anglocentric hierarchical republic. It is probably a stretch worth making to compare his circumstances with those of Burke as he watched his traditional Old Whig aristocratic vision fade as Great Britain's political and cultural ideal. Both Godkin and Burke looked to the patterns of the past as a guide to the structure of the future. As Godkin said in "Aristocratic Opinions": "It may be taken as a general rule, that those who cannot look very far back do not look very far forward. Experience is the nurse of forethought." This was why Godkin was hostile to the frontier mentality, with its "absence of all right of one generation to enter into any obligation that would bind another."[40] Such Burkean sentiments drove Godkin at first to support reforms he saw as restorations of earlier high ideals. Later, as American society diverged farther from his Whiggish vision, Godkin sank into defensive reaction.

Epilogue

Soon after Godkin's retirement from journalism, Theodore Roosevelt's presidency would prominently feature the national personality-split between the impulse to modernize and civilize and the impulse to revert to—or to chase after—the ever-retreating frontier. Other writers were more concerned with developing America over the course of time rather than over the expanse of space, and they turned their attention to refining the culture and politics of an increasingly urban-industrial society still centered in the East. Godkin's friend Charles Eliot Norton, for instance, pioneered the teaching of Western civilization at Harvard. Though he admired Edmund Burke, he mostly produced his own Burkean arguments without referring to their inspirational source.[41] His colleague James Russell Lowell invoked Burke more directly, but he anticipated Woodrow Wilson's twentieth-century interpretation of him as a proto-liberal, and he compared Burke unfavorably with Rousseau. Burke gave the world "some of the profoundest aphorisms of political wisdom," yet Rousseau gave it "some of the clearest principles of political science." The best aphorisms of Burke, in Lowell's opinion, articulated important lessons on human nature as accumulated over the ages. Rousseau, however, "was the foster-father of modern democracy, and without him our Declaration of Independence" would have lacked some of the "longings" and "dreams" that "were at last affirmed as axioms in the manifesto of a nation, so that all the world might hear."[42]

As observed earlier, there were periods in American history in which Burke's name overwhelmingly signaled ideological conservatism, while during other periods Burke was more or less a man for all seasons. Certainly the late nineteenth and early twentieth centuries represented the latter, just as the eras of the French Revolution and Cold War most dramatically represented the former. Yet even during the more eclectic periods, most writers interpreted Burke in light of their own concerns about contemporary political or social issues. (One turn-of-the-century writer presented Burke as an early father of social Darwinism!)[43] That different writers could employ Burke's ever-quotable prose toward divergent ends is unremarkable in itself. The crucial point here is what such exercises revealed about the intramural competition for the right to define American ideals.

Chapter 7

Theodore Roosevelt

Blazing Forward, Looking Backward

Aside from John Adams, the president who invites the closest comparison with Edmund Burke is Theodore Roosevelt (1858–1919). Yet the parallels between Burke and Roosevelt may not be immediately obvious. Many Americans think they know Theodore Roosevelt, but what they know is his mythic image. A good deal of that image was projected by TR himself, and his creation of an unmistakable persona was an early triumph of modern public relations. Over time, his promotional efforts were enhanced by a confederacy of cartoonists, journalists, merchandisers (selling Teddy bears), sympathetic memoirists, and others who reinforced his image as a fearless crusader and as the quintessential American of his era. Politically, Americans remember TR as the first modern president (not to be confused with FDR, who created the modern *presidency*), and as the charismatic leader of Progressive reform. Uniquely among public figures, TR embodied both the refined aristocrat of the East and the rugged ranchman of the West. This cultural combination not only gained him a broad political constituency; it also assured him of wide historical appeal. Nearly everyone, regardless of taste or political persuasion, could find something to like about his adventures or accomplishments. Even TR's personal transformation from a weak, asthmatic child to a dynamic, vigorous leader has attained the status of inspirational myth.[1]

Yet for all the size of Roosevelt's reputation, he has not been adequately understood in a longer historical perspective. That is, because Americans tend to see TR as a potent force behind the *beginnings* of assertive national government, they see him mostly by the light of what has happened *since* his presidency. Hence it is easy to trace the roots of United States superpower hegemony to the American imperialism of TR's day; or to trace the centralized bureaucracies of the New Deal and Great Society to the federal regulation of food, drugs, labor, and industry that began under TR's administration; or to find the origins of modern environmental policy in TR's efforts to conserve America's natural resources and preserve portions of its wilderness; or even to trace the modern "media presidency" to TR's "bully pulpit." ("Speak softly and carry a big stick" may have been the original "sound bite.") There is nothing intrinsically wrong with this "trailblazer" interpretation of TR's ultimate political relevance. Yet it is not complete, because it ignores the more culturally conservative, Victorian, and backward-looking characteristics of Roosevelt's worldview. TR was not exclusively a modernizer. By his own admission, he also wanted to restore traditional conduct in America.[2]

Theodore Roosevelt was born in the middle of the nineteenth century, the century in which he spent most of his life and half of his adulthood. So if after 1900 he personified the "dawn of the American century," he nevertheless must have carried some well-worn notions, attitudes, and expectations into the new day. Moreover, TR was born into a wealthy and distinguished family—genuine patricians who had lived and prospered on the island of Manhattan for seven generations. By means of their social position and public service, Roosevelt's circle stood as the New York Knickerbocker equivalents to the Boston Brahmins. If the United States had a nineteenth-century urban gentry, TR belonged to it. Viewed from another angle, it was no coincidence that when TR died—less than ten years after leaving the White House, and at the age of just sixty—he was already seen as a relic of a bygone age. In part this was because the heroic martial spirit he displayed at San Juan Hill had been discredited by the horrors of the recent world war. But that was only one example of a larger cultural transformation under way in a rapidly modernizing America. As the looming Jazz Age of the 1920s would soon demonstrate, worldly cynicism was supplanting moralistic romanticism among the young, sophisticated elite. Because TR sprang from a more traditional environment, one must keep in mind the lure of older values to which he was perennially receptive. Of these, two beliefs were of paramount importance. The first was that the world remained above all else a moral universe; the second was that the moral universe could only be navigated properly by a man of virtue. In this TR shared a common outlook with both the Whigs and the genteel Victorians—though he considered the genteel Victorians to be effete, ineffectual snobs.[3]

Natural Aristocracy

Another belief he shared with Whigs, Mugwumps, fellow gentry Progressives, and Edmund Burke was that a new elite had usurped power from an older, more legitimate elite. No figure better exemplified that older elite than TR's own father, who was the embodiment of noblesse oblige.[4] Yet his father's energetic public service—and his sheer practical effectiveness—was already atypical among the gentry of his own day. By TR's generation, it was all the more rare. Burke's fears about traditional aristocrats becoming sluggish, inert, and timid, while the dangerous usurpers proved to be vigorous and active men of ability, applied (with the necessary historical adjustments) to the antebellum Whigs' fears of Democratic politicians, the Mugwumps' fears of machine bosses, and the gentry Progressives' fears of predatory capitalists. Though Richard Hofstadter was probably wrong when he portrayed TR as a conservative opportunist (and therefore an unconvincing Progressive), he was probably right when he focused attention on the gentry Progressives' dismay over their loss of leadership status to the plutocrats.[5] TR shared this feeling, which was why he chose to enter what he called the "governing class" of politicians. He often criticized the "malefactors of great wealth," emphasizing the narrowness of their vision, and he considered it his duty to "prevent the upgrowth in this country of the least attractive and most sordid of all aristocracies," that of "a plutocracy, a caste" that was "scant in [its] heirship of Washington and Lincoln." Roosevelt hoped for a "moral regeneration of the business world" and believed that "no amount of commercial prosperity can supply the lack of heroic virtues. . . . The mere materialist is, above all things, shortsighted."[6] Elsewhere, he wrote:

> To the reactionaries, who seem to fear that to deal in proper fashion with the abuses of property is somehow an attack upon property—we would recall the words of Edmund Burke: "If wealth is obedient and laborious in the service of virtue and public honor, then, wealth is in its place and has its use. But if this order is changed and honor is to be sacrificed to the conservation of riches, riches, which have neither eyes nor hands nor anything truly vital in them, can not long survive the well being of . . . their legitimate masters. . . . If we command our wealth we shall be rich and free. If our wealth commands us we are poor indeed."[7]

Roosevelt echoed Burke's homily on wealth and virtue in a lecture he delivered a year before his Progressive "Bull Moose" campaign. "It is a realizable ideal," he told a California audience, "to understand that money is merely a means to an end, and that if you make it the end instead of a means you do little good to yourself and are a curse to everybody else." In this respect, "The chief harm that the multi-millionaire does . . . is that he is apt to give to the rest of us a thoroughly false ideal." TR called for leaders of a more virtuous variety: philanthropists, statesmen, writers, men "of science, of letters, of art, these are the men who will leave their mark on history." He also arrived at a troubling conclusion concerning "very wealthy people." He admitted privately: "The more I see of them the more profoundly convinced I am of their entire unfitness to govern the country, and of the lasting damage they do."[8]

Yet for TR and other gentry Progressives, the plutocrats represented only half of the threat to civilization, and probably the lesser half. The other danger came from the excitable masses—especially if they fell prey to radical ideas or radical leadership. It may surprise today's admirers of TR's image as a "traitor to his class" to learn that he sided against labor and with the repressive forces of property in the aftermaths of both the Haymarket Square bombing in 1886 and the Pullman Strike in 1894. His position stemmed primarily from a hatred of mob violence, but it was also due to the influence within the militant labor movement of "un-American" ideas about socialism, anarchism, and communism. After succeeding to the presidency when William McKinley was shot by a professed (and very confused) anarchist in 1901, TR told Congress: "The anarchist is a criminal whose perverted instincts lead him to prefer confusion and chaos to the most beneficial social order," and he wrote his Brahmin friend Henry Cabot Lodge: "We should war with relentless efficiency not only against anarchists, but against all active and passive sympathizers with anarchists." This, in TR's view, included such fellow-travelers as the yellow press publisher William Randolph Hearst (who fanned the discontent of the underprivileged), former Illinois governor Richard Altgeld (who pardoned three of the Haymarket Square radicals), and the novelist William Dean Howells (who signed a petition in favor of the pardon). Even late into his presidency—long after his Progressive credentials were firmly established—TR ordered the Justice Department to ban a socialist newspaper from the mails and "to prosecute criminally under any section of the law that is available the men that are interested in sending out this anarchistic and murderous publication."[9]

Roosevelt may have repeatedly championed the "plain people" and "democracy" in both public pronouncements and private letters, and no doubt this was not merely lip service on his part. However, like many Americans before and since his time (and not just among the elite), the variety of democracy TR believed in was an orderly, responsible, and "patriotic" sort. Despite TR's crusades for the betterment of the common man, he was never the "great commoner" that William Jennings Bryan was. Nor did he want to be. To the patrician Roosevelt, Bryan exemplified the type of hotheaded, bottom-up, radical class warrior who was more likely to unleash a conservative reaction than to deliver constructive reform. In this TR recalled the example of the French Revolution. He once told the muckraking publisher Samuel McClure: "I wish very much that you could have articles showing up the hideous iniquity of which mobs are guilty, the wrongs of violence by the poor as well as the wrongs of corruption by the rich. . . . At the time of the French Revolution most of what was said about the oppression of the people was true; but inasmuch as the reformers dwelt only on the wrongs done by the noble and wealthy classes, and upon the wrongs suffered by the poorer people, their conduct led up to the hideous calamity of the Terror, which put back the cause of liberty for over a generation." A few weeks later, TR advised the government mint to include the word "Justice" in addition to "Liberty" on newly designed American coins: "For we want to differentiate the kind of liberty we have under this government from the kind of liberty about which the French Revolutionists dreamed dreams of blood."[10]

As these historical references indicated, Roosevelt saw the prospect of class conflict as disastrous—especially if the masses were unleashed on the wealthy by misguided "reformers" and "revolutionists." Like Burke, TR believed that the natural aristocracy—in this case the gentry Progressives like himself—were best suited to play the crucial mediational role in society, and to encourage reform while discouraging disorder. TR's upbringing positioned him in the cultural elite, and he was intuitively conscious of that fact. While a student at Harvard he had written his sister: "I stand 19th in the class. . . . Only one *gentleman* stands ahead of me."[11] For all his genuine commitment to meritocracy, TR shared the common gentry veneration of good breeding. Notwithstanding his cattleman and Rough Rider reputation, the social and intellectual scene at the Roosevelt White House was one of aristocratic sophistication not to be outdone until the Kennedy years.[12] As one historian not distracted by TR's cowboy image observed, Theodore Roosevelt was equipped for his life's work by his "ancestry and outlook."[13] This ancestry and outlook provided TR with his overall approach to the role of government and leadership in America, and also with a sense of how he personally fit into the social order. "He led as if ordained to lead," wrote a minor public figure who had known TR, "as if he were personally responsible for his leadership."[14] His gentry background conditioned him to distrust both the plutocracy and the mob, and to feel morally and culturally superior to both. As president, TR saw it as his responsibility to steer the ship of state between "the Scylla of mob rule and the Charybdis of the reign of a mere plutocracy." Or as he put it without the mythological allusion: "This Government is not and never shall be government by a plutocracy. This Government is not and never shall be government by a mob."[15]

The following year Roosevelt informed the industrialist-turned-philanthropist Andrew Carnegie that he dreaded both the "violent extremists" and the "Bourbon reactionaries" of Europe. Again he harked back to the French Revolution to illustrate his centrist inclinations: "I do not know whether in the French Revolution I have the most contempt and abhorrence for the Marat, Hébert, Robespierre and Danton type of revolutionaries, or for the aristocratic, bureaucratic and despotic rulers of the old regime." Eight years later, TR blamed the same radical cast of characters for bringing on both "the Napoleonic tyranny" and "the tyranny of the Holy Alliance."[16] TR shared the common liberal belief that the French Revolution was a just cause that somehow became perverted, yet he partially subscribed to the conservative critique by condemning the collective psychology of the revolution's Jacobin leaders. He applied a similar judgment to the Russian Revolution: overthrowing the authoritarian czar was a sign of progress, but only if it could be followed by the installation of a responsible democracy. Roosevelt expressed this view in a letter to Ilya Tolstoy (son of Leo Tolstoy) in May 1917, after the February Revolution had displaced the czar but before the Bolsheviks' October Revolution had forestalled the possibility of democracy and capitalism. TR began by introducing himself as a "fellow democrat" and "radical," but he quickly advised the new leaders of the Russian people to proceed "with such moderation and wisdom as to prevent all possibility of reaction." He further cautioned Tolstoy that "the danger, at the point you have reached, comes almost as much from well-meaning, unbalanced extremists who favor the revolution, as from the reactionaries themselves. . . . The torch of enlightenment fired the revolt; see that the light of the torch is not dimmed by any unwise and extreme action, and above all not by any of those sinister and dreadful deeds which a century and a quarter ago in France produced the Red Terror, and then by reaction the White Terror." He implored the Russians to secure the "permanent benefits of the revolution . . . by wisdom and self-control."[17]

During most of his career, TR sought to lead the country toward (as he put it) the political "left center." But in order to accomplish this without either sliding too far to the left or provoking a reaction from the right, he knew that management of reform had to be kept within a relatively small circle of responsible leaders. Although TR learned how to appropriate the language of liberalism—or even of radicalism—to gain popular support (one poet claimed "Roosevelt cursed Bryan and then aped his ways"), he would never willingly cede control of the reform movement to the majoritarians. Along these lines, the historian John Milton Cooper has suggested that "[TR's] 'progressive' self-designation always occurred within a carefully defined conservative framework."[18] A generation earlier, the historian (and editor of TR's letters) John Morton Blum took this interpretation in a more Anglo-traditional direction by comparing TR to Burke:

> Like Edmund Burke, perhaps the greatest of British conservatives, Roosevelt valued the long wash of historical development, sometimes controlled, sometimes accidental, that had given form to the political society in which he lived. Both were wisely careful never to set up a system of their own. Like Burke, Roosevelt delighted in the process by which political achievement and further institutional development were made possible. . . . Roosevelt needed and took his gladness in situations "of power and energy," in government—as Burke described it—"founded on compromise and barter."[19]

Progressive Conservatism

This Progressive conservative approach to government, leadership, and reform determined TR's choice of heroes—and villains. One might expect Roosevelt the reformer and "practical idealist" to have admired the enlightened republican Thomas Jefferson; but instead he despised him and identified with the Federalists Washington and Hamilton. On the day after voters repudiated Bryan's populist "cross of gold" crusade in the watershed election of 1896, TR wrote to Frederick Jackson Turner: "In my estimation Jefferson's influence upon the United States as a whole was very distinctly evil," and he saw "some very unpleasant points of similarity" in Jefferson, Bryan, and Altgeld. During his presidency, Roosevelt informed the Supreme Court justice William Moody: "Heaven knows I despise Jefferson . . . the most incompetent chief executive we ever had. . . . We lived through Jefferson's administration, tho [*sic*] he did us much damage; and we could live thru Bryan or a reactionary; but I do not want to see the experiment tried." (TR did, however, acknowledge Jefferson's "one great virtue . . . he stood for the plain people.")[20] The next year, TR counseled one of his sons on the perceived threats posed by populist agitation: "When we speak of the rising of the democratic tide and feel fear concerning its outcome, it is well to remember that again and again during the past century and a quarter the tide has been higher than at present. Of course the French Revolution was the greatest instance of this. . . . The excesses and follies were much greater . . . when Jefferson was the trusted leader of the people, than they are now." That same year, TR unknowingly reprised the reasoning of the pro-slavery writer Thomas Dew, by recalling the racial turmoil on Haiti [the former Saint-Domingue] "when it yielded to the influence of the French Revolution." Though he did not mention Jefferson by name, he did refer to the "Jacobite [Jacobin] or ultrademocratic movement" of which he considered Jefferson to be the early American champion.[21]

Conservatives stigmatized Jefferson as an apologist for dangerous French enthusiasms and as a defender of the perpetual right to revolution ("every twenty years or so," as he was quoted—too literally—as advocating). "As regards what you say about Jefferson," TR told a Progressive writer, "the revival of the monarchic idea was due partly to the silly inefficiency of men like Jefferson . . . and partly due to the violent excesses of the men such as the French revolutionists." Roosevelt derided Jefferson as a weak executive. He also judged him an impractical idealist for failing to come to grips with the inevitable terminations of the first, or destructive, stages of the great revolutions of his day, and for failing to direct his thoughts instead to the second, more constructive (and necessarily more conservative) stages—as Washington and Hamilton had done. TR differed from Edmund Burke in his support of the French Revolution's original incarnation, but not in the later course it took: "I believe that the French revolutionists," he wrote to a California Progressive, "when, not content with what they had gained in 1789, they pushed forward into four years of red anarchy that culminated in the terror, did more to damage democracy, more to put back the cause of popular government, than any despot or oligarchy from that time to this." He then sounded a more Burkean and anti-Jeffersonian tone, as he dismissed the revolutionaries' utopian hypocrisy: "Remember that these were the men who made a 'religion' of democracy, who typified 'liberty' as a goddess; and who prattled words like these while their hearts were black with murder committed in such names."[22]

On the same occasion, TR recommended Lord Acton's *Lectures on the French Revolution* (1910). This book not only offered the standard liberal assessment of the well-justified revolution taking a bad turn, but also highlighted the strong influence that the American Revolution exerted on events in France. Such an approach was bound to appeal to Americans in general, since it offered an exceptionalist perspective, and to TR in particular, because it paired revolutionary ideals with a practical philosophy of moderation and restraint. Hence Acton's account was liberal and conservative at the same time—much as TR's brand of progressivism proved to be. Acton suggested that the revolution began at a time when Bourbon France was less oppressive than it had previously been, and that its "spark . . . was supplied by the Declaration of Independence." He adhered to both the "whiggest of whigs" and the "clean slate" views of America by recognizing that "the colonies were more advanced than Great Britain in the way of free institutions. . . . They had no remnants of feudalism to cherish or resist. . . . The uprooted Whig, detached from his parchments and precedents, his leading families and historic conditions, exhibited new qualities." Acton bolstered his claim that revolutionary ideas had flowed from the New World to the Old with an unusual example: "The most significant instance of the action of America on Europe is Edmund Burke." Though Burke eventually "became the most strenuous and violent of conservatives," there was "an interval" during the American crisis when "Burke was as revolutionary as Washington. . . . As the strife sharpened and the Americans made way, Burke was carried along, and developed views which he never utterly abandoned, but which are difficult to reconcile with much that he wrote when the Revolution had spread to France." Acton committed four pages to quotations of Burke's liberal arguments about rights and liberties in the context of the American crisis and oncluded: "I cannot resist the inference from these passages that Burke, after 1770, underwent other influences than those of his reputed masters, the Whigs of 1688." In Acton's view, the American Revolution had effectively transformed Burke from an Old Whig into a New Whig. Though Burke's personal transformations did not cease with American independence, his revolutionary example nevertheless paved the way for others in Europe. To paraphrase Acton: if America could inspire Burke to act like a revolutionary, it could certainly inspire popular leaders in France—who had more to gain—to do likewise.[23]

It must have been especially reassuring to TR that Acton placed considerable emphasis on the distinctions between the first and second stages of successful revolutions. As far back as John Adams's *Davila* essays, conservatives in America had sought to separate the responsible construction of the United States from the tragic events of regicide, terror, reactive despotism, and military adventurism in France. Acton, though liberal and British, conformed to this established pattern. As he saw it, "What the French took from the Americans was their theory of revolution, not their theory of government—their cutting, not their sewing." Acton followed exceptionalist precedent when he attributed this to the unspoiled nature of the New

World environment. By way of illustration he quoted the words of a Boston patriot to a departing French officer: "Do not let your hopes be inflamed by our triumphs on this virgin soil. You will carry our sentiments with you, but if you try to plant them in a country that has been corrupt for centuries, you will encounter obstacles more formidable than ours. Our liberty has been won with blood; you will have to shed it in torrents before liberty can take root in the old world." According to Acton, it had been "the ideas of the earlier days [the spirit of '76] that roused the attention of France . . . of James Otis, of Jefferson, of *The Rights of Man*." However, "change followed in 1787, when the Convention drew up the Constitution. It was a period of construction and every effort was made, every scheme was invented, to curb the inevitable democracy." Lamentably, "although France was deeply touched by the American Revolution, it was not affected by the American Constitution. It underwent the disturbing influence, not the conservative."[24]

The need for constructive, controlled idealism was a keynote of TR's political philosophy, and it was in harmony with his gentry code of civic duty and "inner check." The apparent departure from this rule was his attempt to regain the presidency in 1912. Running as the Progressive Party candidate, after failing to unseat William Howard Taft for the Republican nomination, TR pushed such radical proposals as popular referenda to overturn court decisions, and he aimed most of his righteous indignation against "capitalists," "big corporation lawyers," and "the leisured and monied classes." Historians have disagreed over just how anomalous TR's Bull Moose rhetoric was, given his usual penchant for what he claimed to be moderate and reasonable reform.[25] As president, TR had made a point of underscoring the supposedly conservative nature of the progressive measures he favored. For example, he was careful to assure lawmakers that in passing reform legislation, they had "proceeded on sane and conservative lines. Nothing revolutionary was attempted. . . . Nothing radical has been done." The next year, in the wake of his successful *Northern Securities* antitrust case, and his landslide reelection victory, he still found it prudent to warn Congress that "to try to deal with [business corporations] in an intemperate, destructive, or demagogic spirit" would be "harmful." And in 1905, when he proposed that a constitutional amendment might be necessary to guarantee the government sufficient power to regulate business, TR employed an essentially Burkean argument in hopes of making unprecedented federal oversight seem more natural: "This is only in form an innovation. In substance it is merely a restoration." The president claimed that he simply sought "to meet the changed conditions in such manner as will prevent the Commonwealth [from] abdicating the power it has always possessed not only in this country, but also in England before and since the country became a separate nation."[26] In keeping with his proprietary attitude toward responsible leadership, TR dismissed reform journalists as "muckrakers," even while fighting to rectify many of the abuses they publicized.[27] In his autobiography—published the year *after* his "semi-socialistic" Bull Moose campaign—Roosevelt reverted to his earlier desire for a moderate Progressive consensus. He depicted opponents of reform as unreasonable or reactionary men, and he recommended books critical of syndicalism, communism, and socialism, to support his belief that such European designs were not only ill-founded, but irrelevant to the United States—where democracy precluded revolution and where most socialists were "in reality merely radical social reformers, with whom on many points good citizens can and ought to work in hardy general agreement."[28]

Perhaps the keenest insight into the link between TR's leftist insurgency of 1912 and the otherwise "conservative" reform philosophy of his overall career was offered years ago by Elting Morrison. Morrison suggested that because conservatives acted from "intuition and insight in particular situations" [what Burke called "circumstances"], while liberals acted from "a body of principled theory," liberal reasoning could be easily transported from one time or set of conditions to another, while conservative reasoning could not. As a practical matter, this meant that conservatives were at "a distinct disadvantage out of office." Without his own general theories to rely on, the conservative "is left with the argument that if he were put back in office he could run things better."[29] Writers have often viewed TR's seemingly radical rhetoric during the Bull Moose campaign of 1912, and his jingoistic intolerance during the World War, as symptoms of his out-of-office anxiety. Yet such interpretations hinge on TR's psychological thirst for power. By contrast, Morrison's interpretation offers an intellectual (or ideological) explanation for the same behavior, which, if accurate, is more generically useful—since it applies to conservatives regardless of personality type. In addition, Morrison identified other "conservative virtues" that seemed to explain TR's approach to "authority" and the "governing of men." Most crucially, TR possessed the conservative's "unruffled attitude toward power," and the desire to enforce individual moral conduct.[30]

Indeed, when Theodore Roosevelt quoted Edmund Burke in his 1905 Annual Message to Congress (known today as the State of the Union message), it was within the context of his gentry devotion to personal virtue: "It is the man's moral quality, his attitude toward the great questions which concern all humanity, his cleanliness of life, his power to do his duty toward himself and toward others, which really count."[31] After declaring that American government should treat each man "simply and solely on his worth," TR offered up

> the thought so finely expressed by Burke: "Men are qualified for civil liberty in exact proportion to their disposition to put moral chains upon their own appetites; in proportion as they are disposed to listen to the counsels of the wise and good in preference to the flattery of knaves. Society cannot exist unless a controlling power upon the appetite be placed somewhere, and the less of it there be within the more there must be without. It is ordained in the eternal constitution of things that men of intemperate minds cannot be free. Their passions forge their fetters."[32]

This powerful excerpt from Burke's antirevolutionary writings stands as the most conspicuously "official" invocation of Burke by an American president. When read in context, the passage typified the moralizing tone that was a hallmark of TR's writings and speeches, and a staple of Victorian expression. Luckily for TR's popular image, his recurrent sermonizing was more than offset by his colorful plain-speaking. (And luckily for his political legacy, most of TR's policies made sense on a pragmatic level—with or without the moral injunctions.) Roosevelt's moralizing was another example of the backward-looking side of his character, yet it also illustrated an aspect of his political sensibility. As Morrison said of the conservative mind in the liberal age: "The most easily definable thing in the conservative heritage, the scheme of morals which the conservative uses in place of a body of principled theory, becomes, with time, a worn-out or even at times a comic anachronism."[33]

But there is more. Roosevelt's quotation of Burke opens a window on both the nature of TR's conservatism and the extent of its compatibility with Burke's philosophy. TR used Burke's words at least as much to curb the antisocial behavior of plutocrats as to curb the passions of the mob. He immediately followed the quotation with a call for the federal Bureau of Corporations to regulate the insurance industry, and in the next breath he spoke against corporate executives who "take but small note of the ethical distinction between honesty and dishonesty." Interestingly, TR probably got the idea for using Burke's words from an article written by the muckraker Ray Stannard Baker on railroad rate regulation.[34] Both Baker and Roosevelt quoted, in support of reform, from Burke's conservative essay *Letter to a Member of the National Assembly* (1791). TR's Annual Message—composed just after Baker's article appeared—included a proposal for rate regulation, and it decreed: "A heavy penalty should be exacted from any corporation which fails to respect an order" from the government.[35] Obviously TR's approach fit Morrison's "unruffled attitude toward power" like a glove. But considering the even more statist approaches to business regulation favored by the radical left of TR's day, it would be inaccurate to ascribe the ruthless exercise of power to conservatives alone—or even to ascribe it to all conservatives. Edmund Burke, for instance, would have agreed with Lord Acton that absolute power corrupts absolutely, while TR believed that concentrated power in the right hands could be beneficial so long as its duration was limited.[36]

One reason that Burke and Roosevelt seem fraught with contradictions is that we have lost the ability to separate action from character, or ideology from opportunity. To the postmodern sensibility, we are what we do, and our political positions reflect our interests. But TR's outlook was (by present standards) only half modern, and Burke's was less than half. Their political philosophies reflected their visions of civilization, but not with the same straightforward relationship expected today. Recall that in the middle of the nineteenth century George Bancroft differentiated between Burke's character and his political thought—that is, between his value as a man and the value of his work. Such distinctions were not yet extinct in TR's day, at least not among the gentry: "I hope that in my acts I have been a good president," TR wrote to the aristocratic British politician and historian George Otto Trevelyan, "but most of all, I believe that whatever value my service may have comes even more from what I *am* than from what I *do*."[37] Both TR and Burke subscribed to a gentlemen's code; though given their personal idiosyncrasies, their separation in time, and the differences in their national cultures, that code was not consistent in every detail. Like chivalry or noblesse oblige, gentility was more of a Platonic ideal than a definable course of action. Since gentility sought to preserve and perpetuate the best attributes of civilization, it was by nature culturally conservative and respectful of tradition. Yet as both Burke and TR knew, at times it became necessary to take liberal (or progressive) steps in order to protect established ideals.

Here was a kinship between Burke and TR. Both men required the known world to hold steady so that they could substantially improve it. Once it began to change in ways they could neither understand nor control, they found themselves on unfamiliar terrain. Burke's admonition that "to innovate is not to reform" was not just a condemnation of innovation—it was also a defense of reform. Burke, like TR, was an aggressive reformer. To him innovation implied a radical redesign of the existing system, a "change in the substance" of society that would render experience-based reformers like himself irrelevant. Hence part of Burke's hatred of innovation stemmed from its threat to meaningful reform. ("The French revolutionists . . . refused to reform any thing; and they left nothing . . . *unchanged*.")[38] As noted earlier, Burke was not a defender of the status quo, because he was never satisfied with it. But he was a defender—a conservator—of the inherited essences of civilization—the sum total of all the achievements, ideals, and cultural artifacts of what he usually called a "people" and TR often called the "race." This was the sentiment behind TR's belief that his Progressive reform measures only looked like innovations, while actually they were intended to restore civilized behavior. TR claimed that he rejected radicalism because he thought it would induce a reactionary response. But that was his pragmatic side speaking. His intuitive side feared radical change because it would destroy the civilization in which he had invested and achieved so much, along with the natural aristocracy to which he belonged. When TR called Tom Paine a "filthy little atheist," who—during the French Revolution—was undeserving of "the sympathy of an onlooker . . . religious or otherwise," he exhibited a Burke-like inability to separate unorthodox religious thought from political radicalism, as well as a Burke-like hostility toward irresponsible leaders.[39]

Still, there were differences between the Old Whig and Victorian visions. Unlike Burke, TR was aware of the necessity of what is now called "pushing the envelope" in the quest for progress. This was most famously revealed in his reaction to the 1913 New York exhibition of modern art, widely known as the "Armory Show." In an *Outlook* review, TR coined the term "lunatic fringe" to describe cubist, futurist, and "near-impressionist" artists. While the term and its dismissive attitude have achieved immortality, few persons are aware of TR's defense of the need for occasional overreach in the pursuit of human advancement:

> Probably in any reform movement, any progressive movement, in any field of life, the penalty for avoiding the commonplace is a liability to extravagance. It is vitally necessary to move forward and to shake off the dead hand, of the reactionaries; and yet we have to face the fact that there is apt to be a lunatic fringe among the votaries of any forward movement.[40]

At least in theory, TR was modern enough to value the catalytic effect of a radical vanguard, even if such phenomena frightened him in practice. Burke, on the other hand, lived during an age when stability still competed with progress for supremacy as a cultural ideal.

Hence these two reform-conservatives responded differently to the prospect of radical change. Burke overestimated the potential expansion of Jacobinism, and in the process downplayed the serious, even fatal, flaws of the old regime. He did this because, after 1789, he was incapable of conceiving any constructive role for the radical perspective—not even its ability (if only as a lunatic fringe) to accelerate needed reforms. TR may have thought that populist radicalism "was fundamentally an attack on civilization; an appeal to the torch," but he believed that "to decline to recognize the great evils of the present system, and to oppose any effort to deal with them in rational fashion," would "strengthen immensely . . . those who advocate extreme and foolish measures."[41] When faced with revolutionary enthusiasm, Burke dug in his heels and fought the revolution head-on. Roosevelt, who considered revolution in America to be a moot point, sought to deflate radical pressures by eliminating or softening the injustices upon which extremism fed. With this preemptive approach, TR conformed to a now common interpretation of progressivism as a sensible reform movement that was motivated—at least in the push, if not in the pull—by a desire to forestall more-radical changes. This was no less the case during TR's 1912 Bull Moose insurgency than it had been during his years in the White House. As one scholar has pointed out, when Roosevelt spoke in early 1912, "he compared present conditions in the United States to those in prerevolutionary France, and he urged Americans to reject the French example of 'splitting into the two camps of unreasonable conservatism and unreasonable radicalism.'"[42] Fortunately for TR, and in keeping with the American optimism he embodied, it was not too late for Americans to construct a better society. Unfortunately for Europe as Burke saw it, France had already fallen into the abyss, and England was teetering on the edge.

Until the French Revolution stunned Burke with a triumph of theoretical radicalism, he had devoted his career to Whig reform. In part this was a quest for justice, and in part he sought to rectify the problems of the existing system before they could grow more serious and promote extremism. In this respect, Burke's reform activities prior to 1789 resembled TR's variety of progressivism. The major difference was that most political leaders of Burke's day—including the more liberal Whigs—thought it was still possible to control the pace of change. By the middle of the nineteenth century, it became obvious that transformations in the speed of life were developing a momentum of their own. By the early twentieth century, the pursuit of progress pervaded every significant political ideology in America, and disputes centered on what shape progress should take, how it would be measured, and what (or who) had to be left behind in order to achieve it. Even cultural conservatives like TR and Woodrow Wilson accepted this modern expectation of continuous change on a conscious intellectual level. Yet portions of their inner selves remained captives of their less dynamic inherited worldviews, and from time to time their intuitive yearnings for conceptual stability guided their thought and action. There were many traditional values to which TR clung, and many historical traditions to which he assented. Similarly, there was much in Burke's political philosophy to which TR would have proclaimed (as he said in another context): "ditto to Mr. Burke."[43] But—as was the case with other gentry Victorians—many of the Burkean values he admired were moral, rhetorical, and cultural, rather than political. And even those were losing ground to scientific, technological, and economic imperatives.

Americanism

Nowhere did Roosevelt seem to abandon the Burkean sensibility more dramatically than in his life-altering experience in the Dakota Territory during the 1880s. TR's quest for a more primitive, simplified, and strenuous life stemmed partly from the personal anguish of losing his wife and mother within hours of each other in 1884, when he was just twenty-five. Two days earlier he had become a father, and the shocking deaths revived memories of the premature death of his own father in 1878. In addition, 1884 marked TR's first political setback, as he was disowned by reform-oriented Republicans for his failure to repudiate the party's "corrupt" presidential nominee James Blaine. Yet TR had purchased his Dakota ranch before any of these misfortunes struck, and most likely his family tragedies and political frustrations served only to intensify an undertaking to which he was already committed. The Theodore Roosevelt of legend—both the politician of record *and* the iconic popular image—would not have existed had TR not experienced frontier life as an impressionable young man. For one thing, TR could never have achieved fame as a Rough Rider without the physical toughening and close contact with cowboy society that were unavailable in his eastern upper-crust world. Late in life, Roosevelt admitted that he would never have been president without "my years in North Dakota." Before his frontier adventures, TR was a somewhat anomalous eastern aristocrat, an energetic and talented yet semi-comic "swell" or "dude" lacking in gravitas. But as one of his best biographers put it: "Some extraordinary physical and spiritual transformation occurred during this arduous period" in the Badlands, which deepened his character.[44]

It is worth noting that TR first achieved widespread notoriety as the author of such books as *Ranch Life and the Hunting Trail* (1888), *The Wilderness Hunter* (1893), and his four-volume saga *The Winning of the West* (1889–95). Even after he rose to the major political offices of governor of New York and president, he continued to publish works of a similar sort:

The Rough Riders (1899), *The Strenuous Life* (1900), and *Hunting the Grizzly* (1905). TR incurred considerable expense publicizing his image as an accomplished frontiersman and as a cavalry commander, and almost certainly he did this with future political advantage in mind. But it was also likely that TR, far from simply engaging in a cynical manipulation of a gullible public, genuinely believed in his own myth. In other words, he came to view himself as an authentic participant in the great historical drama that was the taming of the wilderness and the building of American civilization. In the opening section of *Winning of the West*, for instance, he traced the "spread of the English-speaking peoples" as they evolved from Germanic to English to American by their conquering of primitive adversaries and settling their lands: "in each case [the victors] undergoing a marked change . . . but in the main retaining . . . the general race characteristics." Those unspecified (yet implicitly beneficial) characteristics, according to TR, resulted from "a perfectly continuous history," as opposed to the "Latin" peoples of Europe, who embodied a mongrel mixture of "blood," "language," "law," "culture," "government system," and "general policy." While TR did not exactly glorify the mythical Anglo-Saxon tribes, he strongly suggested a clearly marked path through time, along which Americans could retrace the progress of their distinctively uncompromised civilization.[45]

But like many Americans, TR wanted it both ways. On the one hand, Americans retained their superior Anglo-Teutonic traits; on the other hand, "When the great western migration began we were already a people by ourselves." TR subscribed to both the new American archetype, which held that Americans were transformed by their revolution, and to some vague version of the frontier thesis, which held that the country's uniqueness was reinforced as each generation pushed westward: "Americans began their work of western conquest as a separate individual people, at the moment when they began their national life. It has been their great work ever since." Roosevelt even anticipated Turner's quotation of Burke (four years *before* Turner wrote) on the frictions between the American East and West: "The statesmen of the Atlantic seaboard were often unable to perceive [the importance of the frontier], and indeed often showed the same narrow jealousy of communities beyond the Alleghenies that England felt for all America. . . . They were yet unable to fully appreciate the magnitude of the interests at stake in the West."[46] Although TR was a scion of the East, he identified greatly with the West, which to him represented the crucial rough edge that prevented American society from turning soft and following Europe into decadence. After Turner's famous essay appeared, TR restated the importance of the frontier more directly in the final volume of *Winning of the West*:

> On the western frontier lay vast and fertile vacant spaces; for the Americans had barely passed the threshold of the continent predestined to be the inheritance of their children. . . . For generations the great feature in the nation's history, next to the preservation of its national life, was to be its westward growth; and its distinguishing work was to be the settlement of the immense wilderness which stretched across to the Pacific. But before land could be settled it had to be won.[47]

Though TR praised the value of Turner's work, he questioned some of its assumptions. Turner rejected the Teutonic-Anglo-Saxon "racial" origin of the American democratic spirit (the "germ theory" of democracy), while TR celebrated it. In Roosevelt's view, the early Americans carried their "genius for self-rule" with them from England. In this sense TR's exceptionalism was less pure than that of Turner—who believed that democracy "was not carried . . . in the *Mayflower*" but that it "came out of the American forest"—as well as more conducive to Anglo-traditionalism.[48] Given Roosevelt's macho reputation, it is surprising that he did not credit the advance of the English-speaking race solely to military prowess (he conceded that "Latins" had conquered as impressively), but instead to an ability to civilize new lands, and in the process to improve itself. This idea of periodic renewal by way of conflict and construction was central to TR's conception of American history.[49] While "taming" the wilderness or "civilizing" indigenous tribes provided the simplest examples of the process, events like the Civil War, or—less obviously—certain types of political crusades, also fit the pattern. He once told a British politician that he had attempted to "radically regenerate" the Republican Party in order to save it, and we may plausibly conclude that the mission of regenerating America was behind his Progressive reforms and his New Nationalism, just as the goal of regenerating his own psyche had led him to the Dakota frontier.[50]

That Roosevelt reveled in symbolic combat with plutocrats, anarchists, horse thieves, and other such malefactors reflected a mental fusion of his own efforts with the advance of his "race." If TR was the quintessential American of his era, it was because he embodied a national sense of regeneration, a feeling that for the first time since Reconstruction the people were fighting to remake American life and government and in the process to revitalize American ideals. TR's unbounded admiration for Abraham Lincoln, for instance, stemmed primarily from Lincoln's moral leadership of America's "new birth of freedom." Indeed, Roosevelt felt that the only thing preventing him from becoming a great president (in the Lincoln-Washington mold) was the lack of a sufficiently apocalyptic crisis, which would have called forth a major national rebirth under his leadership. It has been suggested that "from the romantic historians [TR] learned that at every moment of crisis a hero emerged who encouraged the people to reach their full idealistic potential. . . . This victory of the hero and the people was essentially the triumph of his and their will."[51] Yet it is important to add that TR was always aware of the historical tradition in which he was participating. In keeping with his "race" theory of history, he believed that the civilization he was advancing began in England. He said as much in *Winning of the West*, when, after relating how "England's insular position . . . permitted it to . . . develop a type of nationality totally distinct from . . . the European mainland," he declared: "All this is not foreign to American history. The vast movement by which this continent was conquered and peopled cannot be rightly understood if considered solely by itself."[52] Tellingly, Roosevelt "loved" the writing of the English historian Thomas Babington Macaulay, whose five-volume *History of England* was published around the time of TR's birth, and which was a classic example of the Whig perspective, and he recommended him "above all the authors I know." In fact, TR revealed his belief in the *usefulness* of history by suggesting that Macaulay's "writings will help a man of action . . . [to] be of some account in the world."[53]

TR never ceased to believe that America was an extension of Anglo civilization: a new, better, and separate branch of a very old tree. This was one reason why he made the "special relationship" between the United States and Great Britain the "centerpiece" of his presidential foreign policy.[54] Not only did he intimate this in his published writings, but also in his private correspondence with British elites—pronouncing in one instance that "our two great peoples . . . [are] the only two really free great peoples." The historian David Burton discovered a rich collection of letters in which Roosevelt shared with his British friends "an underlying set of values, sometimes summed up as 'the Whig temperament.'" "After all," the editor of the London *Spectator* wrote TR, "why should not one hold the Whig spirit of enthusiasm as our forefathers did? Moderation and the happy mean have been justly applauded in all ages." This connection enabled upper-crust, culturally conservative reformers in England and America to agree on the dangers of plutocracy, materialism, and socialism in both countries, and to subscribe to a rather Burkean "sympathy of comprehension" regarding their special transatlantic relationship. One English letter to TR suggested Burke's cultural ties, light as air and strong as iron: "The differences of our systems [of government] are superficial, the likenesses fundamental. We speak the same language, recognize the same common law principles in our law and administration, and are inspired by the same political and moral ideals." TR had expressed similar sentiments a few years earlier: "I feel very strongly that the English-speaking peoples['] . . . interests are really fundamentally the same, they are more closely akin, not merely in blood, but in feeling and in principles, than either [the United States or Great Britain] is akin to any other people in the world." At around the same time TR informed his future secretary of state that England was "the country to which we are most closely bound."[55] In fact, he agreed with British liberals that the United States was now the entity best equipped to lead the advance of the English-speaking peoples.

It is ironic that Theodore Roosevelt—the modern American Adam—acknowledged such a strong bond with British civilization (to which, incidentally, he had only a partial blood tie).[56] But one must keep in mind the primacy of Anglocentrism in the worldview of most American elites of TR's day. The Victorian side of TR and his sympathy for British culture are rarely examined, possibly because they grate too harshly against his image as the most exceptional specimen of an avowedly exceptional people.[57] TR himself often projected an image that was almost jingoistically American.[58] He lambasted "Europeanized" Americans and preached a New Nationalism of literature as well as of politics.[59] But even this was misleading, since TR's conception of "foreign" influences really meant "non-Anglo-Saxon." It may at first seem contradictory to accept TR as exceptionalist, ultrapatriotic, frontier-oriented, and a proponent of (in his words) "straight Americanism," and at the same accept him as Victorian, Anglocentric, and culturally Burke-like in many respects. But just as TR struggled to contain the scholar and the man of action, the eastern aristocrat and the western cowboy, the radical and the conservative, so too he contained the desire to be both part of and apart from British culture. Why else would he "take Matthew Arnold along" on his hot pursuit of Dakota horse thieves?[60] In his own exaggerated way TR stood as a microcosm of America's conflicted culture at the turn of the century. Citizens of the United States—especially the middle and upper classes—identified with both Anglocentric Victorianism and Wild West adventurism, while at the same time they were experiencing social, industrial, technological, and cultural changes that bore little connection to either.

If there were few Americans who could be described as fully Burkean before the Civil War, by the turn of the twentieth century their presence was even more negligible. In retrospect, even the antebellum Whigs had been fighting a lost battle when they tried to transplant Anglo-traditionalism and Edmund Burke to American soil. Similarly, when the writers of the genteel tradition followed in their wake, they were already engaging in transatlantic nostalgia. By the time Theodore Roosevelt became president, American conservatism owed even less to the Burkean legacy. It owed more to religious fundamentalism, monopoly capitalism, and "tory" attitudes toward culture and society. Conveniently for the sake of comparison, TR was as uncomfortable with the tory values of his own time as Burke had been with the tory values of the eighteenth century. Furthermore, as John Milton Cooper has noted: "Roosevelt differed in his energy and his imaginative grasp from others who sought to uphold the existing order in the United States. His nervous, dynamic temperament would probably have unfitted him under most circumstances for the calm quiescence normally valued by those who want to maintain things as they are."[61] If Cooper's assessment bears a resemblance to Burke's "twice-born" personality, then perhaps there were psychological *and* cultural similarities between the two statesmen.[62] But in Roosevelt's case, his zigzagging from one extreme to another applied not only to swings between liberalism and conservatism, but to swings between traditionalism and exceptionalism as well.

Chapter 8

Woodrow Wilson

Confronting American Maturity

Although TR retained the more Burke-like sensibility, the American president who outright said the most about Edmund Burke was Woodrow Wilson (1856–1924). Roosevelt and Wilson belonged to opposing political parties and exhibited strikingly different personalities, yet they were much in tune politically. (Ironically, each went to absurd lengths to deny this last point.) As presidents, both men shepherded substantial reform legislation through Congress, and each in his own way asserted the primacy of "the people" over vested economic interests. Both made a show of appealing to morality and high ideals, and both used their offices to expand the limits of government responsibility. When measured by tangible results, Wilson's administration probably accomplished more than Roosevelt's; when assessed symbolically, however, TR's presidency effected a sharper change of national direction.[1] In contrast to the colorful Roosevelt, Wilson has been remembered as somewhat of a cold fish. If TR was all heart, Wilson supposedly was all brain; if TR exuded bravado, Wilson emitted the aura of an aloof and self-righteous scholar.[2] This stereotype was unfair to Wilson. But just as John Adams's reputation as a pompous Puritan was partially self-inflicted, so too Wilson cannot be entirely absolved of blame for his constipated caricature. As with Adams, Wilson's attempts at projecting dignity and moral superiority backfired.

Wilson enjoyed a meteoric political career. He was elected president of the United States barely two years after entering politics for the first time at the age of fifty-three. Nevertheless, he came to the White House remarkably well-prepared intellectually, thanks to a distinguished career as a political scientist and expert on Anglo-American government. In addition, the administrative experience he acquired as president of Princeton University, and (however briefly) as governor of New Jersey, provided him with practical lessons in executive leadership. Yet Wilson's presidency would not have been possible without Theodore Roosevelt. Had TR not split the Republican vote in 1912 by expropriating the party's Progressives, the Democrat Wilson might not have won the election. Furthermore, Wilson could not have enacted his ambitious reform agenda had not TR secured for the presidency extraordinary powers of executive leadership not seen since Lincoln, and not seen in peacetime since Andrew Jackson—if then. Wilson was formidable and committed enough, but he lacked TR's grandstanding personality and his heroic flair for blazing historical trails. Both TR and Wilson were motivated by a similar sense of morality and justice. But while TR relied on epic gestures to signal new policies and to mark the redrawn boundaries of acceptable behavior, Wilson relied more on bureaucratic system building and party discipline to achieve his ends. TR delighted in getting the mule's attention by whacking it with a two-by-four; Wilson took pride in training the mule. Neither man was particularly good at the other's specialty, though neither would have admitted this. One might judge Wilson's approach to be a more mature method of operation; yet it is more useful to observe that (like the destructive and constructive stages of revolutions) each method played its necessary role in the process of sustainable reform. Hence TR's dramatic confrontation with the financier J. P. Morgan, during which he signaled that government would no longer serve as the complacent tool of business, or his intervention (and effectively pro-labor stand) in the coal strike of 1902, or his creation of a Bureau of Corporations with its vital mission yet vague standards and little power, or his attempts at differentiating between "good trusts" and "bad trusts," or even his use of the presidential bully pulpit to preach against greed and materialism, paved the way for Wilson's establishment of the Federal Trade Commission, the Federal Reserve System, the passage of the Clayton Anti-Trust Act, long-overdue tariff reform, and a progressive income tax.[3] Even Wilson's desire to make the world safe for democracy and his postwar crusade for his Fourteen Points, including a League of Nations, revealed an impulse toward international idealism that grew logically from the regenerative imperialism of TR's presidency. Most important, it took a chief executive of TR's volcanic personality to wrestle power away from Congress, where it had resided for three decades; this gave Wilson the "parliamentary" power—as undisputed leader of the majority party—to implement his "second wave" of Progressive reforms.[4]

Thomas Woodrow Wilson (people stopped calling him "Tommie" at about the same point in life that people stopped calling TR "Teedie") belonged to a part of the American gentry far removed from Theodore Roosevelt's Knickerbockers. Yet culturally, and perhaps psychologically, the similarities in their backgrounds were more important than the differences. Both men's fathers were pillars of their local societies; both fathers played humanitarian rather than martial roles in the Civil War; both families saw relatives fight on both sides of that war; both Teedie and Tommie overcame childhood handicaps (asthma, dyslexia); both were inculcated with a sense of noblesse oblige, a belief in moral absolutes, a Whig interpretation of history, an admiration for great men, and a cultural identification with Anglo civilization. Wilson was born in Virginia, where his father, a transplanted Ohioan with Scotch Irish roots, was a Presbyterian minister and educator; his mother was born in England and was herself the daughter of a Scottish Presbyterian minister. While Wilson always considered himself to be a southerner, his southern roots were shallow, and he spent virtually his entire adult life in the North. In addition, he sided with the Union cause in the Civil War: "Because I love the South, I rejoice in the failure of the Confederacy"; and in such areas as education, economic development, and to a lesser degree race relations, he wanted the South to become more like the North.[5] He matched TR's Ivy League education by attending Princeton, and like TR he halfheartedly studied law after graduation (though unlike TR, he went on to halfheartedly practice it). But while TR entered politics early, Wilson entered the Johns Hopkins graduate school and received his Ph.D. in 1886 at age twenty-nine. After short stints teaching at Bryn Mawr and Wesleyan, Wilson joined the Princeton faculty, where in addition to his scholarly achievements he became the most popular lecturer on campus. Nevertheless, it is misleading to think of Wilson as an academic who converted to politics in middle age. Wilson always yearned for political office (as a law student he printed business cards identifying himself as a U.S. senator). But lacking TR's wealth, gregarious personality, and uncontrollable addiction to a life of action, he failed to summon the practical drive required to create his own political opportunities. Almost as a consolation prize, Wilson became the foremost political scientist of his generation, and in the process he grew increasingly enamored of Edmund Burke.

No Vulgar Conservative

Wilson's introduction to Burke came early. When not quite twenty years old, he recorded his noncommittal response to a sketch of Burke's character: "Knowing little of the French Revolution and the history of the latter part of the 18th century I cannot say whether Burke's actions at that time were consistent or not." Yet as a college student he recognized Burke as one of the "greatest and truest" orators, and he advised in the *Princetonian*: "Only as the constant companions of Demosthenes, Cicero, Burke, Fox, Canning and Webster, can we hope to become orators." Shortly thereafter, his mother wrote him: "Your father wishes to send you the enclosed article on Burke." In one of his first professional essays, Wilson quoted Burke, and asked: "Who could not sit at the feet of Burke and learn the principles of legislation?" By 1883 Wilson had not only read Morley's biography of Burke, but had purchased a set of Burke's *Works.* He first demonstrated a critical appraisal in 1884, telling his fiancée that "Burke lived too much with books to know what the French Revolution meant. . . . You'll never find in a *cloister* a fulcrum for any lever which can budge the world."[6] And when Wilson visited England in 1896, one of his pilgrimages was to Burke's tomb in the Beaconsfield church. "My plan," he informed his wife, "is to be in Beaconsfield on Sunday, and attend service in the church where Burke is buried."[7] A few days later, like George Bancroft before him, Wilson shared his impressions of the experience:

> I reached Beaconsfield yesterday forenoon, and was not long in finding what I was in search of. Burke is buried in the church, and with him not only his son and his wife (who survived him more than twenty years) but also his brother Richard. There is a simple, a very simple, tablet in the wall of the plain church, recording the fact of burial without comment or sentiment,—that is all. In the churchyard stands a somewhat elaborate monument to the poet Waller. The local policeman of the quaint village pointed that out readily enough but did not know where Burke was buried.[8]

Wilson seemed surprised that the Beaconsfield locals did not take more obvious pride in Burke: neither in the way they marked his grave, nor in the way they watched over it. Such a reaction is understandable; disappointment is the usual result when the world slights one of our personal heroes. Moreover, one should not exaggerate Burke's influence on Wilson, whose English pilgrimages also included shrines associated with Burns, Wordsworth, Adam Smith, and Walter Bagehot. In fact, scholars have estimated that Bagehot's influence was greater than Burke's during the early part of Wilson's career. And it is likely that Bagehot—a prominent social scientist who edited the London *Economist*—spoke to Wilson's scientific and analytical side while Burke spoke to his intuitive, traditional, inspirational, and rhetorical side. It is also possible that Bagehot's preoccupation with evolution and inevitable progress fed Wilson's liberal optimism, while Burke's Old Whig caution fed his anxiety over social unrest and disorder. In any event, the first of Wilson's two major lectures on Burke presented the French Revolution as a warning to American democracy.[9]

In "Edmund Burke: The Man and His Times" (1893), Wilson marveled at Burke's timeless relevance, and he sought "to account for him as we should wish to penetrate the secrets of the human spirit and know the springs of genius." Fully half of Wilson's lecture related the biographical details of Burke's life, with emphasis on Burke's innate talent, his energy, and his independent spirit. Wilson's first clear assessment of Burke's thinking offered what has since become a platitude of Burkean scholarship: his rejection of abstract theory. Burke's writings "are not purely intellectual productions: there is no page of abstract reasoning. . . . His mind works upon concrete objects. . . . Noble generalizations, it is true, everywhere broaden his matter. . . . But look, and you shall see that his generalizations are never derived from abstract premises. . . . He is not constructing systems of thought, but simply stripping thought of its accidental features. He is even deeply impatient of abstractions in political reasoning, so passionately is he devoted to what is practicable." Wilson correctly observed that in place of speculation Burke relied on moral principles: "[Burke] was afraid of abstract system in political thought, for he perceived that questions of government are moral questions, and that questions of morals cannot always be squared with rules of logic."[10] In noting this Wilson revealed a kinship between the dilemmas of his own political philosophy and those of Burke (and for that matter, those of TR). That is, they each were torn between the impulse to reason, analyze, and engage in logical argument, and the impulse to rely on moral strictures, intuitive judgment, and tradition.

Along similar lines, Wilson's confident declaration that "from first to last Burke's thought is conservative" was less solid than it seemed. In a passage reminiscent of Albert Dicey's defanging of Burkean conservatism in the *Nation*, Wilson equated Burke's conservatism with responsible reform, the restoration of traditional liberties, and a rejection of radicalism. For instance, on America Burke was "with the colonies, against the mother country; but his object was not revolutionary." In the case of Hastings and India, Burke "meant to save the empire . . . by administering it uprightly and in a liberal spirit." And in the case of British government reform, Burke's position was "cleanse Parliament of . . . corruption, and it [will] be restored to something like its pristine excellence as an instrument of liberty." When it came to the French Revolution, Wilson concluded that Burke had been misled both by his excessive aversion to risk and his ignorance of the situation: "Burke was doubtless too timid, and in practical judgement often mistaken. Measures which in reality would operate only as salutary and needed reformations he feared because of the element of change that was in them. He erred when he supposed that progress can in all its stages be made without changes which seem to go even to the substance." As to the factual details: "Let us admit . . . that with reference to France herself he was mistaken. . . . Let us concede that he did not understand the condition of France, and therefore did not see how inevitable that terrible revolution was." Even granting these failures, Burke was worthy of heed because on a more fundamental level he was wrong for the right reasons—even for critical reasons of broad application: "He was not defending France . . . he was defending England:—and the things he hated were truly hateful."[11]

> He hated the French revolutionary philosophy and deemed it unfit for free men. And that philosophy is in fact radically evil and corrupting. No state can ever be conducted on its principles. For it holds that government is a matter of contract and deliberate argument, whereas in fact it is an institute of habit, bound together by innumerable threads of association, scarcely one of which has been deliberately placed. It holds that the object of government is liberty, whereas the true object of government is justice. . . . It assumes that government can be made over at will, but assumes it without the slightest historical foundation. For governments have never been successfully and permanently changed except by slow modification operating from generation to generation.[12]

This was not only a vindication of Burke, but a rejection of the philosophy of Paine and Jefferson and a repudiation of the American liberal tradition. Such a stance does not square with Wilson's image as a Progressive democrat, and it demonstrates that—like many cultural conservatives of the Victorian gentry—Wilson came to progressivism late. Arthur Link has concluded that Wilson's philosophy was first characterized by "a sort of academic conservatism," followed later by a period of "political and economic conservatism," which only yielded to "militant progressivism" well after 1900. Hence Wilson's transformation from conservative to liberal did not occur until the eve of his entry into active politics. Eventually he would praise the Sage of Monticello, and call for Democrats to "act in the spirit of Jefferson."[13] But during the tumultuous years of agrarian populism and labor radicalism, Wilson clearly hoped American society would cling to its British roots and follow Burke's lead: "The history of England is a continuous thesis against revolution; and Burke would have been no true Englishman, had he not roused himself, even fanatically . . . to keep such puerile doctrine out." Furthermore, Wilson saw universal value in the British example, and in Burke's moral approach to politics: "It is both better and easier to reform than to tear down and reconstruct. This is unquestionably the message of Englishmen to the world, and Burke utters it with incomparable eloquence. A man of sensitive imagination and elevated moral sense . . . he stood in the midst of the English nation speaking its moral judgements upon affairs."[14]

In addition to his endorsement of Burke's political principles, Wilson subscribed to the common Victorian view that Burke was to be admired separately for the *way* he said things: "Though his life was devoted to affairs with a constant and unalterable passion, the radical features of Burke's mind were literary. . . . He got knowledge out of books and . . . his mind craved to work its constructive and imaginative effects upon [it]. . . . Burke is not literary because he takes from books, but because he makes books, transmuting what he writes into literature. It is this inevitable literary quality, this sure mastery of style, that mark the man, as much as his thought itself."[15] At some point in Wilson's career, Burke not only displaced Walter Bagehot as Wilson's political guiding light, but he also became his practical model of human genius. This was evident in a letter to Wilson from his first wife, in which she spoke of her pride in his abilities: "[You have] the orator's gift,—the 'personal magnetism' and *all* those gifts which go to make a born leader of men, combined with powers of thought of such a kind that [you] must undoubtedly rank as a *genius*, no less than Burke himself."[16]

Fittingly, Wilson's second lecture on Burke (delivered at Johns Hopkins in 1898) delved more deeply into the nature of the man. Wilson sounded much like TR when he asserted that "Burke makes as deep an impression upon our hearts as upon our minds. . . . [He] was great not so much by reason of what he said or did as by reason of what he was." For a look at the "real Burke" (his term) Wilson chose not the monumental *Reflections*, but the more tragically personal *Letter to a Noble Lord* (1796). Wilson restated his conviction that although Burke was wrong about the revolution's ultimate value to France, he was entirely justified in condemning its principles and in fearing the spread of those principles to England: "The revolution was France's salvation: without it she could not have been set in the way of a free life and a reformed and purified gov't. Frightful as were its excesses, they were but the violent purgings of a wholesome and cleansing disease, and Burke with his knowledge of France and of affairs ought to have seen it." However, so "vulgar" had been the potential "infection" that Burke could not be blamed for his unduly alarmist rhetoric or his blindness to the facts: "If his excitement rose beyond measure in the struggle, who shall say it was an unnatural excitement, or an unhallowed? . . . Who shall say how much this vehement Irishman did to keep ['the dreadful contagion'] out?"[17] In what amounted to a lunatic fringe exemption, Wilson tolerated the radicalism of the revolution as a useful catalyst for liberal progress in France. But he condemned the substance—the ideology—of Jacobin radicalism, and opposed its spread to England. Wilson's position stemmed from his hatred of disorder and radicalism, and his deep admiration for the antirevolutionary British political tradition. In this he was displaying a Burkean instinct that was as old as the American Federalists, and which would later be adopted by Cold War conservatives: factual details were not the issue; the intuitive recognition of evil was what mattered. In this context—and counter to the stereotype—Woodrow Wilson favored guts over brains, or instinctive reaction rather than dispassionate analysis. As Wilson had implied in his earlier lecture, since Burke on France had been wrong for the right reasons, his philosophical position remained valid.

On other grounds, Wilson saw Burke's *Letter* as "a wonderfully perfect mirror in which to see the man and the meaning of his life," because in it Burke justified his public career. The New World democratic side of Wilson (and of his American lecture audience) could appreciate Burke's meritorious rise from comparatively humble beginnings, just as it could identify with his liberal support for the American colonies. Hence Burke's poignant summation of his own achievements, in contrast to those of his high-born critic, the Duke of Bedford, played well in the egalitarian culture of the United States. Yet the more conservative and traditionalist side of Wilson (and of Victorian America) could also find comfort in Burke's criticism of Bedford for his support of the French Revolution, with its ideology that "threaten[ed] to lay waste the whole moral and in a great degree the whole physical world." In addition, Wilson lauded the emotive force and literary excellence of Burke's *Letter*, and—in a particularly imaginative twist—he argued that the evocative quality of Burke's writing made it less speculative and abstract: "Burke is taking you straight to the uplands of the region of thought in which he finds himself,—not so much by deliberation, it would seem, as by instinct." Wilson claimed that Burke's metaphoric use of castles, towers, oaks, and the like enabled him to keep the focus of his essay on the real world, despite his lofty language:

> Burke's thought has, therefore, a certain *visible* quality. It does not seem wholly bred of the mind. It has always about it the scenery and

> atmosphere of action. . . . If images abound, it is because the mind that here speaks conceives the world always thus in concrete and almost tangible shapes. It is because its eye is ever upon the object of its thought. It is not reflecting; it is observing. . . . Its retina is crowded with images and deeply touched with colour, like a little world.

Finally, though with a touch of evasion, Wilson concluded: "It is this vivid realization of the world of fact and spirit as it is that makes Burke's thought seem so conservative, and makes us wonder whether, after all, we should call him a liberal or not. . . . There are visions of the future in [his words], as well as of the past."[18]

Interestingly, Wilson's Johns Hopkins lecture on Burke was followed the next day by his lecture on Walter Bagehot. Among other things, the Bagehot lecture confirmed Wilson's greater admiration for Burke, since he portrayed Bagehot as a follower in Burke's footsteps. To Wilson, Bagehot shared "the social imagination" of Burke and Carlyle, and both Bagehot and Burke were rarities because they obtained their "precocious power" to see "clearly and with . . . penetration" while still in their twenties. Bagehot often sounded like Burke, as when he proclaimed that "the first duty of society, is the preservation of society. By the sound work of old-fashioned generations, by the singular painstaking of the slumberers in churchyards, by dull care, by stupid industry, a certain social fabric exists." Occasionally Bagehot even spoke of Burke, who "first taught the world at large that politics are made of time and place . . . to be determined in every case by the exact exigencies of that case,—in plain English, by sense and circumstances." Crucially, Bagehot agreed with Burke about the "national character" of the French, who were "apt to conceive a great design" or be "swayed by sensations," and were prone to "the sacrifice of old habits to present emergencies." The French simply *thought too much*; as a result they tried to alter things that were better left alone. By contrast, he characterized the English national character as "dull" and "stupid"—and he meant it as a compliment. (As Wilson noted: "The man is a conservative, but his wit is radical.") "Stupidity," in Bagehot's view, was synonymous with "large roundabout common-sense," "good judgement," and "rational forbearance"—all sensible English traits. "A real Frenchman can't be stupid," according to Bagehot, because stupidity was "nature's favorite resource for preserving steadiness of conduct and consistency of opinion: it enforces concentration; people who learn slowly learn only what they must."[19] Clearly this Burkean interpretation of Bagehot revealed that, as the turn of the century approached, Wilson was firmly entrenched in his conservative outlook.

This was equally evident in his address "Princeton in the Nation's Service," delivered as part of the university's sesquicentennial celebration in late 1896.

Coincidentally, this event preceded by just two weeks the watershed election that pitted the establishment figure William McKinley against the evangelical populist William Jennings Bryan. Perhaps the passions of Bryan's "cross of gold" campaign contributed to Wilson's theme of social stability and incremental (that is, nonrevolutionary) progress. Among Wilson's injunctions to the university were: "Help men, but do not delude them," and, "Prepare young men to be wise." He cautioned against scientific speculation, and on that score he alluded to the philosophes: "There is no radical like your learned radical, bred in the schools; and thoughts of revolution have in our times been harbored in Universities as naturally as they were once nourished among the Encyclopedists." On the positive side, Wilson recalled the American Revolution as having been "as fundamentally conservative as the revolution of 1688 or the extortion of Magna Charta. . . . Its object was the preservation of liberties, to keep the natural course of English development in America clear of impediment. It was meant, not in rebellion, but in self-defense." Wilson quoted Burke's *Speech on Conciliation* and endorsed its premise that the American Revolution "was a keeping of faith with the past," in contrast to an English government that had "grown so tyrannous and forgetful of its great traditions." He praised the founding fathers, who were "not radicals" nor "forgetful of the old principles," and who had "built" from "old stuffs whose grain and fibre they knew." In this spirit, Wilson lectured his contemporaries on the error of America's obsession with originality: "The world's memory must be kept alive, or we shall never see an end to its old mistakes. We are in danger to lose our identity and become infantile in every generation." Worse, "The past is discredited among [the masses], because they played no choosing part in it. It was their enemy, they say, and they will not learn of it. They wish to break with it for ever: its lessons are tainted to their taste." And he added that, "In America especially, we run perpetually this risk of newness."[20]

Wilson also applied a Burkean argument to combat the growing tendency toward scientism in the academy, which he saw as a harmful side effect of modernization. Hence he warned educators not to instill a hubris of rationality in their students. Like most conservatives, Wilson believed too much thinking led to dangerous experimentation:

> Science,—our science,—is new. It is a child of the nineteenth century. It has transformed the world and owes little debt of obligation to any past age. It has driven mystery out of the Universe. . . .
>
> . . . We speak of society as an organism, and believe that we can contrive for it a new environment which will change the very nature of its constituent parts; worst of all, we believe in the present and in the future more than in the past. . . .

> It has made the legislator confident that he can create and the philosopher sure that God cannot. Past experience is discredited and the laws of matter are supposed to apply to spirit and the makeup of society. . . .
>
> I should tremble to see social reform led by men who had breathed [such noxious, intoxicating gas]: I should fear nothing better than utter destruction from a revolution conceived and led in the scientific spirit. . . .
>
> We have broken with the past and have come into a new world. Do you wonder, then, that I ask for the old drill, the old memory of times gone by, the old schooling in precedent and tradition . . . as a preparation for leadership in the days of social change?[21]

Scientism was yet another variant of Enlightenment overreach, an outgrowth of speculative theory. As such, it was a natural predator of tradition. With slight adjustments, Wilson's defensive sentiments could have been uttered by Rufus Choate, E. L. Godkin, or any number of nineteenth-century American Burkeans. Given such company (and in a twist on what was earlier said about Burke), one might suggest that had Wilson died at fifty, his legacy would be that of conservative traditionalism rather than Progressive reform or organizational modernization. But while Wilson continued to cite Burke for the rest of his life, he eventually came to emphasize the more proto-liberal side of his thought—while never changing his view of Burke as a voice rooted in morality.

Wilson (like TR) was more impressed with Burke's insight into the tempers, character, and behavior of men than he was with Burke's opinions on the architecture of governments or the mechanics of policy. For example, Wilson's lectures on Burke were devoid of the utilitarian interpretation that was then so widespread on both sides of the Atlantic. And in his other writings, Wilson (who cited Bagehot for utilitarian applications) cited Burke mostly for his general wisdom about human nature. In both his never-published "Government by Debate" (1882) and his most important book, *Congressional Government* (1885), Wilson quoted the passage from Burke's *Thoughts on the Present Discontents* that rebuked the modern adage "Not men, but measures," and which argued that personal conduct could make or ruin any form of government: "The laws reach but a very little way. Constitute Government how you please, infinitely the greater part of it must depend upon the exercise of powers, which are left at large to the prudence and uprightness of ministers of state. Even all the use and potency of the laws depends upon them. Without them your commonwealth is no better than a scheme upon paper; and not a living, active, effective organization." Later in *Congressional*

Government, Wilson allowed Burke to continue this argument: "When men are not acquainted with each other's principles, nor experienced in each other's talents, nor at all practiced in their mutual habitudes and dispositions by joint efforts of business; [with] no personal confidence, no friendship, no common interest subsisting among them; it is evidently impossible that they can act a public part with uniformity, perseverance, or efficacy." Yet Wilson did not ignore the bottom-up threats to responsible government. When he recalled Burke's contention that "the value, spirit, and essence of the House of Commons consists in its being the image of the feelings of the nation," he likened it to the U.S. House of Representatives, and expressed relief that the more dignified Senate was there to curb the excesses of "popular sentiment." Elsewhere, when Wilson quoted *Present Discontents* in an 1891 letter, the focus returned to personal character and disinterested service. Referring to the "moral qualities" and "wisdom" of a magazine editor, Wilson remarked: "Whenever I think of such men I remember that passage in which Burke says, 'When I see a man acting a desultory and disconnected part, with as much detriment to his own fortune as prejudice to the cause of any party, I am not persuaded that he is right; but I am ready to believe he is in earnest.'"[22] Burke's essay on *Present Discontents* was known above all else for its pathbreaking justification of political parties. It is therefore significant that Wilson the political scientist viewed it as a tract on public virtue instead.

Intellectually, Wilson's opinions on Edmund Burke would have been worth noting even if he had risen no higher in life than his Princeton professorship. But because he became president of the United States, his admiration for Burke acquired added importance. To the extent that presidents are reflections of the societies that elect them (or at least they reflect the values and ideals of their constituencies), presidential heroes serve as shadow heroes for the body politic. Not that Wilson had been the only president to select Burke as a mentor. During the Progressive era, for instance, one writer noted that "Garfield was a student of Burke, and it has been said that Garfield in Congress was Burke transferred from the British Parliament." But James Garfield—who was president for seven months in 1881—hardly compared in consequence to Roosevelt or Wilson, who enjoyed longer and more eventful terms of office.[23] One of Wilson's distinctions was that he was the first president since the founding era (and the last president thus far) to have thought long and hard about the constitutional structure of the United States. His *Congressional Government* criticized the relative power of the legislative branch and the relative weakness of the president and cabinet. Hence in terms of ministerial (or executive) efficacy, he judged the American system inferior to the British parliamentary alternative. Given Burke's interest in balancing the branches of government, one might have expected the issue of practical constitutionalism to form a bond between Wilson and Burke. That it did not was yet another indication that Wilson looked to Bagehot for solutions to modern problems of political science, while he looked to Burke for timeless wisdom on the general philosophy of political leadership.[24]

Liberal Turn

What is more, Wilson's ideological transition after 1900 altered his relationship to Burke's thought. Or to put it another way: circumstances caused him to alter what he needed to take from Burke in order to bolster his own arguments. Early in his Princeton presidency (1903) Wilson—while retaining his conservative admiration for Burke's "never . . . philosophical" perspective, which recognized that in politics "reason plays but a small part"—also began to exhibit respect for the liberal spirit of democracy by quoting Burke's "those are free who think they are." Variations on this "freedom" quote would become Wilson's most repeated Burkean sentiment. In his *Constitutional Government* (1908), Wilson combined both Burke's veneration of tradition *and* his pragmatic flexibility in reference to the Magna Charta, the Declaration of Independence, and the Virginia Constitution: "Every generation, as Burke said, sets before itself some favorite object which it pursues as the very substance of its liberty and happiness. The ideals of liberty cannot be fixed from generation to generation. . . . Liberty in fixed and unalterable law would be no liberty at all." The next year, in a speech on liberal education, Wilson again offered a Burkean aphorism that was at once flexible and antirationalist: "Institutions must be adjusted to human nature; of which reason contributes a part, but by no means the principal part."[25] And he suggested a nonanalytical approach to politics that was reminiscent of Burke's mystical evocations, Whitman's transcendental predictions (that poets rather than presidents shall be our "common referee"), and Choate's romantic yearnings for a literary history of the United States in the tradition of Sir Walter Scott: "The best expounders of politics I have ever read outside the pages of Burke have been some of the English poets, who have understood politics better than any systematic writer on that subject with whom I am acquainted. They have felt those great impulses of life which really constitute the consciousness of the nation."[26]

In another speech on education in 1910, Wilson joined the Progressive "revolt against formalism" by observing: "It is as Burke long ago said; the study of law is one of the best of mental disciplines, but it does not in the same degree liberalize the understanding; and so the lawyer merely sticks to the process which stands in the way of progress."[27] By 1914, Wilson (now president of the United States) explained to an interviewer "why a writer was wrong who said he could not be a progressive Democrat if he admired Edmund Burke, and explained his liking for Burke and quoted much from Burke's orations." This was something he did quite often, according to his confidant Colonel House. In a meeting with anti-preparedness leaders in 1916, Wilson contended: "I think in such affairs as we are now discussing, the circumstances are the logic. I remember a sentence of Burke which runs something to the effect: 'If you ask me wherein the wisdom of a certain policy consists, I will say that it consists of the circumstances of that policy.'" That same year Wilson quoted Burke's "famous saying . . . that you can't bring an indictment against a whole people," and two years later he told foreign journalists that he was fond of quoting Burke that "If any man asks me what is a free government, I reply 'A government which those living under it will guard.'"[28]

Once Wilson entered active politics as a Progressive, his citations of Burke were mostly ideologically opposed to the conservative references of his Princeton lectures.[29] After leaving the White House, he spoke of Burke "as knowing, profoundly, the 'wisdom of concession.'" On one occasion, he used "the word *expediency* as Burke would have used it, to mean the wisdom of circumstances." A few months later, he informed a visitor that he had been rereading Burke, "endeavoring to sum up in a phrase the philosophy of expediency," and settled on "the wisdom of circumstances." Wilson in retirement considered writing a biography of Burke, though he dropped the idea, possibly because of ill health. And in a draft of a never-delivered speech, written just twelve days before he died in 1924, Wilson made a note to "See Burke on party," and his text included the line: "I shall take the liberty of quoting in the incomparable English of Edmund Burke" (which was followed by a page reference from Burke's *Works*).[30]

There is little doubt that Wilson was intellectually indebted to Burke; certainly he read and quoted him often. But ultimately Wilson chose the ideology of liberalism in politics, economics, foreign policy, and diplomacy, notwithstanding his cultural (and in some respects social and religious) conservatism. While Wilson hated the speculative radicalism of the French and Bolshevik Revolutions, he learned to accommodate their victories—and he was optimistic that democracy would eventually triumph in Russia. Unlike later Cold War Burkeans, who—like Burke on France—dug in their heals and fought the revolution head-on, Wilson took a realpolitik approach.[31] Like TR, he believed reform liberalism could alleviate the threat of communism's spread. In a 1923 *Atlantic Monthly* essay entitled "The Road Away from Revolution," he wrote:

> Perhaps if we take the case of the Russian Revolution, the outstanding event of its kind in our age, we may find a good deal of instruction for our judgement of present critical situations and circumstances. . . .
>
> What gave rise to the Russian Revolution? . . . The systematic denial to the great body of Russians of the rights and privileges which all normal men desire and must have if they are to be contented and within the reach of happiness. . . . Only the powerful were suffered to secure the rights or even to gain access to the means of material success. . . .
>
> Is the capitalistic system unimpeachable? . . . Is it not . . . too true that capitalists have often seemed to regard the men whom they used as mere instruments of profit . . . to exploit with as slight cost to themselves as possible?
>
> . . . Are offences against high morality and citizenship . . . [or] the blame for the present discontent and turbulence . . . wholly on the side of those who revolt?
>
> The world has been made safe for democracy. . . . But democracy has not yet made the world safe against irrational revolution. That supreme task, which is nothing less than the salvation of civilization, now faces democracy.[32]

Wilson concluded with a plea for justice, sympathy, helpfulness, and a "forgoing of self-interest in order to promote the welfare, happiness, and contentment of others and of the community as a whole."[33] In contrast to Wilson's 1893 lecture on Burke, which repudiated the American liberal tradition, this essay could not have been more supportive of Jefferson's self-evident truths, or more sympathetic to the pursuit of happiness, or more akin to George Bancroft's criticism of a power structure that protected the "happy few." But now Wilson extended the practical application of such ideals to a new world order. That he was able to take Burke along with him, valuing his thoughts on expediency and popular opinion rather than his antirevolutionary bluster and veneration of tradition, testified to Wilson's ideological metamorphosis. While en route to the Paris peace conference to sell his Fourteen Points, he insisted that "the conservatives do not realize what forces are loose in the world at the present time. Liberalism is the only thing that can save civilization from chaos—from a flood of ultra-radicalism that will swamp the world. . . . Liberalism must be more liberal than ever before, it must even be radical, if civilization is to escape the typhoon."[34] Sadly, international liberalism—as Wilson conceived it—was not to be, and civilization would soon face another "typhoon" as a consequence. Domestically as well, liberalism, progressivism, and reform became nearly dormant after the Great War and would not revive for over a decade. When they resurfaced in the 1930s, they were mostly unattached to the moral traditions that were so central to the worldviews of Theodore Roosevelt and Woodrow Wilson—views that enjoyed an unbroken connection to the Whig vision of Edmund Burke. This in part explains why many surviving Progressives did not support Franklin Roosevelt's New Deal. The philosophical distinctions between early twentieth-century Progressives and post-1932 liberals have been discussed elsewhere, and it is enough for our purposes to observe that mid-twentieth-century liberalism had its roots and took its inspiration from sources other than the Burkean legacy. Moreover, due to the post–World War II rise of Cold War Burkean conservatives, Burke became increasingly identified with the antiliberal camp. In this respect, Woodrow Wilson was the last major American figure to apply a roughly equal balance of Burke's reformist and conservative expressions to contemporary affairs.

TR and Wilson have generally been accepted as liberal modernizers who prepared the way for a half century of reform-oriented government that (despite interruptions and setbacks) did not end until the 1980s. The more traditional and conservative aspects of both men's personalities have been de-emphasized in legend because they did not fit the "authorized" narrative of progress. Likewise their Anglocentrism has been forgotten because it conflicted with the exceptionalist nature of American history. This phenomenon has already been examined in TR's case, and here it should briefly be noted that Wilson displayed a similarly split sensibility. He believed that "typical Americans have all been Western men, with the exception of Washington," and he claimed that Jefferson had not been "a thorough American" because of "the strain of French philosophy that permeated and weakened all his thought."[35] Significantly, Wilson has been credited by some writers as a co-inventor (with his friend Frederick Jackson Turner) of the idea that America "was not the transplantation of European civilization to a fresh soil, but one born on native ground and made by hitherto unknown experiences."[36] And clearly Wilson intended an Americanization of the world, in the sense of replacing the "old ways" (his term) of Europe with America's democratic ideals in the aftermath of the Great War.

Yet no small measure of "British philosophy" permeated Wilson's own thought. His devotion to Burke, Bagehot, Gladstone, Smith, even Herbert Spencer (not to mention the purely literary figures), attests to this Anglo influence. Like TR, Wilson admired Macaulay, and he modeled his own *History of the American People* (1902) after the Englishman J. R. Green's popular

Short History of the English People (1874).[37] In fact, Wilson's intended "short history" grew into a five-volume saga that began by depicting the spread of British civilization in a vein (with its unstated Anglocentric premises) akin to TR's approach in *Winning of the West.* Wilson called his first chapter "Before the English Came"; he called his second chapter—which covered from 1607 to the 1690s, and which filled almost all of volume one—"The Swarming of the English"; it concluded by discussing the colonial consequences of England's "Protestant revolution" of 1688. (Incidentally, Wilson referred to or quoted Edmund Burke ten times in the first two volumes, in addition to providing a picture of him.)[38] Wilson—intentionally or not—often presented himself as a hyphenated American, publicly calling attention to his Scotch Irish roots (which were recent) and ascribing certain of his personal traits to his bloodline. Curiously, Wilson occasionally associated sociological tendencies with particular ethnic groups, and this would seem to fly in the face of the "native ground" Americanism that he seemed to endorse elsewhere. Yet this was just another example of the irreconcilable tug of war between traditionalism and exceptionalism that was still raging inside the minds of America's leaders in Wilson's generation.

Coda: Gathering Threats

Theodore Roosevelt, Woodrow Wilson, and their gentry contemporaries carried a romantic-traditionalist sensibility into the new century. But even for them, that sensibility proved to be a recessive trait. When push came to shove in the political arena, the more modern and liberal elements of their character usually won out. Unfortunately, it must also be noted that American society was changing at a pace that was too rapid for men of their ilk to accommodate. And "men of their ilk" no longer constituted the power elite. Not only did the gentry fail to dislodge the plutocrats, but capitalists were forced to share power with a host of new professionals, activist politicians, government bureaucrats, and newly empowered interest groups. Slowly over the decades, citizens other than men of northern European Protestant lineage would gain authority and influence. While the most dramatic breakthroughs toward a more egalitarian society were still years away, such phenomena as woman suffrage, the rise of Jewish and African American intellectuals, and the coalescing of urban "bohemian" circles served as harbingers of future challenges to the presumptive natural aristocracy. Though the Great War itself did not end Victorian culture in America, the energies it released helped accelerate the erosion of patriarchal traditionalism and of many long-accepted verities. The cultural dynamism of the 1920s probably drew much of its nervous energy from the traumas induced by mobilization, demobilization, insidious propaganda, postwar paranoia, the promise and failure of Wilsonian idealism, and the new cosmopolitanism that penetrated artistic and intellectual networks even as the nation lurched toward relative isolation.

All this had tremendous implications for the Burkean perspective, especially the conservative or traditionalist elements of it. Yet the post–World War I climate also proved that conservatism in America diverged sharply from the Burkean organic strain. The reactionary 1920s, which brought Prohibition, the resurgence of the Ku Klux Klan, the Scopes trial, the "return to normalcy" along with the return of the Republican old guard, and which heard Calvin Coolidge declare that the business of America was business (exactly the opposite of what TR and Wilson had been preaching), had no use for Burke's Whig brand of conservatism. Indeed, when the government honored Edmund Burke in 1922 by erecting his statue in Washington, D.C., it cited only his liberal "espousing [of] the cause of the American colonies in Parliament."[39] In 1920 *Living Age* suggested that the American rather than French Revolution was the relevant gateway to Burke's writing, and it linked Burke's passion for freedom with the philosophy of William Penn.[40] The decade's most influential work of American history, Charles and Mary Beard's *Rise of American Civilization*, followed this same liberal pattern: "Burke alone understood American affairs. . . . The burden of Burke's grand argument flowed from reason and moderation."[41] In 1925 the *Quarterly Journal of Speech* offered a nonpolitical assessment of Burke's rhetorical effectiveness, and in 1934 the *Political Science Quarterly* presented Burke not as a conservative sage, but as a participant in the progressive post-Lockean British discourse that took political thought "out of the realm of abstract theory" and into more "utilitarian" "common principles."[42]

But the story of Burke in America did not have this liberal (or nonideological) ending. Already in the interwar years there were harbingers of a future conservative appropriation of Burke. Irving Babbitt, an important conservative intellectual and a critic of Rousseauist "emotional naturalism," anticipated a post–World War II "new conservative" lament in 1924 by observing: "The modern political movement may be regarded in its most significant aspect as a battle between the spirit of Rousseau and that of Burke. Whatever the explanation, it is an indubitable fact that this movement has been away from Burke and towards Rousseau." Babbitt was especially irked by society's abandonment of Burke's "essentials of political wisdom." Hence he pessimistically suggested that Burke's brand of conservatism was no longer of great practical value: "If a true liberalism is to be successfully defended under present circumstances, it will not be altogether by Burke's method.

The battle for prejudice and prescription and a 'wisdom above reflection' has already been lost. It is no longer possible to wave aside the modernists as the mere noisy insects of the hour."[43]

In contrast to TR's or Wilson's criticism of plutocrats and other "interest groups" for their selfishness and lack of social responsibility, Babbitt was rejecting an entire Enlightenment-inspired liberal bias toward irreligious "naturalistic excess." The progressivism of TR and Wilson had been a political philosophy that was on the *offensive* against injustice and abuse; Babbitt's conservatism (or "new humanism") was a *defensive* philosophy erected against the modern liberal worldview. As earlier noted, the conservative Burke has always been more effective in America when used in arguments *against* some threat rather than *for* some cause. And Babbitt's appropriation of him served as an important reminder that liberalism, broadly defined, was the rising intellectual tide. Liberalism's new confidence had been captured in 1912 by the Progressive historian James Harvey Robinson when he suggested that history offered a guide to the "technique of progress" and that "the radical has not yet perceived the overwhelming value to him of a real understanding of the past. It is his weapon by right, and he should wrest it from the hand of the conservative."[44] Still, this gradual encroachment of modern-liberal sensibilities was not enough to spur a sustained counterattack from the right that required resurrecting Burke. It would take the explicitly ideological and apocalyptic climate of the Cold War to return Burke to his 1790s status as an antimodern reactionary.

Part III

Postwar America

Chapter 9

Modern Times

Conjunctions and Consensus

Given the success of Progressive reform and New Deal liberalism in the early decades of the twentieth century (and the technocratic, commercial, and cultural modernization that continued even during the 1920s), as well as the general blurring of Burke's American image, few could have predicted the postwar revival of aggressive Burkean conservatism. Ever since the early nineteenth century, attempts to import or adopt Burke's Anglo-traditionalist sensibility proved to be a fool's errand; America's cultural conservatives admitted this. But following the Second World War hundreds of books and articles about Burke were published, with the great majority emphasizing his conservative principles. Moreover, for the first time since the 1790s, his *Reflections on the Revolution in France* became the centerpiece (to some, virtually the be-all and end-all) of Burkean thought. Of course, few prewar Americans could have foreseen the Cold War, and the extent to which it pervaded the national consciousness.

Past as Prologue

In certain respects the Cold War began soon after World War I (with such events as the first "red scare" and American military intervention in Russia), though for some reason Burke was not called upon to fight it until a generation later. Communism had long been feared in the United States, yet even after 1917 the close analogy between communists and Jacobins was not a major theme. Thus the use of *Reflections* as a timeless antidote for "scientific" revolution was postponed. Surprisingly, given that the reduction of Burke to a simplified "father of modern conservatism" was mostly an American undertaking, the first bold portrait of Burke as a proto-anticommunist appeared in England in 1929. Arthur Baumann's *Burke: The Founder of Conservatism* echoed the new humanists' call for a "recurrence to first principles," and Baumann confessed: "I think that Burke was in the right. But then I am a Tory." He went on to observe that "the Russian Bolsheviks are the spiritual descendants of the French Jacobins, only far more successful." Baumann was ahead of his time in his employment of Burke not only against communism, but against "creeping socialism." He lambasted what conservatives now call the welfare state (calling it "socialist finance") and recalled Burke's criticism of the "plunder of the rich" in France, adding: "I am more afraid of evolution than revolution."[1]

Baumann mourned the demise of deference, and hated "the flotsam and jetsam of universal suffrage." He even condemned the granting of woman suffrage, characterizing it as "a leap into gynocracy." He further declared: "'The conservation of the ancient order of things'—why, Burke's words are a mockery to the present generation!"[2] Baumann's own Tory arguments (and he claimed that Tories were the inheritors of Burkean wisdom, because Old Whigs were conservatives) filled half his book; the second half contained Burke's *Letter to a Noble Lord*. Like Woodrow Wilson, Baumann lauded the literary quality of Burke's *Letter* (calling it "one of the most perfect pieces of composition"), but unlike even the pre-liberal Wilson, he did not admit Burke was misinformed about France. The greatest difference between the two Burkean admirers was that Wilson thought Burke's *Letter* contained "visions of the future, as well as the past," while Baumann dismissed as dangerous almost all of the political changes since Burke's time. He even imagined Burke's "spirit" returning to England and experiencing shock over the triumph of liberalism: "Burke . . . would find . . . the Duke of Bedford [the Noble Lord of his *Letter*], besides being mulcted of half his income by taxation, belonged to a branch of the legislature [the House of Lords] which the malice of radicals and the cowardice of Conservatives had reduced to an impotence hardly superior to that of the Roman senate under the Emperors." Although Baumann referred to Burke's "two speeches on the American War" in his brief preface, there was nowhere in his text any sense of Burke as a dedicated reformer. In presenting Burke's most reactionary side, Baumann anticipated many of the arguments that would dominate Burkean scholarship in the United States after the Second World War.[3]

While England in the 1920s and 1930s witnessed a revival of interest in Edmund Burke—though without any unifying theme—America mostly lost interest in him.[4] This was understandable. Not only were the specific issues on which Burke had spoken settled by the twentieth century, but the death of the Victorians ended the (mostly cultural) legacy of a Burkean sensibility in America. Even Burke's literary and rhetorical methods were apparently outdated, and no longer served as aspirational models. When Burke's legacy was revived after World War II, it was an exercise in intellectual partisanship. In itself this was not unprecedented. What was new was the one-sided nature of the "debate." While Burke's conservative champions adjusted their image of "the father of conservatism" among themselves, the "opposition" displayed little interest. For liberal intellectuals, the action—and the real "fathers" of their age—resided elsewhere.

Nevertheless, almost no intellectual movement begins from absolute zero. Minor antecedents of the Cold War Burkean resurgence in America can be found. The Catholic *Commonweal* had claimed in 1929 that Burke "was surely right in his warning: 'The age of chivalry is gone!'" And it revived the mother of all conservative topics by asking: "Do we not see a vaster, a nobler Burke in those sentences [on] the French Revolution which announce the reaction of a genuine romantic outlook against the diverse pseudo-romanticisms of chaotic dreamers?"[5] In greater detail, and with more obvious passion, the *Saturday Review of Literature* presaged the Cold War perspective by asserting: "The propertyless communist state with its deliberate breach with the past, could he have foreseen it, would have appalled Burke." Yet the essay betrayed its 1933 publication date by pitting Burke against fascism as well: "Only a little less horrifying to him would have been the fascist state. It is true that such a state preserves—indeed glorifies—a national memory, but it stands for power [in a single organ] . . . not through several naturally developed and connected organs." After invoking the French Revolution as the historical parallel, the article cautioned:

> Today, when men of dialectic bear down upon us, we should remind ourselves of Burke's counter-statements. . . . At present, when abstractions and revolutions in the name of abstractions are the order of the day, it is well to think on [Burke's] vision of a flesh and blood society that has progenitors and posterity and to hold the humanity of it against "the organic *moleculae* of a disbanded people" which is being offered us by so many able and earnest people today.[6]

Still, even adding in the new humanists, such examples merely indicate that the Burkean conservative-traditionalist sensibility had not succumbed to extinction. Surely they were no clear signal of that sensibility's imminent expansion.

Challenge to Liberalism

In light of Burke's relative absence from the American scene during the era of the world wars, and given the dubious relevance of Old Whig attitudes in the "atomic age," the "space age," the "youth culture," the "mass market," and in the climate of "consensus," "conformity," and the "organizational man," one might have expected Burke's presence to continue to diminish, and his writings to be of academic interest alone. If Burke was already (in some respects) an anachronism during most of the nineteenth century, surely he was a harmless museum piece by the mid-twentieth.

But at least three factors converged to make Burke timely again. First, his voluminous correspondence (previously inaccessible) was released to scholars in 1948; this resulted in the publication of his letters and in new assessments of his work.[7] Second, an almost desperate effort by conservative intellectuals to counter modern liberalism spawned a subspecies of mostly Roman Catholic writers intent on invoking Burke as a champion of the "natural law" tradition. The third and most important factor was the rise of a Cold War mentality in America, which encouraged writers to apply Burke's anti-Jacobin arguments in the anticommunist crusade. The first factor, taken independently, was a "neutral" event that had no particular ideological valence. The second factor, while more political, probably lacked sufficient strength (and a diverse enough constituency) to spark anything other than a "cult" version of a Burkean revival. But the third factor—the Cold War mentality—was a mass phenomenon that could inflame the passions in ways that discussions of natural law or reassertions of traditionalism could not. The Cold War put Burke back in business in America, though it also distorted his image. Moreover, the simultaneous appearance of all three factors enabled them to reinforce each other, causing interest in Burke to achieve critical mass.

Yet this does not completely address the question of "why Burke, and why now?" Certainly there were other ways to fight liberalism and communism, and names other than Burke's could have inspired the attack. The reasons why Burke was uniquely qualified for conservative sainthood will be examined shortly. But for the moment suffice it to say that (as with John Adams and Federalist conservatism) grand philosophies needed big names attached to them, and that conservatives by the late 1940s felt defeated, endangered, and locked out of the American intellectual mainstream. Despite the political and economic conservatism of the twenties, liberalism was almost universally acknowledged as the secular creed of the twentieth century—or even as the vital force of United States history since the revolution. Such prominent postwar writers as Lionel Trilling, Arthur Schlesinger Jr., Louis Hartz,

Clinton Rossiter, and Allen Guttmann agreed that liberalism dominated conservatism in America. In the mid-1950s, Richard Hofstadter noted "how uneasy Americans still are in the presence of candidly conservative ideas." And as late as the 1970s the conservative publisher Henry Regnery described the "past two generations" as "this liberal age."[8] Influential (and to conservatives, infamous) intellectuals like Margaret Mead and especially John Dewey had helped undermine the moral certainty that supported traditional social behavior. Politically, though New Deal liberalism lost momentum and even suffered some setbacks, its essential framework was preserved even after Republicans recaptured the White House and Congress in 1952. Left-of-center reform was stuck in neutral, but no significant right-of-center agenda other than anticommunism (which liberals shared) was implemented. A telling indicator of this liberal triumph was that Russell Kirk's *The Conservative Mind* (1953)—in retrospect a seminal book of the "new conservative" movement—originally carried the defeatist title "The Conservative Rout," with the equally downbeat "The Long Retreat" as an alternative.[9] Meanwhile, Trilling's *Liberal Imagination* (1949) made the point more directly: "In the United States at this time liberalism is not only the dominant but even the sole intellectual tradition. For it is the plain fact that nowadays there are no conservative or reactionary ideas in general circulation."[10]

There were, however, conservative intellectuals who were eager to broadcast their contrapuntal philosophies, and the unsettled postwar climate gave them an opportunity. Yet just as one should not follow Trilling in exaggerating the triumph of liberalism, one should not overplay the importance or the immediate impact of the postwar conservative revival. It took decades for conservatism to make its way out of the intellectual and political wilderness, and the new conservatives of the 1950s did not necessarily appear bound for success. Indeed, by the early 1970s, intellectual, social, and cultural liberalism seemed more firmly established than ever. Though an antiliberal backlash was already under way politically, its eventual victory was far from certain. Nonetheless, since a conservative political ascendency did emerge beginning around 1980, the postwar conservative intellectuals deserve substantial credit for strengthening the ideological foundations of right-of-center thought. In fact, their collective efforts represented one of the most effective examples of intellectual entrepreneurship in American history. Unlike their liberal counterparts, conservative thinkers did not ride the international tidal wave of modernization. Instead they chose the more difficult task of swimming against it. Coincidentally, their mission was much the same as Burke's had been when he attacked the Enlightenment frame of mind, which was the international liberal tidal wave of his own day.

The intellectual dynamism of the twentieth century centered on replacing the concept of certainty with the inevitability of uncertainty and the novel concept of relativism, and the *ideal of certainty* became increasingly outmoded. That at least was the case for liberal intellectuals in the vanguard of Western thought. But for conservatives, certainty—especially moral certainty—was a key ingredient of civilization, and they were unwilling to dispense with it, or to allow others to dispense with it. Given the recent horrors of Nazism and fascism, and the continuing horrors of communism, postwar conservatives feared the consequences of ideologically imposed regimes that departed radically from any nation's inherited tradition. To them, the war confirmed the dangers of unchecked secular utopianism, just as the Reign of Terror and the rise of Napoleon had done at the end of the eighteenth century. This helps explain why the immediate aftermath of World War II and the first decade of the Cold War provided a window of opportunity for the propagation of conservative ideas that had existed quietly since before the war. And it was not just revolutions or coups that worried conservatives; it was also the incremental decline of civilization at the hands of bureaucratization, secularization, creeping socialism, abstract expressionism, unnerving science, decolonization, and other engines of destabilization. To be sure, from the conservative point of view the postwar decades really did witness a disintegration of the social order. The 1960s and early 1970s accelerated the damage with the civil rights movement, liberal court rulings, the counterculture, the sexual revolution, the women's movement, the gay rights movement, the environmental movement, the explosive growth of government, rock music, drug use, "permissiveness," the decline of academic standards, the erosion of civility, the vogue for self-expression, and the popular tendency to experiment, innovate, or create, rather than to honor or protect existing social structures and institutions. Little wonder, then, that conservatives began to organize and fight back.

By the 1980s, 1990s, and the early twenty-first century, conservatives had organized so well that they not only wrested political power from the liberals, but to a large extent they dictated the nation's economic and social agenda—though on the cultural front they remained mostly reactive. Yet apparently conservatives fell short of actually dethroning liberalism as the dominant intellectual paradigm. In a sense this observation is tautological; in the modern or postmodern age the dominant worldview will always be "liberal" by some definition. But a more meaningful way of approaching the issue is to realize that in a free society no single persuasion or ideology can enjoy monopoly status. It might be useful to think of American liberalism as a continually contested hegemony, rather than as an unassailable cosmology (as medieval Christendom had once been). Painites may have won the original debate with Burkeans in America, but conservatives never stopped coming back to reargue their case. As noted at the onset of this discussion, antimoderns have occasionally been successful. They have often influenced the course of history, even if in the long run they have not been able to control it. As also noted, Americans have always had something of a split personality: liberal ideals, while seldom rejected, have many times been ignored or perverted in the practical arena. Over the course of the last generation, this anti-idealist propensity has been unusually strong. Yet paradoxically, the current conservative craving for Burke is an indication that, despite their political success, conservatives still view liberalism as the controlling national impulse.

As in prior periods, Burke in America remained more useful and effective when invoked as a defense against some identifiable threat. Contemporary conservative railings against a liberal bias in public school curricula, or in the media, or within the "intelligentsia," or (until recently) in Supreme Court decisions that sided with the "educated elite," confirm that in the opinion of the American right, the ghost of liberalism past has not yet been exorcised. After the election of George W. Bush in 2000, a Texas voter interviewed on television pessimistically predicted that it would take a long time to reverse thirty years of liberalism; and no doubt many conservative intellectuals would agree, though they would date the origins of liberalism much earlier. Most fantastically, some conservative writers reverted to Edmund Burke in answer to liberal intellectuals who allegedly justified the September 11, 2001, terrorist attacks on the World Trade Center and Pentagon. No matter that al-Qaeda's Islamic fundamentalism and religious fanaticism embodied the antithesis of liberalism. This was as good a sign as any that using Burke to bolster arguments he could never have imagined was risky (though it was not new). At the very least, it indicated that conservative recursions to Burke needed to be more reflective and less reflexive.

But this is getting ahead of the story. The seeds of the Burkean revival were planted in the early postwar years, and the doctrine of "natural law" provided their nourishment.

CHAPTER 10

Natural Law

A Neo-traditionalist Revival

The idea of "natural law," even if somewhat vague, has a long and venerable history. In various guises it dates back to the ancient Greeks and Romans, and some writers have claimed it belongs also to the Jewish, Muslim, Hindu, Buddhist, and Chinese traditions.[1] Natural law is universal and absolute, since it emanates from God, or from nature. In the Western Christian tradition, it is knowable only to God, though it may be imperfectly discovered by man's reason. During the Middle Ages, when jurisprudence was still a branch of theology, all "customs" and "enactments" were expected to be "in harmony with divine reason," and for Thomas Aquinas natural law was "nothing else than the rational creature's participation in the eternal law."[2] Philosophically, natural law comprised a fundamental "good," a morality not made by man, yet existing in the universe. In the United States, interest in natural law surfaced early: James Wilson—one of the lesser known founding fathers—spoke on the subject, as did the antebellum jurist Joseph Story.[3] Nevertheless, in a country committed to religious pluralism and devoted to the "rights of man," and which was preoccupied in any event with the mechanics of progress, natural law received scant attention outside of legal circles. Because natural law represented a "higher morality" than positive law, it was applicable to liberal causes such as resistance to fugitive slave laws, or to Jim Crow segregation, or to military conscription. But in the twentieth century, liberals never really needed natural law, nor did they feel comfortable with its mysteries, so it remained largely the preserve of conservatives.[4] And not all conservatives at that. It took a particular blend of tradition, religion, and conservatism to bring natural law to a wider audience in the postwar era, and to unite it with the legacy of Edmund Burke.

Catholic Origins

When the University of Notre Dame College of Law held its initial Natural Law Institute in late 1947, organizers saw it as "probably the first gathering in modern times by members of the legal profession for the primary purpose of considering the natural law," and they felt that such an assembly was long overdue. As the Catholic bishop of Buffalo proclaimed in his invocation: "Dry-rot has afflicted our jurisprudence" as had "alien philosophies," hence "the very existence of Natural Law is challenged." In turn, "Some one must challenge the false philosophy that has taken hold of our law schools and our courts." Father John Cavanaugh, president of Notre Dame, blasted the "positivism of Justice Holmes and the relativism of Justice Cardozo" and added that "It is here postulated that the controlling principles of law never change."[5] He stated boldly the creed of natural law and the practical position of its adherents: "[Natural law] is not an ideal; it is a reality. It is not a product of men's minds; it is a product of God's will. . . . Any statute or court decision or system of law which does not conform to natural law simply has no valid binding force."[6]

Notre Dame's law school dean spoke on "The Natural Law Philosophy of [the] Founding Fathers" and argued that American law was forsaking its original wisdom; for instance, he condemned New Deal liberalism for its assault on constitutional limitations. Of even broader scope was Minneapolis lawyer Ben Palmer's discussion, "The Natural Law and Pragmatism," which showcased a conservative hostility to some of the major intellectual trends of the twentieth century. Palmer, a convert to Catholicism, claimed that civilization's recent decline began in 1859, the year Charles Darwin published *Origin of Species* in England and the philosopher John Dewey was born in Vermont. He quoted Sidney Hook to the effect that "the philosophy of John Dewey . . . has carried to completion a movement of ideas which marks the final break with the ancient and medieval outlook upon the world. . . . Organized intelligence is to take the place of myth and dogma in improving the common lot and enriching individual experience." Palmer isolated the "main characteristics" of Dewey's thought with an eye toward its relativistic nature: "There is no absolute truth, no necessary truth. Truth is not transcendent or eternal but only hypothetical and ambulatory. . . . There is no truth but only successive truths, accepted tentatively and provisionally. . . . They are constantly put to the test of experience and discarded as false as soon as they cease to work."[7]

Dewey, of course, could not have destroyed traditional certainties without accomplices; and though Palmer did not exactly call Dewey's cohorts "wicked and designing men," he essentially presented them as such. He criticized the scientist Charles Peirce for believing that truth "varies between persons. . . . What is agreeable to reason is more or less a matter of taste"; and he accused both the psychologist William James and the legal theorist Oliver Wendell Holmes of "winning converts" to Peirce's view. He blamed Harvard president Charles Eliot for bringing a harmful "secular upheaval" to higher education, and he blamed the economist Harold Moulton for acknowledging "the relativity of economic thought." Palmer took issue with anthropologists for perceiving "ethical systems and religions as products of their age and as developments of primitive myths, superstitions and customs," and for stressing "flux, interminable change, [and the] absence of eternal verities and enduring standards." Finally, and comprehensively: "The whole sweep of thought in political science, economics, sociology, anthropology, history, psychology, philosophy, and in legal education during the last hundred years was in the direction of relativism, positivism, [and] empiricism. . . . The emphasis was on change rather than stability, on the temporal and immediate rather than the eternal, on the natural to the exclusion of the supernatural." In a parting shot at Dewey, Palmer cited his explanation of "religious faith, not as belief in a supernatural deity nor in values transcending human life, but as 'the unification of self through allegiance to inclusive ideal ends, which imagination presents to us and to which the human will responds as worthy of controlling our desires and choices.'" Obviously this was an abomination to Catholics, and to other Americans who adhered to a conventional religious orthodoxy. As Palmer saw it, secular innovations yielded a "science that has created a Frankenstein monster which threatens to destroy us and which gives us neither assurance, nor hope, nor wisdom." Hence, "I need not point out how difficult it would be for natural law with its basis in absolutes, in reason, in eternal unchanging verities, to withstand the erosion of [our] philosophical and cultural environment."[8]

These same themes were reinforced by federal judge Robert Wilkin at the second Natural Law Institute in 1948. His "Status of Natural Law in American Jurisprudence" condemned positivism for nullifying the Declaration of Independence, the Constitution, and "twenty-five hundred years of progress in political and legal theory." "In this country," Wilkin continued, "positivism tended to discredit the judicial function and over-emphasize the importance of administrative procedure." He laid the blame precisely where Palmer had laid it the previous year: "Inspired by the pragmatism of Professor John Dewey and the skepticism of Justice Oliver Wendell Holmes, [American judges] arrogated a disdain for Natural Law and discredited all claims of natural right. It then became their habit to assume . . . that 'modern scholars . . . have totally abandoned natural law.'" In consequence, "When the moral and ethical content of our philosophy was abandoned, men felt free to assert without restraint their novel theories." From such a nihilistic condition, it was only a short step to an arbitrary, tyrannical nightmare. According to Wilkin, our law had "lost the distinctive character of Anglo-American jurisprudence and took on a similitude to the arbitrary or fiat rule of totalitarian governments. . . . The champions of statism adopted those principles which soon found expression in the teachings and practices of Machiavelli and later were exemplified in the Fascism of Mussolini and the *Realpolitik* of Hitler."[9]

Wilkin's cry that the nation's judicial sky was falling (or had already fallen) came well before the liberal, activist, and famous rulings of the Warren court, including the landmark civil rights cases. He was reacting against the "go along" legal climate of complicit liberalism that took hold in the thirties, when courts upheld precedent-shattering reforms; and he condemned the new generation of judges and law professors for not defending the natural law tradition and the strict interpretation of the Constitution.[10] As important, Wilkin did not mention Edmund Burke. In fact, none of the participants in any of the five Natural Law Institutes did.[11] Nor did former Harvard Law dean Roscoe Pound's lengthy and important article on "The Revival of Natural Law," which appeared in the *Notre Dame Lawyer* in 1942 and was a precursor to the school's Natural Law Institutes.[12] But natural law conservatism had not yet allied itself with Cold War conservatism. Once it did, Burke easily found employment in both camps.

Nevertheless, the evidence is quite clear that conservatives did not come to natural law by way of Burke. Rather, they rediscovered natural law independently, then retrofitted Burke's legacy to conform to the natural law tradition. Though Burke had been in print for a century and a half, and the idea of natural law had been in circulation for many centuries, the two were not explicitly united until the late 1940s—with most of the action occurring in the 1950s. Notre Dame's conferences demonstrated that, originally, natural law theorists (like new conservatives in general) were traditionalists whose quest for moral and intellectual certainty was inspired by the philosophical and religious coherence of earlier ages. In this respect they stood closer to the prewar new humanism of Irving Babbitt, Paul Elmer More, and their medievalist compatriot Ralph Adams Cram than they did to the more prominent ahistorical strains of postwar conservatism: the libertarianism of free-market economics, and the anticommunism of the Cold War. Most new conservatives would eventually become cold warriors, but many would continue to reject an individualistic society propelled by hedonistic consumption. At least initially, natural law conservatives were—like the new humanists—counter-*evolutionists* making a last stand against insidious but incremental modernization, not antirevolutionaries fighting a foreign threat.

Moreover, the natural law revival was largely a Roman Catholic affair, and it came at a time when Catholicism was struggling to enter the American mainstream. The church's preference for authority, hierarchy, and mystery made it a naturally contrapuntal institution in an era of consensus liberalism. As a prominent account of postwar conservatism explains it: "Both Catholics and conservatives were outsiders. One is even tempted to say that the new conservatism was, in part, an intellectual cutting edge of the postwar 'coming of age' of America's Catholic minority."[13]

At least twenty-five of the "new conservative" writers had some sort of Catholic orientation: fourteen were born Catholic, eight converted to Catholicism, and three others claimed to admire Catholicism.[14] Not only was the Natural Law Institute a creature of the nation's most famous Catholic university, but the Catholic bishops of Buffalo and Indianapolis served as honorary chairmen at the first two conferences; and the invocation at the third conference arrived via cablegram from the pope. Such official sanction hinted that the renewed promulgation of natural law doctrine was partly a denominational crusade. Perhaps it was no coincidence that the postwar Burkean revival itself had notable Catholic roots: the Burke Society of Fordham University, a Jesuit institution, was founded in 1945 to "recall . . . the principles, values, and traditions which are the heritage of . . . Christendom," and for a time Fordham served as a center of Burkean thought.[15] Later, the *Burke Newsletter* was published (1959–67) at the Jesuit University of Detroit. Furthermore, of the first four Americans to publish work in the midcentury Burkean revival, three—Moorhouse Millar, Ross Hoffman, and Paul Levack—were conservative Catholics, and the fourth—Russell Kirk—later converted to Catholicism.

Millar's "Burke and the Moral Basis of Political Liberty" appeared in Fordham's journal *Thought* in 1941. Millar, a Jesuit priest who headed Fordham's graduate department of political philosophy, began by blasting "our present-day severance from the earlier ethical tradition of Western Christendom," and "the corrupted notion of human nature that accounts for the inability of many modern minds to understand any longer the age-old and well-tried principles of which Burke was the last great non-Catholic exponent." He did not use the term "natural law," but parts of his article effectively made a case for it. Millar quoted Burke on "the will of him who gave us our nature, and in giving, impressed an invariable law upon it"; and from Burke's speeches against Hastings, he cited the belief that "we are all born . . . in subjection to one great, immutable, pre-existing law. . . . [Man] is bound by the eternal law of Him, that gave it, with which no human authority can dispense." As if anticipating a secularist, skeptical rebuttal of his theocratic argument, Millar contended that Burke's "magnificent appeal to the eternal law of God as the ontologically fundamental moral barrier to the usurpations of the merely arbitrary in human affairs was no accidental rhetorical flourish." Father Millar also agreed with Burke's condemnation of the French Revolution, with its "radical," "reckless vindication of the 'Rights of Man.'" Though little-known today, Millar's article supplied the prototype for the postwar Burkean revival, especially since he was not just offering a historical review of Burke's politics, but was also issuing a contemporary call to arms. After praising Burke's "realistic vision" and deploring the "human myths" that rejected the "tried principles and traditions that had gone into the making of Western Christendom," Millar delivered a "suggestion for our generation": "So long as we continue the present refusal to allow for any other principles but those of the eighteenth century, which Burke condemned . . . we shall still find ourselves juggling with false issues and committed to the futile attempt to build our future on nothing more solid than quicksand."[16]

Along with Millar, the Burke Society's members included Fordham professors Ross Hoffman and Paul Levack, who in 1948 compiled a single-volume edition of Burke's writings, including a twenty-six-page introduction (written by Hoffman, influenced by Millar), "Burke's Philosophy of Politics."[17] Published the following year, *Burke's Politics* became a handy source for postwar conservative intellectuals. Hoffman was an admirer of medieval Christendom who had earlier left the hostile secular atmosphere of New York University for the more congenial Jesuit setting of Fordham.[18] His essay presented a broadly conservative interpretation of Burke, and its references to natural law are probably more salient in hindsight:

> [Burke] was sure that the first duty of all men was to obey the law ordained by their Creator for their good.
>
> Burke's politics thus were grounded on recognition of the universal natural law of reason and justice ordained by God as the foundation of a good community.

Because he acknowledged the natural law, Burke affirmed men's possession of natural rights.

The universal moral law obliged all rulers and governments to recognize an original right in the subject.

Burke's doctrine of natural rights was in opposition, however, to the "rights of man" philosophy of Paine, Rousseau, and the French Jacobins.[19]

As the final statement revealed, *Burke's Politics* was also an early Cold War document; and unlike the Notre Dame writers, Hoffman assumed an antirevolutionary posture: "All the rationalistic errors of the age of Rousseau and Paine came coursing back with the upsurge of socialism, communism, and fascism. . . . The omnipotent bureaucratic, 'planning' state, which throttled freedom two centuries ago, again has men in its clutches." For Hoffman, postwar American democracy survived as "a majestic creation of the ages and a citadel of prescriptive right in Western Christendom. . . . We emerged from the Second World War as the champions of a conservative cause: the cause of conserving law and liberty against totalitarian despotism."[20] Logically, atheistic communism was as hostile to the natural law tradition as fascism, positivism, relativism, or pragmatism were, and by the late 1950s most new conservatives followed Hoffman's lead in grouping (or conflating) them into a single accretion of modernism run amuck.

Russell Kirk

Foremost among American documents tying Burke to natural law was Russell Kirk's "Burke and Natural Rights," which appeared in Notre Dame's *Review of Politics* in 1951. That very year, Kirk's *John Randolph of Roanoke* portrayed its Old South hero as the "American Burke," and two years later Kirk rallied the Right with his best-selling *The Conservative Mind*, which declared Burke "the greatest of modern conservative thinkers."[21] Kirk (1918–94) quickly became one of the most influential new conservatives, and he was undeniably the most important American Burkean of the twentieth century. More than any single writer, Kirk inspired the postwar glorification of Burke. Allen Guttmann best captured the depth of Kirk's devotion when he remarked: "Kirk moulds almost everyone he admires into the image of Burke, whom he admires most of all."[22] Though he was widely known as a conservative intellectual, Kirk would have been more accurately described as an intellectual entrepreneur. His goal was not scholarship, but the restoration of conservative principles to a society in which "radical thinkers" had "won the day."[23] In this sense Kirk was only a less media-savvy (he refused to buy a television) and less overtly political version of William F. Buckley Jr.—with whom he shared, if not a common vision of conservatism, at least a common contempt for liberalism. Kirk, above all, forged the bond between the postwar conservative resurgence and the American Burkean revival.

Kirk's *Review of Politics* article identified Burke as "at once the chief exponent of . . . natural law, and a chief opponent of the 'rights of man.'" Here Kirk meant to contrast the authenticity of traditional morality with the illegitimacy of speculative morality; but the line between the two was not so distinct. From the start Kirk sought to demonstrate Burke's present-day relevance by suggesting that the core principles of his Old Whig vision still applied: "In our time . . . [with its] simultaneous interest in natural law theory and an enthusiasm for defining 'human rights' . . . Burke's view of natural juridic order deserves close attention." Kirk followed the lead of Millar and Hoffman by taking the then uncommon approach of perceiving Burke through a religious lens: "Burke was a pious man. . . . He takes for granted the Christian cosmos, in which a just God has established moral principles for man's salvation. . . . [Burke] was far more devout [than] his Tory friend Johnson. . . . God gives us our nature, said Burke, and with it he gives us natural law."[24] As noted earlier, a sharply religious view of Burke was open to serious challenge. Burke accepted the "Christian cosmos" because it was an integral part of Europe's inherited civilization, but he probably was neither "pious" nor "devout," and his interest in religion centered on its stabilizing and unifying effect on secular society.[25] Still, if natural law derived from God, Burke as its champion had to be depicted in a theocratic light. "Man's rights exist only when man obeys God's law," declared Kirk, as he initiated his lifelong anti-Enlightenment crusade: "Very different all this is from the 'natural rights' of Locke . . . and we need hardly remark that this concept of natural right is descended from sources very different from Rousseau."[26] Once Kirk found that natural law, like tradition—which presumably was the historical manifestation of "natural right"—could be used as an intellectual trump card, he would play it often.

Yet there was a technical problem. Since Burke actually said little about natural law, Kirk had to explain its relative absence from his writings. He did this by engaging in a defense of the unknowable that was worthy of Burke himself:

> [Burke] did not look upon natural right as a weapon in political controversy. . . . He rarely invokes natural right against his adversaries'

> measures or in defense of his own. He dislikes, indeed, to define it very closely; natural right is an Idea comprehended fully only by the Divine intellect; precisely where it commences and terminates, we are no fit judges. . . . But so far as we can delineate the features of natural justice, Burke suggests, it is the experience of mankind which supplies our partial knowledge of Divine law . . . through history . . . tradition, prejudice, prescription.

It would have been appropriate to mention Burke's situational expediency (that is, the importance of "circumstance") in choosing which traditions to follow, which ones to modify (reform), and which ones to reject. Yet a tactical Burke would not have served the mission at hand. Kirk always intended the "recursion" to Burkean thought to spur a broader "recrudescence" of clear, conservative principles. In any event, and just to cover all the bases, Kirk concluded: "Burke was always on his guard against concepts of natural law that were dangerously vague and concepts that were fatuously exact."[27] This slippery treatment, which posited that humans could not determine where natural law began or ended, and should neither define it too precisely nor too vaguely, *but should be guided by it*, and which argued that Burke's philosophy was informed by (or even based upon) natural law, *yet he chose not to use it as a weapon of discourse*, was logically weak. But it was emotionally persuasive to a particular constituency. Though most new conservatives had not yet adopted Edmund Burke as their mentor, they were already predisposed toward his traditionalist sensibility, not only in their quest for authority and certainty, but in their inclination to sacrifice rational analysis for their more intuitive judgments pitting good against evil.

Kirk continued this antirational approach in his magnum opus, *The Conservative Mind: From Burke to Santayana*, which argued that Burke "was convinced that first principles, in the moral sphere, come to us through revelation and intuition." Stylistically, Kirk presented Burke's philosophy in language that was very close to what Burke himself had used, and one wonders whether this practice was intentional or unconscious: "Revelation, reason, and assurance beyond the senses tell us that the Author of our being exists, and that He is omniscient; and man and the state are creatures of God's beneficence." Kirk even claimed that "Christian orthodoxy is the kernel of Burke's philosophy. . . . And what is our purpose in this world? Not to indulge our appetites, but to render obedience to Divine ordinance." Surely this was going too far. Even if theology played a significant role in Burke's philosophy (which was doubtful), it took a leap of faith to conclude that theology formed its central core. But like Burke at his most feverish, once Kirk began forcing a point he rarely stopped short of climax. In this case: "Contemptuous of the notion of human perfectibility, Burke modelled his psychology on this Christian picture of sin and tribulation." Of course, Burke did no such thing—or at least he never said so in his writings.[28] But possibly Kirk thought he understood Burke's psyche so well that he could speak on his behalf.

Moreover, Kirk's talent for emulating Burke's prose style extended to approximating his worldview and his sense of apocalyptic mission. He even employed certain of Burke's polemical techniques. We have just seen that one such trick was to present mere assumptions or unprovable assertions as authoritative conclusions. Another was to invoke mystery as compensation for lack of evidence. Like Burke, Kirk was perfectly capable of writing a logical argument when the facts were on his side; but he resorted to the vague, the poetic, or the intuitive when reason was either insufficient or counterproductive. Consequently, Kirk and Burke shared the same proselytic fate: they inspired those who already agreed with them, and they failed to convince anyone who did not. Despite its presumed grounding in history and experience, traditionalist conservatism required both a selective memory and a romantic sensibility. One had to feel in one's heart that ideals and practices that had been honored in ages past, or that old values judged to be wise in retrospect, were superior to the ideals, practices, values, and objectives of the present. In addition, one had to reject the slow (and not-so-slow) accumulation of new beliefs and habits that resulted from relatively recent experience. In effect, one could subscribe to Burke's axiom that "the species is wise" only up to some particular year, era, or event; from that moment forward, one had to believe that the species had become foolish. Hence a skeptic might have asked: How many generations—or centuries—of post-traditional society must pass before the yardstick of wisdom is recalibrated? Did even most conservatives, for example, accept the traditionalist Richard Weaver's thesis that Western civilization began to decline once William of Occam broached his nominalist philosophy (denying the existence universals) in the 1300s?[29] It is hard not to like Russell Kirk, or not to enjoy reading him; it may even be hard not to sympathize with him—to a point. But one cannot help sensing that, like Burke in his ultratraditionalist mode, Kirk was speaking eloquently of an already lost world. At his best he rivaled Burke in speaking as if *from* that lost world. This was a rare ability, though perhaps it was rare because few saw any reason to develop it. And we must now come to terms with why so anachronistic a writer as Kirk was able to accomplish so much in "modern times."

What makes the question more intriguing is that Kirk aimed his attack not just at liberalism, but at powerful strains of conservatism as well. Kirk criticized materialism, technology (he called the automobile the "mechanical Jacobin"), big business, the military industrial complex (before Eisenhower coined the term), the permanent war footing of Cold War America, and the big brother government that it justified.[30] Opposing both the positivist-socialist left *and* the most influential, well-financed branches of conservatism (that is, industrial capitalism and statist militarism) could have relegated Kirk to the easily dismissible lunatic fringe. This might well have happened had not conservatism as an articulated public philosophy been in hibernation for at least a generation. Kirk attained celebrity status with *Conservative Mind* because conservatives of disparate stripes were willing, even eager, to unite behind any intellectual leader who could prepare them to take the field against their common liberal or radical foes. One remarkable demonstration of this was that the *other* seminal treatise of postwar conservatism—Friedrich Hayek's *Road to Serfdom* (1944)—was a libertarian tract that implicitly rejected traditionalism (in fact, Kirk and Hayek publicly clashed over fundamental principles).[31] If legend has it right, no two books inspired more American conservatives to step out of the shadows and into the public arena. Yet, excepting their common desire for minimalist government, the two books projected a completely different worldview. Where Hayek was modern, rational, ahistorical, and essentially amoral, Kirk was antimodern, intuitive (some said "aesthetic," others "antirationalist"), historical, and highly concerned with morality. Both authors stood against "social engineering" and the radical redesign of society, but their recipes for avoiding those dangers were at wide variance. Hayek looked backward only a couple of generations, and found his solution in the golden age of laissez-faire; Kirk looked backward to premodern ages, and found his model in the quest for ancient wisdom. As important, Hayek tried to convince his readers by means of utilitarian logic; Kirk, by contrast, sought to inspire his audience with the majesty of a long and honorable tradition. Hayek's goal was to show that economic libertarianism made the most practical sense, while Kirk's mission was to make conservatism respectable again by depicting it as timelessly noble.

Conservatives were not blind to the split personality of their movement. But they chose to explain away the differences rather than to reconcile them. Frank Meyer, in his "fusionist" attempt at uniting the two schools of thought, called the "freedom" and "tradition" versions of conservatism "opposite sides of the same truth." And William F. Buckley Jr. noted that the "differences . . . do not appear to be choking each other off." Buckley recognized the "symbiosis" of the conflicted right.[32] He knew that the dialectic among the various strains of conservatism had piqued the interests and increased the activity levels of sympathetic intellectuals, journalists, politicians, and other interested parties, and in the process sharpened their critique of America's liberal hegemony. As the movement grew in size and strength, most members would reject Kirk's traditionalist ideals (which were Old World in character). Yet at the same time many remained grateful for his entrepreneurial efforts on the conservative revival's behalf. This paradox of praising the messenger while ignoring the essence of his message stemmed from conservatism's postwar inferiority complex. Though the majority of conservatives did not buy the solutions Kirk was selling, all agreed with him that the leftward drift of political, economic, social, and cultural thought had to be reversed by means of any practical alliance.

Kirk had been born and raised in rural Michigan, and he remained a lifelong agrarian organicist.[33] When studying for his master's degree at Duke University, he came to admire the southern agrarians of *I'll Take My Stand* fame, and while researching his thesis on John Randolph he stumbled across Randolph's "preceptor," Edmund Burke.[34] After serving stateside in the army during the war, Kirk earned his D.Litt. at the University of St. Andrews in Scotland, where he developed a love for medieval Christendom and for the Gothic mind. Since his youth Kirk had hated modern "assembly-line society." Now the intellectual adventures of his early adult years began to furnish him with romantic alternatives to it. Kirk was not just an antimodern; he was also an anti-exceptionalist. At the height of the "American Century," he sought to reattach the umbilical cord to mother England. One reason Burke loomed so large in Kirk's vision was that Burke epitomized the Anglo-American historical tradition and cultural sensibility. In turn, Kirk enshrined British culture as the best in the world; he distrusted continental Europe, and events from the French Revolution to the world wars to the triumph of communism seemed to bear out this prejudice. An affinity for British civilization was evident throughout Kirk's writings, though not until late in his career did he publish a book devoted to the subject. Not surprisingly, *America's British Culture* (1992) was a call for conservative action disguised as a historical monograph. Written in the face of threats from "multiculturalists," the book called for "renewing a shaken culture."[35] But specific targets notwithstanding, Kirk was merely updating the same arguments he had made consistently since 1951. Following the lead of Burke and most traditionalists, Kirk took a holistic and inseparable view of civilization. He believed that weakening, replacing, or tampering with any of the existing pillars of the social order would cause the entire edifice to collapse—if not immediately, then eventually. His fixations on religion, common law, constitutions, and (what might be called) an "official" language and a "monopolistic" high culture were manifestations of this view. So sure was he that the past had been more virtuous than the present that he elevated ancient tradition and timeless wisdom above the modern ideals of progress, equity, democracy, and the pursuit of happiness. If we adjust for the passage of time (the way we adjust for inflation), Kirk was far more reactionary than Burke had been. While Burke was a progressive reformer who defended British traditions that were declining but not yet extinct, Kirk condemned liberal reformers and sought to impose ancient, foreign, and vague traditions that had never really existed in the United States.

In this respect Kirk mirrored the Notre Dame natural law scholars in their castigating of liberal politicians and intellectuals, and even in their selection of John Dewey as an ideological lightning rod. Repeatedly in his *Program for Conservatives* (1954), Kirk—although claiming "the terrible events of our time have buried John Dewey"—could not refrain from chasing Dewey's ghost. Because, "the weight of [his] being upon our schools and colleges and universities is the weight of an intellectual corpse." Kirk objected to Dewey's "secular dogma," and he accused Dewey's disciples of "captur[ing] most of our schools" and pushing a "soulless society" of "social collectivism" with a "passion for leveling all orders . . . into one amorphous mass." Decrying the absence of "enduring values" and the passage of the "age of chivalry and of Scholasticism," Kirk grouped John Dewey, William James, David Riesman, and Erich Fromm into the "rigid calculus" of Jeremy Bentham and James Mill.[36] How different Kirk was from the transatlantic Victorians, who had welcomed Burke into the camp of utilitarian progress!

Ironically, Kirk's critique of "dry" social science, and of modern rational, statistical, organizational, or technological approaches to life, would soon become a recurrent theme of the cultural left. The crucial difference, however, between Kirk and the Beats, the New Left, the counterculture, radical feminists, deconstructionists, and related critics was that writers aligned with such movements rejected traditionalism along with liberal rationalism. Paradoxically, a chief mission of the "neoconservatives" during the last quarter of the twentieth century would be to defend old-style liberal rationality against those who undermined it from the left. This bolstered the claim that neoconservatives were actually (or at least substantially) conservative liberals, unlike the postwar new conservatives, who were antimodern traditionalists.[37] While Kirk was a genuine twentieth-century antimodern, Burke, as we have said, was an eighteenth-century half modern. Kirk was more at war with the culture of his age than Burke had been, because by the middle of the twentieth century the wicked and designing men had already won.

Nowhere was this more obvious than in education, an area where once again John Dewey had left his mark. Kirk despised the idea of progressive education, with its encouragement of personal expression and its training for "citizenship." Despite attending graduate school on the G.I. Bill, Kirk held a "swinish multitude" view of educational opportunity: he called for fewer rather than more high schools and colleges, since most students were neither up to nor interested in the intellectual challenge.[38] Unaware that his own educational tastes betrayed a rival version of citizenship training, Kirk saw schools as inculcators of civilized values. In an article blasting Dewey, Kirk made this point in classically Burkean fashion: "Education is the formal means for transmitting culture. Culture is built up slowly and painfully, over the ages, by an elaborate process . . . in custom and habit and precedent. . . . When that conformity is snapped by the impractical reformer, it may be extremely difficult—and sometimes impossible—to atone for the blunder."[39]

Once more the holistic and inseparable vision of civilization was on display, and its harmony extended to style as well as substance. On Kirk's reading, "Dewey's prose is turgid; and . . . a man's style is a man's nature. . . . I do not think anyone is going to read Dewey fifty years from now; and I suspect that his very name, by that time, will be . . . vague and comical."[40] Such thinking was no more wishful—and no less revealing—than Burke's earlier draft of the same resolution: "Who now reads Bolingbroke? Who has ever read him through? Ask the booksellers of London what is become of all these lights of the world. In as few years their few successors will go to the family vault of 'all the Capulets.'"[41] Some years later, Kirk repeated his stability-of-civilization argument almost word for word. But this time he was praising Burke rather than attacking Dewey:

> We call the system of social ideas derived from Burke's later writings, "conservatism." What is conservatism? . . . It is the belief that there are certain abiding standards, moral and social, which change only very slowly, if at all, from age to age; and if we are to touch upon these norms, we must do so only with the greatest caution, for irreparable harm may result from reckless tinkering. Man, through the ages, has built up civilization, law and order, peace and prosperity, by slow and sometimes painful degrees. The radical reformer endangers all this elaborate accomplishment.[42]

Just as Rousseau's progressive ideas on education (published in *Émile*, 1762) reflected his radical political philosophy, so too Dewey's progressive inclination reached beyond the classroom. Conservative traditionalists were right to fear liberalism in *any* field, as a threat to traditional orthodoxy in *every* field. Liberalism and conservatism represented entirely different approaches to past practices. Once the spirit of inquiry and innovation was unleashed, it was unlikely to stay confined to a single sphere. The conservative scholars at Notre Dame and Fordham in the 1940s correctly sensed this. Liberals probably would have acknowledged their expansive tendencies, but since they considered innovation to be the handmaiden of progress, they would have seen the effect as beneficial rather than threatening. Conversely, the new conservatives saw heterodoxy anywhere as merely a separate breach in the common dike. As one 1950s reviewer noted in a slightly different context: "Above all, Burke's consistent aim was to preserve and restore the old harmonious relationship between all the parts of the whole. He wished to preserve the old order and discourage radical solutions and objections."[43] Along related lines, George Nash has observed that "by combining Burke—long the symbol of the appeal to history and expediency—with ["sweeping, universalistic"] natural law theory, conservatives were in effect attempting to bridge the gulf between their libertarian and traditionalist wings."[44] Technically, Nash's reasoning was flawed (neither Burkean traditionalism nor natural law doctrine tolerated libertarianism, thus their union could never yield the desired outcome); but Nash was intuitively alert in sensing that organic unity was what conservatives cherished. At least as an ideal, it was one thing that distinguished true conservatism from liberalism (though weirdly, not from Marxism). We may also suggest here that libertarianism, like neoconservatism, could easily be classified as a type of conservative (or neoclassical) liberalism.

Politically, these inconsistencies did not matter so long as conservatism did not count. The editor of a 1999 anthology of conservative writings still agreed with the conclusions of postwar intellectuals: after the New Deal, "Liberals stopped taking conservatives seriously."[45] Arthur Schlesinger Jr. had even claimed (in 1953) that there was no such thing as a conservative tradition in the United States.[46] Thus in 1957, when Kirk became founding editor of *Modern Age: A Conservative Journal*, he "apologized" for its launching by claiming that most scholarly periodicals were "professedly liberal or radical," whereas "*Modern Age* intends to pursue a conservative policy for the sake of a liberal understanding." He continued: "By 'conservative,' we mean a journal dedicated to preserving the best elements in our civilization; and those best elements are in peril nowadays. We confess to a prejudice against doctrinaire radical alteration, and to a preference for the wisdom of our ancestors." It did not take long for Edmund Burke's name to surface; the very first page of text declared: "With Burke, we take our stand against abstract doctrine and theoretic dogma. But, still with Burke, we are in favor of principle." The first full-length article, "Life without Prejudice," by Richard Weaver, managed to make a perfectly Burkean argument without actually mentioning Burke: "Life without prejudice, were it ever to be tried, would soon reveal itself to be a life without principle."[47] In the journal's second number, Edmund Opitz (reviewing a book on Burke's moral thought) declared postwar conservatism's need for Burke: "Burke's solid utterances on the nature of men and society were provoked by the pernicious ideology which had seeped into the 18th century mind—and still festers among us." Not surprisingly, "Burke saw in the French Revolution . . . a war against man and God." Opitz lamented civilization's sad transition from Christendom to secular rationalism, and he ended by hoping for a renewed Burkean leadership: "When men had an unquestioned sense of being rooted in an order beyond time and nature, they felt linked to other men in societies by this bond. . . . But with the dissolution of the belief in a transcendent order[,] social bonds were attenuated."[48] Ultimately, "Burke did not stem the tide which rose in his day. . . . But after nearly two centuries his realism, his strong religious and historical sense, his appreciation of continuity in the human venture, may yet rally those who are fed up with patchwork remedies and panaceas."[49]

Modern Age eventually embraced a wider range of conservative perspectives. But for our purposes the key event was its spawning (and "spinning off") of a *Burke Newsletter* in 1959. The first few numbers of the *Newsletter* were incorporated into issues of *Modern Age*; it then appeared independently until 1967, when it grew into the journal *Studies in Burke and His Time*—which ran until 1978.[50] As the conservative movement gained momentum, the essentially Old World traditionalist variety of it waned in relative importance. Apparently Burkeans—Kirk chief among them—were most essential in the early days, when some sort of historical authority was needed to undergird conservatism's revival. As previously noted, twentieth-century American conservatism as actually practiced in politics, economics, and social policy has had almost nothing to do with Burke's philosophy. The big exception to this was the antirevolutionary mania of the Cold War, though this was complicated by the fact that mainstream liberals were cold warriors too. Nevertheless, Burke lent an air of respectability to conservatism in general, and Russell Kirk as his self-appointed heir ensured that the "decent drapery" of traditionalist virtue clothed the harsher and seamier aspects of the right-wing's "naked" quest for power. In Kirk's case, there was also a strong desire to argue that no ocean of any size separated Edmund Burke from American society and politics.

> Burke is not *outside* the American tradition; rather, he stands in the greater tradition and continuity—the legacy of our civilization—of which American life and character are a part. And Burke himself was an influence upon America from the end of colonial times to our own day; he has helped to form our society. To seek political guidance from Burke is no more exotic or alien, for Americans, than to seek human insights from Shakespeare, or to seek religious wisdom from St. Paul.[51]

The underlying premises of Kirk's statement were consistent with the general patterns of Anglo-traditionalist thought in America. Yet in his enthusiasm for the Burkean persuasion, Kirk surely exaggerated the historical impact of what had always been a minority view.

While many conservative writers cited Burke, Kirk was unique in the extent to which he presented Burke as *the* oracle of political wisdom. To a substantial extent Kirk's efforts proved successful; no figure has been so widely acclaimed as the father of modern conservatism—despite the incongruities between Burke's philosophy and most schools of conservative thought. Unlike liberalism, which was so secure that it felt no need to certify its patrimony, conservatism—if only for its own self-confidence—sought the legitimacy of a respected father. Burke was far better suited for this role than any other conservative thinker: Gentz was too obscure, Metternich too authoritarian, de Maistre too royalist, Henry Maine too legalistic, Dr. Johnson too Tory, Cardinal Newman too Catholic, Disraeli too reformist and eccentric, Churchill too recent (still living, when it counted), Coleridge and Carlyle too literary and romantic. Napoleon lacked legitimacy, and those with supreme legitimacy—the American fathers—were spoken for: Washington belonged to everyone, Hamilton to economic interests, Adams to blue bloods, Calhoun and Randolph to southerners. Conservatives tried to claim Lincoln, but the Great Emancipator refused to oblige.[52]

Burke, by default, was a perfect choice. First of all he was British (his Irish roots notwithstanding), and the Anglo-American bond was strong among conservatives. This worked in his favor both positively (in tying him to the Whig tradition of measured progress) and negatively (in separating him from the taint of "un-American" Continental "isms"). Second, Burke was Protestant; even better, he was Anglican—close enough to Catholicism to allow for hierarchy, mystery, and High Church ceremony, far enough from dissenters to reject the "protestantism" of rebels. Third—and as a practical matter of crucial importance—Burke had sympathized with the American Revolution. This alone set him apart from other conservatives, and to some extent neutralized his monarchism and his inherent Old Worldism. Fourth, Burke was a self-made man; he may have defended the aristocracy, but brains rather than birth explained his impact. Burke's career also anticipated the Victorian middle-class challenge to the hereditary elite; his alleged preference for the laissez-faire implications of Smithian economics played to this interpretation. On some level this (like his sympathy with the colonists) made Burke quasi-American in sensibility. Moreover, this view opened the only door to a libertarian reading of his work. The fifth reason was historical: ever since the Paine debates of the 1790s, political conservatives felt that Burke was on their side. In this respect Burke was present at the creation of American ideology (granted, as a counterweight to the dominant persuasion). Hence there was a unique structural connection between Burke and American discourse. Reason six was that Burke's antirevolutionary writings perfectly fit the anticommunism of the 1950s; and during that decade nothing defined American conservatism more than anticommunism. Finally, the seventh reason was what made Burke exceptional: his mastery of the English language. Without this factor, none of the others—nor all of them combined—would have elevated Burke to the father of anything.

In Edmund Burke's case Russell Kirk's assertion was apt: a man's style *was* his nature. If not for the way Burke expressed his ideas, it is doubtful they would have provided the "magazine of wisdom" that Gladstone or anyone else would have celebrated. Aside from the King James Bible and the works of Shakespeare, few English language sources yield as many quotable quotes as the writings and speeches of Burke. Furthermore, as should be second nature to us by now, one did not have to share Burke's politics in order to quote him effectively. Or to put it another way: one could usually interpret Burke's ideas to conform to one's own. The fact that in his day Burke was as much a progressive as he was a conservative made resorting to his words even more convenient. Curiously, once one becomes sensitized to the existence of Burkean quotations, one tends to stumble across them in surprising places. For example, no less a postwar liberal than John F. Kennedy began his Pulitzer-winning *Profiles in Courage* with an epigraph from Burke's eulogy to Charles James Fox ("He may live long, he may do much. But here is the summit. He never can exceed what he does this day"). In any event, Burke's rhetoric was his ticket to immortality. While he deserves *some* credit as an original thinker, his true status stems from his ability to articulate ideas already in the air better than anyone else. Most likely the main reason conservatives quoted him more than the others was that he was more quotable than the others.

Peter Stanlis

If Russell Kirk was the chief champion of Edmund Burke, then his friend Peter Stanlis was the most important Burkean scholar in the natural law tradition. Stanlis (1920–2011) edited both the *Burke Newsletter* and the most comprehensive Burkean bibliography.[53] Compared to Kirk, Stanlis was not as burdened by his entrepreneurial mission; thus he did not subjugate scholarship to ideology to the same egregious degree. This did not prevent him from reading too much natural law into Burke's philosophy.[54] If Stanlis was excessively passionate about anything, it was natural law itself, and he turned to Edmund Burke merely as its agent. The book that made Stanlis's reputation, *Edmund Burke and the Natural Law* (1958), expanded on themes introduced by Millar, Hoffman, and Kirk—and by the "halfway" Burkean Leo Strauss.[55] Stanlis acknowledged that Burke rarely mentioned natural law, but claimed that his devotion to it was embedded in his veneration of the constitution: "Burke's appeals were almost always indirect, through the British constitution, which was for him merely the practical means of guaranteeing the 'rights' of Natural Law throughout the empire."[56] This claim made Stanlis's task more manageable, though it made his the strangest of the major postwar American books on Edmund Burke.

Thanks to Stanlis's smooth, straightforward style—unlike Kirk, he attempted no subliminal messages via quasi-Burkean language—the project's shortcomings were perhaps not readily apparent. Yet they were substantial, and they hinged on Stanlis's inability to deliver what his title promised. That is, the book did not prove the thesis that Burke's philosophy was derived from or guided by natural law doctrine. Instead, it accepted the link between natural law and the constitution, and examined Burke's views from the safety of that premise. What the book actually achieved was a depiction of how Burke's Whig traditionalism (of which the unwritten constitution was a central element) provided a ready alternative to the rights-of-man philosophy of the Enlightenment. To put it another way, Stanlis used Burkean conservatism and its reliance on prudence as a means of discrediting rationalism. In so doing, he attacked not only the philosophe radicals of Burke's day, but the positivist utilitarians and utopians of his own: the "secular contemporary sociologists who deny the existence of all moral norms and standards."[57] If the sentiment sounds familiar, one need only recall the natural law theorists of Notre Dame and Fordham who made the same case with or without the use of Burke. This exposed another strange element of *Edmund Burke and the Natural Law.* Namely, it was not so much about Edmund Burke, as it was a defense of natural law and Catholicism.

Burke was portrayed as a Christian humanist, because Stanlis believed that was what the modern world needed.

In his highly charged chapter on church and state, Stanlis (an Augustinian Catholic) pressed Burke into the Roman Catholic mold. This was informed by Stanlis's awareness that Catholicism had long been the premier repository of natural law doctrine. Hence, since Burke's conservative constitutionalism served as a surrogate for the natural law tradition, Burke at heart must have been a philosophical Catholic. According to Stanlis, "Burke's own religious convictions might well be described as Catholicism qualified by British nationalism." In effect, Stanlis considered Burke to be Anglican in political form and Catholic in moral substance: "Burke was strongly attached to the Catholic elements in the Anglican Church. A constant yet semi-detached adhesiveness marked Burke's connection to the Anglican Church. In his theological convictions he was essentially Catholic; in his loyalty to the sovereign authority of his church he was a true Protestant." Furthermore, Stanlis thought that Burke viewed the Church of England as "essentially Catholic in her inherited doctrines and forms of worship."[58] And in Stanlis's mind there was good reason for pursuing such unity:

> Catholicism was . . . the great unbroken chain of historical continuity, and was the closest in spirit to that "wisdom of our ancestors" which connected men and nations with the classical Natural Law. No theology was more in harmony with the ancient traditions of Natural Law than that of Roman Catholicism. Throughout its history the conservative spirit of Catholicism had retained an unbroken spiritual and cultural continuity among its adherents.[59]

No doubt the redundancy was intentional, and it nicely infused the passage with hints of a liturgical chant. Stanlis occasionally got carried away when praising either Catholicism or natural law. This was excusable in a writer of strong commitment. Less excusable was his twisting of Burke's thought to conform to a flawed paradigm. The problematic nature of Stanlis's reasoning showed through in his technique. Each time he made an unsupported claim about Burke's reliance on natural law, he qualified it with an excuse as to why Burke could only translate the doctrine into political thought in ways that were vague to the point of meaninglessness. For instance: "Faith in the classical and Scholastic conception of Natural Law is Burke's ultimate political principle. But prudence prevented him from seeking to apply the normative ethical principles of Natural Law as though they were mathematical theorems." Since none of the great natural law writers (Cicero, Aquinas, Hooker) applied their doctrines as if mathematical theorems, readers might have wondered why anyone expected Burke to do so. But at least the genuine exponents of natural law spoke openly about it; here readers might have expected Stanlis to explain why Burke alone needed to obscure natural law with the British constitution or the "principle of prudence." Stanlis noted that natural law theorists from Aristotle to the medieval Scholastics favored "practical" over "speculative" reason. So did Burke. This may have placed them all in methodological opposition to the philosophes, but it still did not explain why the other "practical" thinkers articulated their ideas on natural law while Burke remained suspiciously silent.[60]

Stanlis further undermined the validity of natural law by letting situational expediency slip into the picture. Burke's "principle of prudence" led him to "his belief that Natural Law was a part of practical reason," which depended on "circumstances" and "contingent matters." Incredibly, "Burke conceived of Natural Law with a *changing content* and *dynamic method* . . . subject to growth by the recognition of *new values* emerging from the historical development of civilization." Clearly this clashed with Stanlis's own summary of Natural Law's "basic principles." Specifically, that "Natural Law was an eternal, unchangeable, and universal ethical norm or standard . . . at all times, in all circumstances and everywhere it bound all individuals, races, nations, and governments."[61] Granted, Stanlis and other natural law advocates admitted that while God's law was absolute, its mortal application relied on man's "right reason." Yet this only introduced more difficulties. Since natural law conservatives rejected pragmatic or utilitarian standards of choosing what was "right," and at the same time argued that historical traditions must guide men's decisions in (often) completely novel situations, there was not much to fall back upon except moral intuition. In fact, "moral intuition" was probably the best term available to describe in a nutshell the basic operating principle of Burkean conservatism. Yet Stanlis and a host of new conservatives sought something more mysterious, grandiose, and permanent. In their retreat to the mists of natural law, they perhaps were running from the implicit subjectivity and relativism of their own beliefs.

Leo Strauss

Less theological and evasive than either Kirk or Stanlis was the Austrian-born political philosopher Leo Strauss (1899–1973). Strauss fled Nazi Europe for America in the late 1930s and taught at both the New School for Social Research and the University of Chicago. Although he shared the new conservatives' distaste for Enlightenment thought, he was in other respects a harbinger of the neoconservatives (Jewish rather than Catholic, reasoning rather than mystical). Strauss was a keen student of natural right, but unlike Stanlis and Kirk, he was also a critic of Edmund Burke. His *Natural Right and History* (1953) expressed considerable skepticism over the soundness and relevance of Burke's philosophy. Like Stanlis, Strauss recognized that the British constitution provided the framework for Burke's political vision. But while Stanlis believed that the constitution was a repository of natural law morality, Strauss thought that Burke's attachment to constitutional precedent negated the authority of natural law—which was universal and timeless rather than national and historical. According to the neoconservative writer Irving Kristol, Strauss "did not . . . much admire Edmund Burke, a modern conservative icon, because he felt that Burke's emphasis on 'prescription' as the basis for social order was too parochially British, and too vulnerable to the modern insistence that we should, in the words of Tom Paine (echoed by Jefferson), 'let the dead bury the dead.'"[62] Strauss agreed with the new conservatives that "the contemporary rejection of natural right leads to nihilism—nay, it is identical with nihilism."[63] Yet he could not agree that Edmund Burke belonged to the beneficial natural law tradition.

New conservative writers like Kirk and Stanlis occasionally stretched the conservative interpretation of natural law to allow for some accommodation of benign liberalism. These (unconvincing) attempts were implied rather than clearly articulated, and apparently they were intended to suggest that natural law was the sort of umbrella doctrine that could include both traditional values and such popular modern ideals as Jefferson's self-evident truths and the antitotalitarian concept of international human rights. Committed Burkeans chose to hint at, but not pursue, the liberal ramifications of natural law philosophy, since liberal inertia was the intellectual force they wanted to restrain. Strauss, by contrast, was unconcerned with preserving the organic holism that derived from medieval Christianity; instead he broke natural right (or beliefs that were in accordance with natural law) into two distinct traditions. The classic—or conservative—tradition was virtuous and grounded in universal moral values. The modern—or liberal—tradition was relativistic and effectively valueless, because it held that competing values merited equal consideration. Consequently, "Liberal relativism has its roots in the [modern] natural right tradition of tolerance or in the notion that everyone has a natural right to the pursuit of happiness as he understands happiness; but in itself it is a seminary of intolerance." Perhaps Strauss's personal experience of watching the Nazis grab power in his homeland led him to the erroneous conclusion that "generous liberals" were so "uninhibited" in their "cultivation of individuality" that "intolerance appeared as a value equal in dignity to tolerance" in modern civilizations.

The bad men of Strauss's liberal natural right tradition included Rousseau, who "abandoned himself to modernity" and "jettisoned important elements of classical right"; John Locke, "the most influential of all modern natural right teachers," who erred by succumbing to "nonteleological natural science"; Thomas Hobbes, the "atheistic," "mathematical," "founder of liberalism"; and (as an exogenous precursor) Niccolò Machiavelli, "that greater Columbus, who had discovered the continent on which Hobbes could erect his structure." Machiavelli's sin was that he replaced wisdom with realism; he based his political philosophy on the way men actually lived rather than the way they ought to live; in effect, he substituted the attainment of results for the pursuit of virtue. Meanwhile, the good men of the classic natural right tradition included Aristotle, Cicero, Aquinas, and the Spanish scholastic philosopher Francisco Suarez.[64] It is worth observing that the last good man (Suarez) died about halfway through the lifetime of the first bad man (Hobbes); this overlap worked nearly as well if the English theologian Richard Hooker was recognized as the last good man, though the entire scheme required counting Machiavelli as an influential outsider.[65] The net effect of Strauss's biographical chronology was that an altered and in many ways incompatible new understanding of natural law diverged from the long-established version at the dawn of the age of reason—a century before the life of Edmund Burke.

Strauss credited Burke with attempting "at the last minute" a "return to the premodern conception of natural right" by siding with "Cicero and Suarez against Hobbes and against Rousseau." But while Burke may have been philosophically sympathetic to the men of virtue, neither the "practical character" of his political career nor the historically specific nature of his conservatism enabled him to adhere to the classic tradition of natural law. In the first instance, Burke "did not hesitate to use the language of modern natural right whenever that could assist him in persuading his modern audience of a policy which he recommended. He spoke of the state of nature, of the rights of nature or of the rights of man, and of the social compact or of the artificial character of the commonwealth." On the other hand, "he may be said to integrate these notions into a classical or Thomastic framework." In Strauss's opinion, Burke used fragments of scholastic thought (derived selectively from Aquinas and Aristotle) to fight against abstract or theoretical reasoning. But instead of countering modern rationalism with classical reasoning and faith in universal truths, Burke fell back on English tradition: "For almost all practical purposes . . . the established constitution, is the highest authority. . . . The root of legitimacy is not so much consent or contract as proved beneficence, i.e., prescription. . . . The people is so little the master of the constitution that it is its creature. . . . The people, or for that matter any other sovereign, is still less master of the natural law; natural law is not absorbed by the will of the sovereign or by the general will."[66]

This was the crux of the Burkean problem for Strauss, who believed that "Burke's remarks on the problem of theory and practice are the most important part of his work." Burke's retreat to history as an antidote to speculative theory proved in the end to be merely a successful stopgap measure. That is, it was an effective move against the Jacobins, but it offered no long-term solutions in the form of affirmative guiding principles. Because historical experience is merely "concerned with the particular and the changeable," while theory is "concerned with the universal and unchangeable[,] . . . political rules derived from experience . . . are . . . inapplicable to new situations" and "history is only of very limited value." Moreover, Burke's belief that the best constitution was unwritten, unplanned, accidental, natural, and that it accumulated over many years "without guiding reflection, continuously, slowly, not to say imperceptibly," contradicted the classic tradition, which held that "the best constitution is a contrivance of reason, i.e., of conscious activity or of planning on the part of an individual or of a few individuals. . . . It is a work of design . . . directed toward a variety of ends. . . . The best constitution is therefore directed particularly toward that single end which is by nature the highest." That highest end was "the perfection of human nature," which meant the pursuit of virtue.[67]

Somewhat anomalously for a conservative writer, Strauss depicted Burke as prudent yet conflicted and confused. Strauss identified Burke's chief concern as "personal liberty" or "individuality" (because it was the brave new impulse of his age), but at the same time he concluded that "Burke himself was still too deeply imbued with the spirit of 'sound antiquity' to allow the concern with individuality to overpower the concern with virtue."[68] Burke was unable to join the emerging liberals, but he was equally unequipped to apply classical reason to the issues of his day, since the constitution upon which he founded his political philosophy was impervious to active reason. For Burke, "designing men" could never be virtuous; or more precisely, while individuals could be virtuous, political virtue could never result from collective human design. (He saw the Glorious Revolution as a restoration, not an innovation.) This was the idealistic opposite of Strauss's belief in the conscious exercise of classical reason in the pursuit of public virtue. Still, it seems that several postwar writers (and some writers since) assumed that Strauss agreed with Burke across the board. One scholar remarked that while Hoffman, Kirk, and Stanlis championed Burke outright, Strauss seemed to nod with approval from the sidelines.[69] Anyone who did not read Strauss carefully could easily mistake his condemnation of modern liberalism and his respect for classic natural law as endorsements by default of Burkean conservatism.[70] So strong was Burke's reputation as the quintessential traditionalist conservative that "virtuous" conservatives who did not subscribe to his vision (such as Strauss and Richard Weaver), and professedly "descriptive" analysts (such as Clinton Rossiter), sometimes found themselves mistakenly lumped into the Burkean camp.

Critical Reaction

It did not take long for critics of the new conservative Burkeans to mount an opposition. Even some admirers of Burke voiced skepticism over the extent of his devotion to natural law. Gertrude Himmelfarb responded (in 1949) to the claims of Millar, Hoffman, and Levack by noting that "for every citation from Burke demonstrating his submission to 'the universal natural law of reason and justice ordained by God as the foundation of a good community,' there are two others conclusively establishing his contempt for theories of natural law and abstract, absolute values." Himmelfarb eventually grew sympathetic to the natural law interpretation, at least as it applied to *Reflections*. But she refused to repudiate her initial opinion, and confessed: "I myself may be of two minds about [Burke]."[71] Since the new conservatives were appropriating Burke for a tradition of their own construction, certain liberal writers seemed to take pleasure in exposing the abuse. The *New Republic* spoke to the matter in 1956, when it expounded on the absurdity of applying ancient tradition in the modern age: "We are told . . . that we must erect new shrines to our grandfathers; one devotee of the 'New Conservatives' has even stated . . . that 'we must think through the graveyard.'"[72]

> It is not surprising that in this plethora of ancestor fetishism, the name of Edmund Burke should be on the lips of its modern defenders. . . . Many of Burke's followers in modern times tend to see in historic forms of class rule a spirit of *noblesse oblige* which ordinary historians, unequipped with Burkean lenses, cannot discern. . . .
>
> . . . It would seem that our ancestors, while sometimes wise, were as frequently stupid, and that we of this generation suffer from their stupidities. . . . We need . . . a new and viable radicalism; not the stone of the ancestor-worship that Burke has bequeathed to us.[73]

Another *New Republic* writer observed that "The only kind of conservatism, or liberalism for that matter, which was legitimate for Burke was that which emerged from, and was required by the *actual historical situation*."

In other words, the importance of circumstances was key. The natural law, the ancient constitution, prescription, and custom, bent to the specifics of the moment, not the other way around. "But our new conservatives, by displaying what is essentially a mood as a philosophy of politics, deny to statesmen that flexibility." This perception captured the intuitive nature of new conservative traditionalism, which represented a sensibility rather than a program. Still, many new conservatives (because they were more philosophe than philosopher) yearned for concrete applications of their antimodernist impulses. Singling out Russell Kirk for special censure on this point (in part because he attacked "Deweyites"), the *New Republic* complained that "Kirk has sought to convert the art of conservative statesmanship into a theory of political conservation and use."[74] Of course, since new conservatives had little to lose but their irrelevance, there was no such thing as bad publicity. Prominently placed dismissals of their ideas by liberal intellectuals only heightened their profile, and were therefore encouraging. "Nothing is more revealing of Positivism's extremity," claimed a letter to the *Burke Newsletter* in 1960, "than the irresponsible manner in which its partisans attack Burke, as the symbol of a conservatism they now recognize to be a threatening antagonist."[75] Such confidence was still premature; but the new conservatives had at least succeeded in rejuvenating a moribund intellectual tradition, and they had effectively installed Edmund Burke as its figurehead.

Yet while acknowledging their achievements, one must confront head-on the legitimacy of the marriage they forced between Burke and natural law. Not only was natural law the original doctrine of the Burkean revival; it also symbolized an essential feature of contemporary Burkeanism: what one writer called "the appeal of the everlasting in an age of revolution."[76] Stanlis and others showed that some of Burke's statements *could be* extrapolated into an essentially religious ideology, centered on a strict construction of conservative natural law. But none of the new conservative writers provided a convincing enough argument that such an interpretation *should be* accepted. The new schoolmen of the natural law tradition made a case that was not entirely groundless; but was it wise? Even if some general awareness of natural law contributed to Burke's philosophy, did natural law doctrine as its postwar champions understood it stand at the very core of his worldview? This seems unlikely, since both Burke's thought and the idea of natural law were so multifaceted. For example, the Jesuit scholar Francis Canavan (another Fordham professor, and a moderate Burkean conservative) has cautioned that any conclusions about the "net effect" of Burke's religious beliefs on his philosophy "will necessarily be the judgement of the one making [it] and therefore, if you will, subjective."[77] And Benjamin Fletcher Wright's study of *American Interpretations of Natural Law* (1931)—which appeared well before the rise of the new conservatives—concluded that "the natural law concept has been used in many ways and for many purposes. It has aided in the defense of the most diverse causes. It has, in other words, not been a narrowly confined group of changeless rules, but rather a flexible instrument." Tellingly, Wright's substantial book contained no mention of Edmund Burke.[78] Given the many interpretations of Burke over the course of American history, it seems doubtful that such an ideologically motivated attempt at Burkean revisionism should be accepted as anything other than interesting, convenient, and clever.

In the first place, the doctrine of natural law itself is open to challenge. No need to embark here on a tangent that could easily extend to infinity. Suffice it to say that establishing a working intellectual consensus about whether there is such a thing as natural law, and if so exactly what form it takes, and how that form might be practically applied to public policy, is an impossibility.[79] Furthermore, it seems logical to argue that the idea of natural law was exactly the sort of abstract theoretical construct that Burke claimed to reject as a useful guide to human behavior. But even if Burke evaded his own advice on such matters (which he often did), and intuitively accepted that some "natural" or "divine" rules governed man's "nature" and therefore his activities and his morality, did he not also believe that such rules were inscrutable and shrouded in mystery? Hence it is likely that Burke's caveat (in *Reflections*) concerning man's "pretended rights" applied as well to "natural right" or to "natural law." That is,

> Rights entering into common life, like rays of light which pierce a dense medium, are, by the laws of nature, refracted from their straight line. Indeed . . . rights of men undergo such a variety of refractions and reflections, that it becomes absurd to talk of them as if they continued in the simplicity of their original direction. The nature of man is intricate; the objects of society are of the greatest possible complexity; and therefore no simple disposition or direction of power can be suitable either to man's nature, or to the quality of his affairs.[80]

One would assume that this cautionary view would have rejected the simple disposition or direction of natural law along with the "metaphysic rights" of the philosophes. While on the subject, one might also take issue with the natural law conservatives' use of "right reason" as a moral trump card. Indeed, their assertion (taken from Cicero) that "its commands and prohibitions always influence good men, but are without effect upon the bad," sounds strikingly similar to Burke's sarcastic remark (taken from Samuel Butler's *Hudibras*) regarding men who "have lights where better eyes are blind, as pigs are said to see the wind."[81] This "right reason" mentality—ascriptively classical and Catholic—suspiciously smacked of the self-righteousness of the Protestant Calvinist elect, who saw in their own elite standing and worldly success the signs of their salvation—and by implication the damnation of everyone else.

Natural law was not the key to understanding Burke's Whig vision, or even the portion of it that today we call conservatism. Though there is nothing wrong with using the natural law hypothesis as a heuristic device for probing Burke's philosophy, it can be used effectively only if combined with, and tested against, other approaches. Nevertheless, the historical importance of the idea of natural law as a major component in the postwar Burkean revival should not be underestimated.

Chapter 11

The Cold War

Existential Threat Redux

While natural law remained an esoteric concern during the 1950s, the Cold War became a major preoccupation of the American public, and it provided the apocalyptic context for political and social debate. The communist menace was cited repeatedly on such issues as the Marshall Plan, McCarthyism, the fluoridation of water supplies, civil rights, math and science education, the interstate highway system, and management of the "mixed economy." Moreover, fear of "godless communism" was not just theoretical; the threat of nuclear attack by the Soviet Union made it primal. Suburbanites did not build fallout shelters and schoolchildren were not taught to "duck and cover" because the secular relativists were coming. Mainstream liberals, including such relativists among them, were as engaged in the struggle to protect the "free world" and the "American way of life" against "totalitarianism" as the conservatives were—though their efforts were less emotionally extreme. More to the point, the expansion of communism provided a historical parallel to the spread of Jacobinism in Burke's day. As Ross Hoffman put it in 1949: "The rise of the doctrines of Karl Marx and communism to a commanding influence over men's minds has been a phenomenon comparable to the ascending movement of the doctrines of Rousseau and the kind of democracy that was called Jacobinism."[1]

Return of the Jacobins

Of course there were fundamental differences between the French and Russian Revolutions. But as the editors of an American collection of Burke's writings pointed out in 1960 (not long after Castro's victory in Cuba), their practical effects were identical:

> The Russian Revolution did not appeal to abstract reason as the French Revolution did. . . . Yet the result is the same in essence: reason is separated from experience and becomes the enemy of morals. A nation is created which is . . . the center of a world-wide revolution, which exists to foment civil war everywhere. Its end is a new social organization opposed to the spirit—moral, social, religious—of Western civilization as it has developed up to now.[2]

After quoting Burke's assertion that "a sect of fanatical and ambitious atheists" was "aiming at universal empire . . . beginning with the conquest of France," the editors observed: "Burke sounds as though he were talking of Communists, not Jacobins, and he sounds that way over and over because he is talking about the same issue." In particular, "Communism is totalitarian; it differs from ordinary despotism because it enters every area of life." Moreover, "It is usually assumed that totalitarianism is a twentieth-century creation. Yet Burke found that Jacobinism governed too much, that its hand was on every aspect of life. . . . In a word, he found it totalitarian."[3] A very similar connection between Jacobins and Bolsheviks had appeared in *Newsweek* in 1953 (just months after the Korean armistice), when Raymond Moley praised the "final distillation of Burke's thought in his *Reflections*." Moley noted that while schoolboys knew Burke for his oratory on the American Revolution (confirming that Burke had survived more as a rhetorician than as an antiradical), conservatives knew him for his still relevant attack on the French Revolution. Moley had been a key member of FDR's "Brain Trust," but he deserted the New Deal when he felt it had become too pro-labor and antibusiness. Defecting to the Republican Party, Moley befriended Herbert Hoover and became an adviser to conservative heavyweights including Taft, Nixon, and Goldwater. Moley's adaptation of Burke to the politics of anticommunism reflected his ongoing reaction against leftist overreach: "We face the same rejection of civil order, justice, morality, and religion in the polluted Marxian wake of the revolution in Russia. Like Burke, we cannot compromise with this 'offspring of cold hearts and muddy understanding.' We must have the courage of our conservatism."[4]

Lest one pronounce too harshly against the anticommunist paranoia of the 1950s, it should be noted that a steady stream of events at home and abroad had convinced Americans of the worldwide communist ascendency. Even before the war ended, FDR's perceived capitulation to Stalin over the fate of Eastern Europe set the mood for Churchill's postwar lament that an Iron Curtain had descended across the Continent, dividing freedom from totalitarianism. The Berlin Crisis of 1948, the "loss" of China in 1949, the invasion of South Korea in 1950, the Viet Minh victory in French Indochina in 1954 (which led Eisenhower to speak of the "falling domino principle" of communism), the Soviet invasion of Hungary in 1956, Soviet development of atomic weapons in 1949 and of the hydrogen bomb in 1953, followed by its launching of the Sputnik satellite in 1957: all contributed to the belief in America that democracy and capitalism were losing their global advantage. In addition, as Republican senator Robert A. Taft wrote in 1951: "If [the communists] are convinced that they cannot achieve world conquest by military means they are likely to turn to their old love of propaganda and infiltration. . . . [which is] well-fitted to [their] missionary ardor."[5] There is no need to recount here the excesses and abuses of the search for communist infiltrators in the army and the State Department, in Hollywood studios, labor unions, and elsewhere. But if the tactics were often inexcusable, the climate in which they operated made them at least understandable. Indeed, the retrospective image of Senator Joseph McCarthy as a reckless buffoon is unfair not because it misjudges his character, but because it absolves from censure the millions of citizens who willingly marched to his tune. Historical circumstances spawned the hysteria; the unexceptional man who personified it was mostly a symptom.

Yet therein lies another similarity with the French Revolution. If McCarthy (as the saying went) believed that a communist was hiding under every bed, then Burke believed that there were Jacobins in every closet, pulpit, and port. Akin to Taft's reasoning, Burke believed that if radicals could not conquer Britain by military invasion, they would attempt to do so by propaganda and infiltration. The full title of his masterwork said as much: *Reflections on the Revolution in France and on the Proceedings in Certain Societies in London Relative to That Event.* Burke was referring to Dr. Richard Price's enthusiastic endorsement of France's "ardor for liberty" in a sermon he preached before the London Revolution Society. Price's declaration that the revolutions of 1688, 1776, and 1789 were equally "glorious" amounted to a naive and dangerous conflation, in Burke's view.[6] Certainly Burke hoped that the French would regain their senses and revert to their traditional mode of government (with necessary reforms); but he wrote *Reflections* to save Britain from following the French example. What is more, his *Letter to a Noble Lord* revealed that high rank was no shield against suspicion of collusion with the enemy, or of being too soft in one's opposition to the enemy's insidious presence. George Marshall, a former five-star general, secretary of state, and secretary of defense, and Robert Oppenheimer, the former Manhattan Project director, would learn this lesson through bitter personal experience during the red scare. McCarthyites and Burkeans (the two camps may be compared ideologically without combining them intellectually) believed that under extreme circumstances, overreaction was better than complacency, and that sympathy or compromise was treason.

This attitude accounted for much of the sweep and creep of anticommunism, which casually equated liberalism with subversion. The postwar conservative reaction against the established liberal hegemony did not last long, but it made a distinct impression. In 1950, *Life* magazine pronounced that America was undergoing a "conservative revival." Its editorial "hypothesis" was "that this country is going conservative—with a little *c*," which represented "the opposite, all in all, of the spirit identified with the name and era of Franklin Roosevelt." This meant "that such old-fashioned words and concepts as 'right' and 'wrong' are returning powerfully to American life." Among the wrongs were too much government spending and a growing sense of public entitlement. But the chief wrong, which inspired *Life* to call for the defeat of Truman Democrats, was the big *C*: "Communism is *wrong*. Therefore it is hostile to all that is good, solid and enduring in the American spirit." Consequently, "the rightness of the anti-communist purpose ought not to be in question."[7] *Life*'s declaration trailed closely in the wake of McCarthy's newfound ability to capture national headlines, and was a salient example of the ideological atmosphere within which conservatives reprised Burke's antirevolutionary arguments.

Less prominently, a *Thought* editorial in 1949 entitled "Burke and Our Present Discontents" virtually cried eureka. "Here is the Burke we have all been looking for," proclaimed historian Crane Brinton, who was impressed by "the special timeliness of Burke today" and who praised his attack on the "Jacobin perversion into totalitarianism." From Brinton's perspective, the historical parallel was unmistakable: "We call totalitarians by other names today, but the evil is the same. The Jacobin and the Bolshevik, the totalitarian, the humanitarian, the earthly perfectionist, though their concrete programs may seem antithetical, they have this in common: they cannot really abide, let alone understand, men and women." The fact that Brinton was an "optimistic rationalist" rather than a pessimistic conservative signaled that anticommunism had pervaded the political spectrum (absent only from the hard left).

It typified as well the tendency of some old-generation liberals (like Walter Lippmann) to display quasi-conservative impulses.[8] A similar reaction had previously overtaken certain old-generation Progressives during the 1930s, when they moralistically attacked the secular socialism of the New Deal. This cyclical phenomenon (which would happen again in the late 1960s) demonstrated that while conservatism could sidestep the notion of perpetual progress, liberalism had to extend itself every generation—often to the distress of its old champions. Significantly, Brinton was not only an expert on Jacobins and revolutions, but was also a major figure in the teaching of the history of Western civilization in the United States. True to the patterns of Edmund Burke and American Burkeans, Brinton attacked radicalism because he feared it was on the verge of destroying the world as he knew it.

The same year as Brinton's article, the genuinely conservative Peter Viereck (who had coined the terms "new conservatives" and "Burkean new conservatism") published his *Conservatism Revisited*, a slimmer and more narrowly focused anticipation of Kirk's *Conservative Mind*. Viereck paid homage to Metternich more than to Burke, but he credited Burke with founding the political conservatism that Metternich learned from (his assistant) Gentz. And he echoed Brinton's *Thought* editorial by recognizing the contemporary relevance of Burke: "A Burkean conservative opposes tyranny from above as well as from below. . . . Americans will find none timelier than Burke though his *Reflections on the Revolution in France* are dated 1790. He teaches us to answer world revolution not by out bidding it with a leftism of our own nor by a reactionary rightist tyranny but by conserving the free institutions of the west." Remarkably, Viereck was a defender of New Deal economics and—like Kirk—a critic of capitalist materialism, which testified to an affinity with the culturally conservative progressives and the (not so progressive) new humanists, and to an antipathy to the Republican old guard.[9] This served as yet another indication that conservatives were united less by what they stood for, than by what they fought against.

A more fully developed link between Burke and anticommunism surfaced in Francis Graham Wilson's *Case for Conservatism*, which appeared in 1951 but—according to Russell Kirk—"made no great immediate stir." Wilson's two main points were that "Burke's writings are the doctrinal source of modern conservatism" and that "Marxism . . . has changed profoundly the conservative opposition to revolution." Because Marxism denied the "essential intellectual positions" of both "Western conservatism" and "Western liberalism," it threatened the very survival of Western civilization.[10] Therefore, conservatism in the postwar era had necessarily become an anticommunist crusade. Wilson believed there were at least five affirmative "characteristics" of Western conservative thought, and he feared that the political triumph of Marxism would endanger them all.[11] Interestingly, although Wilson alluded to the horrors of totalitarianism, he shied away from using that ubiquitous word. In fact, he hardly spoke of "communism," and instead resorted to such substitutes as "Slavic ideology," "revolution from the East," or "revolutionary tyranny." Perhaps Wilson's willingness to avoid the clichés of the hour accounted for both his failure to make an impression in 1951 and his belated appeal as a thoughtful advocate of anticommunist Burkeanism. Contrary to Leo Strauss, Wilson preferred Burke's "historical rationalism" to the classical or "ancient" variety. The historical conservatism of Burke, Vico, Montesquieu, and Hegel "taught . . . that . . . each nation had to learn its own lesson from its own national tradition."[12] Again in contrast to Strauss, Wilson thought that this "timely" rather than "timeless" approach (my terms) was a good thing, as it acknowledged the importance of temporal circumstances.

Upon reading Wilson's *Case for Conservatism* today, one encounters a fine synthesis of some of the nobler strands of Burkean traditionalism in the American setting. Certainly it was anticommunist, but the emphasis was on the preservation of a free and progressive civilization: "Burke's system was a defense of the national tradition, and of the nation-state as the context of the good life." Hence, "the benefits of a historically continuous civilization must be realized." Moreover, "the long-run conservative tradition has believed that government must represent the total body of social interests; it has drawn its standards from the moral tradition of the West. . . . [That] is the kind of conservatism that wrote the Constitution of the United States, and it is the kind of conservatism that has enabled the British system to change and to persist through many and startling phases of history." Furthermore, "Ideas and a common spirit can unite a people, but material interests must surely divide." Most Burkean of all, the "conservative spirit in America is thus never simply a defense of things as they are, for at height it seeks to blend the fading past and the emerging future into an imaginative present." Wilson's ultimate Whiggish conclusion was that "modern tyranny is, perhaps, merely the symbol of the failure of the conservatives to perform their constant, historical task."[13] It might be suggested here that many modern tyrannies (fascism, Nazism, numerous right-wing dictatorships) materialized because certain types of conservatives performed their tasks so well. But this would be making a separate point. Surely if conservatism can be equated with the enlightened application of Burke's Whig vision of progressive traditionalism, Wilson's argument becomes easier to appreciate.

The Burkean Moment

During our initial discussion of Edmund Burke's reputation, it was noted that without *Reflections* he would have remained a minor historical figure. *Reflections* immortalized Burke and inserted his antirevolutionary message into countless textbooks and lectures on Western civilization, Anglo-European history, political philosophy, and also the books and articles of political journalists and assorted intellectuals. Ironically, despite this book's desire to counterbalance the "gatekeeper" effect of *Reflections*, it probably would not have been written had not the Cold War political climate inspired the comparison of Jacobinism and communism. The postwar antitotalitarian crusade lent a relevance and immediacy to the Burkean revival that the new conservative movement, the natural law resurgence, the diffuse remnants of Anglo-American traditionalism, and the appreciation of great rhetoric did not. In consequence, a "Burkean moment" occurred. Revivalists consciously reshaped the manner of Burke's appearance in light of problems they identified as crucial to the survival of civilization as they chose to see it. Their entrepreneurial efforts yielded a revised and proprietary image of Burke that supplanted all prior interpretations, and this resulted in a paradigm shift in the application of Burkean thought that has set the pattern to this day. Cold War Burkeans may not have been able to copyright Burke's legacy, but the effect of their appropriation was the same. Of course, this was easy to accomplish when the ideological opposition did not object. Remember that because Burke defended kings and queens while denouncing calls for liberty and equality, he was rejected, dismissed, or ignored by the American intellectual mainstream. But by neglecting one of the world's greatest polemicists, liberal writers not only impoverished their own (implicit) canon, but also ceded the Burkean legacy to illegitimate heirs.

It has become almost obligatory for historians to debunk the myth of postwar consensus; yet relative to earlier and later traumas, American society from the mid-1940s to the mid-1960s approximated consensus more than it exemplified conflict, turmoil, or fragmentation. Despite the noise from the right wing, most politicians and opinion makers of the era were at heart either liberal conservatives or conservative liberals. Hence the practical gap between centrist conservatives (of the "me too" Republican variety) and mainstream liberals was bridgeable on many issues. Excepting the (then tiny) radical left, all segments of the political spectrum could have agreed with the essentials of Burke's arraignment of ideological tyranny, even if most would not have accepted his monarchism, mysticism, Old World traditionalism, and many of the finer points of his argument.[14] Moreover, the parallels certain writers drew between eighteenth- and twentieth-century totalitarianism would likely have seemed valid to all but the most intellectually fastidious observers. Yet the postwar subscription to Burke's antirevolutionary philosophy became partisan rather than general. This outcome was not inevitable; in fact one of the earliest uses of *Reflections* as a Cold War document came not from the new conservatives but from a mainstream academic.

In a 1946 lecture sponsored by the Burke Society of Fordham University, the historian Geoffrey Bruun observed that "People today are in a mood to learn from Burke, perhaps in a more percipient mood than at any time since 1815." Bruun declared *Reflections* to be "the most profound criticism of Jacobin principles and practices which has ever been offered," for in it Burke attacked the dangerous "process of depersonification" that was unleashed by the "rationalists" of his day. Thereafter: "In the nineteenth century this attitude persisted in the positivist schools of sociology, and in the twentieth it shaped the thinking of many totalitarians." Anticipating the cruel hypocrisy of ideological dictatorships, "Burke thought [the Jacobins'] zeal for social justice disguised a lust for power," and "like the philosophes, their masters, they cared more for the power than for the principles or forms of government." Thus began the "technique" of totalitarian rule that was "not yet perfected" in 1790, but has been thoroughly perfected since: "Jacobins gave to the technique of revolution its modern form. All revolutions since 1789 have partaken in some measure of the Jacobin spirit, have drawn upon the Jacobin example, [and] have exploited the Jacobin heritage."[15]

As heated as such statements might sound, Bruun's lecture was no right-wing rant. Judging by his Unitarian Universalist affiliation and some of his other writings, Bruun was of a generally moderate persuasion. Hence he took great pains not to "indict the French Revolution and all its works." Indeed, he credited it with advancing the "democratic tide" in the nineteenth century, and with starting a "great era of constitutionalism, of representative and responsible government, [and] of popular enfranchisement" in "Western society," along with "an advance in human welfare unique in history." Unlike the new conservatives, Bruun made sure he did not throw the liberal baby out with the radical bathwater. On this point, however, he wrongly assumed that Burke shared his optimistic view that the French Revolution was a leap of progress tainted by troubling side effects: "It was not the genuine humanitarian aims of the French Revolution that Burke attacked, and it is not the benefits which followed the revolution that are in question here. But unfortunately the great revolution loosed something more upon society than a program of liberal reforms." Bruun's otherwise excellent insight could be faulted for not recognizing that Burke's hatred of the revolution foreclosed any possibility of acknowledging its potential for good. On the other hand, since Bruun's focus was elsewhere, his enthusiastic ode to the revolution's good intentions and its long-term benefits was offered merely as an aside.[16]

The main purpose of Bruun's lecture was to comb *Reflections* for the criticisms of Jacobinism that were relevant to twentieth-century totalitarianism. Bruun was concerned with fighting revolutionary fanaticism, not with reviving Burke's traditionalism or romanticism. He took from *Reflections* only what he needed for that task: Like modern totalitarianism, the Jacobin system "meant the destruction of everything opposed to it. . . . There was no place for [a] loyal opposition." Jacobinism had initiated "the essential and exclusive role to be played by the Party. . . . The one party dictatorships of the twentieth century prove that the Jacobin experiment was not fortuitous or unique." Another similarity was "anti-clericalism," which attempted "to justify political authority by secular sanctions." Bruun condemned such "godless philosophy" and feared its determination to "control education, culture, even the consciences of the citizens." Equally familiar to twentieth-century observers was "an inhuman cruelty towards enemies of the Revolution. . . . The Jacobin Utopia . . . had no place for political dissenters, and recalcitrant groups were faced by the threat of exile or extermination." In addition, the Jacobins anticipated the communists in their holding of sham elections, and in the state's "monopoly of propaganda." According to Bruun, the "Jacobin heritage" gave to the modern word "a mood and a technique," which he described as "psychopathic" "political despotism." Finally, Bruun saw Maximilien Robespierre as the prototype for modern utopian dictators, who "idealized humanity but . . . disliked people."[17] Coincidentally, Bruun's little-known lecture was delivered just days before the diplomat George F. Kennan sent his secret "Long Telegram" from Moscow to the State Department, analyzing the nature of Soviet communism. And it was published just before Kennan began expanding that document to include a strategy of global containment.[18]

Published anonymously in 1947 as "The Sources of Soviet Conduct," Kennan's analysis—which quickly became famous and influential—bore striking similarities to Bruun's lecture. Though Kennan mentioned neither Jacobins nor Burke, his portrayal of communism's mood and technique shared with *Reflections* a psychological and methodological understanding of the modern ideological state. For example, Marxism (like Jacobinism) served as a "highly convenient rationalization" and a "pseudo-scientific justification" for the revolutionaries' "yearning for power." Stalin and his operatives (like Robespierre and his) would "not . . . tolerate rival political forces in the sphere of power which they coveted." More Burkean still: "Their particular brand of fanaticism, unmodified by any of the Anglo-Saxon traditions of compromise, was too fierce and jealous to envisage any permanent sharing of power." Again like the Jacobins, their plans for a "positive program" once they achieved power were "nebulous, visionary and impractical." Ultimately, "in seeking that security of their own rule they were prepared to recognize no restrictions, either of God or man, on the character of their methods. And until such time as that security might be achieved, they placed far down on their scale of operational priorities the comforts and happiness of the peoples entrusted to their care." Even more dangerous (and inviting comparison with France in the 1790s), "ideology . . . taught them that the outside world was hostile and that it was their duty eventually to overthrow the political forces beyond their borders."[19]

To the extent that Kennan resembled Burke on the nature of totalitarianism (or the extent to which Burke presciently anticipated Kennan), the bipartisan acceptance of Kennan's analysis demonstrated once again that Burkean arguments were most potent when employed against some identifiable threat. Liberals and conservatives both could have agreed with Burke's characterization of revolutionary tyranny. What separated liberals from conservatives was the extent to which conservatives were willing to accept some of the things Burke was defending as well as to reject those he was fighting. *Reflections* was a long and meandering work, and the parts of it that generically attacked revolutionary tyranny and theoretic dogma were comparatively few and far between. Yet it was exactly those sections that saved the larger work from practical obsolescence. (The overwhelming majority of *Reflections* dealt in specifics about England or France, or in the details of political activity in 1789–90 such as the proceedings of the National Assembly—in other words, in the kinds of "facts" that were tied to particular circumstances.)[20] To Burke, all strands of his argument were inextricably intertwined, including his yearning for chivalry, the "conservative" interpretation of the Glorious Revolution, the admiration of the British as a "dull, sluggish race," and the willingness to venerate that which could not be understood; and these sentiments were holistically joined to his abhorrence of Jacobinism. But for most twentieth-century American readers, swallowing Burke whole would have been impossible. Those few who came close—Kirk, for instance—would have found it difficult to spread Burkean philosophy beyond a limited circle without the benefit (or the "hook") of his timely antiradicalism.

Nevertheless, since the Bolsheviks themselves had acknowledged the connection between the French and Russian Revolutions, one did not have to be particularly imaginative to perceive the postwar relevance of Burkean antiradicalism.[21] Certainly *Reflections* contained its share of quotable condemnations of Jacobin tyranny that were applicable to the Soviet regime. Indeed, *Reflections* anticipated many of the judgments that Geoffrey Bruun, George Kennan, and others made about Russian communism. Stalinist duplicity and barbarity, the supremacy of doctrine over reason, the infamous Soviet rewriting of history, and the triumph of "true believer" extremism all seemed to be current incarnations of old Jacobin devices. Hence Burke's critical remarks about them sounded like timeless truths. *Reflections* offered "free world" intellectuals—liberal as well as conservative—some profound adages that could easily have been written with post-1917 Russia in mind:

> Amidst assassination, massacre, and confiscation . . . they are forming plans for the good order of future society.
>
> Tenderness to individuals is considered as treason to the public.
>
> Liberty is always to be estimated perfect as property is rendered insecure.
>
> The usurpation . . . will hold power by arts similar to those by which it has acquired it.
>
> Their liberty is not liberal. Their science is presumptuous ignorance.
>
> Their humanity is savage and brutal.
>
> They commit the whole to the mercy of untried speculations; they abandon the dearest interests of the public to . . . loose theories.
>
> Such is the effect of the perversion of history, by those who, for the same nefarious purposes, have perverted every other part of learning.
>
> Of all things, wisdom is the most terrified with epidemical fanaticism.[22]

Contrary to the usual tendency of equating anticommunism with conservatism, one must note here that Burke's remarks were fundamentally liberal. They valued human rights, freedom of thought, and civil liberties, and they condemned the abuse of power and ideological fanaticism. Liberals have always been more fearful of police states than conservatives have; outrage against the Haymarket convictions, the Palmer Raids, McCarthyism, and (initially) the Patriot Act did not come from the Right. To put it in Burkean terms: liberals have been quicker than conservatives to "snuff the approach of tyranny in every tainted breeze." Probably this was a function of the liberal emphasis on freedom and the conservative emphasis on order. In any event, in postwar America outright support for communism was rare, and sympathy for socialism among liberals served a particular (and notably nonrevolutionary) strategic role: the specter of socialism encouraged—by threat and by example—the mediation of capitalism along New Deal and Great Society lines. This had previously been the strategic approach of Progressive-era politicians, who presented their reform programs as compromises between laissez-faire capitalism and outright socialism; thus reform acted as a tonic against the spread of radical ideologies. (Recall TR's belief that most socialists were merely radical reformers with whom most Americans could work in general agreement.) Economic and welfare policies aside, the war had reinforced the collective American revulsion against undemocratic, authoritarian governments. Yet even this nearly universal sentiment was not monolithic in nature. Liberals hated totalitarianism mostly because it was repressive, inhumane, and militaristic; conservatives hated it mostly because it was evil, godless, and anticapitalist. (After the defeat of fascism and Nazism, conservatives continued to fight communism while often accommodating right-wing dictatorships that allowed business and religious institutions to operate.) Mainstream liberals saw Stalinism as a perversion of humanitarian socialism; conservatives saw it as the logical outcome of secular positivist thought. This was the key to why Cold War conservatives rushed to embrace the comprehensive traditionalist message of *Reflections*. They agreed with Burke that the breakdown of religion, custom, deference, hierarchy, the sanctity of property, the natural aristocracy, the veneration of history, and other such vestiges of yore had created a vacuum into which totalitarian movements—which were the unharnessed expression of human will—were drawn.

Both liberal and conservative camps saw the Enlightenment as the intellectual and psychological impetus for the French Revolution, but they differed as to whether its effect on history was positive or negative. Likewise, both sides saw Marxism as the wild child of post-Enlightenment rationalism. But to conservatives, the progeny was proof that the ascent of reason led inevitably to the overreach of social engineering. To liberals, the realization that Russia had never experienced the Enlightenment, nor the Reformation, nor the Renaissance, nor the Age of Revolution, nor even—practically speaking—the Industrial Revolution until very late, was proof that it was not a mature society capable of funneling innovation into constructive channels. Conservatives usually ended the story of the French Revolution with the Reign of Terror or with Napoleon; yet France spent the bulk of the nineteenth century inching fitfully toward constitutional democracy. Russia, by contrast, never did achieve that goal; even after the collapse of communism it found that democracy, freedom of the press, and civil liberties were hard to sustain. To conservatives, modernism begat communism; while to liberals this conclusion was disproved by the reality that communism first achieved success in a country that had not yet modernized, and that by 1917 had achieved a stage of development that might well be called neo-feudalism. A similar historical explanation—with all due allowances for the uniqueness of nations—applied to China.

Anticommunism in Perspective

As aggressive a document as *Reflections* may have been, it was more a spirited defense of what Burke wanted to preserve than an offensive assertion of a political philosophy (as, for instance, Marx's writings were). Its defense of traditionalism, rather than its attack on totalitarianism, gave *Reflections* its conservative appeal. Burke's antimetaphysical argument—so highly touted by postwar revivalists—was at heart a distraction and a platitude. Nearly all political agents claimed to be practical rather than theoretical; even Marxists claimed to be scientific. Anyway, rejecting abstract reason was beside the point: postwar Americans did not need to be talked out of communism, whatever its intellectual underpinnings, just as Americans of myriad political stripes did not need to be told why totalitarianism was a bad idea. It is more pertinent to observe that both the content and tone of *Reflections* appealed to conservatives as a unified body of thought, a sensibility, and a worldview. Liberals, on the other hand, had to sift through *Reflections* in search of the comparatively few insights they found useful. Understandably, most chose to spend their time and energy elsewhere.

While the excerpts already cited addressed the horrors of totalitarianism, a more representative passage in *Reflections* explained *why* totalitarianism came to be. That is, it described the modern, post-traditional state of mind:

> These enthusiasts do not scruple to avow their opinion, that a state can subsist without any religion better than with one; and that they are able to supply the place of any good which may be in it, by a project of their own—namely, by a sort of education they have imagined, founded in a knowledge of the physical wants of men; progressively carried to an enlightened self-interest, which, when well understood, they tell us will identify with an interest more enlarged and public. The scheme of this education has been long known. Of late they distinguish it . . . by the name of a Civic Education.[23]

Within these few sentences, some of the major bugaboos of twentieth-century conservatism made their debut. In a faintly derisive tone (and derision itself became pro forma when conservatives spoke of liberalism or worse), Burke mocked the hubris of the radicals, hinted at the conspiratorial nature of their project, and, without actually using the word (which had not yet been coined), classified their school of thought as positivist. He also attacked the antireligious nature of their approach, effectively identifying it as secularist. Burke lived too early to concern himself with the threat of relativism, but he did provide a precocious criticism of the scientistic mentality that would later be used (by classical liberals) to justify the economic marketplace. And since he applied it to morality instead of economics, conservatives could accept his critique without dissent. Finally, his scorn for the educational scheme of the philosophes (presumably derived from Rousseau and Condorcet) presaged the postwar conservatives' hostility to the progressive educational "ideology" of John Dewey and his "school." As Russell Kirk pointed out, education was a means of transmitting values and therefore of preserving civilization; thus those who controlled the spirit of education controlled the future. Conservatives did not need Edmund Burke in order to fight the Cold War. That campaign already had plenty of spokesmen. But they did need his help in the less popular crusade of combating liberalism and the historical rise of the leftist tide. Fortunately, since his anti-Jacobin arguments seemed to fit anticommunism so perfectly, it was easy for conservatives to stretch the wisdom of *Reflections* to cover the perceived threats of humanitarian activism and liberal reform.

In this respect Burke was not only the father of conservatism, but also of modern conservatism's chief debating ploy: the "slippery slope" argument. This tactic implied that if a single step to the left was taken, the worst-case scenario would likely unfold. Limiting the power of the aristocracy would lead to mob rule; disestablishing religion would lead to moral and social collapse; and imposing business regulations would lead to the "serfdom" of a centrally planned economy (so convenient did the myth of the slippery slope become, that even libertarians—who were otherwise champions of innovation—adopted it). Under this ideological law of gravity, liberalism inevitably slid toward socialism, and socialism toward communism. So too with Enlightenment thought: reason slid to rationalism, and in turn to positivism, secularism, relativism, and ultimately to nihilism. Ideally, the best place to stop leftist radicalism was at its tradition-shattering, Enlightenment source. But since that opportunity had long past, and liberalism was now the dominant persuasion of Western civilization, any talk of preemption was meaningless. Where, then, could the brakes be applied? Burke knew that reasonable steps to the left were periodically necessary in order to forestall either social stagnation or political explosion. He even learned through experience that the required steps often turned out to be fairly large ones. Practically speaking, the difference between reform and innovation—just as between revolution and restoration—was in the eye of the beholder. Or to put it another way, the distinction depended on the particular circumstances and on the subjective judgment of the individual. As Burke explained (remarkably, in one of his antirevolutionary essays): "In all situations of difficulty men will be influenced in the part they take, not only by the reason of the case, but by the peculiar turn of their own character. The same ways to safety do not present themselves to all men, nor to the same men in different tempers."[24] Burke even went so far as to warn against "a false reptile prudence, the result not of caution but of fear."[25] With these sentiments, Burke cast himself counter to type—that is, against his unyielding conservative image. Yet the notion of psychological—and therefore ideological—ambivalence is not surprising to anyone familiar with the more complete Burkean record. Of course, a complex and flexible Burke was not the sort of figure that Cold War conservatives chose to present to America. Indeed, if one focused solely on *Reflections*, then the simplicity of good versus evil, or of tradition versus totalitarianism, seemed obvious. Likewise, by focusing on anticommunism, his modern admirers found it easy to keep Burke conservative by keeping him simple.

To assert that the Cold War distorted Burke's reputation, or that the postwar conservatives were not his true heirs, is not to suggest that Burke's antirevolutionary radicalism was not genuine or that it had no twentieth-century application. Nor is there much doubt that Burke would have hated communism or that he would have subscribed (at least loosely) to some version of the domino theory.[26] Yet this says little of importance about the "father of conservatism," since liberals and moderates also opposed communism and feared its spread. It bears repeating that on a fundamental level, antitotalitarianism was a manifestation of the liberal (antiauthoritarian) worldview. As for the slippery slope, liberals inverted that metaphor by interpreting each step to the left as an advance up the inclined plane of civilization. Hence more democracy, more freedom of thought, more "rights," more tolerance, less superstition, less injustice, and so on, moved humanity toward a greater potential for personal happiness. To liberals, reform was the political path to progress. But postwar Burkean conservatives fought both innovation and reform. While Burke declared that a state without some means of change was without a means of its own conservation, traditionalist and right-wing conservatives rejected most of the changes that had taken place in recent generations. They did not seek merely to apply the brakes; they wanted American civilization to reverse course.

Most important, the useful antitotalitarian observations in *Reflections* did not by themselves validate the conservative traditionalists' reliance on the "wisdom" of entailed inheritance, natural law, religion, prescription, chivalry, ancient rights, and so on. That is, to the modern mind such matters were separable from the critique of utopian radicalism. Only the organic holism adhered to by certain conservatives required accepting everything in *Reflections* as comprising a mutually supportive system, with each element indispensable. While traditional orders did prevent dangerous experimentation so long as they remained healthy, the breakdown of such systems did not necessarily lead to horrible outcomes: liberal democracies as well as totalitarian dictatorships followed the Age of Revolution. In fact, Burke's Whig sensibility, as well as the broader Whig interpretation of history, rested on the premise that a nation's ability to make incremental reforms determined its prospects of avoiding harmful revolutions. In other words, the right kinds and the proper doses of liberal activism kept radicalism in check. The primary error of postwar conservatives was to misunderstand this—or perhaps to misinterpret it for partisan advantage. It was ironic that while the postwar Burkeans held a most holistic worldview, they subscribed to the most narrow construction of Burke's philosophy.

Cold War conservatives were wrong to equate liberalism with communism, and wrong to suggest that liberal reform greased the slippery slope to tyranny. The modern emphasis on reason (and assertive human agency) could not have taken hold if the traditional methods of understanding and governing society had been more effective. Furthermore, the ramifications of the Age of Revolution were ongoing; they did not conclude with the American Constitution, or the Reign of Terror, or with the rise or fall of the Soviet regime. While it is logical to suppose that Burke—exhumed and vitalized—would have been a cold warrior, it is less clear what his positions would have been on a variety of other issues. As earlier noted, Burke's Whig vision seemed to be fairly congruent (making the necessary historical adjustments) with that of certain turn-of-the-century Progressives. It is no great risk to suggest that Burke would have rejected leftist radicalism, but mainstream liberalism was another matter. Perhaps a postwar Burke might have been a political moderate: slightly liberal on some matters, slightly conservative on others. One must not overreact to the Cold War interpretation of Burke by ignoring his genuine conservatism; but one must not pretend that Burke—before or after 1789—thought that all kinds of conservatism were beneficial, or that civilization could ever stand still. Burke often sided with reformers, or even with radicals, against conservatives. The right-of-center revivalists should not be condemned for claiming a piece of Burke, but for claiming the whole of him. Equally so, their left-of-center intellectual counterparts might be chastised for leaving Burke completely unclaimed and unattended.

Chapter 12

Contemporary Conservatives

Victories and Illusions

Unlike the Cold War, which many believed offered clear alternatives between good and evil and right and wrong, most social and political concerns in the final decades of the twentieth century did not lend themselves to such all-or-nothing analysis. (The loudest exception to this rule was the clash over abortion rights, a battle that Burke was not asked to join.) Plenty of writing on Edmund Burke has appeared since the 1970s, but much of it has not been useful for tracing the course of American ideals. In part this represented a maturation of Burkean scholarship, as well as a diversification of it.[1] Yet with Burke, as with political thinking in general, any post–Cold War "end of ideology" proved to be illusive, exaggerated, or merely transitory. The partisan deployment of Burke may no longer be the only Burkean game in town, but it has seemingly found a permanent niche. Still, perhaps the "father of conservatism" has mostly served his purpose, and his name—already enshrined in the pantheon—will be stitched on fewer battle flags. The impact of ideological publications on Burke has mirrored the general trend of American conservatism since the war: as the right has gained respectability and power, its traditionalist strain—which had been so instrumental to the revival of the 1940s and 1950s—has declined in relative importance. Eventually the postwar casting of Burke as a conservative oracle inspired some countervailing revisionism—though it took nearly a generation to surface.

Half Modern

If one ignores the conservative stereotype, Burke is best understood as a transitional thinker. Compared to, say, Maistre and Metternich, he was no royalist reactionary, and in contrast to, say, Marx or Freud, he did not introduce major new concepts to the world. Instead he sought to reconcile customary ways with the spirit of new ideas (while often rejecting the ideas themselves). Burke was a "half modern" during the last generation in which that worldview was still defensible, or at least understandable. In the twentieth century, Burke became the father of conservatism because his disciples refused to fully adopt the post-Enlightenment frame of mind: a posture that became less comfortable with each passing decade. Meanwhile, more-neutral commentators tried to understand Burke's historical placement. Such writings as Isaac Kramnick's *The Rage of Edmund Burke: Portrait of an Ambivalent Conservative* (1977) and Richard Boyd's article "Edmund Burke's Defense of Civil Society" (1999) highlighted this transitional (rather than traditional) element in Burke's thought.[2]

Kramnick's insights provided a refreshing alternative to the conservative analysis of Burke that had become routine by 1977. For our purposes, the psychological origin of Burke's "ambivalence" is less important than are the historical and intellectual tensions between Burke's traditionalist and his progressive impulses. As Kramnick saw it:

> In late eighteenth-century England a bridge was being forged between two great periods of western Christiandom [*sic*]. The aristocratic age was passing and the bourgeois epoch dawning. . . . [Burke's] basic ambivalence . . . matched most perfectly the historical identity crisis then being experienced by the advanced societies of England and France. . . . There was a long and confused period of transition when men and women were buffeted by the pulls and tugs of both the old and the new order. For sheer dramatic personification of this crisis in the western identity Burke dominates the period as a towering symbol of its "internal strife."[3]

One need not accept every particular of Kramnick's psycho-historical argument in order to understand—or even to agree with—his broader portrayal of Burke as a conflicted participant in the painful transition to modernity.

Two decades later, Boyd jettisoned Kramnick's psycho-historical approach but made virtually the same points from a conventionally political and economic perspective:

> [Burke] could fully envision neither the democratic age of mass opinion . . . nor the modern commercial society that lurked just around the

> corner. . . . His position [was] midway between a premodern world of prescriptive intermediary institutions and a modern society in which commerce and social mobility shattered once and for all these ascriptive bonds. Burke's treatment of intermediary institutions shares that ambivalence.[4]

Boyd even agreed that Burke (along with Tocqueville) was the sort of "liberal conservative" that presaged our present-day neoconservatives.[5] This last point was incorrect. But that Burke could be misclassified as a neoconservative demonstrated once again the timeless truth that his Whig vision tended to warp in the mind of the beholder.

It is unfortunate that the transitional character of Burke's philosophy (whether described as a case of "ambivalence" or as a search for "balance") has not gained wider recognition. Since the conservative stereotype of Burke offers only half of the picture, one is left to wonder why the other half has been so effectively eclipsed. Perhaps the reason lies in the deceptive clarity and single-mindedness of postwar and contemporary conservative writers. When Burkean ideas become tools of persuasion (disguised or not), they are often applied to the task with unjustifiable certainty. Conversely, when Burke's thoughts are analyzed from a less adversarial position, their circumstantial expediency tends to dominate. To understand Burke fully, one must view him in his own historical setting, and a balanced or ambivalent Burke does not travel as well as the ideological caricature. Modern conservatives have had few qualms about bringing Burke, or any part of him (even if it was twisted), anywhere they thought he was needed. Such efforts have become second nature; they serve to dignify the increasingly strident criticisms of liberal culture.

Post-1960s Reaction

What is wrong with America today depends on who is doing the complaining. Those who are most likely to invoke Burke—that is, certain conservatives—are convinced that American civilization is in a state of decline, though exactly when that decline began varies with the source. As we have seen, conservatives have been lamenting the nation's moral and social declension since the end of the Revolution. In the twentieth century, natural law advocates and new conservatives blamed the descent on the encroachment of positivism, relativism, and secularism, all of which Cold War Burkeans linked to communism. For contemporary conservatives, the latest wave of cultural deterioration began with the events of the 1960s and early 1970s.

While liberals generally view "the sixties" as a colorful, liberating, and creative watershed, conservatives view the period as destructively utopian, and needlessly rebellious. The sixties encouraged personal license, social experimentation, and political radicalism; as Abbie Hoffman put it, they were a time of "revolution for the hell of it" (not that he was complaining). In the post-sixties era, conservatives have entrusted themselves with the task of picking up the pieces of American civilization and gluing them back together. Aside from the futility of that effort, not all Americans would agree that their society has been shattered, or that the (nostalgically) perceived coherence of "fifties culture" deserves reclamation. Many liberals believe that American ideals came closer to fruition during the sixties than at any time since the Civil War. Actually, the sixties witnessed a climax and a synthesis of cultural trends that had started much earlier. What was unique about the sixties was the diffusion and popularization of an advanced-modern sensibility, which had previously been confined to intellectuals, artists, and other elites. This blend of modernism and postmodernism made the traditional conservatism associated with Burke less applicable than ever in the United States, where it had never been widely appreciated to begin with. Eventually, the cultural trauma induced by the sixties shocked some conservatives into redoubling their efforts at restoring the nation's virtue.

For example, the writings of Daniel Ritchie and Bruce Frohnen in the 1990s were grounded in religion, virtue, traditionalism, and antirationalism; as such they amounted to a "baby boomer" extension of postwar new conservatism. Ritchie even dedicated a 1990 collection of Burkean appraisals "to the generation of Burke scholars who revived and redirected our knowledge of Edmund Burke after World War II."[6] Ritchie (b. 1955) received his Ph.D. in English from Rutgers in 1985, where his dissertation addressed Burke's "literary significance" for nineteenth-century English romantic writers. Given his literary specialty, Ritchie would seem a curious choice to edit and introduce Burke's overtly political essays in *Further Reflections on the Revolution in France* (1992)—until the ideological leanings of his publisher (Liberty Fund) are taken into account. Even so, the combination of Ritchie (an avowed Christian conservative), Burke (a progressive-traditionalist Whig), and the Liberty Fund (a conservative libertarian organization) made strange bedfellows. Ritchie's introduction to Burke's antirevolutionary writings contained an uneasy mix of libertarian values, justifications for community and state regulation of individual behavior, and odes to the aristocratic gentlemen's code, the mysteries of "art," and "natural law." On the one hand, Ritchie claimed that Burke stood for "security of property, a free market for labor, freedom from confiscatory taxation, and freedom of expression."

But on the other hand, Ritchie acknowledged that because "morality and liberty were dependent upon each other," the imposition of external controls was unavoidable. Toward this end, he reprised the Burkean language that TR had quoted to Congress in 1905. That is, "Society cannot exist unless a controlling power upon will and appetite be placed somewhere, and the less of it there is within, the more there must be without." Yet in relying on this general axiom, Ritchie was dodging the crucial point: it is the practical reconciliation of liberty and order—not the broad recognition that they must somehow balance each other—that feeds the ideological conflicts of modern political thought. But instead of affirming that Burke offered concrete remedies to this omnipresent dilemma, Ritchie resorted to a nebulous evasion worthy of Russell Kirk: "Nature is mediated through art, natural law, through social institutions, the acts of a people through the leadership of a natural aristocracy. Burke's view of practical liberty is complex, but its complexities are those of human life. Its satisfactions are limited, but its limitations are those of human life as well."[7]

Elsewhere, in a book intended as a refutation of multiculturalism, feminism, and other liberal maladies, Ritchie offered an unabashedly religious approach to Burke, confessing: "My own perspectives are rooted in biblical faith [which] provides the most thorough response to ideological criticism. . . . My study proposes a revived religious humanism. . . . My approach to literature, or 'poetics,' comes from the Bible as it has been received by the Christian church." Amazingly, Ritchie claimed that "faith commitments affect literary study . . . but they do not determine outcomes as ideology does." Later, he avowed that "biblical faith is not an ideology," without recognizing that religion applied to politics usually becomes ideological. In his discussion of Burke's impeachment of Warren Hastings, Ritchie began by asserting: "Burke located the foundation for his sympathy with other peoples in his and their common creation in God's image." He declared Burke to have been an adherent of natural law, and he explained Burke's "pluralistic multiculturalism" by means of a scriptural argument regarding the Tower of Babel and the Pentecost.[8] There is little cause to delve into the details of Ritchie's biblical exegesis, since objections to his method need not hinge on interpretive specifics. Instead, one may suggest that Ritchie's theological approach to Burke will appeal mainly to those who share his brand of conservative Christianity, or at least share his anti-secular bias. For anyone else—at the risk of belaboring the point—Ritchie's writing explained Ritchie's world, not Edmund Burke's. It did however offer an implicit critique of contemporary American culture—a task for which Burke continued to be useful. The strained nature of Ritchie's use of Burke demonstrated that applying

Burke's thought to daily politics in the post–Cold War and post-sixties era was no easy task. Feminists, multiculturalists, deconstructionists, and liberal intellectuals may all be descendants of Rousseau; but by now that relationship is distant, and the inheritance has become diluted, adulterated, mutated, and recombinant. Hence the devil Burke thought he knew no longer walks among us. Moreover, many of today's political hot spots (environmentalism, stem cell research, gay marriage, globalization, international terrorism, abortion, affirmative action, gun control, creationism) are so far removed from the issues Burke addressed that extrapolating his philosophy to cover them becomes highly speculative.

Nevertheless, Ritchie seemed especially bent on transporting Burke past his known world. He even claimed that "[Burke] would note that three of the major founders of modern philosophy—Rousseau, Marx, and Nietzsche—all inspired cults and, later, revolutions by men and women claiming to be their followers, and yet many modern intellectuals have tried to exonerate the philosophers themselves of the sufferings caused by those revolutions. Burke, however. . . . does not feel free to divorce ideas from unforeseen consequences."[9] One may wonder (as apparently Ritchie did not) if Burke must be held accountable because his ideas were used to defend slavery, utilitarianism, and social Darwinism. Or more broadly, how responsible was Edmund Burke for the later behavior of self-styled Burkeans? The sensible answer is that Burke must be praised, damned, or otherwise judged for what he said and did within the context of his life. He is not answerable for what later advocates *think* he meant, or (as in Ritchie's last quote) for what they think he *might* say now. As to America's current "culture wars," it seems that Burke's writings are a poor source of practical advice. Burke had enough trouble grasping the early modern sensibility; to expect his Whig vision to comprehend the advanced modern consciousness would be absurd. This does not mean that Burke can no longer be relevant, only that readers must be careful not to stretch him too far, or to take him completely out of his element (this point will be revisited).

A God-centered, resurgent new conservative view of Burke has also been prominent in the work of Bruce Frohnen. Frohnen (b. 1962) studied political science under Kramnick at Cornell, and his dissertation was *Virtue and the Promise of Conservatism: The Legacy of Burke and Tocqueville* (1993). Although a relatively short book, *Virtue* addressed several important themes. In part it was a renewed attempt at fusing together the apparently contradictory strains of conservatism (libertarian, neoconservative, traditionalist); in part it sought to reconcile republican liberalism with conservatism; philosophically, it called for an essentially classical commitment to the good life, and for an essentially medieval commitment to the primacy of natural law. Along the way, Frohnen presented his own take on Tocqueville and Burke. His need for Burke was rooted in a (by now familiar) belief that Western civilization was in its "seeming twilight" because of "the rationalistic innovations set forth by the philosophical prophet Jean Jacques Rousseau in the eighteenth century and first instituted, with murderous efficiency, by the French revolutionary despot Robespierre." Predictably, "The French Revolution, like its Marxian progeny in Russia and elsewhere, was essentially an attempt to substitute man's will for God's." Thus, "The conservative need not apologize for throwing stones at the false prophet who would sacrifice us to the god of his own delusions." But in addition to standing in Burkean opposition to rationalism (a cliché by 1993), Frohnen updated the argument by aiming his wrath at the perceived moral vacuum of post-sixties society: "Whatever their behavior, all men now claim their right to monetary support from the government, along with the security for self-esteem provided by assurances that all actions will be deemed equally moral. Thus the contemporary conservative must find a basis on which to defend a society tragically divorced in its very spirit from the pursuit of the good life." While Frohnen's quest for civic virtue seems quaintly genuine, his premises are badly flawed. In fact, "all men" do not expect a check from the government, nor do they (even if they are liberals) believe that all actions are equally moral. And since when did conservatives gain a monopoly on pursuing (or in defining) the good life? But it is enough here to identify Frohnen's preconceptions concerning "the corrupt times in which we live."[10]

The Burkean gloss in Frohnen's vision mirrored the natural law perspective pioneered by Peter Stanlis, whom Frohnen explicitly credited with "pathbreaking" work. According to Frohnen, "It is to the traditional, uncorrupted doctrine of natural law that the conservative turns in facing the corruptions of his day." As noted in our discussion of Stanlis and his peers, such an approach required both a leap of faith and an acceptance of a particular conception of natural law; and Burke had to be read with a predisposition toward identifying such natural law as the basis of his philosophy. No doubt this worked for readers who were so inclined, just as earlier readers had performed similar exercises in the cause of utilitarian philosophy. Conversely, readers who approached Burke with different predilections were unlikely to be convinced. Frohnen knew that a narrow reading of Burke would appeal to a narrow audience, and choosing to preach to the religiously conservative choir was intentional. Clearly there was no mistaking his anti-secular animus: "Conservative political philosophy rests on recognition of man's God-given limits. It unabashedly asserts man's need for God. . . . Burke and Tocqueville added to this recognition that we must acknowledge the sovereignty of God."[11] Ultimately, according to Frohnen, Burke believed that

> each man has a specific place in the natural, hierarchical Great Chain of Being, be he peasant, squire, or monarch. And each man must accept his place, itself often bestowed at birth in aristocratic societies, as a manifestation of the will of God. We each have our station in life, a station that determines the nature and extent of our capacity and of our right to act.[12]

It goes without saying that such an outlook conflicted with American egalitarian ideals, and it is doubtful that it would play well today in most of the industrialized world. Aside from its theological rigidity, it implied that most citizens had a duty to obey their "natural superiors" without question, and that they had little or no right to effect change or fight injustice, regardless of their own sufferings under existing conditions. Even if one accepts Frohnen's opinion that such thoughts were an essential feature of Burke's vision, one might suggest that they were obsolete vestiges of Old Whiggery that would be better left for dead. Moreover, it seems that Frohnen's fixation on religion is unlikely to impress secular conservatives—though to him that term is probably an oxymoron.[13] In his view some combination of divinity, hierarchy, tradition, and virtue (probably in that order) constituted the essence of Burke's conservatism. Frohnen even suggested that "perhaps the most famous passage from Burke's writings" was the one that asserted "The awful author of our being is the author of our place in the order of existence." This was a strange claim, considering the competition. Even more suspect was Frohnen's reduction of Burke's philosophy to a virtual commandment: "We must accept our place in the Great Chain of Being lest we defy the will of God. The virtuous man works humbly . . . to fulfill the obligations of his station in life. Men must accept the existing structure of society as a given . . . because unquestioning adherence to traditional forms and practices is itself a virtue."[14]

Here, in true Burkean fashion, a critical reader might submit that if the cheerful acceptance of one's lowly place in society has long ceased to be "natural" behavior, then there were good reasons—if not necessarily provable ones—as to why our "species" has chosen to alter its habits. Even in the Old World, adherence to a strict construction of inherited hierarchy has become extinct. And if Americans had followed Frohnen's advice (which was not quite Burke's), women would never have gotten the vote and blacks would still be slaves. Moreover, both the American economy and its political system would have been deprived of many of its greatest leaders, who sprang from modest beginnings. Like it or not, the modern ambition (or expectation) of men and women to exceed their station at birth has become a driving force behind the phenomenon called "progress." Granted, traditionalists like Frohnen are skeptical of progress (as are many critics on the left, for entirely different reasons), but economic libertarians and neoconservatives could not live without it. Like the new humanists and new conservatives before him, Frohnen seemed less concerned with promoting American ideals than with reverting to some vague semblance of neo-Christendom. While technically this may not constitute utopianism, psychologically it comes very close.

As a practical matter, the theological approach to Burke offered by Ritchie and Frohnen is open to a more pedestrian criticism: even if intellectuals of the secular majority were not their intended audience, it is doubtful that the religious conservatives—who presumably were—had much need for Burke. The beliefs of the religious right today derive from evangelical fundamentalism, not Anglo-traditionalism. With no need for historical mediation, there is little need for apostles like Burke—even if he did conform to the theocratic regime to which Ritchie and Frohnen have assigned him. As for the more Scholastic idea of natural law, a similar criticism applies. Catholic and quasi-Catholic conservatism (now politically allied with Protestant fundamentalism) has grown beyond any necessity for a Burkean slant. Religious conservatism in America would be just as healthy today if Edmund Burke had never existed, or if his name was entirely absent from the writings of God-centered intellectuals. Conversely, the secular liberal intellectuals who (by Ritchie's and Frohnen's own account) present the major obstacle to conservative Christian thought are not susceptible to arguments that allow religious belief to trump reasoned analysis. Hence those who are most sympathetic to arguments proclaiming "God's Burke" do not need them, and those who (allegedly) need them most do not want them. But these tactical considerations aside, writers like Ritchie and Frohnen demonstrated that natural law and new conservatism were back in bloom, and that the ideologically handy Edmund Burke had not been forgotten.

Recent Invocations

Meanwhile, a new variant of Cold War conservatism has sprouted, one that again links liberalism to evil, and occasionally invokes Burke. This time, liberalism stands accused of being soft on terrorism. After the events of September 11, 2001, conservatives effectively added a new verse to their old song. In a *New Criterion* article on Burke (part of a 2002 series on "the survival of culture"), Martin Greenberg called for a renewed seriousness and thoughtfulness among politicians and intellectuals: "But our intellectuals are not up to the task. Steeped in a utopianism whose origins lie far back in religious dissent, they exhibit an ignorant romanticism that finds innocence abroad and evil-doing at home."[15] More specifically:

> Today's left-wing intellectuals, and the troops of the enlightened who trail after them in public and private life, are not moved by ordinary emotions of fear and anger when their country comes under deadly terrorist attack—they are full of *understanding*. Their moral vainglory would cut the throat of liberty once again, threatening the survival of culture, so as to satisfy the sense of their own virtuousness. How well Edmund Burke understood this, two centuries ago.[16]

Similarly, in his introduction to a new American edition of *Reflections* (2003), Frank M. Turner not only lauded Burke's conservative wisdom, but also depicted Burke's adversary Richard Price as the first in a long line of foolish modern liberals: "Price . . . was not badly intentioned, but he was exceptionally naive. . . . Many later academic historians would effectively follow Price and his contemporaries in their general approval of the French Revolution, downplaying or even approving its destructiveness, anticlericism, property confiscation, state violence against French citizens, and ultimately military despotism."[17] Therefore,

> Price was the forerunner of so many later, otherwise peaceful, even personally timid, intellectuals in the West who from the French Revolution to the Russian Revolution to the revolutionary disturbances in the former colonial world to the attack on the United States on September 11, 2001, would voice support for violence and terror or demand that it be "understood" as somehow justified or even deserved in the larger order of things.[18]

Of course, intellectuals (or journalists, or politicians, or citizens) who sought to understand the phenomenon of Islamic terrorism—by asking "Why do they hate us?"—were not implying that they condoned it. An urge for retribution was the initial response to "9/11" on the part of many liberals, as well as most conservatives. Nevertheless, it was possible for responsible Americans to be morally appalled by the World Trade Center and Pentagon attacks and at the same time to be aware that al-Qaeda did not exist in a vacuum, and that misguided support for the likes of Osama bin Laden had to be understood in order to be successfully countered. In other words, not only must the mass murders themselves be (as the euphemism puts it) "brought to justice," but the conditions that create terrorists must be altered. To recognize that American policy in the Middle East helped spawn Islamist terrorism is far from claiming that terrorism's victims "deserved" their fate—or that the United States in general deserved such a catastrophe. Rather, it is a recognition that the government must be more aware of the unintended (and harmful) consequences of its economic and foreign policies, and also of the nation's vulnerability to small groups of committed enemies. While mass murder itself can never be justified, the reasons why fanatical agents might commit it can be explained—and they should be. Furthermore, to equate Jacobinism or communism with religious fundamentalism was inaccurate. Devout Muslims seeking their martyr's passport to paradise were far removed from the worldly enthusiasm of Marxists or secular liberals. Operationally speaking, religious fundamentalists had no use for abstract theory; they had the word of God on their side. And while secular radicals were obsessed with improving the earthly future, religious fanatics found their authority in ancient scripture and were driven by faith in a spiritual afterlife. Even on a basic philosophical plane, religious fundamentalism was at greater odds with liberalism than it was with conservatism.[19]

As was the case with Cold War anticommunism, liberals were no less antiterrorist than conservatives were. But conservatives seemed to be more concerned with talking and acting tough—and with denigrating liberals for not doing the same. Ironically, in their haste to paint the world in simple black and white, conservatives adopted an orientation that was closer to that of the Islamist terrorists than it was to that of the mainstream intellectual community. In their war against terror, fear or anger trumped reason or analysis. Historically, this represented a major blow to the legacy of the Enlightenment.[20]

This anti-Enlightenment sensibility, which had long been an element of conservative thought, has lately come to dominate conservative politics. Not only has political conservatism overtaken political liberalism since 1980, but conservatism has become more reactionary. In the intellectual arena, the right-wing hostility to secular reason resulted in the strange practice of some conservatives being dismissed by others for their lack of atavism. For instance, the same year (1987) that liberals defeated judge Robert Bork as a Supreme Court nominee, he was attacked in *Commonweal* (an otherwise progressive Catholic journal) as "the illegitimate child of contemporary American liberalism." Bork's crime—or perhaps his sin—was to be "skeptical of higher law."[21] Though Bork claimed to be a follower of Burke, his use of Burkean prescription lacked a sufficiently religious foundation. Apparently the *Commonweal* view of Burke comported with the Catholic natural law school, and its indictment of Bork's secularism was reminiscent of the postwar Notre Dame essays (except for the implicit blame on sixties culture):

> It is ironical that Bork's positivism follows logically from the moral relativism promoted by the culture of liberalism for the past twenty years or so. If there is no higher law, and right and wrong are largely matters of personal preference, then there is no philosophically responsible alternative to some form of legal positivism. Despite his temperamental conservatism, Robert Bork is the logical outcome of the liberal revolution in moral thinking that has swept America during the last third of the twentieth century.[22]

Curiously, a decade later Bork spoke of "original sin" in the only paragraph of his best-selling *Slouching towards Gomorrah* (itself a biblical reference) that directly mentioned Edmund Burke. Judge Bork may or may not have been as secularist as *Commonweal* charged, though certainly religion was not his central concern. Bork's main theme was modern liberalism's excessive devotion to personal freedom. On this topic he chose to side with Burke against John Stuart Mill: "Burke, unlike the Mill of *On Liberty*, had a true understanding of the nature of men, and balanced liberty with restraint and order." At the heart of Bork's conservatism was a desire to impose discipline on modern man. Prescription, legal formalism, and judicial restraint were but specific formulations of his general compulsion to control the excesses of individualism—or what liberals might call the pursuit of happiness.[23] During the 1990s Bork became a high-profile critic of "the Sixties" (the capital *S* was Bork's; possibly it reflected the scale of his horror). To Bork, that era was characterized by the inability of American institutions to manage and properly train the younger generation. He acknowledged that "the Sixties" had merely accelerated existing trends, but still blamed that "malignant decade" for implanting "the moral and political assumptions of those who now control and guide our major cultural institutions." In other words, "Sixties radicals" eventually became the "modern liberals" who were leading society astray.[24]

The following year, and along related lines, the conservative writer Mark Henrie blamed the "ideology of liberalism" for America's "ever increasing social pathology." Henrie asked: "Why can't we turn back the clock? Or, rather, to be more faithful to Burke, who was himself no believer in simple reaction, why may we not address . . . the negative social and cultural effects which follow from the normal operation of liberal political, economic, and social institutions[?] . . . How may we heal a society that has overdosed on liberalism?"[25] Like Bork, Frohnen, Ritchie, and other late twentieth-century conservatives, Henrie took the sickness of American society for granted. What is more, all writers of their ilk blamed rampant liberalism for the disease. Although their proposed (or implied) remedies sometimes differed, they unanimously identified the Enlightenment as the original—and lasting—threat to the health of civilization. By contrast, to sixties-style liberals and leftist radicals, America's illness had little to do with personal license or the decline of old-time religion. When Martin Luther King Jr. (who was no secularist) spoke of a "sick society," he was referring to racism, poverty, and the Vietnam War. Others on the left used the term to indict capitalism (or its excesses), militarism, sexism, and—more diffusely—the perceived corruption and repressiveness of "the system" or "the establishment." Hence, while left-of-center activists attacked liberal society for not being liberal enough, and for not living up to its professed ideals, conservative crusaders faced the more daunting challenge of convincing Americans that the liberal traditions of the past few centuries—of which their nation stood as the proud (if flawed) exemplar—should be either abandoned or taken with a grain of salt. Edmund Burke's role in this conservative counterrevolution (or "counter-Enlightenment") has been prominent, though the ultimate effect of his participation remains to be fully understood.

Burke's relationship to Enlightenment thought was complicated. In matters of science, economics, agriculture, history, and "normal politics," Burke was a proponent and practitioner of reasoned analysis. Furthermore, he was a believer in progress. When faced with the prospect of radical change, however, Burke despised, mocked, rejected, and attacked any hint of the Enlightenment sensibility. What separated Burke from his twentieth-century followers was that Burke had two sides to his Whig vision (one side was reformist, progressive, and rational, the other was traditionalist, reactionary, and mystical), while America's postwar and contemporary conservatives had (and have) only one side to their worldview (namely, antiliberal or anti-Left). Effectively, the Burkeans' Burke remains a Tory. In stark repudiation of the Whig interpretation of history, Burke's disciples believe that reason and progress have moved civilization backward.

Conclusion

A World without Fathers

There is currently no clear American consensus on the value of Burke's political philosophy, and there is not—and never has been—any meaningful agreement about Burke's relevance to American history. Furthermore, direct interest in Burke has been confined to a relatively small handful of scholars, journalists, and political advocates; elsewhere, even among educated Americans, Burke's name usually goes unrecognized. Yet this belies the significance of Burke's legacy. Burke was not the only thinker to have influenced Americans who—in a climate suspicious of intellectuals—supposedly acquired their beliefs simply because certain ideas were "in the air." Many Americans absorbed elements of Burke secondhand, through the writings and opinions of others. The question is *why* the intermediaries felt Burke was needed in America to begin with. The second chapter of this book cited some of the reasons why Burke's vision and American civilization seemed to be fundamentally mismatched. In simplified terms: America represented a future-oriented culture of innovation, while Burke represented a past-oriented culture of tradition. Inherent in such a dichotomy were competing preferences for either progress or stability. Because the United States was the first truly modern nation, it was devoted (more consciously than any other nation) to the encouragement of rapid change. This had not necessarily been the goal at the time of the revolution, but it became so soon thereafter. Within a generation or two, democracy, egalitarianism, innovation, and the freedom to chart one's own destiny—all components of the "American liberal tradition"—became (to borrow a phrase) a process of "creative destruction." Old habits, practices, and beliefs had to be discarded to make way for the new. As a twentieth-century cabinet officer (surprisingly, a Hoover Republican) explained it: "Tradition is the enemy of progress." In such an environment, progress too became a force of creative destruction, and—like liberalism—it tended to be messy, unstable, and prone to excesses and mishaps. Liberalism and progress were not for the faint of heart, just as conservatism—with its dedication to the tried and true—was not for the bold. Liberalism was always risky, but the rewards of progress were often worth the pain, danger, and inevitable setbacks.

Dynamic Tension

But this explanation, though it satisfies the requirements of exceptionalism and modernization, is simply too one-sided. If all adherence to tradition and all impulses toward conservatism could have been removed from American soil after the revolution, the result would have been disaster. So too, if conservatism could be banished today, American civilization would quickly crash and burn. The United States successfully pioneered the practical ideal of a free and modern nation because of a continually contested liberal hegemony—not an absolute liberal monopoly. Ideological monopolies reign both in traditional societies and in radically repressive societies. Liberal societies, by their very nature, must be pluralistic or at least dualistic. Liberalism and conservatism not only need each other, but also help define each other (recall Emerson's yin-yang conception of their symbiotic relationship). Nevertheless, their dynamic tension does not amount to a struggle between equals. While the forces of restraint and innovation are codependent, the power of evolutionary progress must—in modern societies—be somewhat greater than that of changeless order. To put it another way: conservatism must be there to feather the brakes when liberalism gains too much speed, and it must grab the wheel if radicalism changes the course too abruptly. But it must never throw society into reverse, nor make an outright U-turn. Early in this discussion, American Burkeanism was likened to a loyal opposition: strong enough to influence the agenda, but not strong enough to set it. Something similar can be said about American conservatism over the long haul. (Though during certain contrary periods, it holds sway while liberalism regenerates itself.) When Burke enters the picture, it is not in the straightforward manner that his champions might expect. It seems doubtful that Burke's post-1789 reactionary traditionalism can serve either as a blueprint for some particular conservative agenda, or as a model for a successful assault on post-Enlightenment thought. Yet whatever its drawbacks as a practical guide to policy, the Burkean legacy has long been a significant intellectual counterpoint to liberal American ideals. In this respect, it serves as a sort of "alternative mirror" that reflects the shape and direction of the conservative response to threat.

Burke first surfaced in the Federal period as a voice opposed to the Painean militancy that sought to sustain the rebellious spirit of the first stage of the American Revolution. Later, as the democratic sensibility spread, Burke represented less a realistic political alternative and more a cultural reminder of an ancestral civilization that still depended on a natural aristocracy. Burke was briefly drafted to combat abolitionism, before the cultural appropriation of his thought was revived by genteel writers as a counterweight to frontier barbarity, rapid technological change, industrialization, political corruption, and the potential fragmentation of an increasingly multiethnic society. Around the turn of the century, Burke played a (less obvious) role in support of culturally conservative Progressive reform, because by then the main threat to society was perceived to be coming from the irresponsible plutocracy. Following the Second World War, Burke was dragged into contemporary debate more forcefully than at any time since the 1790s: first as a natural law opponent of modern positivism, secularism, relativism, and liberalism; then as an anticommunist cold warrior. More recently, Burke has been asked to pronounce on the apparently irreparable damage inflicted on society by the revolutionary 1960s: not only the acceleration of moral relativism, but the growth of new manifestations of it such as radical feminism and multiculturalism. It is no coincidence that God's Burke—as presented in the writings of Ritchie and Frohnen—peaked at a time when the religious Right became extremely influential—and therefore earned the privilege of defining threats to the nation's moral survival. Finally, that some writers have now discovered Burke to be an antiterrorist philosopher should be no surprise. As always, Burke will be heard to say whatever needs to be said.

Applied Ideology

The reception of Burke in America has been tied to the subordinate nature of conservatism itself.[1] Arthur Schlesinger Jr. was not quite correct when he claimed that the United States had no consistent conservative tradition. If consistency (or constancy) were the issue, then liberalism too was disjointed, often contradictory, and had occasionally been upstaged, arrested, or even defeated by alternative persuasions. Both the Left and Right have experienced periods of apparent dormancy, as well as periods of potency. Schlesinger and Samuel Huntington were largely justified in seeing modern conservatism as a reactive phenomenon rather than as an affirmative philosophy, but that in no way lessens its legitimacy. Conservatism's natural (contrapuntal) role is to curb the excesses of dominant liberalism. One can argue over whether or not the habitual exercise of that role constitutes a tradition in the full sense of the term. But even if it represents a countertradition, conservatism has been part and parcel of American thought since the beginning. More than one scholar has observed that conservatism as we now conceive it did not exist before the French Revolution. In other words, ideological conservatism is exclusively a modern phenomenon, and it is roughly contemporaneous with the life span of the United States. In this respect, Burke's antirevolutionary writings do make him (more than any other figure) the father of conservatism.[2] Moreover, *if* the ideologically important Burke was the anti-Jacobin crusader of the Burke-Paine debates, then in a sense Burke (not Adams, Hamilton, or anyone else) was the father of conservatism in America. Yet in sparking the ideological process by rejecting the legitimacy of revolution, Burke's status in American culture was precarious from the start.

The United States was founded upon principles of "fresh start" liberalism. But Burke's ideological passion was aimed at theoretical radicalism, and his temperamental devotion was to Old World traditionalism. Burke and most conservatives accepted the American Revolution as a restoration of traditional (constitutional) rights, not as an experiment in political design.[3] However, this view soon ran counter to the national creation myth, with its emphasis on reasoned human agency in a virgin landscape. Furthermore, the new American archetype owed much to the spirit of the Enlightenment, as became obvious when most Americans initially welcomed the French Revolution as a duplication of their own. Even after events in France turned ugly, the conservative Federalists lost ground to the liberal Jeffersonians, possibly (in part) because anti-Jacobinism was not relevant to life in the new nation. Indeed, it would not be especially relevant until the middle of the twentieth century, when it was linked to anticommunism. As noted in the Cold War context, antirevolutionary conservatism was needed to fight radicalism, not liberalism. But the American right wing has habitually erred in its identification of the enemy. When it perceived the danger correctly (as with communism, anarchism, or terrorism), most liberals were in agreement. In fact, the last time democratic capitalism was seriously threatened in the United States (during the 1930s), it was saved by aggressive liberalism. So it was ironic that by the 1940s conservatives were blaming liberalism for destroying America from within. While it is convenient to claim Rousseau, Marx, and

Nietzsche as fathers of utopian radicalism, it is a mistake to add names like Paine, Jefferson, Holmes, Dewey, the Roosevelts (TR, FDR, and Eleanor), John Kenneth Galbraith, Ken Burns, Hillary Clinton, or Barack Obama to the totalitarian bloodline.

In light of the dramatic differences between authoritarian radicalism and historical liberalism, it is worth asking: What if the ideological Burke is not of particular importance to the United States, because both the Right and (all but the most extreme segments of) the Left are—and have been—in agreement with his antiradical critique of theoretical schemes to redesign society and to reconstruct human nature? That is, what if mainstream liberalism represents the impulse to reform the existing system (itself a product of liberalism) rather than to replace it with something else? If this is the case, then despite the eloquence, power, and passion of *Reflections*, the anti-Jacobin Burke is not the "father" American civilization needs. He may, however, be the father American conservatives want—for two mutually supportive reasons. First, the most effective way to attack liberalism is to stoke fears about what liberalism might become: that is, liberalism greases the slippery slope to radicalism and thence to either nihilism or totalitarianism. Second, the traditionalism of *Reflections*, while seemingly irrelevant to modern life, actually resonates with certain constituencies by (incorrectly) evoking the harmony of older, simpler, more virtuous times, which Enlightenment liberalism allegedly has destroyed. This was central to the mentality of the antebellum Whigs, the writers of the genteel tradition, the new humanists, and the new conservatives, just as it is central to the illusions of contemporary Americans who are nostalgic for the Victorian era or the 1950s. Conservatives today may not yearn for a hereditary aristocracy or an established church, but they yearn for a society that, once established, remains fundamentally unchanged. As the technocratic liberal Buckminster Fuller might have put it: to conservatives, civilization is a noun; to liberals, civilization seems to be a verb.

The element of action, of change, of movement, has always blurred and confused the conservative picture of the world. Such was the case when the Darwinian theory of evolution replaced the static and unalterable creation of Genesis. Similarly, conservatives were (and are) uncomfortable with the progressive side of Burke and his emphasis on the novelty of circumstances, because to acknowledge the need for progress or situational flexibility would undermine the idea of timeless wisdom—and thus the prospect of a changeless political philosophy. In this respect, Burkean conservatives seem to be (at least temperamentally speaking) more fundamentalist than traditionalist.[4] When Burke's disciples refused to adopt a post-Enlightenment frame of mind, they were failing to recognize that the static cosmology of premodern times is not retrievable. Contemporary observers must bring themselves to acknowledge that social mores, scientific theories, cultural sensibilities, and intellectual premises are inevitably fluid (and implicitly relative). In America and other "advanced" countries, the dominant worldview (or collection of paradigms) now tends to shift every generation or so—sometimes incrementally, other times profoundly. Such changes are due less to the concoctions of utopian dreamers than to the practical consequences of real-world developments in the economic, technological, scientific, political, and cultural "markets." New ideas will only grow in fertile soil, and they will not dominate until old ideas have begun to weaken. Yet Burkean conservatives fail to ask themselves why so many long-standing traditional societies have succumbed to both liberal and radical alternatives. In other words: if traditional civilizations were—as conservatives claim—superior in moral value to post-traditional varieties, why were they not strong enough to prevail? Why, despite the mighty efforts of today's reactionaries, does traditional society show no sign of returning?

Supposedly, Burke rejected the "speculative" French Enlightenment but accepted the "practical" Scottish one. The same distinction has been made about the American Revolution, in that the construction of the United States embodied the "common sense" rather than "utopian" tradition. But in reality, the United States was a product of both. Its ideals of life, liberty, and the pursuit of happiness sprouted from the same tree as the ideals of liberty, equality, and fraternity, and the revolutionaries of both America and France sought to establish global precedents for other nations to follow. On the other hand, the American experience has also shown that high ideals seldom intruded into the nitty-gritty (or calculated behavior) of daily life. Thus the pursuit of happiness has often equated to the pursuit of wealth. While in today's environment the "greed is good" mentality of "free enterprise" is associated with conservative politics, it has traditionally run counter to the strain of conservatism associated with Burke. Like Burke's religious beliefs, his economic philosophy is open to conflicting interpretations. Some writers have made the case that he was an early advocate of laissez-faire capitalism; others have pointed out that unfettered economic competition was sure to destroy Burke's traditional world of prescriptive institutions ruled by a hereditary aristocracy. This is not the place for a detailed examination of the topic, which has never been more than a sideshow among Burkean conservatives.[5] But it is helpful to suggest that in Burke's day no one could have envisioned the large-scale industrial capitalism or the culture of mass consumption that lay ahead. Both Burke and his friend Adam Smith died while the Industrial Revolution was in its infancy. It took another half century before even the historically precocious Marx began to perceive the world-historical transition that was under way—and to conclude that capital-intensive manufacturing and finance were permanently displacing agriculture as the dominant economic activity. One need not be a Marxist to realize that when land (as a means of production) shrinks in relative importance, the political power of the landed gentry and aristocracy diminishes. In addition, since by their very nature industrial and service economies are more dynamic than are agricultural or extractive ones, the familiar pace of life that is a precondition for a traditional society eventually ceased to exist.

It is clear that Burke possessed not only a brilliant mind full of diverse interests, but also the energy of genius. But unlike certain other great thinkers of the modern era, Burke lacked the vision to anticipate the future. This, of course, flies in the face of his legendary ability to predict the disastrous outcome of the French Revolution. Yet even in that celebrated instance—which his admirers have exalted beyond measure—he was (mostly) right about the near term, and completely wrong about the long term. Not only was he ultimately in error about France, but about the future of Great Britain and America as well. The England of Disraeli and Gladstone (not to mention of Charles Dickens) would have been a foreign country to him, and as one of the most perceptive studies of American conservatism noted (at the height of the postwar Burkean revival): "If Burke had lived to see nineteenth-century America, he would have had to conclude that it too had gone the way of revolutionary France. Indeed . . . the liberal Conservative [*sic*] distinction between the American and French Revolutions, which began with Burke, is based on both theoretical contradictions and historical illusion."[6] Most of the political, economic, and social developments of the nineteenth and twentieth centuries would have surprised Burke. As it turned out, history did not progress in the direction he would have preferred; and (excepting totalitarianism) many of the trends he saw as damaging became widely accepted as beneficial. The rise of liberalism (broadly defined) in the West, and the decline of traditionalism, may well have constituted the overarching intellectual theme of the past two centuries. In this respect the "conservative" or "antimodern" Burke clearly backed the wrong horse.

Again, New Soil

But it should be equally clear by now that the Burke of the conservative stereotype is not the only Burke available to the dispassionate observer. While his counterrevolutionary arguments attacked radicalism and lauded traditionalism, they completely overlooked nascent liberalism. If Burke is to be relevant in today's America, his complete Whig vision—comprising both his progressive and conservative instincts—must be considered. It is a fundamental inconsistency on the part of contemporary Burkeans to claim that they value the past more than liberals do, while they refuse to respect the path history has taken for the last two hundred years. Unlike his modern disciples, Burke did not choose to consider only those parts of the past that were congenial to him; rather, he accepted the whole past as having shaped the traditions and conditions of the present. Therefore it is foolish for his "heirs" to assume that most of what transpired in the West since the French Revolution is somehow less legitimate than almost everything that happened previously. In the American context: exceptionalism, democracy, egalitarianism (social, political), equalitarianism (racial, ethnic, gender, religious), individualism, liberalism, competitiveness, populism, innovation, civil rights, civil liberties, environmentalism, reproductive rights, and other modern mentalities have over time combined with—and fleshed out—the "glittering generalities" of life, liberty, and the pursuit of happiness, to become legitimate traditions themselves. American traditions do not derive their authenticity by persisting since "time out of mind" (as Burke's Anglo-traditions did). Quite the contrary; they are cherished because Americans believe that fellow Americans invented (or at least perfected) them. As noted above, the vital force of human agency began to spread beyond the founding fathers even while many of those founders still walked the earth. What conservatives fail to grasp is that—symbolically speaking—the process of diffusing agency has continued to expand ever since. Moreover, in America, as in Western civilization overall, such modern trends as secularism and relativism have become culturally embedded because they were logical products of reason.[7] Indeed, they were the historical offspring of the spirit of skeptical inquiry that initiated the modern age. As such, they are inextricably intertwined with the rest of contemporary life (which also contains many strands of premodern thought: religious, classical, medieval, and—presumably—primordial).

Society cannot go backward, and it would be counterproductive to try. But citizens should heed Nietzsche's warning that no matter how fast man runs, he drags the chain of his past with him. Or as William Faulkner more famously put it: the past isn't dead; it isn't even past. Late-modern Americans must realize that with any new approach, history is never starting from square one. Even the founding fathers believed they were transcribing the best ideas of the Old World onto the clean slate of the New, and that their young civilization was to be a fresh branch of an existing tree. The almost immediate and widespread acceptance of new American traditions (based on the ideals, events, and heroes of the revolution) demonstrated that, far from becoming obsolete, national traditions were indispensable. This is why Burke's role as a transitional figure (or a progressive-traditionalist) is more important than his superfluous role as an antiradical. Since we live in transitional times, we are forced to wonder (as did Burke) just how much longer our principles, values, and assumptions will comport with reality. Consequently, who among us is not ambivalent about the ever-changing society in which we live? What person over the age of forty (including liberals, who presumably age slower) does not feel that the world he or she once knew has already been supplanted by a more confusing one? Even freshman undergraduates (whom I have asked directly) are nervous about such things as genetic engineering, the high-tech monitoring of individual activity, and the prospect of renewed religious strife. As a society, the United States has experienced bouts of "future shock" throughout its existence; but the sensation of being overwhelmed by the pace of change has lately become more intense. Unfortunately, the nation has shown no signs of developing any resistance to this psycho-socio-cultural ailment, though over time its symptoms have been reclassified as neurasthenia, angst, malaise, and (recently) fear.

With fear the spotlight may rightly return to Burke. For it is fear rather than conservatism that pervades both *Reflections*—which launched his antirevolutionary crusade—and *Letters on a Regicide Peace*—which extended it.[8] As previously noted, Burke was afraid that Jacobin radicalism would destroy British and Western civilization as he knew it, either by invasion or infiltration. His almost irrational fear of rationalism, which caused him to exaggerate the possibility of worldwide Jacobin dominance, triggered his reversion to mystery, monarchy, and—virtually for the first time in his career—personal alignment with reactionaries. Burke failed to see that the best inoculation against radicalism would have been a renewed commitment to reform (as was proven—both positively and negatively—in Great Britain, Europe, and America, during the nineteenth century). After September 11, 2001, "fear" was the simple explanation in the United States for everything from conservative election victories, to a spike in church attendance, to renewed preferences for "comfort foods" (chicken soup, meat loaf with mashed potatoes), to a reawakened appreciation of one's own family, to increased gun sales, and demand for ever-larger sport utility vehicles (including those customized with armor and bulletproof glass). There is no doubt that the "9/11 effect" was substantial. But, at least as it informs this discussion, the effect was mostly catalytic. Many of the trends that accelerated after 9/11 had been under way for quite some time. In fact, American society had been mired in a state of new-age insecurity since the breakdown of liberal hegemony in the 1970s. Just as Americans in the nineteenth century learned that democracy was no cure-all, their counterparts in the twentieth century learned the same lesson about modernization. In the wake of such disillusionment, the advanced-modern sensibility (which was liberalism's latest creation) was not the cultural comfort food that a nervous nation craved.

For roughly the last forty years, the cultural and intellectual Left has been preaching that since uncertainty is inevitable, persons should learn to live with it, or even celebrate it as a new type of freedom. Meanwhile, the cultural and intellectual Right has been preaching a return to certainties that are so dated that (with the exception of biblical injunctions) they are difficult to retrieve, pin down, or agree upon. While the postmodern vanguard urges Americans to step beyond reason, the antimodern rear guard claims that they should never have adopted reason in the first place. It is too much to hope that these camps will cancel each other out. More likely, both extremes will continue to savage each other, while everyone else will dread the prospect of either side emerging victorious. Those in the middle are in a historical situation akin to Burke's, except that they are viewing modern history from the end rather than the beginning. Burke lived at a time when mystery, custom, religion, and aristocracy were giving way to reason, democracy, liberalism, and (just over the horizon) modernization. At the dawn of the twenty-first century, Americans are awakening to the realization that reason (in the form of modernization) has failed to deliver the psychic goods that liberals had expected or that conservatives might have accepted. In response, some segments of society have retreated to fundamentalism, social repressiveness, militarism, hyper-materialism, and similar security blankets, while other segments have pursued "meaning" via New Age obscurantism, health foods and exercise programs, the revival of a countercultural sensibility (sometimes linked to political agendas, sometimes eschewing politics), personal adventurism, career changes, and the like. It is not too early to predict that if American civilization is to find a central, unifying theme for the twenty-first century, it will not be any of these.

Here is where Burke's work may serve as both an example and a warning. At his political and intellectual best, Burke was pretty much in step with his time. He was devoted to incremental change and to responsible, left-of-center reform. Moreover, his writings and speeches displayed both reasoned analysis and a respect for existing establishments, traditions, and modes of thought. At the same time he was willing to challenge many entrenched interests (slavery, penal laws, the East India Company, the crown) when he felt justice was at stake. Contrary to popular opinion, Burke favored a good deal of change, so long as it traveled in the proper direction. Most important, Burke viewed Great Britain as a civilization, not just a body politic. And he knew that the only way to assure historical continuity was to treat the past as a magazine of wisdom rather than as a useless encumbrance. Perhaps his wisest insight was that "people will not look forward to posterity who never look backward to their ancestors." Of course, at his worst Burke lost his sense of balance and claimed that the beliefs of long-dead generations bound the behavior of the living. But that stance was no more mistaken than its modern polar opposite, which claimed that the past had no value because the present generation had no part in creating it.

Where We Stand

Today ignorance of history is one of society's chief maladies. Another is the increasing unwillingness of individual Americans to think in terms of belonging to a civilization, not just to an interest group, a religious or sexual persuasion, a regional identity, a racial or ethnic hyphenate, an ideological camp, a lifestyle category, a generational cohort, an economic class, a vocational specialty, or a cultural profile—all of which are consciously intended to divide persons into incompatible subsets. A great nation's goal should be the preservation and advancement of a civilization that is pluralistically dynamic yet cohesive enough to instill a common sense of purpose. Instead, America's current impulse toward fragmentation seems to be yielding not a civilization, but a polycentric society that is incapable of finding common ground or agreeing on common goals.[9]

Nearly a century ago George Santayana (an outsider living and working in the United States) explained: "To be an American is of itself almost a moral condition, an education, and a career. Hence a single ideal figment can cover a large part of what each American is in his character, and almost the whole of what most Americans are in their social outlook and political judgements."[10] Assuming that Santayana's "ideal figments" were analogous to Burke's "pleasing illusions" or O'Brien's "Platonic ideals," they represented symbolic values rather than observable patterns of agreement. Even so, that Santayana (often viewed as a Continental conservative who was skeptical of liberalism) would paint such a cohesive portrait of American culture is surprising. From the twenty-first-century vantage point, the important issue is not how homogenized, harmonized, or united Americans actually were in Santayana's day or earlier; it is how much they valued the ideal of a common national spirit. For if idealistic unity was an illusion, it was a pleasing, healthy, and useful one. Now that the "consensus" school of American historiography is passé, and both the heroism of the "frontier thesis" and the myth of exceptionalism stand exposed as naive, and especially since today's "culture wars" promote divisive crusades instead of civilization building, even liberals might be forgiven a touch of nostalgia: not for simpler times that never existed, but for the bygone belief that a nation was a community writ large. Currently, there are many debates raging (actually, they more resemble parallel monologues): some parties concern themselves with identifying who America's legitimate intellectual fathers (and occasionally, mothers) were—or who they ought to be; others disagree over our generation's right to pick them; still others see no need for any remembrance of (let alone any homage to) intellectual parents—since we are free to make our own destiny without historical fetters; in response, the historically inclined caution that if we declare ourselves to be orphans, we make ourselves aliens instead.

Clearly the past is not past, as long as we argue about its meaning. History does not provide clear lessons; but our understanding of the past shapes our view of the present, and therefore influences our hopes and expectations for the future. When it was suggested above that American Burkeans were trying to preserve the nation's ideals by restraining its idealism, it was with this sort of historical continuum in mind. To conservatives, the American Revolution was a restoration of British liberty that *ended* with the practical implementation of the Constitution during the Federal period. To liberals, the revolution *started a process* that never can end if America is to survive as a global ideal. American conservatives viewed the events of 1776–89 much like the Old Whigs viewed the events of 1688–89; that is, both "glorious revolutions" settled the big political questions—if not permanently, then for a very long time. American liberals, by contrast, believed (and believe) that the "spirit of '76" initiated the modern political age, which the Civil War and Reconstruction, woman suffrage, the civil rights movement, and other such advances continued, and which continues still. This is why the typical American hero was a breaker of tradition, rather than a defender of it. Great Americans were improvers, not apologists. Burke obviously was both. But his record as an improver has been sidetracked, not only because he "turned conservative," but because there were other champions of improvement and progress whose philosophies were more straightforward, bold, accessible, and convenient.

The point on which to end is this: In Burke's day, history mostly was the story of tradition; even the (sometimes substantial) changes that had taken place were nonrevolutionary by later standards. If conservatism did not yet exist, it was because the challenges to the existing order were not yet rapid or extreme enough to create it. In our time, history—especially American history—is mostly the story of change and progress. Thus tradition now includes liberalism (as well as conservatism), and one may now defend civilization by promoting the liberal worldview. James Harvey Robinson was exaggerating when he claimed that history could now be a guide to the "technique of progress," but he was nearer the mark when he recognized that it could now be wrested from the hands of conservatives. It seems that those who invoke Burke to promote premodernism are irrelevant, and those who employ him to advocate right-wing agendas are perverting his legacy by misrepresenting his Whig vision. On the other hand, those on the Left who are too postmodern to grant the idea of civilization its due, or who are too sophisticated to speak of American civilization without irony or sarcasm, are rejecting not just Burkean Anglo-traditionalism, but the idea that any voice from the past can speak with authority, wisdom, purchase, or grandeur. Perhaps it is better to identify with the great oaks, rather than the mere flies of summer. And rather than offer a "nebulous evasion" of our own, let us endorse Francis Graham Wilson's "historically continuous" sentiment, and propose that Americans might extract from the comprehensive Edmund Burke a spirit that "seeks to blend the fading past and the emerging future into an imaginative present."[11]

Notes

Most sources appearing in the notes are cited in full on the first reference in each chapter. Works frequently cited are identified by the following abbreviations:

AJL	Lester J. Cappon, ed. *The Adams-Jefferson Letters.* Chapel Hill: University of North Carolina Press, 1959.
Corres.	Thomas W. Copeland, ed. *The Correspondence of Edmund Burke.* 10 vols. Chicago: University of Chicago Press, 1958–78.
Further Reflections	Edmund Burke. *Further Reflections on the Revolution in France,* edited by Daniel E. Ritchie. Indianapolis: Liberty Classics, 1992.
Reflections	Edmund Burke. *Reflections on the Revolution in France,* introduction by Conor Cruise O'Brien. New York: Penguin Books, 1986.
TR Letters	Elting E. Morrison, ed. *The Letters of Theodore Roosevelt.* 8 vols. Cambridge, Mass.: Harvard University Press, 1951–54.
WJA	Charles Francis Adams, ed. *The Works of John Adams, Second President of the United States: With a Life of the Author.* 10 vols. Boston: Charles C. Little and James Brown, 1851.
WJQA	Worthington Chauncey Ford, ed. *The Writings of John Quincy Adams.* 8 vols. New York: Macmillan, 1913.
WSEB	Paul Langford, ed. *The Writings and Speeches of Edmund Burke.* 9 vols. Oxford: Clarendon Press, 1981–99.
WW Papers	Arthur S. Link, ed. *The Papers of Woodrow Wilson.* 69 vols. Princeton, N.J.: Princeton University Press, 1966–94.

Introduction

1. Jeffrey Goldberg, "What Douglas Feith Knew, and When He Knew It," *New Yorker,* May 9, 2005. Feith was undersecretary of defense for policy.

2. Edmund Burke, *Reflections on the Revolution in France* (1790; London and New York: Penguin Books, 1986), 171.

3. See Raymond Williams, *Culture and Society, 1780–1950* (1958; New York: Columbia University Press, 1983), 11. The concept that a nation "is made by . . . tempers, dispositions, and moral, civil, and social habitudes of the people" (as Burke

put it) was, as Williams noted, "to be called the 'spirit of a nation'; by the end of the nineteenth century, it was to be called a 'national culture.'" Likewise, "ideology" is a nineteenth-century concept (coined 1812) but is traceable to debates over the French Revolution.

4. For example, Joanne B. Freeman, *Affairs of Honor: National Politics in the New Republic* (New Haven, Conn.: Yale University Press, 2001), blends the honor code, most dramatically evident in dueling, with political behavior. Jeffrey L. Pasley, *The Tyranny of Printers: Newspaper Politics in the Early American Republic* (Charlottesville, University of Virginia Press, 2001), examines the partisan political agency of the press. More in line with this discussion of Burke in America is an earlier, more intellectualized conception of "political culture" by Daniel Walker Howe as "an evolving system of beliefs, attitudes, and techniques for solving problems," in *The Political Culture of the American Whigs* (Chicago: University of Chicago Press, 1979), 2.

1. Burke in Brief

1. A widely available version of *Reflections on the Revolution in France* is the paperback Penguin Classics edition, introduction by Conor Cruise O'Brien (New York: Penguin Books, 1986). Several follow-up pieces are included in Edmund Burke, *Further Reflections on the Revolution in France*, ed. Daniel E. Richie (Indianapolis: Liberty Classics, 1992).

2. *Speech on Conciliation with the Colonies* [or, *with America*] (March 1775), in *The Writings and Speeches of Edmund Burke*, 9 vols., ed. Paul Langford (Oxford: Clarendon Press, 1981–99), 3:164 (henceforth cited as *WSEB*).

3. Burke to Richard Shackleton, August 10, 1757, and Burke to Charles O'Hara, July 10, 1761, in *The Correspondence of Edmund Burke*, 10 vols., ed. Thomas W. Copeland (Chicago: University of Chicago Press, 1958–78), 1:123 and 1:141 (henceforth cited as *Corres.*).

4. William and Edmund Burke, *An Account of the European Settlements in America*, vols. 1 and 2, 3rd ed. (London: R&J Dodsley, 1760).

5. See for instance Gordon S. Wood, *The Radicalism of the American Revolution* (New York: Vintage Books, 1991), 15, 110.

6. "Speech on Declaratory Resolution" (February 1766), *WSEB*, 2:50.

7. *Speech on Conciliation*, *WSEB*, 3:124.

8. See Pauline Maier, "John Wilkes and American Disillusionment with Britain," *William and Mary Quarterly* 20 (1963): 373–95.

9. See "Speech on the Middlesex Election," *WSEB*, 2:227; "Speech on Parliamentary Incapacitation," *WSEB*, 2:234.

10. "Speech on the Middlesex Election," *WSEB*, 2:229; *Thoughts on the Present Discontents*, *WSEB*, 2:295–98, 300.

11. *WSEB*, 2:252.

12. *Speech on Conciliation*, 251, in *Select Works of Edmund Burke*, vol. 1, ed. E. J. Payne (1874; Indianapolis: Liberty Fund, 1999); *Letter to the Sheriffs of Bristol on the Affairs of America* (April 1777), *WSEB*, 3:317.

13. Quoted in Bertram D. Sarason, "Burke's Two Notes on America," *Burke Newsletter* 6:2 (Winter 1964–65): 390–94.

14. "Notes for a Speech on Capital Punishment" (1777), *WSEB*, 3:338–39.

15. "Some Thoughts on the Approaching Executions" and "Additional Reflexions on the Executions" (both 1780), *WSEB*, 3:613–14, 615–18.

16. "Speech on Mutiny" (1780), *WSEB*, 3:586–88.

17. "Speech on Pillory" (1780), *WSEB*, 3:583–86.

18. D. B. Horn and Mary Ransome, eds., *English Historical Documents, 1714–1783* (London: Eyre & Spottiswoode, 1957), 12.

19. "Speech on Insolvent Debtors Bill" and *Speech at Bristol before Election* (both 1780), *WSEB*, 3:552–53, 3:634–37.

20. "Sketch of a Negro Code," *WSEB*, 3:563–81, quote 563.

21. Burke to Henry Dundas, *Corres.*, April 9, 1792, 7:122–24.

22. Burke to William Windam, *Corres.*, March 28, 1796, 8:451.

23. Burke to William Burgh, February 9, 1775, *Corres.*, 3:112.

24. *Tract on the Popery Laws* (1765), *Address at Bristol on the Gordon Riots and the Catholic Question* (1780), in Isaac Kramnick, ed., *The Portable Edmund Burke* (New York: Penguin, 1999), 310, 311.

25. "Brief for Lord Rockingham" (1778), "Draft Address for Catholics" (1778), *WSEB*, 3:378, 385.

26. Warren Hastings (1732–1818) entered East India Company service in 1750 and spent most of the next thirty-five years in India, becoming governor general in 1773. He returned to England in 1785; the impeachment proceedings began in 1788 and ended with his acquittal in 1795. See P. J. Marshall, *The Impeachment of Warren Hastings* (Oxford: Oxford University Press, 1965); Geoffrey Carnall and Colin Nicholson, eds., *The Impeachment of Warren Hastings* (Edinburgh: Edinburgh University Press, 1989); Conor Cruise O'Brien, *The Great Melody: A Thematic Biography of Edmund Burke* (Chicago: University of Chicago Press, 1992), 255–385.

27. *Speech on Fox's India Bill*, *WSEB*, 5:386, 389, 402, 415.

28. *WSEB*, 5:383.

29. Gerald W. Chapman, *Edmund Burke: The Practical Imagination* (Cambridge, Mass.: Harvard University Press, 1967), 263.

30. *Oxford English Dictionary*, 2nd ed., s.v. "rationalism," def. 2.c. The word dates from slightly after Burke's death, though "rationalists" dates from the 1600s.

31. *Reflections*, 90.

32. Richard M. Weaver, *The Ethics of Rhetoric* (Chicago: Henry Regnery, 1953), chap. 3, "Edmund Burke and the Argument from Circumstance," 58.

33. *Reflections*, 151–52.

34. *Reflections*, 211–12.

35. *Thoughts on French Affairs* (December 1791), *WSEB*, 8:341.

36. J. C. D. Clark, introduction to Burke, *Reflections on the Revolution in France* (Stanford, Calif.: Stanford University Press, 2001), 67, note 135.

37. *Reflections*, 92; *Letter to a Noble Lord*, in *Further Reflections*, 290 (emphasis in the original).

38. J. G. A. Pocock, "Burke and the Ancient Constitution: A Problem in the History of Ideas," *Historical Journal* 3 (1960): 125–43; see also *The Ancient Constitution and the Feudal Law: English Historical Thought in the Seventeenth Century* (New York: W. W. Norton, 1967).

39. *Reflections*, 173, 191. Both statements were qualified and reasonable in their original context; they are (and have been) usually quoted out of context.

40. *Reflections*, 181, 183.

41. "Speech on Clerical Subscription" (1772). Burke continued: "[Better] to impose upon a few individuals perhaps a disagreeable restraint, rather than introduce disorder and confusion into the whole body politic." *WSEB*, 2:361.

42. *An Appeal from the New to the Old Whigs*, in *Further Reflections*, 199.

43. *Reflections*, 121.

44. *Reflections*, 92.

45. "Speech on Divorce Bill" (1771), "Speech on Clerical Subscription" (1772), *WSEB*, 2:357, 359.

46. *Speech on Conciliation*, *WSEB*, 3:127.

47. *Reflections*, 170–71.

48. O'Brien, *Great Melody*, 376–77.

49. *Reflections*, 171–72, 245.

50. *Reflections*, 377.

51. See *Appeal from the New to the Old Whigs* (1791), in *Further Reflections*, 168.

52. Burke to the Duke of Richmond, post November 15, 1772, *Corres.*, 2:377 (emphases added).

53. William James, *The Varieties of Religious Experience* (1902; New York: Mentor, 1958), 83, 141–42, 281.

54. Respectively, the year of the Glorious Revolution, Burke's birth, his election to Parliament, and the last year of the ancien régime in France.

2. Old Seeds, New Soil

1. Robert A. Ferguson, *The American Enlightenment, 1750–1820* (Cambridge, Mass.: Harvard University Press, 1997), 34.

2. Bernard Bailyn, *The Ideological Origins of the American Revolution*, rev. ed. (Cambridge, Mass: Belknap Press of Harvard University Press, 1992), x.

3. See Henry Steele Commager, *The Empire of Reason: How Europe Imagined and America Realized the Enlightenment* (Garden City, N.Y.: Anchor Press / Doubleday, 1977). If nothing else, Commager's thesis that "the Old World imagined, invented, and formulated the Enlightenment, the New World—certainly the Anglo-American part of it—realized it and fulfilled it" exactly fits the common myth of the early United States.

4. The claim here is that the three elements of the archetype—clean slate, human agency, hence a better society—were widely accepted by 1863. The acceptance of racial equality was another matter.

5. A fitting example of this was in Will and Edmund Burke's *Account of the European Settlements in America*, 3rd ed., 6 vols. (London: R&J Dodsley, 1760): "[Columbus's] whole time was spent in fruitless endeavours to enlighten ignorance, to remove prejudice, and to vanquish incredulity, which is of all others the greatest enemy to improvement, rejecting everything as false and absurd, which is ever so little out of the track of common experience" (1:8).

6. The statement is from Indian agent T. W. Davenport in 1850, as quoted in Ted Morgan, *Wilderness at Dawn: The Settling of the North American Continent* (New York: Simon & Schuster, 1993), 19.

7. Federalist No. 14, in Isaac Kramnick, ed., *The Federalist Papers* (1788; London: Penguin Books, 1987), 144–45.

8. Gordon S. Wood, *The Creation of the American Republic* (Chapel Hill: University of North Carolina Press, 1998), 614.

9. See also Ernest Cassara, *The Enlightenment in America* (Lanham, Md.: University Press of America, 1988), and Henry F. May, *The Enlightenment in America* (New York: Oxford University Press, 1976).

10. Jack P. Greene, *The Intellectual Construction of America: Exceptionalism and Identity from 1492 to 1800* (Chapel Hill: University of North Carolina Press, 1993), 207. Greene notes that the United States seemed "to offer a blueprint for the future" and that America had "radical differences from the Old World" (209).

11. See Eric Foner, *Tom Paine and the American Revolution* (New York: Oxford University Press, 1976), esp. 211–70; and Harvey J. Kaye, *Thomas Paine and the Promise of America* (New York: Hill & Wang, 2005); also useful is Christopher Hitchens, *Thomas Paine's Rights of Man: A Biography* (Vancouver: Douglas & McIntyre, 2006).

12. See Michael Lienesch, *New Order of the Ages: Time, the Constitution, and the Making of Modern American Political Thought* (Princeton, N.J.: Princeton University Press, 1988), 172.

13. Cabot to Hamilton, November 29, 1800, in *The Papers of Alexander Hamilton*, 27 vols., ed. Harold C. Styrett et al. (New York: Columbia University Press, 1961–87), 25:248 (emphasis added).

14. See Clinton Rossiter, *Conservatism in America: The Thankless Persuasion* (Knopf/ Vintage, 1962); Arthur Schlesinger Jr., *The Age of Jackson* (Boston: Little, Brown, 1953), 277–82; Louis Hartz, *The Liberal Tradition in America: An Interpretation of Political Thought since the Revolution* (1955; Harvest / Harcourt Brace, 1991); Allen Guttmann, *The Conservative Tradition in America* (New York: Oxford University Press, 1967).

3. Federalist Persuasions

1. See Russell Kirk, *The Conservative Mind* (Chicago: Henry Regnery, 1953); Peter Viereck, *Conservatism: From John Adams to Churchill* (Princeton, N.J.: D. Van Nostrand, 1956); Clinton Rossiter, *Conservatism in America: The Thankless Persuasion* (Knopf/Vintage, 1962); and Larry E. Tise, *The American Counterrevolution: A Retreat from Liberty, 1783–1800* (Mechanicsburg, Pa.: Stackpole Books, 1998), 398–413. See also Randall B. Ripley, "Adams, Burke, and Eighteenth-Century Conservatism," *Political Science Quarterly* 80, no. 2 (1965): 216–35.

2. Charles Francis Adams, ed., *The Works of John Adams, Second President of the United States: With a Life of the Author*, 10 vols. (Boston: Charles C. Little and James Brown, 1851), 1:405–6 (henceforth cited as *WJA*).

3. Adams to Jefferson, December 25, 1813, in *The Adams-Jefferson Letters*, ed. Lester J. Cappon (Chapel Hill: University of North Carolina Press, 1959), 410 (henceforth cited as *AJL*).

4. Adams to Benjamin Rush, September 27, 1809, in *The Spur of Fame: Dialogues of John Adams and Benjamin Rush, 1805–1813*, ed. John A. Schutz and Douglas Adair (San Marino, Calif.: Huntington Library, 1966), 155.

5. Adams to Francis Vanderkemp, July 5, 1814, quoted in Joseph J. Ellis, *Passionate Sage: The Character and Legacy of John Adams* (New York: W. W. Norton, 1993), 146, and in Edward Handler, *America and Europe in the Political Thought of John Adams* (Cambridge, Mass.: Harvard University Press, 1964), 158.

6. See James H. Hutson, "John Adams' Title Campaign," *New England Quarterly* 41 (1968): 30–39; see also Stanley Elkins and Eric McKitrick, *The Age of Federalism: The Early American Republic, 1788–1800* (New York: Oxford University Press, 1993), 46–50.

7. *WJA*, 4:380, 392, 583. *Defense* was written in 1786–87 and published in three volumes in 1787–88.

8. *WJA*, 6:256.

9. Adams to Jefferson, July 13, 1813, *AJL*, 356.

10. *WJA*, 4:290–91. See also 6:456–58.

11. In Zoltan Haraszti, *John Adams and the Prophets of Progress* (Cambridge, Mass.: Harvard University Press, 1952), 201.

12. Adams to Benjamin Rush, January 8, 1812, in Schutz and Adair, *Spur of Fame*, 205, for "enemies" [*sic*] quote; see Adams to Rush, August 28, 1811, ibid., 191–95, or in *WJA*, 9:635–40, for Adams's thoughts on being misunderstood.

13. Adams to Henry Channing, November 3, 1820, *WJA*, 10:393.

14. Adams to David Sewall, May 22, 1821, *WJA*, 10:399.

15. *Appeal from the New to the Old Whigs*, in Edmund Burke, *Further Reflections on the Revolution in France*, ed. Daniel E. Ritchie (Indianapolis: Liberty Classics, 1992), 200–201.

16. Burke to the Duke of Portland, September, 14, 1794, *Corres.*, 8:12; to Walker King, September 17, 1794, and to William Pitt, September 19, 1794, 8:16–17; to Countess Spencer, October 1, 1794, 8:27; and to William Windham, October 16 and 20, 1794, 8:42, 52.

17. "Motion for Papers on Hastings" (February 17, 1786), *WSEB*, 6:48.

18. John Adams, *Discourses on Davila: A Series of Papers on Political History* (1791), in *WJA*, 6:223–399, quote 6:246.

19. John Adams, *Defense of the Constitutions of Government of the United States of America* (written 1786–87, published 1787–88), in *WJA*, 4:271–588, 5:3–486, 6:3–220, quote 6:219.

20. *WJA*, 4:200; *Davila*, *WJA*, 6:234; for virtue is "chimerical" see John Adams to Samuel Adams, October 18, 1790, *WJA*, 6:415; for virtue and balanced government see *Defense*, *WJA*, 6:206–11.

21. *Reflections*, 172.

22. See Haraszti, *Prophets of Progress*, 12, 25.

23. Adams to Jefferson, August 24, 1815, *AJL*, 455.

24. *WJA*, 4:292–93.

25. Ellis, *Passionate Sage*, 150, 151, 153.

26. Elkins and McKitrick, *Age of Federalism*, 531–37; Gordon S. Wood, *The Creation of the American Republic* (Chapel Hill: University of North Carolina Press, 1998), 567–92.

27. "Dissertation on the Canon and the Feudal Law" (1765), "Instructions of the Town of Braintree" (1765), "Novanglus Papers" (1774), "Thoughts on Government" (1776), and sections of vol. 1 of *Defense of the Constitutions* (1787), *WJA*, 3:448–64, 465–68, 4:11–177, 193–267, 283.

28. For example, compare Adams to Josiah Quincy, February 9, 1811, *WJA*, 9:629, with Adams to Jefferson, July 16, 1814, *AJL*, 435.

29. Elkins and McKitrick, *Age of Federalism*, 529.

30. Merle Curti, *The Growth of American Thought*, 3rd ed. (New York: Harper & Row, 1964), 151. The previous two debates in America (over independence in the 1770s and over ratification of the Constitution in 1787–88) were settled once they ended, but the debates over the French Revolution not only never ended, but, in part because of their perpetuity, can be said to have founded political ideology in the United States. For the renewed interest in Enlightenment writers during the 1790s see Henry F. May, *The Enlightenment in America* (New York: Oxford University Press, 1976), 225–27.

31. An excellent, if ancient, account is Charles Downer Hazen, *Contemporary American Opinion of the French Revolution* (Baltimore: Johns Hopkins University Press, 1897), pt. 2: "Opinion of Americans at Home," 139–299. See also R. R. Palmer, *The Age of the Democratic Revolution: A Political History of Europe and America, 1760–1800*, 2 vols. (Princeton, N.J.: Princeton University Press, 1964), 2:522, May, 225–77, and Charles Warren, *Jacobin and Junto, or, Early American Politics as Viewed in the Diary of Dr. Nathaniel Ames, 1758–1822* (Cambridge, Mass.: Harvard University Press, 1931).

32. Adams to Rush, October 10, 1808, in Schutz and Adair, *Spur of Fame*, 123.

33. *The Journal of William Maclay* (New York: Albert & Charles Boni, 1927), 151 (September 18, 1789).

34. Adams to Richard Price, April 19, 1790, *WJA*, 9:563–64.

35. A week after Adams's letter to Price, Maclay recorded: "[Adams] told how many late pamphlets he had received from England; how the subject of the French Revolution agitated English politics; that for his part he despised them all but the production of Mr. Burke, and this same Mr. Burke despised the French Revolution," *Journal of William Maclay*, 243 (April 26, 1790).

36. Adams to Jefferson, July 13, 15, 1813, *AJL*, 356, 357; see also 594–96.

37. Letter no. 23 to John Taylor, *WJA*, 6:496 (post–April 15, 1814); Haraszti, *Prophets of Progress*, 209.

38. Haraszti, *Prophets of Progress*, 213; *WJA*, 3:172.

39. Madison to Jefferson, June 23, 1791: "An attack on Payne has appeared in a Boston paper under the name of Publicola, and has an affinity in the stile [*sic*] as well as sentiments to the discourses on Davila"; Jefferson to Madison, June 28, 1791: "Nobody doubts who is the author of Publicola, any more than of Davila"; both in *The Republic of Letters: The Correspondence between Thomas Jefferson and James Madison, 1776–1826*, 3 vols., ed. James Morton Smith (New York: W. W. Norton, 1955), 2:691, 693.

40. Madison to Jefferson, July 13, 1791, in *The Papers of Thomas Jefferson*, 26 vols. to date, ed. Julian P. Boyd et al. (Princeton, N.J.: Princeton University Press, 1950–2000), 20:298.

41. Monroe to Jefferson, July 25, 1791, ibid., 20:304.

42. Charles Francis Adams, "Memoir of John Quincy Adams," *Proceedings of the Massachusetts Historical Society* 2 (1880): 400 (April 1848).

43. Jefferson to Adams, August 30, 1791, *AJL*, 250.

44. *Letters of Publicola*, in *The Writings of John Quincy Adams*, 8 vols., ed. Worthington Chauncey Ford (New York: Macmillan, 1913), 1:65–110 (henceforth cited as *WJQA*). The letters originally appeared in the *Columbian Centinel* between June 8 and July 27, 1791; quotes on 1:66, 67, 70.

45. *WJQA*, 1:70–73, 81.

46. *WJQA*, 1:91, 108, 110.

47. John Quincy (in London) to John Adams (in Philadelphia), August 31, September 11, 19, 21, 1797, *WJQA*, 2:198–216; quotes 198, 201, 205–7.

48. *WSEB*, 8:335–499. These "memorials" contained *Thoughts on French Affairs* and *Remarks on the Policy of the Allies*. In *WJQA*, 2:206, 207, C. F. Adams mistakenly identifies them as Burke's *Letters on a Regicide Peace*.

49. *WJQA*, 2:206–9.

50. Marshall Smelser, "The Federalist Period as an Age of Passion," *American Quarterly* 10 (1956): 391–419, quote 407.

51. *AJL*, 260–61, February 28, April 6, 1796.

52. Friedrich von Gentz, *The Origin and Principles of the American Revolution, Compared with the Origin and Principles of the French Revolution*, translated by "An American Gentleman" [J. Q. Adams] (1800; Delmar, N.Y.: Scholars' Facsimiles & Reprints, 1977).

53. Adams to Gentz, June 16, 1800, *WJQA*, 2:463.

54. *WJA*, 6:223–403; Davila's *History of the French Civil Wars* was published in Italian in Venice in 1630; Adams worked from a French translation, though he also owned an English edition; Haraszti, *Prophets of Progress*, 165.

55. *WJA*, 6:228.

56. *WJA*, 6:232–33.

57. *WJA*, 6:234.

58. See Douglas Adair, *Fame and the Founding Fathers* (New York: W. W. Norton, 1974), 3–26.

59. *WJA*, 6:252.

60. *WJA*, 6:276–77.

61. In light of this argument, it is an extremely interesting coincidence that John Adams was the first person known to use the word "ideology" in the English language (the term itself was coined by Napoleon); *Oxford English Dictionary*, 2nd ed., s.v. "ideology," def. 2. For the Adams quotes (he used the term twice in the same letter) see Adams to Jefferson, July 13, 1813, *AJL*, 355.

4. Democratic America

1. Henry Adams, great-grandson and grandson of John and John Quincy respectively, put it this way in his history: "In 1787, John Adams . . . and other constitution-makers, might . . . indulge in speculations more or less visionary in regard to the future character of a nation not yet in its cradle; but in 1814 the character of people and government was formed; the lines of their activity were fixed." *History of the United States of America*, 9 vols. (1889–90; New York: Scribner's, 1931), 1:195.

2. A famous example of this concept is Francis Fukuyama, *The End of History and the Last Man* (New York: Free Press, 1992). "The end of history would mean the end of wars and bloody revolutions. Agreeing on ends, men would have no large causes for which to fight" (311).

3. Dorothy Ross, "Historical Consciousness in Nineteenth-Century America," *American Historical Review* 89 (1984): 909–28, quotes 912.

4. This does not, and for the American mainstream never did, imply an equality of talent, character, position, or wealth; but it does imply "the acceptance of what can be called 'individualism,' that is, the belief that ordinary men and women have a dignity and value in their own right, and that they are sufficiently trustworthy to be allowed a measure of autonomy in their lives." Daniel Walker Howe, *Making the American Self: Jonathan Edwards to Abraham Lincoln* (Cambridge, Mass: Harvard University Press, 1997), 9; Howe ties this into the influence of the Scottish Enlightenment in America (48–77).

5. Robert V. Remini, *Andrew Jackson*, vol. 3, *The Course of American Democracy, 1833–1845* (Baltimore: Johns Hopkins University Press, 1984). Remini expands on Jackson's quote: "[He had a] full commitment to the democratic philosophy of government. He believed totally in the concept of popular rule as expressed through the ballot box. No longer did he subscribe to republicanism with its fears and hesitations about democracy, fears that allowed [elites] to alter the popular will when necessary" (25). For Jackson's view of this as a continuation of Jeffersonian principles see Arthur Schlesinger Jr., *The Age of Jackson* (Boston: Little, Brown, 1953), 356, and Harry L. Watson, *Liberty and Power: The Politics of Jacksonian America* (New York: Noonday Press, 1990), 10.

6. "In Memory of Thomas Paine" (1877), in *Walt Whitman: Prose Works, 1892*, 2 vols., ed. Floyd Stovall (New York: New York University Press, 1963), 1:140–42, quote 141.

7. May 3, 1847; as quoted in *Social Theories of Jacksonian Democrats: Representative Writings of the Period 1825–1850*, ed. Joseph L. Blau (New York: Hafner Publishing, 1947), 131.

8. Several editions (most of them abridged) of Tocqueville are available; one is Richard D. Heffner, ed. (New York: Mentor, 1984); quoted section headings begin on 112, 192. For Tocqueville's own approximation of democratization as an end of history see "Why Great Revolutions Will Become More Rare," 263–74.

9. James Fenimore Cooper, *Notions of the Americans: Picked Up by a Travelling Bachelor* (Albany: SUNY Press, 1991); Nathan O. Hatch, *The Democratization of American Christianity* (New Haven, Conn.: Yale University Press, 1989).

10. George H. Callcott, *History in the United States, 1800–1860: Its Practice and Purpose* (Baltimore: Johns Hopkins University Press, 1970), 13.

11. In 1832 Noah Webster published his *History of the United States*, which was widely used in American schools; while he overplayed the Christianity card, Webster otherwise conformed to the exceptionalist pattern: "[Puritan founders] rejected all distinctions among men . . . [They] established institutions on republican principles. . . . Their liberal and wise institutions, which were then novelties in the world, have been the foundations of our republican governments." From Harry R. Warfel, *Noah Webster: Schoolmaster to America* (New York: Macmillan, 1936), 399–400.

12. Ephram Douglas Adams, *The Power of Ideals in American History* (New Haven, Conn.: Yale University Press, 1926), xi (emphasis in the original).

13. For example, the Federalist Fisher Ames, in his antidemocratic "The Dangers of American Liberty" of 1805, makes a fairly Burkean argument without mentioning Burke. In *Works of Fisher Ames*, 2 vols., ed. W. B. Allen (Indianapolis: Liberty Classics, 1983), 1:120–82.

14. Bancroft to William Prescott, August 17, 1847, in *Life and Letters of George Bancroft*, 2 vols., ed. M. A. DeWolfe Howe (1908; New York: Da Capo Press, 1970), 2:22. Burke's estate, located near the village of Beaconsfield, was named the Gregories. English poet Edmund Waller (b. 1606) had been a previous owner.

15. Bancroft (1800–91) held no academic post. He became the de facto Democratic boss of Massachusetts and was the party's unsuccessful nominee for governor in 1844; thereafter he served as secretary of the navy (he founded the academy at Annapolis) and U.S. ambassador to Great Britain. He was an antislavery Democrat and Lincoln supporter during the Civil War.

16. George Bancroft, *History of the United States from the Discovery of the American Continent*, 10 vols. (original eds. 1834–75; Boston: Little, Brown, 1866–75); vol. 5 first published in 1852, vol. 6 in 1854. In 1876–79 Bancroft revised the work into a six-volume "Centennial Edition," which he again revised in 1883–85. Twenty-five editions of the *History* appeared during Bancroft's lifetime.

17. Bancroft, *History*, 5:302.

18. Ibid., 6:521–22.

19. Burke said of the old French constitution: "You possessed in some parts the walls, and in all the foundations of a noble and venerable castle. You might have repaired those walls; you might have built on those old foundations." *Reflections*, 121.

20. See Stow Persons, *The Decline of American Gentility* (New York: Columbia University Press, 1973), esp. chap. 1, "Democracy and Gentility," 1–28.

21. Delivered July 4, 1826, at Northampton, Massachusetts; Howe, *Life and Letters*, 1:186.

22. Bancroft believed he was an unbiased practitioner. When the German historian Leopold Ranke praised Bancroft's *History* as "the best book ever written from the democratic point of view," Bancroft disagreed: "I deny the charge; if there is democracy in the history it is not subjective, but objective . . . and so has necessarily its place in history and gives its colour as it should." Howe, *Life and Letters*, 2:183.

23. On Bancroft's approach to his *History* see Bert James Loewenberg, *American History in American Thought* (New York: Simon & Schuster, 1972), 247, 329. Gordon Wood, in *Imagined Histories*, states (147): "More than any other work, Bancroft's *History of the United States* contributed to the belief that the American republic was showing the world the way toward true liberty and democracy. . . . [His] view was highly whiggish; he saw the past as simply an anticipation of the present and future."

24. See Russel B. Nye, *George Bancroft: Brahmin Rebel* (New York: Alfred A. Knopf, 1944), 96–97, 101.

25. Delivered July 4, 1836, at Springfield, Massachusetts; Howe, *Life and Letters*, 1:216.

26. Lilian Handlin, *George Bancroft: The Intellectual as Democrat* (New York: Harper & Row, 1984), 330.

27. For details on this periodical see Frank Luther Mott, *A History of American Magazines, vol. 1, 1741–1850* (Cambridge, Mass.: Harvard University Press, 1938), 677–84. The *Democratic Review* ran (under slightly altered titles) from 1837 to 1859; John L. O'Sullivan was a founding editor, and it was in the *Review* that he coined the term "manifest destiny" in 1845.

28. *United States Magazine and Democratic Review* 1 (October 1837): 2; this article has been reprinted in several books, including Blau, *Social Theories of Jacksonian Democrats*. For Bancroft on this point see Blau, 263–73, esp. 267.

29. "Edmund Burke," *United States Magazine and Democratic Review* 27 (1850): 305–19; quotes 316, 319.

30. "Edmund Burke," *United States Magazine and Democratic Review* 34 (1854): 70–87, quotes 70, 81, 82, 83, 86.

31. "Edmund Burke," *Methodist Quarterly Review* (January 1858): 100–110; quotes 105, 108.

32. "Edmund Burke" (March 1835), in *The Early Lectures of Ralph Waldo Emerson, vol. 1, 1833–1836*, eds. Stephen E. Whicher and Robert E. Spiller (Cambridge, Mass.: Harvard University Press, 1959), 184–201.

33. Ibid., 190, 194. As noted above, "conservative" attained its modern usage after Burke's death; the *OED* dates the first four occurrences between 1830 and 1832.

34. Ibid., 196, 201. To be precise, Emerson devoted one complete paragraph (201) and one long sentence in another paragraph (196) to the revolution. His excuses for withholding judgment are at 185–86. According to editors Whicher and Spiller, Emerson defended the French Revolution in a Lyceum debate a month before giving his Burke lecture; in his journal, however, he defended political conservatism (183).

35. "The Conservative" (December 1841), in *Ralph Waldo Emerson: Essays and Lectures*, ed. Joel Porte (New York: Library of America / Penguin Books, 1983), 171–89.

36. Emerson, "Burke," 190–94; "Conservative," 173, 174, 183; this lecture alternately contrasted "conservatism" with either "reform" or "innovation."

37. Emerson, "Conservative," 189. In a separate "Lecture on the Times" (December 1841), Emerson made this same yin-yang kind of argument (Porte, *Essays and Lectures*, 153–70, on 159); he also employed remarkably Burkean language (154).

38. Emerson acknowledged the influence of the past, witness his "Politics": "In dealing with the State, we ought to remember that its institutions are not aboriginal . . . [not] rooted like oak trees . . . there are no such roots and centers." Porte, *Essays and Lectures*, 7, 559; see also Paul F. Boller Jr., *American Transcendentalism, 1830–1860: An Intellectual Inquiry* (New York: G. P. Putnam's Sons / Capricorn Books, 1974), xxii.

39. See Boller, *American Transcendentalism*, 99–133. An excellent, more recent treatment of this entire topic is Philip F. Gura, *American Transcendentalism: A History* (New York: Hill & Wang, 2007). The American Adam refers to the idea of the American as the new "archetypal man"; see R. W. B. Lewis, *The American Adam: Innocence, Tragedy and Tradition in the Nineteenth Century* (Chicago: University of Chicago Press, 1955).

40. Merle Curti, *The Growth of American Thought*, 3rd ed. (New York: Harper & Row, 1964), 196–97.

41. Octavius Brooks Frothingham, *Transcendentalism in New England: A History* (1876; Gloucester, Mass.: Peter Smith, 1965), 136.

42. The average birth year of the twelve leading transcendentalists was 1805; *Encyclopedia of Philosophy*, 1972 reprint of 1967 1st ed., s.v. "New England Transcendentalism." Watson, *Liberty and Power*, 11, makes the interesting point that while the

Democratic-Republicans often called themselves "Republicans" for short during the early 1800s, by the 1830s they were calling themselves "Democrats"; this seems to demonstrate linguistically the strength of the democratization process and the abandonment of the classic republican reliance on mediation and (as Watson also notes) on a natural aristocracy.

43. Something of this "personal is political" sensibility in transcendentalism (beyond only Thoreau) is captured in John T. Lysaker, *Emerson and Self-Culture* (Bloomington: Indiana University Press, 2008).

44. British and German romanticism dealt with the heroic artist and nature, but transcendentalism dealt with the common man and nature. One must go back to European folktales to find the common focus—and then the role of nature is often not a positive one. While this is not the place to develop the argument, it also appears that Old World romanticism was more socially and less individualistically colored as well. To my reading, for example, this is a difference between Thomas Carlyle and R. W. Emerson ("the American Carlyle").

45. Van Wyck Brooks to Lewis Mumford, July 19, 1940, in *The Van Wyck Brooks–Lewis Mumford Letters: The Record of a Literary Friendship, 1921–1963*, ed. Robert E. Spiller (New York: E. P. Dutton, 1970), 187 (emphasis in original).

5. American Whigs

1. The magisterial study of Whig Party history is Michael F. Holt, *The Rise and Fall of the American Whig Party: Jacksonian Politics and the Onset of the Civil War* (New York: Oxford University Press, 1999), 26–34, esp. 28–29, for the party's origins; 118–21 for Whig ideology and attributes. A less detailed but more accessible alternative is Robert V. Remini, *Andrew Jackson*, vol. 3, *The Course of American Democracy, 1833–1845* (Baltimore: Johns Hopkins University Press, 1984), 119, 132–41; see also his source notes on 551.

2. *New England Magazine* 7 (November 1834): 344–50. According to Frank Luther Mott, this Boston-based magazine supported the Whigs Webster and Everett and opposed the Democrat Van Buren. The Whig Party formed in 1834 and died in 1856. See Mott, *A History of American Magazines, vol. 1, 1741–1850* (Cambridge, Mass.: Harvard University Press, 1938), 599–603.

3. For Burke's *Thoughts on the Present Discontents* see *WSEB*, 2:251–323.

4. *New England Magazine* 7 (November 1834): 344, 348.

5. This last point is now commonly accepted; possibly the first historian to make it was Arthur Schlesinger Jr.; see *The Age of Jackson* (Boston: Little, Brown, 1953), 38, 275–77.

6. The successful Whig "log cabin and hard cider" campaign of 1840 adopted the techniques of democratic politics without accepting its spirit: "I have no faith . . . in this democracy, but it is the road to success. I tell you I have no faith in it, but . . . no fellow shall out democrat me," said a Kentucky Whig in 1840; quoted in Harry L. Watson, *Liberty and Power: The Politics of Jacksonian America* (New York: Noonday Press, 1990), 212 (italics removed).

7. Both the Federalists and Whigs have been presumed to be less accepting of the need for the machinations of party politics than their respective political rivals. While such views have been refuted—see, for example, David Hackett Fischer, *The*

Revolution of American Conservatism: The Federalist Party in the Era of Jeffersonian Democracy (New York: Harper & Row, 1965), and Holt, *Rise and Fall*—there is probably some kernel of truth to the presumption. See Ronald P. Formisano, "Political Character, Anti-partyism and the Second Party System," *American Quarterly* 21 (1969): 683–709. See also Lynn L. Marshall, "The Strange Stillbirth of the Whig Party," *American Historical Review* 72 (1967): 445–68. Jacksonians were voter oriented; proto-Whigs were leader oriented (448–49).

8. Daniel Walker Howe, *The Political Culture of the American Whigs* (Chicago: University of Chicago Press, 1979).

9. Holt, *Rise and Fall*, 116, 118; 115–21, provides details on the Whig constituency.

10. Lewis M. Ogden to William Meredith, February 26, 1801, quoted in Fischer, *Revolution of American Conservatism*, 97.

11. "Burke and Milton," *Monthly Anthology* 9 (July 1810): 19–20. Rush to Adams, October 2, 1810, *Letters of Benjamin Rush*, 2 vols., ed. L. H. Butterfield (Princeton, N.J.: Princeton University Press, 1951), 2:1066–67. Mott, *History of American Magazines*, 1:223–46, quote 227. "Prior's Memoir of Mr. Burke," *Port folio*, 5th ser., vol. 19 (1825), 38–52, quote 52. Claude M. Fuess, *The Life of Caleb Cushing*, 2 vols. (New York: Harcourt, Brace, 1923), 1:83 (diary entry January 27, 1829).

12. Herman Melville, *Moby Dick* (1851; New York: Modern Library, 1926), xvii.

13. On "sensibility" see Howe, *Political Culture of the American Whigs*, 219–20.

14. Dana was a Massachusetts aristocrat who enjoyed a successful legal career as an expert on admiralty law. Active in politics, he at one point described himself as "a Whig of the old school; . . . a highly conservative Whig." Dana was best known, however, as a writer-lecturer and as the author of the autobiographical maritime adventure *Two Years before the Mast* (1840). The quote is from Dana's remarks at a Free Soil meeting, July 7, 1848; Samuel Shapiro, *Richard Henry Dana, Jr., 1815–1882* (East Lansing: Michigan State University Press, 1961), 33. Dana certainly qualified as a Burkean, though a minor one; a short analysis of his political congruency with Burke can be found ibid., 73–74.

15. Robert F. Lucid, ed., *The Journal of Richard Henry Dana, Jr.*, 3 vols. (Cambridge, Mass.: Belknap Press of Harvard University Press, 1968), 2:775–76, August 6, 1856. According to his son, "Burke's speeches and essays . . . [Dana] read and reread, learning passages by heart." Richard Henry Dana 3rd., ed., *Richard Henry Dana, Jr., Speeches in Stirring Times and Letters to His Son* (Boston: Houghton Mifflin, 1910), 15 (see also 436).

16. *American National Biography* (New York: Oxford University Press, 1999), s.v. "Everett, Edward" (entry written by Daniel Walker Howe).

17. John Tyler, the nominally Whig vice president who assumed the presidency upon Harrison's death in 1841, had been a states' rights Democrat and a supporter of Jackson in 1828 and 1832, only to break with Jackson later. As president, Tyler rejected Whig policies and was in turn rejected by the Whig Party. Millard Fillmore, who became president at Zachary Taylor's death in 1850, alienated the "conscience" Whigs with his compromise position on slavery; this resulted in his rejection by the Whig Party convention of 1852.

18. When Frederick Douglass sought to learn the art of oratory he turned to the 1832 edition of *The Columbian Orator*, which "had more selections from . . . Edward

Everett than from any other author"; Daniel Walker Howe, *Making the American Self: Jonathan Edwards to Abraham Lincoln* (Cambridge, Mass: Harvard University Press, 1997), 150. See also Ronald F. Reid, *Edward Everett: Unionist Orator* (Westport, Conn.: Greenwood Press, 1990). The other book-length biographies of Everett are Paul A. Varg, *Edward Everett: The Intellectual in the Turmoil of Politics* (Selinsgrove, Penn.: Susquehanna University Press, 1992), and Paul Revere Frothingham, *Edward Everett: Orator and Statesman* (Boston: Houghton Mifflin, 1925).

19. Edward Everett, *Orations and Speeches on Various Occasions*, 4 vols. (Boston: Little, Brown, 1850–68); 1:vii, 1:120, 3:560, 3:163. In light of Everett's many references to Burke, it is curious that none of the three biographies cited above note the Burkean influence.

20. Ibid., 4:182, 183; Varg, *Edward Everett*, 61; *North American Review* 71 (1850): 445.

21. Varg, *Edward Everett*, 67, 74–75, 157–71, quote 171.

22. Reid, *Edward Everett*, 23–25; "The Character of Washington" is reprinted 145–74.

23. Everett, *Orations and Speeches*, 1:108, 126–27.

24. It was cited in a footnote to the published version of his speech on charitable institutions; it is worth noting here as an indication of Everett's familiarity with even Burke's less-known writings. Everett, *Orations and Speeches*, 3:591.

25. Ibid., 1:515, 2:517, 589, 3:639, 4:57–59, among other places.

26. Ibid., 1:64–65.

27. Ibid., 1:396, 2:655, 3:336–37.

28. "The Importance of Agriculture" (Buffalo, N.Y., 1857), ibid., 3:537–67, quote 561.

29. Ibid., 3:224–31, quotes 226–28.

30. For reactions to Everett's Gettysburg speech see Reid, *Edward Everett*, 94–106.

31. "The National Cemetery at Gettysburg," in Everett, *Orations and Speeches*, 4:622–59. Illegitimacy of rebellion on 626–28, quotes on 644, 646, 647; historical wars, 653–56.

32. Everett, *Orations and Speeches*, 4:659.

33. Everett all but spelled this out in his 1833 oration "The Seven Years' War[,] the School of the Revolution," ibid., 1:377–401. The "principles," "institutions," reforms," and "experiments" ushered in by the revolution had produced a happy ending (399).

34. Remarks of Henry Chapin, *Proceedings of the American Antiquarian Society at a Special Meeting, January 15, 1865, in Reference to the Death of Their Former President, Hon. Edward Everett*, 28–29.

35. See Daniel Walker Howe, *The Unitarian Conscience: Harvard Moral Philosophy, 1805–1861* (Middletown, Conn.: Wesleyan University Press, 1988), 287.

36. Claude M. Fuess, *Rufus Choate: The Wizard of the Law* (New York: Minton, Balch, 1928).

37. Howe, *Political Culture of the American Whigs*, 225–26; Jean V. Matthews, *Rufus Choate: The Law and Civic Virtue* (Philadelphia: Temple University Press, 1980) 3, 5. Both authors call Choate a Burkean; see also *American National Biography*, s.v. "Choate, Rufus" (entry by Jean Matthews).

38. Officially *Dartmouth College v. Woodward*, this decision (issued February 2, 1819) freed corporations from control by state governments by means of the contract clause (art. I, sec. 10) of the Constitution.

39. Reuben D. Mussey to Leverett Saltonstall, July 18, 1816, quoted in Robert V. Remini, *Daniel Webster: The Man and His Time* (New York: W. W. Norton, 1997), 150–51.

40. Samuel P. Huntington, "Conservatism as an Ideology," *American Political Science Review* 51 (1957): 454–73; quotes 459, 470; most points about Burke, 461–63.

41. Choate to Sumner, n.d. (possibly 1844), in Joseph Neilson, *Memories of Rufus Choate* (Boston: Houghton, Mifflin, 1884), 428.

42. Fuess, *Rufus Choate*, 214–15 (exclamation point in the original).

43. David Bradstreet Walker, "Rufus Choate: A Case Study in Old Whiggery," *Essex Institute Historical Collections* 94 (October 1958): 334–55; quotes 343, 345.

44. Choate to E. W. Farley and members of the Maine Whig State Central Committee, August 9, 1856, in *The Works of Rufus Choate with a Memoir of His Life*, 2 vols., ed. Samuel Gilman Brown (Boston: Little, Brown, 1862), 1:215. Emerson objected to Choate's "glittering generalities" and called the ideals of the Declaration "blazing ubiquities" (Matthews, *Rufus Choate*, 222).

45. Speech at Lowell (Mass.), October 28, 1856, in Brown, *Works of Rufus Choate*, 2:387–414, quotes 405, 406, 407, 412, 413.

46. The use of Burke by anti-abolitionist and pro-slavery writers will not be pursued here in the interest of space; I intend to publish on this interesting matter elsewhere.

47. For an analysis of Choate's courtroom oratory see John W. Black, "Rufus Choate," in *History and Criticism of American Public Address*, ed. William Brigance (New York: McGraw-Hill, 1943), 434–58.

48. Brown, *Works of Rufus Choate*, 1:86, 88, 90 (journal entries, June, July, and August 1844; some italics removed from original); other references to Burke can be found on 1:93, 235, 351.

49. "The Importance of Illustrating New-England History by a Series of Romances Like the Waverly Novels," ibid., 1:319–46; quotes 320, 321, 323, 333, 334; see 338–39 for Choate's thoughts on the benefits of history.

50. Ibid., 1:414–38 (July 3, 1845).

51. Ibid., 423, 424.

52. Ibid., 430–31.

53. Ibid., 431 ("grave" = "engrave").

54. Ibid., 432. This speech contained another Burkean passage on "successive flights of summer flies, without relations to the past or duties to the future" (417).

55. "Speech on the Judicial Tenure," July 14, 1853, ibid., 2:284–310; quotes 308–10.

56. As reported in the *Boston Daily Advertiser*, July 17, 1851 (no page numbers visible on microfilm used). Incredibly this speech is not included in Brown's *Works of Rufus Choate*, though a few sentences from it are excerpted (1:172–73) in the "Memoir of His Life" section.

57. For an example of the internal split see [anonymous], "The Duty of Conservative Whigs in the Present Crisis: A Letter to the Hon. Rufus Choate, by a Conservative Whig" (Boston, 1856).

58. *WSEB*, 2:361.

59. *Boston Daily Advertiser*, July 17, 1851. Compare Burke's "great lights" passage in his *Appeal from the New to the Old Whigs*.

60. *Boston Daily Advertiser*, July 17, 1851. For a brief note on the history of the "glittering" phrase see Matthews, *Rufus Choate*, 302, note 75.

61. Jefferson thought Story, at age thirty-two, "too young" and "unquestionably a tory," but Madison (without enthusiasm) nominated him, and he was confirmed in November 1811. The first court session to include Story began in February 1812. James McClellan, *Joseph Story and the American Constitution: A Study in Political and Legal Thought* (Norman: University of Oklahoma Press, 1971), 40.

62. See William W. Story, ed., *Life and Letters of Joseph Story*, 2 vols. (Boston: Little and Brown, 1851), 1:9–12 for his father's revolutionary activities.

63. This is especially true of his extrajudicial writings. His magnum opus, *Commentaries on the Constitution*, his encyclopedia articles on "Natural Law" and on legal codes, and his pamphlet on the history and future prospects of the law all were published 1831–35. His power on the high court began to wane after Taney succeeded Marshall as chief justice in 1836.

64. Joseph Story, *Commentaries on the Constitution of the United States*, 3rd ed., 2 vols. (orig. 3 vols., 1833; Boston: Little, Brown, 1858), 1:235 (emphases in original).

65. For instance, James P. McClellan, "Judge Story's Debt to Burke," *Burke Newsletter* 3, no. 3 (Spring 1966): 583–86, exaggerates both the "weight" of Story's citations of Burke and the natural law angle of Story's reasoning—and by implication of Burke's reasoning.

66. Story to George Ticknor, March 6, 1828, in W. W. Story, *Life and Letters*, 1:536; Gerald T. Dunne, *Justice Joseph Story and the Rise of the Supreme Court* (New York: Simon & Schuster, 1970), 338; the remainder of this passage, however, identifies Cicero as the most important.

67. On this topic see chap. 2, "Law over Politics," in R. Kent Newmyer, *Supreme Court Justice Joseph Story: Statesman of the Old Republic* (Chapel Hill: University of North Carolina Press, 1985), 37–72.

68. See R. Kent Newmyer, "A Note on the Whig Politics of Justice Joseph Story," *Mississippi Valley Historical Review* 48 (1961): 480–91.

69. Newmyer, *Joseph Story*, 190, 233.

70. For instance, *The Federalist*, the *Journal of the Constitutional Convention*, Blackstone's *Commentaries*, James Kent's *Commentaries on American Law* (1826–30), James Wilson's *A View of the Constitution* (1825), William Rawle's *Commentaries on the Constitution* (1792), and Nathan Dane's *Abridgement and Digest of American Law* (1823) were each cited more than Edmund Burke's writings.

71. Story, *Commentaries*, 1:206–53; quotes 216–17, 219, 227, 233.

72. Ibid., 1:285, 293, 297.

73. Ibid., 1:325; the quote is Story's paraphrase of Burke.

74. *WSEB*, 3:316–17.

75. Story repeated Burke's aphorism later in *Commentaries*, 1:403.

76. Ibid., 1:397, 398. "Mr. Burke . . . has treated . . . the mischiefs of an *indirect* choice only . . . in a masterly manner" (397 note 5); see also 407 note 2, and notes on 408–9.

77. For an unconvincing defense by Story's son see W. W. Story, *Life and Letters*, 2:392.

78. In *Luther v. Borden* (1849) the Supreme Court partially rejected Story's extreme repression of the Dorr rebels as circuit judge; see Newmyer, *Joseph Story*, 360–65.

79. Quoted (from 1842 and 1843) in Newmyer, *Joseph Story*, 356.

80. Story described the historical value of the independence of judges in England in his *Discourse on the Past History, Present State, and Future Prospects of the Law* (1835 pamphlet), reprinted in McClellan, *Joseph Story*, 325–49, quote 331.

81. Written by Kent (March 18, 1835) in his copy of Story's *Commentaries*; quoted in McClellan, *Joseph Story*, 79 note 67.

82. See Newmyer, *Joseph Story*, 175; and Leonard L. Richards, *The Life and Times of Congressman John Quincy Adams* (New York: Oxford University Press, 1986).

83. Howe, *Unitarian Conscience*, 125.

84. [Charles Francis Adams], "An Appeal from the New to the Old Whigs, by a Whig of the Old School" (Boston, 1835), 1.

85. *American Whig Review* (November 1845): 393; *Littell's Living Age* (1844), 598; see Mott, *History of American Magazines*, 1:748, for *Littell's* connection to leading Whigs.

86. *North American Review* 93 (1861): 391–417, quotes 400, 417.

87. *Littell's Living Age* (1861), 291–304, quotes 294, 295, 296.

6. The Gilded Age

1. For the early history of the *Nation* see Frank Luther Mott, *A History of American Magazines, vol. 3, 1865–1885* (Cambridge, Mass.: Harvard University Press, 1938), 331–44. Quote of intentions is from the original prospectus (July 6, 1865) as reprinted in Katrina Vanden Heuvel, ed., *The Nation, 1865–1990: Selections from the Independent Magazine of Politics and Culture* (New York: Thunder's Mouth Press, 1990), 1–2. For an earlier collection see Gustav Pollak, *Fifty Years of American Idealism: The New York Nation, 1865–1915* (Boston and New York: Houghton Mifflin, 1915), which includes an introductory essay on the magazine's editors and contributors, 4–83.

2. The phrase "genteel tradition" was coined by the philosopher George Santayana in 1911; see Douglas L. Wilson, ed., *The Genteel Tradition: Nine Essays by George Santayana* (Cambridge, Mass.: Harvard University Press, 1967). John Tomsich, *A Genteel Endeavor: American Culture and Politics in the Gilded Age* (Stanford, Calif.: Stanford University Press, 1971) is useful on the general characteristics at play, though narrow in its cast of characters.

3. See Richard Clarke Sterne, *Political, Social, and Literary Criticism in the New York Nation, 1865–1881: A Study of Change in Mood* [reprint of 1957 Harvard dissertation] (New York: Garland, 1987), "Morals, Manners and Taste," 151–91, 312–15. James Bryce's *American Commonwealth*, 2 vols. (1888; New York: Macmillan, 1924) was playing some of the same themes (1:79). Bryce was a contributor to the *Nation*, and a friend of Godkin.

4. See Sterne, *Political, Social, and Literary Criticism*, 94, 101. For Godkin's dislike of southerners and westerners see William M. Armstrong, *E.L. Godkin: A Biography* (Albany: State University of New York Press, 1978), 41, 94, 108, 180.

5. "Mr. John Morley on Edmund Burke," *Nation*, December 19, 1867, 497–98. Book reviews in the *Nation* were not signed; attribution is from Clara I. Gandy and Peter J. Stanlis, *Edmund Burke: A Bibliography of Secondary Sources* (Westport, Conn.: Greenwood Press, 1994), source no. 899.

6. *Nation*, December 19, 1867, 497.

7. Ibid., 498.

8. E. J. Payne, ed. and intro, *Burke: Select Works*, vol. 1, rev. ed. (1874; Oxford: Clarendon Press, 1875); this contained an excellent fifty-nine-page introduction and Burke's *Thoughts on the Present Discontents*, *Speech on American Taxation*, and *Speech on Conciliation with America.*

9. The quote on Dicey's (1835–1922) classic law book (1885) is from *Webster's New Biographical Dictionary* (1988), s.v. "Dicey, Albert Venn." For a more in-depth study see Richard A. Cosgrove, *The Rule of Law: Albert Venn Dicey, Victorian Jurist* (Chapel Hill: University of North Carolina Press, 1980), chap. 4, "The Constitutional Expert: Law and the Constitution," 66–90.

10. *Nation*, October 15, 1874, 253–54. Attribution to Dicey is from Gandy and Stanlis, *Bibliography*, source note no. 916.

11. *Nation*, October 15, 1874, 254.

12. Ibid.

13. Cosgrove, *Rule of Law*, xiii.

14. John Morley, *Burke*, in the English Men of Letters series (London: Macmillan; New York: Harper & Bros., 1879); this is not the same book reviewed by Godkin in 1867.

15. "Four writers whom I read with perpetual profit & enjoyment on all constitutional matters are Burke, Paley, Macaulay & Bagehot." Dicey to Godkin, June 26, 1900; quoted in Cosgrove, *Rule of Law*, 69.

16. "Morley's Burke," *Nation*, October 9, 1879, 244–45. Attribution to Dicey is from Gandy and Stanlis, *Bibliography*, source no. 380.

17. "Burke as a Prophet," *Nation*, January 20, 1876, 48–49.

18. Ibid., 49. The passage (which the *Nation* quoted but did not identify) is consistent with Tocqueville's *The Old Regime and the Revolution* (1856).

19. See Alan S. Kahan, *Aristocratic Liberalism: The Social Thought of Jacob Burckhardt, John Stuart Mill, and Alexis de Tocqueville* (New York: Oxford University Press, 1992).

20. "Edmund Burke," in *Orations and Essays by Edmund Burke, with a Critical and Biographical Introduction by Edwin Lawrence Godkin* (New York: D. Appleton, 1900), iii–x.

21. See, for example, Godkin's rage at the Haymarket Square defendants, "The Execution of the Anarchists," *Nation*, November 10, 1887; reprinted in Heuvel, *Nation*, 15–19.

22. *Orations and Essays by Edmund Burke*, iii–vi.

23. Ibid., vii.

24. Ibid., viii.

25. Ibid., x.

26. Armstrong, *E.L. Godkin*, 198, 201, note 3.

27. Brander Matthews, *These Many Years: Recollections of a New Yorker* (New York: Charles Scribner's Sons, 1917), 173.

28. Ibid., 174.

29. Vernon Louis Parrington, *Main Currents in American Thought*, vol. 3, *The Beginnings of Critical Realism in America, 1860–1920* (New York: Harcourt, Brace, 1930), 162.

30. Richard Hofstadter, *The American Political Tradition and the Men Who Made It* (1948; New York: Vintage, 1989), 214.

31. Armstrong, *E. L. Godkin*, 198–99.

32. Edwin L. Godkin, *Unforeseen Tendencies of Democracy* (Boston and New York: Houghton Mifflin, 1898), iii–vi.

33. Ibid., vi, and "Peculiarities of American Municipal Government," ibid., 145–82.

34. Edwin L. Godkin, "Aristocratic Opinions of Democracy," *North American Review* 100 (January 1865): 194–232.

35. For Turner: "The Significance of the Frontier in American History," in *History, Frontier, and Section: Three Essays by Frederick Jackson Turner*, ed. Martin Ridge (Albuquerque: University of New Mexico Press, 1993), 64, 65, 75, 76.

36. Turner, "Significance of the Frontier," 84–85. The Burke quote is from *Speech on Conciliation with America*; see *Select Works of Edmund Burke*, ed. E. J. Payne (1874; Indianapolis: Liberty Fund, 1999), 1:247, or *WSEB*, 3:128–29.

37. See Gerald D. Nash, *Creating the West: Historical Interpretations 1809–1990* (Albuquerque, University of New Mexico Press, 1991); Allan G. Bogue, *Frederick Jackson Turner: Strange Roads Going Down* (Norman: University of Oklahoma Press, 1998), 102–4 for Godkin's influence; and Ray Allen Billington, *The Genesis of the Frontier Thesis: A Study of Historical Creativity* (San Marino, Calif.: Huntington Library, 1971), 69–70 for Godkin.

38. *Speech on Conciliation with America*, *WSEB*, 3:129.

39. William and Edmund Burke, *An Account of the European Settlements in America*, 3rd ed. (London: R&J Dodsley, 1760), 2:201. Burke was addressing German-speaking settlements in Pennsylvania; this line was quoted by Turner in "Significance of the Frontier" (76). As with his other Burkean quote, Burke's reference to regulation on the same page was omitted.

40. Godkin, "Aristocratic Opinions of Democracy," 219.

41. See, for example, Charles Eliot Norton, "Some Aspects of Civilization in America," *Forum* 20 (1896): 641–51; or "The Lack of Old Homes in America," *Scribner's Magazine*, May 1889, 636–40.

42. *The Works of James Russell Lowell*, 10 vols. (Boston: Houghton Mifflin, 1890), 6:197–98 (taxation); "Rousseau and the Sentimentalists" (1867), 2:232–71, quotes 233, 234, 264.

43. Kate Holladay Claghorn, "Burke: A Centenary Perspective," *Atlantic Monthly*, July 1897, 84–95, esp. 91–92.

7. Theodore Roosevelt

1. Interest in TR's early life was invigorated by Edmund Morris's Pulitzer Prize–winning *The Rise of Theodore Roosevelt* (New York: Coward, McCann & Geoghegan, 1979), and by David McCullough, *Mornings on Horseback* (New York: Touchstone, 1981); the excellent Carlton Putnam, *Theodore Roosevelt: The Formative Years* (New York: Scribner's, 1958), made less of an impression.

2. See George E. Mowry, *Theodore Roosevelt and the Progressive Movement* (Madison: University of Wisconsin Press, 1946) and his *The Era of Theodore Roosevelt and the Birth of Modern America* (New York: Harper Torchbooks, 1958); Lewis L. Gould, *The Presidency of Theodore Roosevelt* (Lawrence: University of Kansas Press, 1991); John Morton Blum, *The Republican Roosevelt* (1954; 2nd ed., Cambridge, Mass.: Harvard University Press, 1977); Edmund Morris, *Theodore Rex* (New York: Modern Library, 2001); H. W. Brands, *TR: The Last Romantic* (New York: Basic Books, 1997). James MacGregor Burns and Susan Dunn, *The Three Roosevelts: Patrician Leaders Who Transformed America* (New York: Atlantic Monthly Press, 2001), presents a holistic portrait of TR, FDR, and Eleanor Roosevelt.

3. TR to Ray Stannard Baker, June 3, 1908, in *The Letters of Theodore Roosevelt*, 8 vols., ed. Elting E. Morrison (Cambridge, Mass.: Harvard University Press, 1951–54), 6:1048 (henceforth cited as *TR Letters*); and Theodore Roosevelt, *American Ideals* (New York: G. P. Putnam's Sons, 1897), 37.

4. See Burns and Dunn, *Three Roosevelts*, 21; McCullough, *Mornings on Horseback*, 29–32; Putnam, *Theodore Roosevelt*, 112–13. TR called his father "the best man I ever knew. He combined strength and courage with gentleness, tenderness, and great unselfishness." *Theodore Roosevelt: An Autobiography* (1913; New York: Da Capo Press, 1985), 7.

5. Richard Hofstadter, *The Age of Reform: From Bryan to F.D.R.* (New York: Vintage, 1955), 135, 137, 166–67, 240.

6. TR to George Otto Trevelyan, January 1, 1908, and TR to Charles Joseph Bonaparte, January 2, 1908, *TR Letters*, 6:883, 687; Roosevelt, *American Ideals*, 11.

7. TR to James Eli Watson, August 18, 1906, *TR Letters*, 5:375–76. For Burke's original words see *WSEB*, 9:194.

8. Theodore Roosevelt, *Realizable Ideals: Earl Lectures of Pacific Theological Seminary Delivered at Berkeley, California, in 1911* (San Francisco: Whitaker & Ray-Wiggin, 1912), 10, 13, 18. TR to William Henry Moody, September 21, 1907, *TR Letters*, 5:802.

9. Theodore Roosevelt, *First Annual Message*, December 1, 1901, in *A Compilation of the Messages and Papers of the Presidents*, 12 vols., ed. James D. Richardson (New York: Bureau of National Literature and Art, 1910), 9:6641; TR to Henry Cabot Lodge, September 9, 1901 (written after McKinley was shot but before he died), *TR Letters*, 3:141; TR to Department of Justice, March 20, 1908, *TR Letters*, 6:977.

10. TR to Samuel Sydney McClure, October 4, 1905, and TR to [Treasury Secretary] Leslie Mortimer Shaw, November 24, 1905, *TR Letters*, 5:45, 94.

11. TR to Anna "Bamie" Roosevelt, 1879, *TR Letters*, 1:41–42 (emphasis added).

12. See Owen Wister's remark, quoted in John Milton Cooper Jr., *The Pivotal Decades: The United States, 1900–1920* (New York: W. W. Norton, 1990), 42.

13. "Ancestry and outlook" quote from Arthur M. Schlesinger Jr., *The Crisis of the Old Order, 1919–1933* (Boston: Houghton Mifflin, 1957), 19.

14. J. Hampton Moore, *Roosevelt and the Old Guard* (Philadelphia, 1925), 7. Moore was president of the Republican Club and a member of the U.S. Industrial Commission.

15. TR to George Otto Trevelyan, January 1, 1908, *TR Letters*, 6:882; *Fifth Annual Message* (1905), in Richardson, *Messages*, 10:7366.

16. TR to Andrew Carnegie, August 6, 1906, and TR to Raymond Robins, August 12, 1914, *TR Letters*, 5:345, 7:798.

17. TR to Ilya Lovovich Tolstoi, May 1, 1917, *TR Letters*, 8:1186.

18. Cooper, *Pivotal Decades*, 73. The "cursed Bryan" line was by Vachel Lindsay, quoted in Mowry, *Roosevelt and the Progressive Movement*, 11.

19. Blum, *Republican Roosevelt*, 87.

20. TR to Turner, November 4, 1896, and TR to William Henry Moody (who had also served as TR's secretary of the navy and attorney general before his appointment to the court), September 21, 1907, *TR Letters*, 1:564, 5:802–3.

21. TR to Theodore Roosevelt Jr., November 20, 1908, and TR to Ray Stannard Baker, June 3, 1908, *TR Letters*, 6:1372, 1046. (On Haiti see also 7:255.)

22. TR to Cora Miranda Older, June 12, 1911, and TR to Charles Dwight Willard, April 28, 1911, *TR Letters*, 7:285, 251.

23. John Emerich Edward Dalberg-Acton (first Baron Acton), *Lectures on the French Revolution* (1910; New York: Noonday Press, 1959) [from Acton's Cambridge history lectures, 1895–99], 20–31, quotes 20, 21, 26, 27, 31. According to the *Dictionary of National Biography* (sup. vol. 23, 1921), s.v. "Acton, John": "He never wavered from his unflinching and austere liberalism . . . no historian is less impartial and more personal in his judgements than Acton appears in [his] *French Revolution*."

24. Acton, *Lectures*, 32, 34, 35.

25. On TR in 1912 see Martin J. Sklar, *The Corporate Reconstruction of American Capitalism, 1890–1916* (New York: Cambridge University Press, 1988), 351; Burns and Dunn, *Three Roosevelts*, 129.

26. TR, *Third Annual Message* (1903), *Fourth Annual Message* (1904), *Fifth Annual Message* (1905), in Richardson, *Messages*, 9:6859–60, 10:7029, 10:7355.

27. TR first used the term in an unpublished Gridiron Club speech in January 1906; he repeated it in a public speech in Washington on April 14, 1906; see "Muck-Rakers," in *The Roosevelt Policy: Speeches, Letters, and State Papers*, 2 vols. (New York: Current Literature, 1908), 2:367–78. See also Roosevelt, *Realizable Ideals*, 139.

28. Roosevelt, *Autobiography*, "Appendix: Socialism," 514–15 (see also 497). The books were John Graham Brooks, *American Syndicalism: The I.W.W.* (New York: Macmillan, 1913), and Vladimir G. Sinkhovitch, *Marxism versus Socialism* (New York: Columbia University Press, 1913). That TR chose to end his autobiography with his presidency rather than his 1912 crusade is further indication of his reversion to antiradicalism.

29. Elting E. Morrison, editor's introduction in *TR Letters*, 5:xxii–xxiii.

30. Ibid., 5:xxii.

31. TR, *Fifth Annual Message* (1905), in Richardson, *Messages*, 10:7365–66.

32. Ibid., 10:7366. For Burke's words in context see *Further Reflections*, 69 (or *WSEB*, 8:332). Burke said something similar in *Reflections*, 151.

33. *TR Letters*, 5:xxiii.

34. "The Railroad Rate: A Study in Commercial Autocracy," *McClure's* 26, no. 1 (November 1905): 47–59. Baker used a single sentence from Burke's passage as an epigraph (47).

35. TR, *Fifth Annual Message*, in Richardson, *Messages*, 10:7357.

36. In true Old Whig fashion Burke "resisted power" and wrote: "Those who have been once intoxicated with power . . . even though but for one year, never can willingly abandon it. They may be distressed in the midst of all their power; but they will never look to any thing but power for their relief." *WSEB*, 8:301, or *Further Reflections*, 35.

37. TR to George Otto Trevelyan, June 19, 1908, *TR Letters*, 6:1087.

38. *Letter to a Noble Lord*, in *Further Reflections*, 290–91 (or *WSEB*, 9:156), italics in the original. Burke continued: "It was . . . my hatred of innovation, that produced my Plan of Reform" (292 or 9:157).

39. Theodore Roosevelt, *Gouverneur Morris* (Boston: Houghton Mifflin, 1888), 289.

40. Theodore Roosevelt, "A Layman's Views of an Art Exhibition," *Outlook*, March 29, 1913, 718–20, quote 719.

41. TR to Albert Shaw, November 4, 1896, and TR to James Eli Watson, August 18, 1906 ["ing" dropped from "strengthen"; this was the same letter in which TR quoted Burke on wealth], *TR Letters*, 1:565, 5:375.

42. John Milton Cooper, *The Warrior and the Priest: Woodrow Wilson and Theodore Roosevelt* (Cambridge, Mass.: Belknap Press of Harvard University Press, 1983), 157.

43. TR to Henry Cabot Lodge, March 1, 1910. The phrase was a clever way of saying "I agree with you and have nothing of value to add." *TR Letters*, 7:51.

44. Morris, *Rise of Theodore Roosevelt*, 374, 303.

45. Theodore Roosevelt, *The Winning of the West*, 4 vols. (1889–95; New York: G. P. Putnam's Sons, 1907), 1:6, 13 [1889].

46. Ibid., 1:24–25.

47. Ibid., 4:1 [1895]. On Turner's influence see TR to Frederick Jackson Turner, February 10, 1894, *TR Letters*, 1:363.

48. For hints of this distinction see TR to Turner, April 10 and 26, 1895, *TR Letters*, 1:440–41, 546. For a succinct explanation see Ernst A. Breisach, *American Progressive History: An Experiment in Modernization* (Chicago: University of Chicago Press, 1993), 79, from which Turner's quote is taken.

49. An excellent examination of this is Richard Slotkin, "Nostalgia and Progress: Theodore Roosevelt's Myth of the Frontier," *American Quarterly* 33 (1981): 608–37.

50. TR to Arthur Hamilton Lee, August 14, 1912, *TR Letters*, 7:597. (Lee was a baron and a viscount, as well as a conservative MP and cabinet minister.)

51. David W. Noble, *The Progressive Mind, 1809–1917* (Chicago: Rand McNally, 1970), 157, 161.

52. Roosevelt, *Winning of the West*, 1:8.

53. Edward Wagenknecht, *The Seven Worlds of Theodore Roosevelt* (New York: Longmans, Green, 1958), 56.

54. William N. Tilchin, *Theodore Roosevelt and the British Empire: A Study in Presidential Statecraft* (New York: St. Martin's, 1997), 242. I do not—as Tilchin does not—dismiss the "realpolitik" behind TR's policy; but it would be absurd to ignore the cultural connections.

55. TR to Arthur Hamilton Lee, August 4, 1900; St. Loe Strachey to TR, October 1, 1904, and March 10, 1906; TR to Lee, November 25, 1898; and TR to Elihu Root, September 2, 1899, in David H. Burton, "Theodore Roosevelt and His English Correspondents: A Special Relationship of Friends," *Transactions of*

the American Philosophical Society 63 (1973): 3–70; quotes on 9, 19–22, 26, 37. The other correspondents covered are Cecil Spring Rice, James Bryce, and George Otto Trevelyan.

56. TR was predominantly of Dutch ancestry on his father's side, with much smaller doses of Irish, Scotch Irish, Welsh, English, and German; on his mother's side the roots were mainly Scottish, with a bit of French.

57. Here and there, brief discussions of TR and British culture can be found; for instance, "The Glory of Albion," in Wagenknecht, *Seven Worlds*, 50–57.

58. Several selections in Herman Hagedorn, *The Americanism of Theodore Roosevelt: Selections from his Writings and Speeches* (Boston: Houghton Mifflin, 1923), serve as blatant examples.

59. See "'On Deck' with Roosevelt during the Campaign for American Cultural Independence," in Lawrence J. Oliver, *Brander Matthews, Theodore Roosevelt, and the Politics of American Literature, 1880–1920* (Knoxville: University of Tennessee Press, 1992), 112–44.

60. Morris, *Rise of Theodore Roosevelt*, 323.

61. Cooper, *Warrior and the Priest*, 33.

62. See the end of chapter 1 for the "twice-born" personality.

8. Woodrow Wilson

1. See the discussion of Wilson's accomplishments in John Milton Cooper, *The Warrior and the Priest: Woodrow Wilson and Theodore Roosevelt* (Cambridge, Mass.: Belknap Press of Harvard University Press, 1983), 229–47.

2. The term "righteous scholar" is taken from David H. Burton, *The Learned Presidency: Theodore Roosevelt, William Howard Taft, Woodrow Wilson* (Rutherford, N.J.: Fairleigh Dickinson University Press, 1988), 136.

3. The income tax required a constitutional amendment, which passed Congress in the first year of Taft's administration (with Taft's lukewarm approval) and was ratified a month before Wilson took office. The tax itself was enacted under Wilson.

4. Arthur S. Link, *Wilson: The New Freedom* (Princeton, N.J.: Princeton University Press, 1956), 146, 152.

5. Arthur S. Link, *Wilson: The Road to the White House* (Princeton, N.J.: Princeton University Press, 1947), 1. See also Cooper, *Warrior and the Priest*, 15–26, 44–58 (45 for Civil War quote). TR's mother was a southerner; her brothers fought for the Confederacy; his father served with the civilian Sanitary Commission (a relief agency). Wilson's father served as a Confederate chaplain; his uncles from Ohio fought for the Union. As a boy Wilson witnessed aspects of the war in Georgia (though not actual battles), while TR witnessed Lincoln's funeral procession as it passed his grandfather's New York home.

6. Wilson's diary, October 6, 1876; editorial in *Princetonian*, June 7, 1877; letter from Janet Woodrow Wilson, November 6, 1877; "Government by Debate" (1779); Wilson to Ellen Louise Axon, November 9, 1884, all in *The Papers of Woodrow Wilson*, 69 vols., ed. Arthur S. Link (Princeton, N.J.: Princeton University Press, 1966–94), 1:204, 275, 580, 2:239, 3:314 (henceforth cited as *WW Papers*). For Wilson's reading of and about Burke, 8:316.

7. Wilson to Ellen Axon Wilson, c. July 23, 1896, *WW Papers*, 9:546. See Arthur Walworth, *Woodrow Wilson*, 2 vols. in one (New York: W. W. Norton, 1978), 1:73 for the other shrines on Wilson's tour.

8. Wilson to Ellen Axon Wilson, July 26, 1896, *WW Papers*, 9:547.

9. See editorial note, *WW Papers*, 8:317. Walter Bagehot (1826–77) tended toward nineteenth-century scientism and an overreliance on the analogy of biological evolution. In his *English Constitution* (1864) he spoke of the (presumably natural) decay of the House of Lords; in *Physics and Politics* (1875) he applied the principles of natural science to human activity.

10. "Edmund Burke: The Man and His Times," c. August 31, 1893, *WW Papers*, 8:318–43, quotes 319, 328, 334. Apparently this was delivered at Johns Hopkins and again at Princeton; a revised version appeared in Wilson's *Mere Literature and Other Essays* (1896).

11. *WW Papers*, 8:335, 340–41.

12. *WW Papers*, 8:341.

13. Link, *Road to the White House*, 31–32, 107.

14. *WW Papers*, 8:341.

15. *WW Papers*, 8:343.

16. Ellen Axon Wilson to Woodrow Wilson, April 3, 1892, *WW Papers*, 7:542.

17. "Edmund Burke: A Lecture," February 23, 1898, *WW Papers*, 10:408–23; quotes 409, 414, 416 (later published in *Century Magazine*, September 1901).

18. *WW Papers*, 10:415–16, 417, 419–21.

19. "Walter Bagehot.—A Lecture," February 24, 1898, *WW Papers*, 10:423–42, quotes 428–32, 439.

20. "Princeton in the Nation's Service," October 21, 1896, *WW Papers*, 10:9–31, quotes 22–25 ("preparing" changed to "Prepare").

21. Ibid., 10:29–30.

22. *WW Papers*, 2:228, 4:14, 127; Wilson to Albert Shaw, July 14, 1891, 7:245; the editor under discussion was W. T. Stead of the London *Review of Reviews*. For Burke's words in context, *WSEB*, 2:277, 278, 292, 314, 318.

23. B. J. Hoadley, "Edmund Burke—an Apostle of Conservatism," *Methodist Review* (January 1905): 102–7, quote 106. The published collections of Garfield's writings contain only two brief mentions of Burke.

24. See Link, *Road to the White House*, 16–17, 32–33. See also "A Memorandum," c. June 19, 1896, *WW Papers*, 9:522. Probably Barack Obama (as a professor of constitutional law) has thought as deeply about the Constitution, though with concerns different from Wilson's.

25. "Conversation with Graham Elliot," January 5, 1903; *Constitutional Government in the United States*, March 24, 1908; "The Meaning of a Liberal Education" (address to NYC school teachers association), January 9, 1909, all in *WW Papers*, 14:322, 324; 18:71; 18:594.

26. "Liberal Education," *WW Papers*, 18:601.

27. "Arts as Opposed to Professional Courses. . . . " Madison, Wisconsin, January 5, 1910, *WW Papers*, 19:726.

28. "Interview by Samuel G. Blythe," December 5, 1914; (according to the dairy of Colonel House, November 7, 1914: "He spoke often of himself as a disciple of Burke and Bagehot. This is literally true, for he is always quoting from one or the other, mostly from Bagehot"); "A Colloquy with a Group of Anti-preparedness

Leaders," May 8, 1916; "Press Conference," September 29, 1916; "Remarks to Foreign Correspondents," April 8, 1918; all in *WW Papers*, 31:403; (31:279); 36:645; 38:291; 47:288; see also 53:355.

29. A notable exception (in 1899): "I never have been able to understand how people thought *Reflections* was a hysterical production," *WW Papers*, 11:256. See also August Heckscher, *Woodrow Wilson* (New York: Scribner's, 1991), 112.

30. Wilson to Bainbridge Colby, February 24, 1922; diary of Ray Stannard Baker, April 4, 1922 (italics added); "Notes and Passages for an Acceptance Speech," January 21, 1924 [I have been unable to match Wilson's page reference to any of the nineteenth-century *Works* editions available to me], all in *WW Papers*, 67:556; 67:585; 68:541. On Wilson's rereading of Burke and for second "expediency" quote see Cooper, *Warrior and the Priest*, 265 (W. W. talk with William Gorham Rice, May 2, 1922).

31. See Georg Schild, *Between Ideology and Realpolitik: Woodrow Wilson and the Russian Revolution, 1917–1921* (Westport, Conn.: Greenwood Press, 1995), and Lloyd C. Gardner, *Safe for Democracy: The Anglo-American Response to Revolution, 1913–1923* (New York: Oxford University Press, 1984).

32. *WW Papers*, 68:393–95, July 27, 1923 (*Atlantic Monthly*, August 1923).

33. *WW Papers*, 395.

34. Charles Seymour's notes, "Conference on [the ship] *George Washington* with Wilson," December 10, 1918, quoted in Gardner, *Safe for Democracy*, 1.

35. Walworth, *Woodrow Wilson*, 1:64; Link, *Road to White House*, 33.

36. Heckscher, *Woodrow Wilson*, 112 (Heckscher quotes an editorial statement from *WW Papers* that "it is simply impossible to ascribe the authorship of the theme either to Wilson or to Turner" (unfortunately the page reference given is incorrect, and I have been unable to locate it). Apparently this view originated in 1919 during the writing of William E. Dodd's *Woodrow Wilson and His Work* (Garden City, N.Y.: Doubleday, Page, 1920), though Dodd watered this down before publication, settling for the more general "Wilson surely influenced Turner and lent new earnestness to his historical independence" (28). See Wendall H. Stephenson, "The Influence of Woodrow Wilson on Frederick Jackson Turner," *Agricultural History* 19 (October 1945): 249–57; Wilson modestly "disclaimed all originality," and the only specific influence Turner credited to Wilson was his suggestion of the word "hither," as in "the hither side of free land."

37. See note 3, *WW Papers*, 8:279.

38. Woodrow Wilson, *A History of the American People* (1901–2; New York: Harper and Bros., 1906). All the Burkean references pertained to the American crisis and the Wilkes Affair; *Thoughts on the Present Discontents* was specifically mentioned; only the "liberal" side of Burke was portrayed; 1:305, 2:105 (picture on 106), 106–7, 123, 124, 153, 211, 213, 215, 217.

39. The bronze statue by J. Harvard Thomas is at Massachusetts Ave. and 11th St. NW.

40. F. W. Raffety, "Edmund Burke and America: From a British Point of View," *Living Age* 305 (June 12, 1920): 669–72.

41. Charles A. Beard and Mary R. Beard, *The Rise of American Civilization*, one-volume ed. (New York: Macmillan, 1930), 206, 284.

42. Robert Hannah, "Burke's Audience," *Quarterly Journal of Speech* 11 (April 1925): 145–50; M. Einaudi, "The British Background of Burke's Political Philosophy," *Political Science Quarterly* 49 (December 1934): 576–98.

43. Irving Babbitt, *Democracy and Leadership* (Boston: Houghton Mifflin, 1924), 115–16. Babbitt (1865–1933) was professor of French literature at Harvard from 1912 to 1933.

44. James Harvey Robinson, *The New History* (New York: Macmillan, 1912), 252, 266.

9. Modern Times

1. Arthur Anthony Baumann, *Burke: The Founder of Conservatism* (London: Eyre & Spottiswoode, 1929), [3], 12, 52, 73, 75–76, 79 (see also 47, 56, for the Jacobin-Bolshevik link). Baumann (1850–1936) was born in Glasgow and educated at Oxford; he was a member of the bar and briefly an MP (1885–86) and edited the *Saturday Review*, 1917–21.

2. Ibid., 40, 49, 60, 69.

3. Ibid., [3], 59; see 53–54 for a defense of laissez-faire economics.

4. With few exceptions, books on Burke in the interwar years were published in England rather than in American. See note 3, xiii, in Ross J. S. Hoffman and Paul Levack, eds., *Burke's Politics: Selected Writings and Speeches of Edmund Burke on Reform, Revolution, and War* (New York: Alfred A. Knopf, 1949).

5. "Orator for Chivalry," *Commonweal* 9 (January 30, 1929): 362–63.

6. Padraic Colum, "Burke and the Present Order," *Saturday Review of Literature*, September 30, 1933, 141–42; the "organic *moleculae*" quote is from *Reflections* (106, or *WSEB*, 8:72); referring to the English Restoration of 1660 and the Glorious Revolution of 1688, Burke praised the participants for keeping "the shape of their old organization" and for preserving the "principles" of "conservation and correction."

7. See *Corres.*, 1:vii, on the release of Burke's papers.

8. Lionel Trilling, *The Liberal Imagination: Essays on Literature and Society* (1949; New York: Viking Press, 1951); Arthur Schlesinger Jr., "The New Conservatism in America: A Liberal Comment," *Confluence: An International Forum* 2 (December 1953): 61–71; Louis Hartz, *The American Liberal Tradition: An Interpretation of American Political Thought since the Revolution* (1955; New York: Harvest, 1991); Clinton Rossiter, *Conservatism in America: The Thankless Persuasion* (Knopf /Vintage, 1962); Allen Guttmann, *The Conservative Tradition in America* (New York: Oxford University Press, 1967); Richard Hofstadter, *The Age of Reform: From Bryan to F.D.R.* (New York: Vintage, 1955), 14; "This Liberal Age: A Critical Appraisal" (1975), reprinted in Henry Regnery, *A Few Reasonable Words: Selected Writings* (Wilmington, Del.: Intercollegiate Studies Institute, 1996), 3–31.

9. Regnery, *Reasonable Words*, 87.

10. Trilling, *Liberal Imagination*, ix (December 1949).

10. Natural Law

1. See *University of Notre Dame Natural Law Institute Proceedings* 5 (1953).

2. Charles Grove Haines, *The Revival of Natural Law Concepts* (Cambridge, Mass.: Harvard University Press, 1930), 13, 15, 278. Haines's failure to mention Burke was true to the norms of the 1920s–1930s.

3. Philadelphia lawyer James Wilson (1742–98) signed both the Declaration of Independence and the Constitution and was an original member of the U.S.

Supreme Court. See James McClellan, *Joseph Story and the American Constitution: A Study in Political and Legal Thought* (Norman: University of Oklahoma Press, 1971), 65–82; Story wrote an *Encyclopedia Britannica* article on natural law, which is reprinted ibid., 313–24.

4. See Knud Haakonssen, *Natural Law and Moral Philosophy: From Grotius to the Scottish Enlightenment* (Cambridge: Cambridge University Press, 1996), 330–31 (including notes 55 and 56).

5. *Notre Dame Natural Law Institute Proceedings* 1 (1949), [i, iii, iv] (conference held December 12–13, 1947). On Oliver Wendell Holmes and this topic see Michael H. Hoffheimer, *Justice Holmes and the Natural Law* (New York: Garland, 1992), which declares: "Holmes did not just refuse to acknowledge the influence of natural law; he attacked natural law jurisprudence repeatedly and effectively. . . . His antipathy to natural law is well documented" (11).

6. *Notre Dame Natural Law Institute Proceedings* 1, 1.

7. Ben W. Palmer, "The Natural Law and Pragmatism," *Notre Dame Natural Law Institute Proceedings* 1, 30–64, quotes 33, 36–37.

8. Ibid., 34, 35 ["ing" added to "win"], 40, 48, 56, 61–63.

9. Robert Wilkin, "Status of Natural Law in American Jurisprudence," *Notre Dame Natural Law Institute Proceedings* 2 (1949), (December 10–11, 1948), 125–49, quotes 127–31.

10. Ibid., 144. Wilkin thought that "constitutionalism, the essence of Western civilization, is dependent on two things: The Natural Law theory of a higher law . . . and [i]ndependent courts, *presided over by men of learning who are consecrated to judicial service, with authority to restrain*" (emphasis added). By some interpretations, O. W. Holmes had been the John Dewey of American law; see Morton White, *Social Thought in America: The Revolt against Formalism* (1949; Boston: Beacon Press, 1957), 59–75.

11. Burke's name appears only once in the five Law Institute volumes (4:124), and it is in a quote from Bryce's *American Commonwealth* (1888) that does not tie him to natural law.

12. *Notre Dame Lawyer* 17, no. 4 (June 1942) [four lectures delivered at Notre Dame College of Law, January 1942]: 287–372. This contains an excellent, clearly written history of natural law thought; even those not persuaded by the idea of natural law would benefit from reading it, if only to understand the doctrine's historical roots.

13. George H. Nash, *The Conservative Intellectual Movement in America* (New York: Basic Books, 1976), 80–81.

14. The "list" of twenty-five is compiled from Patrick Allitt, *Catholic Intellectuals and Conservative Politics in America, 1950–1985* (Ithaca, N.Y.: Cornell University Press, 1993), 3, 56–57.

15. Nash, *Conservative Intellectual Movement*, 68; Allitt, *Catholic Intellectuals*, 55.

16. Moorhouse F. X. Millar, "Burke and the Moral Basis of Political Liberty," *Thought: Fordham University Quarterly* 16, no. 60 (March 1941): 79–101, quotes 81, 87, 92, 93–94, 100–101.

17. Ross J. S. Hoffman and Paul Levack, eds. (intro. by Hoffman), *Burke's Politics: Selected Writings and Speeches of Edmund Burke on Reform, Revolution, and War* (New York: Alfred A. Knopf, 1949). Hoffman and Levack give credit to Millar in their preface (viii).

18. On Hoffman see Allitt, *Catholic Intellectuals*, 49–51.

19. Hoffman, *Burke's Politics*, xiv–xvi.

20. Ibid., xxxiv–xxxv. Hoffman explicitly made the connection between the "French Revolution of 1789" and the "Petrograd and Moscow enslavement of 1917" (xxxvi).

21. Russell Kirk, "Burke and Natural Rights," *Review of Politics* 13, no. 4 (October 1951): 441–56; *John Randolph of Roanoke: A Study in American Politics* (1951; Chicago: Henry Regnery, 1964), quote 26; *The Conservative Mind: From Burke to Santayana* (Chicago: Henry Regnery, 1953), quote 3.

22. Allen Guttmann, *The Conservative Tradition in America* (New York: Oxford University Press, 1967), 159.

23. Kirk, *Conservative Mind*, 4.

24. Kirk, "Burke and Natural Rights," 441. Kirk used the term "natural right(s)" to mean that which is moral according to natural law.

25. Fellow new conservative Peter Viereck said that while "Burke praised Catholicism as 'the most effectual barrier' against radicalism. . . . Such praise sounds as if motivated by secular expediency, not spiritual fervor." Viereck, *Conservatism: From John Adams to Churchill* (Princeton, N.J.: D. Van Nostrand, 1956), 16.

26. Kirk, "Burke and Natural Rights," 442.

27. Ibid., 442–43.

28. Kirk, *Conservative Mind*, 24, 26, 31.

29. Richard Weaver, *Ideas Have Consequences* (Chicago: University of Chicago Press, 1948). As was the case with Kirk's *Conservative Mind*, Weaver's "new conservative" book was originally submitted with a pessimistic title: "The Fearful Descent" (Nash, *Conservative Intellectual Movement*, 39).

30. See, for example, Russell Kirk, *A Program for Conservatives* (Chicago: Henry Regnery, 1954), 104–5, 267–68.

31. Friedrich Hayek, *The Road to Serfdom* [finally, a pessimistic title that survived to publication!] (Chicago: University of Chicago Press, 1944). See Hayek's "Why I Am Not a Conservative" (1960), 88–103, in Frank S. Meyer, ed., *What Is Conservatism?* (New York: Holt, Rinehart and Winston, 1964).

32. Frank S. Meyer, "Freedom, Tradition, Conservatism," 9, and William F. Buckley Jr., "Notes toward an Empirical Definition of Conservatism," 226, both in Meyer, *What Is Conservatism?*

33. On Kirk's life and work see Nash, *Conservative Intellectual Movement*, 69–76, and W. Wesley McDonald, *Russell Kirk and the Age of Ideology* (Columbia: University of Missouri Press, 2004); McDonald's book began as a dissertation at the Catholic University of America. Two sketches by Henry Regnery are highly favorable introductions to Kirk's work: "Russell Kirk: Making of the Conservative Mind," in Regnery, *A Few Reasonable Words: Selected Writings* (Wilmington, Del.: Intercollegiate Studies Institute, 1996), 83–120 (also published in *Modern Age*, fall 1977), and "Russell Kirk: An Appraisal," in Charles Brown, *Russell Kirk: A Bibliography* (Mount Pleasant: Clarke Historical Library, Central Michigan University, 1981), 127–41.

34. John Crowe Ransom et al., *I'll Take My Stand: The South and the Agrarian Tradition* (New York: Harper, 1930). For an analysis see Paul Murphy, *The Rebuke of History: The Southern Agrarians and American Conservative Thought* (Chapel Hill: University of North Carolina Press, 2001).

35. Russell Kirk, *America's British Culture* (New Brunswick, N.J.: Transaction Publishers, 1992).

36. Kirk, *Program for Conservatives*, 10, 62, 63, 65, 68, 69, 72, 87, 88, 92, 231. A decade later, in *Edmund Burke: A Genius Reconsidered* (1967; Wilmington, Del.: Intercollegiate Studies Institute, 1997), 8–9.

37. New conservatives and neoconservatives were different animals, even if in translation they shared the same name. New conservatives—the term was coined by Peter Viereck in "But I'm a Conservative!" *Atlantic Monthly*, April 1940, 543—were traditionalists; neoconservatives were former liberals or leftists (mostly centered in New York City) who exhibited no nostalgia for the virtues of premodern, preindustrial times; instead they accepted modern social science, democracy, economic theory, and so on, while criticizing liberal excesses, failures, and counterproductive policies. New Conservatives ascended in the 1950s, neoconservatives in the 1970s and 1980s. See McDonald, *Russell Kirk and the Age of Ideology*, 206–12, for the neoconservative rejection of Kirk; see also Godfrey Hodgson, *The World Turned Right Side Up: A History of the Conservative Ascendency in America* (Boston: Houghton Mifflin, 1996), 128–57, and Irving Kristol, *Neoconservatism: The Autobiography of an Idea* (New York: Free Press, 1995).

38. See McDonald, *Russell Kirk and the Age of Ideology*, 170–200.

39. Russell Kirk, "John Dewey Pragmatically Tested," *National Review*, June 21, 1958, 11–12, 23, quote 23.

40. Ibid., 11.

41. *Reflections*, 186.

42. Russell Kirk, introduction to *Edmund Burke: Reflections on the Revolution in France* (New Rochelle, N.Y.: Arlington House, 1965), xviii.

43. Robert A. Smith, "The Consistency of Edmund Burke," *Yale Review* 45, no. 4 (June 1956): 607. The context was Burke's thoughts concerning the British Empire during the American crisis; Smith was reviewing Ross Hoffman's *Edmund Burke: New York Agent.*

44. Nash, *Conservative Intellectual Movement*, 166.

45. Robert M. Crunden, *The Superfluous Men: Conservative Critics of American Culture, 1900–1945* (Wilmington, Del.: ISI Books, 1999), xxii. Though first published in 1977, the new introduction from which the quote is taken was written in 1998.

46. Arthur Schlesinger Jr., "The New Conservatism in America: A Liberal Comment," *Confluence: An International Forum* 2 (December 1953): 65. He added: "The New Conservatives must realize that the aristocratic conservatism they so deeply admire has little substantial basis in the actualities of American life" (69).

47. Russell Kirk, "Apology for a New Review," 2–3, and Richard Weaver, "Life without Prejudice," 4–9, quote 8, in *Modern Age: A Conservative Journal* 1, no. 1 (Summer 1957).

48. Edmund A. Opitz, review of Charles Parkin, *The Moral Basis of Burke's Political Thought* (Cambridge University Press, 1956), *Modern Age* 1, no. 2 (Fall 1957): 202–3.

49. Ibid., 203.

50. *Studies in Burke and His Times* was revived in 2002 as an annual edition.

51. From Kirk's review of Clinton Rossiter's *Conservatism in America*, in *Burke Newsletter* 4, no. 2 (Winter 1962–63): 192.

52. All these conservative icons have been taken from Kirk's *Conservative Mind* and from Peter Viereck's *Conservatism*.

53. Stanlis was a professor of English at the University of Detroit and later at Rockford College; the previously cited bibliography (1983) was coedited with Clara Gandy.

54. We shall focus mostly on Stanlis's "big book," which is cited below; others include: Peter J. Stanlis, ed., *The Relevance of Edmund Burke* (New York: P. J. Kennedy & Sons, 1964) [papers from Burke Symposium at Georgetown University], includes Stanlis, "Edmund Burke in the Twentieth Century," 21–57; Stanlis, ed., *Edmund Burke: The Enlightenment and the Modern World* (Detroit: University of Detroit Press, 1967) [papers from Burke Symposium at University of Detroit], includes Stanlis, "Edmund Burke and the Scientific Rationalism of the Enlightenment," 81–116; Stanlis, *Edmund Burke: The Enlightenment and Revolution* (New Brunswick, N.J.: Transaction, 1991), introduction by Russell Kirk. Stanlis also edited a selection of Burke's works (1963).

55. Peter J. Stanlis, *Edmund Burke and the Natural Law* (Ann Arbor: University of Michigan Press, 1958), from his Ph.D. dissertation, "Burke's Politics and the Law of Nature," University of Michigan, 1951.

56. Stanlis, *Burke and Natural Law*, 48.

57. Ibid., 15.

58. Ibid., 201–2.

59. Ibid., 201.

60. Ibid., 113–14.

61. Ibid., 7, 112 (emphasis added), 114.

62. Kristol, *Neoconservatism*, 9. Kristol cites Trilling and Strauss as the two writers most influential to his own emerging conservatism (6). See McDonald, *Russell Kirk and the Age of Ideology*, 92–93 (including note 14) for an explanation hostile to Strauss and favorable to Kirk and Burke. In Gandy and Stanlis, source no. 967, the claim is made that Stanlis "reached his conclusions wholly independently from any reading of Strauss."

63. Leo Strauss, *Natural Right and History* (Chicago: University of Chicago Press, 1953), 4, 5.

64. Ibid., 5, 6, 170–71, 178, 181–82, 252.

65. The lives in play here were Suarez, 1548–1617; Hooker, 1553–1600; Hobbes, 1588–1679 (and Machiavelli, 1469–1527).

66. Strauss, *Natural Right and History*, 296, 299. But see Strauss's entire Burke section, 294–323.

67. Ibid., 303–6, 314.

68. Ibid., 322–23.

69. Harvey C. Mansfield Jr., introduction to *Selected Letters of Edmund Burke* (Chicago: University of Chicago Press, 1984), 4, note 4.

70. This thumbnail sketch of Strauss's view is not meant to deny the interesting similarities between Burke and Strauss (which is why I earlier called Strauss a "half-way Burkean"); see for instance *Reflections*, 176 and 258–59.

71. Gertrude Himmelfarb, *Victorian Minds* (original essays 1949 and 1967; Gloucester, Mass.: Peter Smith, 1975), 3, 4, 7. Himmelfarb specifically cited the writings of Millar et al. (p. 5, notes 4 and 5), so there was no mistake about whom

she was responding to. For a criticism of the natural law claims see (the British political writer) Frank O'Gorman, *Edmund Burke: His Political Philosophy* (Bloomington: Indiana University Press, 1973), 11–14, and notes on 12–13.

72. Mulford Q. Sibley, "Burke and the New Ancestor Worship," *New Republic*, March 12, 1956, 24–25.

73. Ibid.

74. Morton J. Frisch, "Burke vs. the New Conservatives," *New Republic*, April 23, 1956, 17.

75. Letter from Reginald D. Lang, *Burke Newsletter* 2 (Fall 1960): 64.

76. In full: "The rediscovery of Burke since 1949 demonstrates the appeal of the everlasting in an age or [*sic*] revolution." Stephen J. Tonsor, "Who's Afraid of Edmund Burke," *National Review*, February 9, 1965, 112. Tonsor was not specifically making the connection to natural law.

77. Francis Canavan, *Edmund Burke: Prescription and Providence* (Durham, N.C.: Carolina Academic Press, 1987), 62.

78. Benjamin Fletcher Wright Jr., *American Interpretations of Natural Law: A Study in the History of Political Thought* (Cambridge, Mass.: Harvard University Press, 1931), 327.

79. A recent work that "pushes the envelope" on this subject is David Braybrooke, *Natural Law Modernized* (Toronto: University of Toronto Press, 2001).

80. *Reflections*, 152–53, or *WSEB*, 8:112.

81. Robert Wilkin, *Notre Dame Natural Law Institute Proceedings*, 2:148; Burke, "Appeal from New to Old Whigs," in Edmund Burke, *Further Reflections on the Revolution in France*, ed. Daniel E. Ritchie (Indianapolis: Liberty Classics, 1992), 147.

11. The Cold War

1. Ross J. S. Hoffman and Paul Levack, eds., *Burke's Politics: Selected Writings and Speeches of Edmund Burke on Reform, Revolution, and War* (New York: Alfred A. Knopf, 1949), xiii.

2. Louis I. Bredvold and Ralph G. Ross, eds., *The Philosophy of Edmund Burke* (Ann Arbor: University of Michigan Press, 1960), introduction, 8.

3. Ibid., 8–9.

4. Raymond Moley, "Indestructible Burke," *Newsweek*, December 28, 1953, 72.

5. Robert A. Taft, *A Foreign Policy for Americans* (Garden City, N.Y.: Doubleday, 1951), 79, 114.

6. Richard Price (1723–91) was a dissenting minister and influential moral philosopher. His sermon was delivered on November 4, 1789, at London's "Old Jewry" meetinghouse; published in book form (which included the French National Assembly's Declaration of the Rights of Men and of Citizens), it became a best-seller and provoked Burke's *Reflections*. A recent facsimile edition (introduction by Jonathan Wordsworth) is *A Discourse on the Love of Our Country* (New York: Woodstock Books, 1992), quotes 50–51.

7. "The Conservative Revival," *Life*, May 15, 1950, 38 (italics in original).

8. Crane Brinton, "Burke and Our Present Discontents," *Thought* 24, no. 93 (June 1949): 197–200, quotes 199–200. The editorial recommended Hoffman and Levack's *Burke's Politics*. Brinton (1898–1968) was influenced by Laski on the left and

Babbitt on the right; see *American National Biography*, s.v. "Brinton, Crane." He was a scholar of the French Revolution who published the unflattering study *The Jacobins: An Essay in the New History* (New York: Macmillan, 1930), which did not mention Burke. Brinton taught at Harvard from 1942 to 1968; in 1955 he coauthored a widely used text, *History of Civilization.* He said he went from being "a liberal with at least an initial capital" to "a liberal in inverted commas"—"my earlier optimistic rationalism has been tempered by an awareness of the place of prejudices, sentiments, the unconscious and the subconscious, in human life." *Contemporary Authors Online* (2003), s.v. "Brinton, (Clarence) Crane."

9. Peter Viereck, *Conservatism Revisited: The Revolt against Revolt, 1815–1949* (New York: Scribner's, 1949), quotes 13, 84. Viereck did more than just echo the *Thought* editorial; he quoted from another Crane Brinton article as well (84–85). The next year, Viereck praised Brinton's *Ideas and Men* in a *New York Times* review. See Viereck's attacks on Manchester liberalism and the Gilded Age laissez-faire philosophy of the Republican Party in his "The Philosophical 'New Conservatism,'" in *The New American Right*, ed. Daniel Bell (New York: Doubleday, 1963), esp. 165–68. Viereck also took Kirk to task for supporting Barry Goldwater.

10. Francis Graham Wilson, *The Case for Conservatism* (1951; New Brunswick, N.J.: Transaction, 1990), 5, 10, 11 (intro. to new edition by Kirk, quote xii).

11. Wilson's five characteristics of conservatism differed from Kirk's more famous six "canons" of conservatism; the direct overlaps were the defense of property and the recognition of a moral order in the universe.

12. Wilson, *Case for Conservatism*, 13.

13. Ibid., 8, 18, 19, 51, 74.

14. Arthur M. Schlesinger Jr., *The Vital Center: The Politics of Freedom* (Boston: Houghton Mifflin, 1949) is the classic example of a New Deal Democrat's anticommunism; see his chapter "The Failure of the Left" (35–50) for his criticism of American leftists and "fellow travelers."

15. Geoffrey Bruun, "The Heritage of Jacobinism," in *The Centenary Charter Lectures in Modern Political History, 1945–1946*, ed. William J. Schlaerth, S.J. (New York: Fordham University Press, 1946), 26, 30–31. Bruun (1898–1988) was a Canadian citizen but taught history at six U.S. institutions; he was at Columbia at the time of this lecture.

16. Ibid., 27.

17. Ibid., 31–34.

18. Kennan's telegram was sent on February 22, 1946; Bruun's lecture was delivered on February 11, 1946.

19. Mr. X [George F. Kennan], "The Sources of Soviet Conduct," *Foreign Affairs* 25 (July 1947): 566–82; quotations are from a reprint in Richard L. Watson Jr., ed., *The United States in the Contemporary World, 1945–1962* (New York: Free Press, 1965), 46–64, quotes 48–51.

20. For an illustration of this point see the table of contents to J. C. D. Clark, ed., *Edmund Burke: Reflections on the Revolution in France* (Stanford, Calif.: Stanford University Press, 2001), which breaks *Reflections* into subsections.

21. See François Furet, *Interpreting the French Revolution* (Cambridge: Cambridge University Press, 1981), 4–7, 85–89, for the Bolshevik-Jacobin connection.

22. *WSEB*, 8:119, 129, 131, 132, 192, 202, 214. I have altered the order of these quotes to place like thoughts in sequence and to effect a logical flow; this arrangement in no way distorts their original meaning.

23. Ibid., 8:197.

24. *First Letter on a Regicide Peace* (1796), *WSEB*, 9:193.

25. Ibid., 193.

26. As Burke said in 1793: "If Spain goes, Naples will speedily follow. Prussia is quite certain. . . ." *Remarks on the Policy of the Allies*, *WSEB*, 8:483.

12. Contemporary Conservatives

1. Much new writing on Burke came from literary and cultural scholars (over the past twenty years, more dissertations on Burke addressed his "sublime" aesthetic theory than any other topic); separately, some liberal portrayals of Burke have gained wide recognition, such as those by Kramnick and O'Brien; and most recent contributions by political scientists have been devoid of obvious ideological bias.

2. Isaac Kramnick, *The Rage of Edmund Burke: Portrait of an Ambivalent Conservative* (New York: Basic Books, 1977); Richard Boyd, "'The Unsteady and Precarious Contribution of Individuals': Edmund Burke's Defense of Civil Society," *Review of Politics* 61, no. 3 (Summer 1999): 465–91. Kramnick has been professor of political science at Cornell since 1972; Boyd received his Ph.D. from Rutgers in 1998.

3. Kramnick, *Rage*, 190, 193.

4. Boyd, "Edmund Burke's Defense," 489.

5. For Burke as a neoconservative see Sanford Lakoff, "Tocqueville, Burke, and the Origins of Liberal Conservatism," *Review of Politics* 60, no. 3: 435–85 (Boyd cites this article in his note 7).

6. Daniel E. Ritchie, *Edmund Burke: Appraisals and Applications* (New Brunswick, N.J.: Transactions Publishers, 1990), [v].

7. Edmund Burke, *Further Reflections on the Revolution in France*, ed. Daniel E. Ritchie (Indianapolis: Liberty Classics, 1992), x, xix.

8. Daniel E. Ritchie, *Reconstructing Literature in an Ideological Age: A Biblical Poetics and Literary Studies from Milton to Burke* (Grand Rapids, Mich.: William B. Eerdmans, 1996), esp. chap. 4, "From Babel to Pentecost: George Psalmanazar's 'Formosa,' Burke's India, and Multiculturalism," 180–231, quotes 13–14, 211, 222, 230.

9. Daniel E. Ritchie, "Desire and Sympathy, Passion and Providence: The Moral Imaginations of Burke and Rousseau," in *Burke and the French Revolution: Bicentennial Essays*, ed. Steven Blakemore (Athens: University of Georgia Press, 1992), 120–43, quote 123.

10. Bruce Frohnen, *Virtue and the Promise of Conservatism: The Legacy of Burke and Tocqueville* (Lawrence: University Press of Kansas, 1993), 2, 4, 10, 214. Frohnen teaches at the Catholic University of America; another example of his extremely God-centered politics can be found in "Commitment and Obligation," in George W. Carey and Bruce Frohnen, eds., *Community and Tradition: Conservative Perspectives on the American Experience* (Lanham, Md.: Rowman & Littlefield, 1998), 165–86. For example: "The ultimate source of obligation [is] transcendent, God-centered

principles"; "Societies necessarily reflect a common vision of God's dictates if they are to survive" (166).

11. Frohnen, *Virtue*, 9.

12. Ibid., 23.

13. Several of the conservative American Burkeans we have encountered were far from religious in their outlook. A recent acknowledgment of this phenomenon is in Stephen J. Tonsor, "Mistaken Assumptions," *Modern Age* 44, no. 1 (Winter 2002): 58.

14. Frohnen, *Virtue*, 53, 65.

15. Martin Greenberg, "Burke and Political Liberty," *New Criterion* 20, no. 7 (March 2002): 4–14, quote 4.

16. Ibid.

17. Frank M. Turner, ed., introduction to Edmund Burke, *Reflections on the Revolution in France* (New Haven, Conn.: Yale University Press, 2003), xviii.

18. Ibid.

19. Incidentally, many liberal intellectuals *did* express "fear and anger"—along with shock and sadness—after 9/11; but those emotions did not destroy their reason, nor blind them to the complexities of that tragic event.

20. See Gary Wills, "The Day the Enlightenment Went Out," *New York Times*, November 4, 2004.

21. David R. Carlin Jr., "Bork, Burke, and Moral Relativism," *Commonweal* 114, no. 22 (December 18, 1987): 729–30.

22. Ibid. For another sample of Carlin's extreme anti-secularism and his conservatism on social issues see his "The Gay Rights Movement and Aggressive Secularism," *America* 173 (September 23, 1995): 12–16.

23. Judicial restraint—or its opposite, judicial activism—can be applied in either the liberal *or* conservative direction; Bork and contemporary conservatives are open to fair criticism for presenting judicial activism (or "legislating from the bench") as if it were always liberal.

24. Robert H. Bork, *Slouching towards Gomorrah: Modern Liberalism and American Decline* (New York: Regan, 1996), 53, 64.

25. Mark C. Henrie, "Edmund Burke and Contemporary American Conservatism," in *The Enduring Edmund Burke: Bicentennial Essays*, ed. Ian Crowe (Wilmington, Del.: Intercollegiate Studies Institute, 1997), 198–212, quotes 203 (italics removed), 212.

Conclusion

1. My repeated references to the United States as a liberal nation may be especially hard to swallow for younger readers (those who cannot remember much before, say, the 1980s). My suggestion to such readers is to live as long as possible; it is likely that conservatism will again revert to a "thankless persuasion" within their lifetimes, if not my own. I also repeat here my earlier contention that liberalism (broadly defined) remains the majority view within the intellectual community; though conservatism has made substantial inroads, I do not see it taking over.

2. See Thomas Short, "Divergent Sources of Conservatism," *Modern Age* (Winter 2002): 51.

3. To cite one of the most popular "consensus" postwar historians on this point, Daniel J. Boorstin, *The Genius of American Politics* (Chicago: University of Chicago Press, 1953): "The ablest defender of the Revolution—in fact, the greatest political theorist of the American Revolution—was also the great theorist of British conservatism, Edmund Burke" (72–73).

4. This view is also manifest in the belief among conservatives of the "strict constructionist" or "original intent" school that the Constitution can (and should) be interpreted the same way in 1800, 1900, or 2000, regardless of the dramatically different conditions existing at each of those moments, not to mention the impossibility that judges—or anyone else—could accurately revert to a worldview that has not existed for generations.

5. Since Burke experienced only "premodern" economic conditions, I feel his pronouncements on economics are mostly of historical interest. Nevertheless, the following sources deserve citation, beginning with Burke's *Thoughts and Details on Scarcity* (1795, but published posthumously in 1805), *WSEB*, 8:119–45. An interesting but virtually unknown work is Ruth A. Bevan, *Marx and Burke: A Revisionist View* (LaSalle, Ill.: Open Court, 1973); a more conventional piece is George Fasel, "'The Soul That Animated': The Role of Property in Burke's Thought," *Studies in Burke and His Time* 17, no. 1 (Winter 1976): 27–41; for an important revisionist view see C. B. Macpherson, *Burke* (New York: Hill & Wang, 1980); many of the competing interpretations are incorporated into Francis Canavan, *The Political Economy of Edmund Burke: The Role of Property in His Thought* (New York: Fordham University Press, 1995); for differences between Burke and Smith see Donald Winch, *Riches and Poverty: An Intellectual History of Political Economy in Britain, 1750–1834* (Cambridge: Cambridge University Press, 1996), chap. 7, "Burke's Creed: Politics, Chivalry and Superstition."

6. M. Morton Auerbach, *The Conservative Illusion* (New York: Columbia University Press, 1959), 270. Auerbach's book deserves more attention than I give it here; I urge readers to discover it.

7. Recently, scientific discoveries about how reason operates in the human brain have been explained to the layman in such books as George Lakoff, *The Political Mind: Why You Can't Understand 21st-Century Politics with an 18th-Century Brain* (New York: Viking, 2008); these new findings of cognitive science challenge the long-held confidence in rational persuasion and in inevitable progress. While *Edmund Burke in America* (essentially completed before these writings became prominent) does not engage this subject, such findings may help explain the continued appeal of anachronistic Burkeanism (and other contra-liberal or antimodern beliefs).

8. The last of the four letters (1795–97) remained unfinished at his death; only two were published during his lifetime. See *WSEB*, vol. 9, or Edmund Burke, *Letters on a Regicide Peace*, ed. E. J. Payne (1878; Indianapolis: Liberty Fund, 1999).

9. See Daniel T. Rodgers, *Age of Fracture* (Cambridge, Mass.: Belknap Press of Harvard University Press, 2011).

10. "Materialism and Idealism in America" (1919), in George Santayana, *Character and Opinion in the United States* (London: Constable, 1924), 168.

11. See chaps. 8 and 11 for Robinson and Wilson.

Index